The *Revels*
History of Drama
in English

GENERAL EDITOR
T. W. Craik

The *Revels* History of Drama in English

VOLUME VIII American Drama

Travis Bogard, Richard Moody
& Walter J. Meserve

LONDON
Methuen & Co Ltd
Barnes & Noble Books
NEW YORK

First published in 1977 by
Methuen & Co Ltd
11 New Fetter Lane, London EC4P 4EE

ISBN 0 416 13090 9 (hardbound)
ISBN 0 416 81400 X (paperback)

and by Barnes & Noble Books
10 East 53rd Street
New York NY10022

ISBN 0–06–470625–7 (hardbound)
ISBN 0–06–470626–5 (paperback)

Library of Congress Catalog Number
LC 75–321430

Typeset by
William Clowes & Sons Ltd
London, Beccles and Colchester
Printed in Great Britain by
Richard Clay (The Chaucer Press), Ltd
Bungay, Suffolk

BH

Contents

List of illustrations

Preface

The devoting of a volume of the *Revels History of Drama in English* to the whole of American drama has necessitated a somewhat different structure from that followed in the 'English' volumes, each of which covers a different historical period. The physical development of the English playhouse, for example, is being recorded, for each period, in the other volumes: there seemed, therefore, little useful purpose in recording, in less detail, the corresponding American development in the course of over two centuries. Instead more space has been allotted to the account of the actors and actresses who performed in these changing theatres. Again, the three contributors have been encouraged to find common ground and not to feel inhibited from venturing into one another's territory: it is hoped that, as a result, the reader will more easily find his bearings in the various sections than might otherwise be the case. There is, inevitably, some consequent overlapping between the contents of these three sections, but the effort has been made to achieve coherence and avoid mere duplication. The compilation of the chronological table (in which, as in the selection of illustrations, the general editor gratefully acknowledges the assistance of the contributors) has raised in an acute form the problem of selection, because of the length of the period to be covered and because of the need to take some account of the copious literary and theatrical activity of Britain and of Europe; the choice of items has been governed by such factors as (on the one hand) absolute importance and (on the other) relevance to matters American and matters theatrical.

Chronological
table

Date	Historical events	Theatrical events within the USA
1492	Columbus discovers America	
1587	'Lost Colony' left on Roanoke Island	
1620	*Mayflower* lands Pilgrims at Massachusetts; Plymouth Colony	
1627	Charter granted to the Massachusetts Bay Colony	
1637	Harvard College established	
1675	King Philip's War (ended 1676)	
1691	New Massachusetts charter destroys church control of government	
1703		Anthony Aston gives first professional performance at Charleston, S. Carolina
1713	Treaty of Utrecht	
1714		
1718		First American theatre, Williamsburg, Virginia
1737		
1741		
1748		
1751		
1752		First professional theatre company, led by Lewis Hallam, comes to America at Williamsburg
1754		
1756	Seven Years' War begins; French and Indian War in America	
1757		

4	5	6 Birth and death dates of	7
Non-dramatic literary events	First performance of American plays	notable American playwrights	Theatrical events outside America

	Hunter, *Androboros* (published)		
		R. Hunter d.	
			Début of Garrick
		H. H. Bracken- ridge b.	
			Sheridan b.
Jonathan Edwards, *Freedom of the Will*			Diderot, *Le Père de famille*
		R. Tyler b.	

1	2	3
Date	*Historical events*	*Theatrical events within the USA*
1758		David Douglass with company of actors arrives in New York
1763	Treaty of Paris	
1765	Stamp Act	
1766		Southwark Theatre, Philadelphia
1767		John Street Theatre, New York
1768		
1770		
1771		
1773	Boston tea riots	
1774		
1775		
1776	Declaration of Independence (definitive peace 1783)	
1777		
1779		
1781		

4	5	6 Birth and death dates of notable American playwrights	7
Non-dramatic literary events	First performance of American plays		Theatrical events outside America
		W. Dunlap b.	
John Dickinson, *Letters from a Farmer in Pennsylvania*	Godfrey, *The Prince of Parthia*		
			Mrs Pritchard d.
	Mumford, *The Candidates* (published)		
Benjamin Franklin, *Autobiography* (Part I)	Anon., *The Trial of Atticus* (published)		
			Goethe, *Goetz von Berlichingen*; Gold- smith, *She Stoops to Conquer*
Burke, *Speech on American Taxation*; Goethe, *Werther*			Goldsmith d.
Burke, *Speech on Con- ciliation with America*; Johnson, *Taxation no Tyranny*			Début of Sarah Siddons; Beaumarchais, *Le Barbier de Séville*
Declaration of Independence; Paine, *Common Sense*			Garrick retires; Sheridan assumes control of Drury Lane
			Sheridan, *The School for Scandal*
			Garrick d.
Jefferson, *The Rights of British America*; Rousseau, *Confessions*; Kant, *Kritik der reinen Vernunft*			Lessing d.; Schiller, *Die Räuber*

1	2	3
Date	Historical events	Theatrical events within the USA
1783		
1784		
1787	American Constitution	
1788		
1789	Washington's First Inaugural Address; French Revolution begins	
1791		
1792		
1793		
1794		Federal Street Theatre, Boston; Chestnut Street Theatre ('Old Drury'), Philadelphia
1796		
1798		Park Theatre, New York
1799		
1800	Jefferson elected President	
1801		First theatre in Cincinnati
1802		
1804		
1805		

4	5	6 Birth and death dates of	7
Non-dramatic literary events	*First performance of American plays*	*notable American playwrights*	*Theatrical events outside America*
			Début of J. P. Kemble as Hamlet
		J. N. Barker b.; R. Mumford d.	Beaumarchais, *Le Mariage de Figaro*
J. Adams, *Defence of the Constitution*	Tyler, *The Contrast*	S. Woodworth b.	
Federalist Papers			Kemble manager of Drury Lane
Blake, *Songs of Innocence*			Kotzebue, *Menschenhass und Reue* ('The Stranger')
Paine, *The Rights of Man*		J. H. Payne b.	
H. H. Brackenridge, *Modern Chivalry*			Goldoni d.
Blake, *America*			
Blake, *Songs of Experience*; Ann Radcliffe, *Mysteries of Udolpho*			
Joel Barlow, *Hasty Pudding*; Lewis, *The Monk*			
C. B. Brown, *Wieland*; Wordsworth and Coleridge, *Lyrical Ballads*	Dunlap, *André* (revised 1803)		Pixérécourt, *Victor*
			Sheridan, *Pizarro*
		J. A. Stone b.	Schiller, *Maria Stuart*
			Hugo b.
			Début of W. H. B. Betty (the 'Infant Roscius')
Scott, *The Lay of the Last Minstrel*			Schiller d.

1	2	3
Date	Historical events	Theatrical events within the USA
1806		
1807		
1808		
1809		
1810		George Frederick Cooke's US début at Park Theatre
1811		Richmond Theatre fire (26 December), 70 killed
1812	War between USA and Britain begins	
1813		First theatre in Albany
1814		
1815	Battle of Waterloo	
1816		
1817		
1818		
1819		

4	5	6 *Birth and death dates of*	7
Non-dramatic literary events	*First performance of American plays*	*notable American playwrights*	*Theatrical events outside America*

		R. M. Bird b.; W. H. Smith b.	
Barlow, *The Columbiad*; Wordsworth, *Poems in Two Volumes*			
Ingersoll, *Rights and Wrongs of the USA*			Goethe, *Faust* I (completed; *Faust* II completed 1832)
J. G. Adams, *American Principles*; Freneau, *Poems Written During the American Revolutionary War*; Irving, *History of New York*			Début of Ludwig Devrient
Byron, *Childe Harold's Pilgrimage*			Sarah Siddons retires
Jane Austen, *Pride and Prejudice*			
Scott, *Waverley*		Mercy Warren d.	Edmund Kean's début as Shylock
Key, 'The Star-Spangled Banner'; *North American Review* established			
		H. H. Brackenridge d.	Macready's London début; Sheridan d.
			J. P. Kemble retires; Tom Taylor b.
	Payne, *Brutus*		
Irving, *Sketch Book*		Anna Cora Mowatt (Ritchie) b	

Date	Historical events	Theatrical events within the USA
1820	George IV becomes King of England	Chestnut Street Theatre and Park Theatre destroyed by fire; Edmund Kean's US début at Anthony Street Theatre, New York
1821		Park Theatre rebuilt; Junius Brutus Booth's US début there
1822		Chestnut Street Theatre rebuilt
1823	Monroe Doctrine promulgated	
1824		First Mobile, Alabama, theatre; Camp Street Theatre, New Orleans; Noah Ludlow, Sol Smith acting in Mississippi region
1825		
1826		First Nashville, Tennessee, theatre; Bowery Theatre, New York; W. C. Macready's US début at Park Theatre
1827		Tremont Theatre, Boston
1828	Andrew Jackson elected President	Bowery Theatre burned and rebuilt; Arch Street Theatre, Philadelphia; Edwin Forrest's first (of seven) playwriting contest
1829		
1830	William IV becomes King of England; revolutions in Europe	
1831		Showboat theatre begins on the Ohio and Mississippi with William Chapman's 'drama barge'

4 Non-dramatic literary events	5 First performance of American plays	6 Birth and death dates of notable American playwrights	7 Theatrical events outside America
Keats, *Lamia*, etc.; Shelley, *Prometheus Unbound*			Scribe, *Un Verre d'eau*
Bryant, *Poems*; Cooper, *The Spy*			
Irving, *Bracebridge Hall*		D. Boucicault b.	
			J. P. Kemble d.; Frédéric Lemaître plays Robert Macaire in Paris
	Barker, *Superstition*; Payne and Irving, *Charles the Second*		
	Woodworth, *The Forest Rose*		
Cooper, *The Last of the Mohicans*		R. Tyler d.	
			Début of Charles Kean; Hugo, preface to *Cromwell*
Webster, *American Dictionary of the English Language*			Ibsen b.
Jefferson, *Autobiography*; Balzac, *Comédie humaine* (begun)	Stone, *Metamora*		
Channing, *Remarks on American Literature*			Hugo, *Hernani*
Poe, *Poems*; Stendhal, *Le Rouge et le noir*	Bird, *The Gladiator*, *The Broker of Bogota*		Sarah Siddons d.

1	2	3
Date	*Historical events*	*Theatrical events within the USA*
1832		Fanny Kemble as Juliet at Park Theatre
1833		
1834		
1835		St Charles Theatre, New Orleans
1836		
1837	Victoria becomes Queen of England	
1838		Bowery Theatre burned (rebuilt 1839)
1839		
1840		
1841		Boston Museum; Barnum's Museum
1842		
1843		Virginia Minstrels at Bowery Amphitheatre, New York; Macready tours USA

4 Non-dramatic literary events	5 First performance of American plays	6 Birth and death dates of notable American playwrights	7 Theatrical events outside America
Irving, *The Alhambra*; Tennyson, *Poems*; Frances Trollope, *Domestic Manners of the Americans*			Goethe d.
Dana, *Poems and Prose Writings*		D. Thompson b.	Edmund Kean d.
		J. A. Stone d.	
Kennedy, *Horse-Shoe Robinson*; Simms, *Yemassee*			
Dickens, *Pickwick Papers*; Holmes, *Poems*			Büchner, *Woyzeck*; Gogol, *The Inspector- General*
Emerson, *The American Scholar*; Hawthorne, *Twice-Told Tales*		W. D. Howells b.	London début of Samuel Phelps
		A. Daly b.	Irving b.; Rachel plays Camille in Corneille's *Horace* in Paris
Longfellow, *Hyperion*; Stendhal, *La Chartreuse de Parme*		J. A. Herne b.; W. Dunlap d.	Lytton, *Richelieu*
Cooper, *The Pathfinder*; Dana, *Two Years before the Mast*; Poe, *Tales of the Grotesque and the Arabesque*			
Browning, *Dramatic Lyrics*; Cooper, *The Deerslayer*			Boucicault, *London Assurance*
Dickens, *American Notes*; Longfellow, *Ballads and Other Poems*		B. Howard b.; S. MacKaye b.; S. Woodworth d.	Pitt, *Sweeney Todd*
Dickens, *Martin Chuzzlewit*			

I	2	3

Date	Historical events	Theatrical events within the USA
1844		
1845		Bowery Theatre burned and rebuilt; Castle Garden, New York
1846	US War with Mexico	Howard Athenaeum, Boston
1847		First Chicago theatre
1848	Marx and Engels, *Communist Manifesto*; revolutions in Europe	Park Theatre burned; Macready's final US tour
1849	Gold rush to California begins	Astor Place Riots in New York result from rivalry of Forrest and Macready; Eagle Theatre, Sacramento, California
1850	Fugitive Slave Law	Jenny Lind Theatre, San Francisco
1851		
1852		
1853		
1854	Crimean War begins; Kansas–Nebraska Act	Academy of Music, New York

4	5	6	7
Non-dramatic literary events	First performance of American plays	Birth and death dates of notable American playwrights	Theatrical events outside America
Dumas, *Les Trois Mousquetaires*; Emerson, *Essays* (second series); Lowell, *Poems*	Smith, *The Drunkard*	E. Harrigan b.	Sarah Bernhardt b.
Mérimée, *Carmen*; Poe, *Tales of Mystery and Imagination*	Anna C. M. Ritchie, *Fashion*		
Melville, *Typee*; Webster, *Bunker Hill Speeches*			
Charlotte Brontë, *Jane Eyre*; Emily Brontë, *Wuthering Heights*; Emerson, *Poems*; Longfellow, *Evangeline*; Melville, *Omoo*; Thackeray, *Vanity Fair*	Brougham, *Metamora* (burlesque)		
Lowell, *The Biglow Papers*			Royal theatricals begin at Windsor Castle
Thoreau, *Civil Disobedience*; *A Week on the Concord*			Ellen Terry b.
Emerson, *Representative Men*; Hawthorne, *The Scarlet Letter*; Melville, *White Jacket*			
Hawthorne, *House of the Seven Gables*; Melville, *Moby Dick*			Macready retires
Hawthorne, *The Blithesdale Romance*; H. B. Stowe, *Uncle Tom's Cabin*		J. H. Payne d.	Boucicault, *The Corsican Brothers*; Dumas *fils*, *Camille*; Ibsen becomes stage director and dramaturge at Bergen
		D. Belasco b.	
Thoreau, *Walden*		J. N. Barker d.; R. M. Bird d.	

1	2	3
Date	*Historical events*	*Theatrical events within the USA*
1855		
1856		Laura Keene's Varieties, New York; Edwin Booth's New York début
1857	Indian Mutiny	McVickers Theatre, Chicago
1858		
1859		
1860	Abraham Lincoln elected President	
1861	Civil War begins at Fort Sumter	Wallack's Theatre, New York
1862	Homestead Act opens the west	Salt Lake City Theatre
1863		Piper's Opera House, Virginia City, Nevada
1864		

4	5	6	7
		Birth and death dates of	
Non-dramatic literary events	First performance of American plays	notable American playwrights	Theatrical events outside America
Browning, *Men and Women*; Longfellow, *Hiawatha*; Melville, *Benito Cereno*; Tennyson, *Maud*; Whitman, *Leaves of Grass*	Boker, *Francesca da Rimini*		
			Shaw b.
Atlantic Monthly established; Baudelaire, *Les Fleurs du mal*; Melville, *The Confidence Man*; Spencer, *Essays*	Boucicault, *The Poor of New York*		
Holmes, *The Autocrat at the Breakfast Table*; Longfellow, *The Courtship of Miles Standish*	Pratt, *Ten Nights in a Bar Room*		Dumas *fils*, *Le Fils naturel*; Rachel d.
Darwin, *The Origin of Species*	Boucicault, *The Octoroon*		Boucicault, *The Colleen Bawn*
Emerson, *The Conduct of Life*; Hawthorne, *The Marble Faun*			
Holmes, *Elsie Venner*; Mrs Henry Wood, *East Lynne*			Edwin Booth's first English tour; Scribe d.
Hugo, *Les Misérables*		L. Mitchell b.	Sarah Bernhardt's début at Comédie-Française
Hawthorne, *Our Old Home*; Lincoln, *Gettysburg Address*; Longfellow, *Tales of a Wayside Inn*; Thoreau, *Excursions*			Taylor, *The Ticket-of-leave Man*; Stanislavsky b.
Thoreau, *Maine Woods*; *Cape Cod*			

1	2	3
Date	Historical events	Theatrical events within the USA
1865	Civil War ends; Lincoln assassinated	Opera House, New York (vaudeville)
1866		
1867	Reconstruction Act	
1868		
1869		Booth's Theatre, New York
1870	Franco-Prussian War begins	
1871		Union Square Theatre, New York
1872		
1873	Financial panic hits USA	Augustin Daly's New Fifth Avenue Theatre, New York
1874		
1875		

4 Non-dramatic literary events	5 First performance of American plays	6 Birth and death dates of notable American playwrights	7 Theatrical events outside America
Browne, *Artemus Ward: his Travels*; Lewis Carroll, *Alice in Wonderland*; Shaw, *Josh Billings: his Sayings*; Whitman, *Drum-Taps*	Jefferson and Boucicault, *Rip Van Winkle*	C. Fitch b.	
Whittier, *Snow-Bound*			
Mark Twain, *The Celebrated Jumping Frog*; Marx, *Das Kapital*; Whittier, *Maud Muller*	Daly, *Under the Gaslight*		Robertson, *Caste*
Louisa M. Alcott, *Little Women*; Browne, *Artemus Ward: his Book*; Long-fellow, *New England Tragedies*			
Louisa M. Alcott, *Good Wives*; Mark Twain, *The Innocents Abroad*		E. A. Robinson b.; W. V. Moody b.	
Harte, *The Luck of Roaring Camp*		Anna Cora Mowatt Ritchie d.	
Darwin, *The Descent of Man*; Edward Eggleston, *The Hoosier Schoolmaster*; George Eliot, *Middle-march*		C. R. Kennedy b.	H. Irving appears in L. Lewis's *The Bells*; Robertson d.
Holmes, *The Poet at the Breakfast Table*		W. H. Smith d.	
Mark Twain and C. D. Warner, *The Gilded Age*			Macready d.; Zola, preface to *Thérèse Raquin*, proclaims naturalism
		Josephine Marks b.	
Mary Baker Eddy, *Science and Health*	Daly, *Pique*	P. MacKaye b.	Ellen Terry appears as Portia; Tennyson, *Queen Mary*; Gilbert and Sullivan, *Trial by Jury*

1	2	3
Date	Historical events	Theatrical events within the USA
1876		Broad Street Theatre, Philadelphia
1877		
1878		
1879		Broadway Theatre, New York, renamed Daly's Theatre
1880		Steele MacKaye's Madison Square Theatre, New York
1881		
1882		Wallack's Theatre, New York
1883		Irving's first US tour
1884		
1885		Lyceum Theatre, New York
1886	Haymarket Square riot in Chicago; American Federation of Labor organized	

4	5	6	7
		Birth and death dates of	
Non-dramatic literary events	*First performance of American plays*	*notable American playwrights*	*Theatrical events outside America*
James, *Roderick Hudson*; Mark Twain, *Tom Sawyer*			Ibsen, *Peer Gynt*; Wagner's Bayreuth Theatre established; Lemaître d.
James, *The American*; Zola, *L'Assommoir*			
Hardy, *The Return of the Native*; James, *Daisy Miller*	Howells, *Yorick's Love*	Rachel Crothers b.	
James, *The Europeans*	Belasco and Herne, *Hearts of Oak*; Harrigan, *The Mulligan Guard Ball*; MacKaye, *Hazel Kirke*		Ibsen, *A Doll's House*
Harris, *Uncle Remus*; Mark Twain, *A Tramp Abroad*; Wallace, *Ben Hur*			T. Taylor d.
James, *The Portrait of a Lady*			Ibsen, *Ghosts*
Howells, *A Modern Instance*	Campbell, *The White Slave*; Howard, *Young Mrs Winthrop*	Susan Glaspell b.	Ibsen, *An Enemey of the People*; H. A. Jones, *The Silver King*
Harris, *Nights with Uncle Remus*; Nietzsche, *Also sprach Zarathustra*			
Mark Twain, *Huckleberry Finn*			Ibsen, *The Wild Duck*
Howells, *The Rise of Silas Lapham*; Zola, *Germinal*			
James, *The Bostonians, The Princess Casamassima*; Nietzsche, *Jenseits von Gut und Böse*; Stevenson, *Dr Jekyll and Mr Hyde*	Thompson, *The Old Homestead*	E. Sheldon b.	

1	2	3
Date	*Historical events*	*Theatrical events within the USA*
1887		
1888		
1889		
1890	Sherman Anti-Trust Act	Harrigan's Theatre, New York (later renamed Garrick Theatre)
1891		
1892	Ford completes his first automobile	
1893		Empire Theatre, New York
1894		
1895		Steele MacKaye's Scenitorium
1896		First Theatrical Syndicate agreement signed
1897		

4	5	6	7
Non-dramatic literary events	First performance of American plays	Birth and death dates of notable American playwrights	Theatrical events outside America
		G. Kelly b.	Strindberg, *The Father*; A. Antoine founds Théâtre Libre, Paris
Bellamy, *Looking Backward*	Howard, *Shenandoah*	M. Anderson b.; E. O'Neill b.	
		G. S. Kaufman b.	Strindberg, *Miss Julie*; O. Brahm founds Freie Bühne, Berlin
Emily Dickinson, *Poems*	Herne, *Margaret Fleming*	M. Connolly b.; D. Boucicault d.	Ibsen, *Hedda Gabler*; Maeterlinck, *Les Aveugles*
Bierce, *Tales of Soldiers and Civilians*; Howells, *Criticism and Fiction*; Shaw, *Quintessence of Ibsenism*; Wilde, *The Picture of Dorian Grey*		S. Howard b.	J. T. Grein founds Independent Theatre Society, London
	Fitch, *The Girl with the Green Eyes*; Howells, *A Letter of Introduction*; Hoyt, *A Temperance Town*	A. MacLeish b.; Edna St V. Millay b.; E. Rice b.	Hauptmann, *Die Weber*; Shaw, *Widowers' Houses*; Wilde, *Lady Windermere's Fan*
	Herne, *Shore Acres*; Howells, *The Unexpected Guests*	S. N. Behrman b.	Pinero, *The Second Mrs Tanqueray*
Mark Twain, *Pudd'nhead Wilson*		P. Green b.; S. MacKaye d.	Schnitzler, *Liebelei*; Wedekind, *Earth Spirit*
Crane, *The Red Badge of Courage*; Wells, *The Time Machine*; Yeats, *Poems*	Belasco, *The Heart of Maryland*; Gillette, *Secret Service*	J. H. Lawson b.	Wilde, *The Importance of Being Earnest*
Jewett, *The Country of Pointed Firs*		P. Barry b.; R. Sherwood b.	Chekhov, *The Seagull*; Jarry, *Ubu roi*
James, *What Maisie Knew*; *The Spoils of Poynton*		T. Wilder b.	Chekhov, *Uncle Vanya*; Jones, *The Liars*; Rostand, *Cyrano de Bergerac*

1	2	3
Date	*Historical events*	*Theatrical events within the USA*
1898	Spanish-American War	
1899		
1900		Shubert Brothers in New York
1901	President McKinley assassinated; Theodore Roosevelt becomes president; Edward VII becomes King of England	
1902		Republic Theatre, New York, renamed Belasco Theatre
1903	Ford Motor Company established; Wright brothers' first sustained flight in powered aeroplane at Kitty Hawk, NC	
1904		
1905		
1906		

4 Non-dramatic literary events	5 First performance of American plays	6 Birth and death dates of notable American playwrights	7 Theatrical events outside America
			Shaw, *Mrs Warren's Profession*; Stanislavsky founds Moscow Art Theatre
Norris, *McTeague*	Gillette, *Sherlock Holmes*	L. Riggs b.; A. Daly d.	Shaw, *Caesar and Cleopatra*; Yeats, *The Countess Cathleen*
Conrad, *Lord Jim*; Marie Corelli, *Boy*; Dreiser, *Sister Carrie*	Belasco, *Madame Butterfly*		
Mann, *Buddenbrooks*	Fitch, *The Climbers*		Chekhov, *The Three Sisters*
Gide, *L'Immoraliste*; James, *The Wings of the Dove*			Gorky, *The Lower Depths*
James, *The Ambassadors*; London, *The Call of the Wild*			
Conrad, *Nostromo*; O. Henry, *Cabbages and Kings*; Steffens, *The Shames of the Cities*		M. Hart b.	Abbey Theatre, Dublin, opened; Synge, *Riders to the Sea*; Chekhov, *The Cherry Orchard*; Puccini, *Madama Butterfly*
Forster, *Where Angels Fear to Tread*; James, *The Golden Bowl*; Edith Wharton, *The House of Mirth*			Shaw, *Major Barbara*
Adams; *The Education of Henry Adams*; Galsworthy, *The Man of Property*; O. Henry, *The Four Million*; London, *White Fang*; Sinclair, *The Jungle*; Wallace, *The Four Just Men*	Mitchell, *The New York Idea*; Moody, *The Great Divide*	Lillian Hellman b.; S. Kingsley b.; C. Odets b.	Ibsen d.

1	2	3
Date	Historical events	Theatrical events within the USA
1907		David Belasco builds Stuyvesant Theatre (now Belasco Theatre)
1908		
1909		New Theatre, New York (closed 1911); George Pierce Baker first teaches 'Techniques of the Drama' at Harvard (as 'English Course 47')
1910	George V becomes King of England	Drama League of America established
1911		
1912		Dramatists' Guild established
1913		Actors' Equity Association established
1914	First World War begins	
1915		Provincetown Players (to 1929) established; Washington Square Players (to 1918) established

4 Non-dramatic literary events	5 First performance of American plays	6 Birth and death dates of notable American playwrights	7 Theatrical events outside America
Conrad, *The Secret Agent*	Kennedy, *The Servant in the House*		Synge, *The Playboy of the Western World* causes riots at Abbey Theatre; Chinese Spring Willow Society adapts and produces *Uncle Tom's Cabin* in Tokyo and Shanghai
Bennett, *The Old Wives' Tale*	P. MacKaye, *The Scarecrow*; Walter, *Paid in Full*, *The Easiest Way*	W. Saroyan b.; B. Howard d.	Barrie, *What Every Woman Knows*; Strindberg, *The Ghost Sonata*
Florence M. Barclay, *The Rosary*	Fitch, *The City*; Sheldon, *The Nigger*	C. Fitch d.	Galsworthy, *Strife*; Molnár, *Liliom*
Forster, *Howards End*		J. A. Herne d.; W. V. Moody d.	
Lawrence, *The White Peacock*; Edith Wharton, *Ethan Frome*	Belasco, *The Return of Peter Grimm*; Rachel Crothers, *He and She*; Sheldon, *The Boss*	E. Harrigan d.; D. Thompson d.	Puccini, *La Fanciulla del West* (première, New York)
Dreiser, *Jennie Gerhardt*			Strindberg d.
Willa Cather, *O Pioneers!*; Frost, *A Boy's Will*; Lawrence, *Sons and Lovers*; Mann, *Der Tod in Venedig*; Proust, *A la recherche du temps perdu* (to 1928)		W. Inge b.	Copeau founds Théâtre du Vieux-Colombier
Frost, *North of Boston*; Joyce, *Dubliners*		T. L. Williams b.	Shaw, *Pygmalion*; Lilian Baylis founds Old Vic, London
Dreiser, *The Genius*; Lawrence, *The Rainbow*; Maugham, *Of Human Bondage*; Virginia Woolf, *The Voyage Out*		A. Miller b.	

1	2	3
Date	Historical events	Theatrical events within the USA
1916		Theatrical Syndicate dissolved
1917	US troops in France; Russian Revolution	First Equity contract signed
1918		Theatre Guild established
1919	Treaty of Versailles; Communist International organized in USSR	Actors' Equity strike
1920	XIX Amendment to US Constitution	
1921	Communist Party organized in China	
1922		
1923		
1924		
1925		Guild Theatre, New York

| 4 | 5 | 6 Birth and death dates of | 7 |
Non-dramatic literary events	First performance of American plays	notable American playwrights	Theatrical events outside America
Moore, *The Brook Kerith*; E. A. Robinson, *The Man Against the Sky*; Sandburg, *Chicago Poems*	O'Neill, *Bound East for Cardiff*		
Eliot, *Prufrock*	Williams, *Why Marry?*		
Willa Cather, *My Antonia*		A. Laurents b.	Kaiser, *Gas* I (II, 1920)
Anderson, *Winesburg, Ohio*; Cabell, *Jurgen*; Mencken, *Prejudices, The American Language*	Edna St V. Millay, *Aria da Capo*		Maugham, *The Circle*; Toller, *Masse-Mensche* (*Masses and Men*)
Fitzgerald, *This Side of Paradise*; Lawrence, *Women in Love*; Lewis, *Main Street*; Pound, *Umbra*; Edith Wharton, *The Age of Innocence*	O'Neill, *Beyond the Horizon, The Emperor Jones*	W. D. Howells d.	
	Susan Glaspell, *The Verge*; O'Neill ,'*Anna Christie*'		Capek, *R.U.R.*; Pirandello, *Six Characters in Search of an Author*
Eliot, *The Waste Land*; Fitzgerald, *The Beautiful and the Damned*; Joyce, *Ulysses*; Lewis, *Babbitt*	O'Neill, *The Hairy Ape*	Josephine Marks d.	
	Lawson, *Roger Bloomer*; Rice, *The Adding Machine*	P. Chayefsky b.	Flecker, *Hassan*; Shaw, *Saint Joan*
Forster, *A Passage to India*	Anderson and Stallings, *What Price Glory?*; Howard, *They Knew What They Wanted*; Kelly, *The Show-off*; O'Neill, *Desire under the Elms*	J. Baldwin b.	Coward, *Hay Fever*; O'Casey, *Juno and the Paycock*
Dreiser, *An American Tragedy*; Fitzgerald, *The Great Gatsby*; Kafka, *Der Prozess*; Anita Loos, *Gentlemen Prefer Blondes*	Kelly, *Craig's Wife*; Lawson, *Processional*		

Date	Historical events	Theatrical events within the USA
1926		Civic Repertory Theatre established by Eva Le Gallienne
1927		
1928		
1929	Stockmarket crashes, 29 October; beginnings of the Great Depression	
1930		
1931		Group Theatre (to 1941) established
1932	Franklyn Delano Roosevelt elected President	
1933		
1934		

4 Non-dramatic literary events	5 First performance of American plays	6 Birth and death dates of notable American playwrights	7 Theatrical events outside America
Edna Ferber, *Show Boat*; Hemingway, *The Sun Also Rises*; Kafka, *Das Schloss*	Green, *In Abraham's Bosom*; Howard, *The Silver Cord*; O'Neill, *The Great God Brown*		Galsworthy, *Escape*
Hemingway, *Men Without Women*; Lewis, *Elmer Gantry*; Sandburg, *The American Songbag*; Sinclair, *Oil!*; Wilder, *The Bridge of San Luis Rey*	D. and Du B. Heyward, *Porgy*	N. Simon b.	
Benét, *John Brown's Body*; Jeffers, *Cawdor and Other Poems*	Barry, *Holiday*; O'Neill, *Lazarus Laughed, Marco Millions, Strange Interlude*	E. Albee b.	Brecht, *Die Dreigroschenoper*; Sherriff, *Journey's End*
Faulkner, *The Sound and the Fury*; Hemingway, *A Farewell to Arms*; Wolfe, *Look Homeward, Angel*	Rice, *Street Scene*		
Dos Passos, *The 42nd Parallel*	Anderson, *Elizabeth the Queen*; Barry, *Hotel Universe*; Connelly, *The Green Pastures*; Kaufman and Hart, *Once in a Lifetime*	Lorraine Hansberry b.	Besier, *The Barretts of Wimpole Street*
	O'Neill, *Mourning Becomes Electra*; Riggs, *Green Grow the Lilacs*	D. Belasco d.	
Caldwell, *Tobacco Road*; Farrell, *Studs Lonigan*; Runyon, *Guys and Dolls*	Behrman, *Biography*; Howard, *The Late Christopher Bean*		
Cozzens, *The Last Adam*; Thurber, *My Life and Hard Times*; West, *Miss Lonelyhearts*	O'Neill, *Ah, Wilderness!*		Lorca, *Blood Wedding*
Cain, *The Postman Always Rings Twice*; O'Hara, *Appointment in Samarra*	Lillian Hellman, *The Children's Hour*; Odets, *Awake and Sing!*		Cocteau, *La Machine infernale*

1	2	3
Date	*Historical events*	*Theatrical events within the USA*
1935	Works Progress Administration Act; Social Security Act	Federal Theatre (to 1939) established
1936	Spanish Civil War begins	
1937		
1938		Playwrights' Company (to 1961) established
1939	Second World War begins	
1940		
1941	Pearl Harbor, 7 December; USA enters the war	
1942		
1943		

4	5	6	7
Non-dramatic literary events	First performance of American plays	Birth and death dates of notable American playwrights	Theatrical events outside America
Steinbeck, *Tortilla Flat*; Wolfe, *Of Time and the River*	Anderson, *Winterset*; Kingsley, *Dead End*; Odets, *Waiting for Lefty*; Sherwood, *The Petrified Forest*	L. Mitchell d.; E. A. Robinson d.	Eliot, *Murder in the Cathedral*; Giraudoux, *La Guerre de Troie n'aura pas lieu*
Faulkner, *Absalom, Absalom!*; Margaret Mitchell, *Gone With the Wind*; Sandburg, *The People, Yes*	Green, *Johnny Johnson*; Kaufman and Hart, *You Can't Take It With You*; Sherwood, *Idiot's Delight*		Auden and Isherwood, *The Ascent of F6*; Rattigan, *French Without Tears*
Steinbeck, *Of Mice and Men*; Stevens, *The Man with the Blue Guitar and Other Poems*	Green, *The Lost Colony*; Lawson, *Marching Song*; Odets, *Golden Boy*		Priestley, *Time and the Conways*
	Sherwood, *Abe Lincoln in Illinois*; Wilder, *Our Town*		
Katherine Anne Porter, *Pale Horse, Pale Rider*; Steinbeck, *The Grapes of Wrath*	Lillian Hellman, *The Little Foxes*; Kaufman and Hart, *The Man Who Came to Dinner*; Saroyan, *My Heart's in the Highlands*, *The Time of your Life*	S. Howard d.	Eliot, *The Family Reunion*
Chandler, *Farewell My Lovely*; Greene, *The Power and the Glory*; Hemingway, *For Whom the Bell Tolls*; Wolfe, *You Can't Go Home Again*	Sherwood, *There Shall Be No Night*		
			Brecht, *Mother Courage*
	Wilder, *The Skin of our Teeth*		Sartre, *Les Mouches*; Brecht, *Galileo*
Eliot, *Four Quartets*; Betty Smith, *A Tree Grows in Brooklyn*	Rodgers and Hammerstein, *Oklahoma!*		

Date	Historical events	Theatrical events within the USA
1944		
1945	VE Day, 7 May; atomic bombs dropped on Japan; VJ Day, 14 August; United Nations Charter signed in San Francisco, 24 June	
1946		
1947		
1948		
1949		
1950	Start of Korean War	
1950–4	'McCarthyism' (1950 Senator McCarthy's allegations concerning Communists in the State Department; 1954 McCarthy censured by Senate)	
1951		
1952		

4 Non-dramatic literary events	5 First performance of American plays	6 Birth and death dates of notable American playwrights	7 Theatrical events outside America
	Williams, *The Glass Menagerie*		Anouilh, *Antigone*; Sartre, *Huis clos*
Orwell, *Animal Farm*	Laurents, *Home of the Brave*		
Jeffers, *Medea*; Carson McCullers, *The Member of the Wedding*; Warren, *All The King's Men*; Wilson, *Memoirs of Hecate County*	O'Neill, *The Iceman Cometh*	E. Sheldon d.	
Camus, *La Peste*; Lewis, *Kingsblood Royal*; Steinbeck, *The Pearl*	Williams, *A Streetcar Named Desire*		Brecht, *The Caucasian Chalk Circle*
Faulkner, *Intruder in the Dust*; Mailer, *The Naked and the Dead*		Susan Glaspell d.	Fry, *The Lady's Not For Burning*
	Miller, *Death of a Salesman*; Rodgers and Hammerstein, *South Pacific*	P. Barry d.	Eliot, *The Cocktail Party*
	Inge, *Come Back, Little Sheba*	C. R. Kennedy d.	Ionesco, *La Cantatrice chauve*
Capote, *The Grass Harp*; Faulkner, *Requiem for a Nun*; Salinger, *The Catcher in the Rye*	Williams, *The Rose Tattoo*		
Hemingway, *The Old Man and the Sea*		Edna St V. Millay d.	Beckett, *En attendant Godot*; Rattigan, *The Deep Blue Sea*

Date	Historical events	Theatrical events within the USA
1953	Truce ends fighting in Korea	
1954	*Brown v. Board of Education of Topeka* (Supreme Court judgement reversing, in the field of education, the 'separate but equal' doctrine of *Plessey v. Ferguson* (1896) supporting racial segregation)	
1955		
1956		
1957	Little Rock: Governor Faubus of Arkansas uses National Guard to keep Negro children out of public schools	
1958		
1959		
1960		Association of Producing Artists established by Ellis Rabb (to 1969)
1961	Bay of Pigs: US abortive invasion of Cuba	La Mama Experimental Theatre Club established by Ellen Stewart
1962	Col. John Glen: first American in space; Cuban missiles crisis	

4	5	6 Birth and death dates of	7
Non-dramatic literary events	First performance of American plays	notable American playwrights	Theatrical events outside America
	Inge, *Picnic*; Miller, *The Crucible*; O'Neill, *A Moon for the Misbegotten* (in Stockholm); Williams, *Camino Real*	E. O'Neill d.	Greene, *The Living Room*
Amis, *Lucky Jim*; Golding, *Lord of the Flies*		L. Riggs d.	Whiting, *Marching Song*
Nabokov, *Lolita*	Inge, *Bus Stop*; Miller, *A View from the Bridge*; Williams, *Cat on a Hot Tin Roof*	R. Sherwood d.	
Wilson, *Anglo-Saxon Attitudes*	O'Neill, *Long Day's Journey into Night*	P. MacKaye d.	Osborne, *Look Back in Anger*
	O'Neill, *A Touch of the Poet* (in Stockholm); Williams, *Orpheus Descending*		
	MacLeish, *J.B.*; O'Neill, *Hughie* (in Stockholm); Williams, *Suddenly Last Summer*, *Sweet Bird of Youth*	Rachel Crothers d.	Pinter, *The Birthday Party*
Bellow, *Henderson the Rain King*	Albee, *The Zoo Story*; Chayefsky, *The Tenth Man*; Lorraine Hansberry, *A Raisin in the Sun*	M. Anderson d.	Arden, *Serjeant Musgrave's Dance*; Ionesco, *Rhinocéros*; Wesker, *Roots*
	Kopit, *Oh Dad, Poor Dad*		Bolt, *A Man for All Seasons*; Pinter, *The Caretaker*
Heller, *Catch 22*	Albee, *The American Dream*; Williams, *The Night of the Iguana*	M. Hart d.	
	Albee, *Who's Afraid of Virginia Woolf?*; O'Neill, *More Stately Mansions* (in Stockholm)	G. S. Kaufman d.	F. Dürrenmatt, *The Physicists*

	1	2	3

Date	Historical events	Theatrical events within the USA
1963	Civil Rights march on Washington; assassination of President Kennedy	Repertory company formed for the Lincoln Center for Performing Arts
1964	Gulf of Tonkin Resolution: Congressional authority to increase American involvement in Vietnam	Black Arts Repertoire Theatre School established
1965	Watts County race riots	
1966		
1967		
1968	Assassinations of Dr Martin Luther King and Robert Kennedy	Negro Ensemble Company established; Theatre Development Fund launched
1969	Col. Neil Armstrong: first man lands on the moon	
1972	Ceasefire in Vietnam; Watergate break-in	
1973		
1974	Resignation of President Nixon	
1975		

4	5	6 Birth and death dates of	7
Non-dramatic literary events	First performance of American plays	notable American playwrights	Theatrical events outside America
		C. Odets d.	
	Albee, *Tiny Alice*; Jones, *Dutchman*; Miller, *After the Fall, Incident at Vichy*; Williams, *The Milk Train Doesn't Stop Here Anymore*		Shaffer, *The Royal Hunt of the Sun*; P. Weiss, *Marat/Sade*
	Fraser, *The Odd Couple*; Williams, *Slapstick Tragedy*	Lorraine Hansberry d.	Bond, *Saved*
	Albee, *A Delicate Balance*		
	Feiffer, *Little Murders*; Heller, *We Bombed in New Haven*	E. Rice d.	Stoppard, *Rosencrantz and Guildenstern are Dead*
	Miller, *The Price*; Williams, *The Seven Descents of Myrtle*		
		S. N. Behrman d.; W. Inge d.	
		G. Kelly d.	
		T. Wilder d.	

Acknowledgements

The authors and publisher wish to thank the following for permission to reproduce the following copyright material:

Plates 3, 5, 19, 24, 25, 30, 31 by courtesy of the Theatre and Music Collection, Museum of the City of New York

Plate 4 by courtesy of The New York Historical Society

Plates 7, 12, 16 by courtesy of the Richard Moody Collection, Bloomington, Indiana

Plates 8, 14, 15 by courtesy of the Bancroft Library, University of California, Berkeley (Fred G. Ross Collection)

Plates 9, 10, 11, 13, 17 from the private collection of Professor J. Peter Coulson, Southwest Texas State University

Plates 18, 23, 27, 28, 29 by courtesy of the Theatre Collection, Library of the Performing Arts, New York Public Library

Plate 20 by courtesy of the University Research Library, University of California, Los Angeles (Kenneth Macgowan Collection)

Plate 21 by courtesy of Sheldon Cheney.

Plate 26 by courtesy of The Beinecke Library, Yale University (Vandamm photograph)

I The American drama: its range of contexts

Travis Bogard

1 Actors in the land

The memories of many Americans reach easily back through more than a quarter of their nation's history, to a time of simple wonders – crystal sets and World Fairs and mail planes – and to cities not quite urban, where streetcars moved through open fields. Laced inextricably with such images are memories of theatres, and sentences of recall come readily to the lips: '*Ben Hur* with real horses . . .' or 'Nazimova in *Ghosts*', or 'Katharine Cornell, Ruth Gordon *and* Judith Anderson in Chekhov!' The names fall easily and form a small litany acknowledging service rendered and pleasure given, part of the gentle recollection of a lost world.

Like everything else in the United States, the theatre had to be created in a hurry from nothing, under conditions of real hardship, not the least of which was the size of the expanding nation. In the beginning, in the young nation that hugged the eastern seaboard, the drama could not be expected to flourish. In a world whose cultural life was dominated by the very Puritans who a hundred years earlier had delivered the *coup de grâce* to the moribund Caroline theatre, there was little hope that even amateur theatre could prosper. Furthermore, what less auspicious time could there be for a theatre to emerge than the latter half of the eighteenth century, when theatres in all nations were barely existing, devoid of energy and imagination? In a nation struggling to know itself, there was little incentive to create a drama that could serve as a central reflector of what the nation was.

Instead, America received the theatrical benefits any colony might expect. In the metropolitan centres, touring companies from England, bolstered on occasions with local talent, presented the derivative repertory that London gave its audiences and went on the road to cities and towns within Britain. With perhaps this difference: that the actors coming as far afield as America were not clearly displaying the intrepidity of a Columbus or a Drake, but were, rather, seeking work. No actor would cross the Atlantic and endure the uncertainties and hardships, the censorship, the meagre financial rewards of the eighteenth-century American theatre, if he could have survived in London, or, it must be assumed, anywhere in England. The actors of the Hallam company, who performed with varying degrees of success in Williamsburg, New York, Philadelphia and Charleston at mid-century, were following dollars, not their stars. Although their playbills and their petitions to local governments for the privilege of performing cast a pious halo of good works around their activities, the Hallam associates could have been no more than hardworking barnstormers of moderate talent. Content with the routine repertory of the eighteenth century – Rowe, Lillo, Farquhar, Steele and some Shakespeare – theirs was not a cultural mission. It was a struggle for survival.

Hardship was normal. So long as no city had achieved the important centrality in relation to the rest of the country that New York City was to attain by the end of the nineteenth century, the actor was forced to travel. He proved capable of mighty effort. As the nation developed, following its 'manifest destiny' to the west, the actors appeared, amateurs on the wagon trains, strolling players like Mark Twain's King and Duke in *Huckleberry Finn*, relatively sophisticated troupes on showboats, bringing theatre to the towns along the Mississippi and Missouri rivers, touring companies in the deserts and the Sierra Nevada. With extraordinary hardihood, they sought audiences and were enthusiastically, gratefully received.

A sample of what their life was like in the early nineteenth century is provided by the diary of an itinerant actor, Sol Smith, who in 1830 was so heavily in debt that he had to play alternate nights in two Mississippi towns, Port Gibson and Natchez, fifty miles apart. An extract from his journal describes three days in his muddy *Künstlerleben*:

> *Wednesday*. Rose at break of day. Horse at the door. Swallowed a cup of coffee while the boy was tying on leggins. Reached Washington at 8. Changed horses at 9 – again at 10 – and at 11. At 12 arrived Port Gibson.

Attended rehearsal – settled business with stage manager. Dined at 4. Laid down and endeavored to sleep at 5. Up again at 6. Rubbed down and washed by Jim (a negro boy). Dressed at 7. Acted the *Three Singles* and *Splash*. To bed at 11½.

Thursday. Rose and breakfasted at 9. At 10 attended rehearsal for the pieces of next day. At 1 leggins tied on and braved the mud for a 50 miles' ride. Rain falling all the way. Arrived at Natchez at half past 6. Rubbed down and took supper. Acted *Ezekiel Homespun* and *Delph* to a poor house. To bed (stiff as steelyards) at 12.

Friday. Cast pieces – counted tickets – attended rehearsals until 1 P.M. To horse again for Port Gibson – arrived at 7. No time to eat dinner or supper! Acted in the *Magpie and the Maid*, and *No Song No Supper*, in which latter piece I managed to get a few mouthfuls of cold roast mutton and some dry bread, they being the first food tasted this day . . . BUT I PAID MY DEBTS![1]

Granted that Smith's problems were severe, the exhausting journey for meagre theatrical accomplishment was normal in the actor's career. Judged by any standard, the life was unbearable. Eugene O'Neill, himself the son of an itinerant actor, describes something of the squalor of the actor's life in the persons of James and Mary Tyrone, the names he gave to the characters representing his father and mother in *Long Day's Journey into Night*. Mary speaks of the many nights her husband has been brought home drunk to the squalid hotel rooms they inhabited on theatrical tours:

> I had waited in that ugly hotel room hour after hour. I kept making excuses for you. I told myself it must be some business connected with the theatre. I knew so little about the theatre. Then I became terrified. I imagined all sorts of horrible accidents. I got on my knees and prayed that nothing had happened to you – and then they brought you up and left you outside the door, . . . I didn't know how often that was to happen in the years to come, how many times I was to wait in ugly hotel rooms. I became quite used to it.[2]

To extrapolate a picture of the hardships of empty lives in lonely hotel rooms from the rueful words takes no special act of imagination. Once the railroads had come, a large company of forty or more actors would have special coaches and firm arrangements to facilitate their travel; an established star

[1] Sol Smith, *Theatrical Management in the West and South for Thirty Years* (New York and London, 1968), p. 64.
[2] Eugene O'Neill, *Long Day's Journey into Night* (New Haven, Conn., 1955), p. 113.

would have at least a compartment on a train and a vestige of privacy and
comfort. For small companies and for most of the travelling actors, such
luxuries were unknown. They took their places in the day coaches, along with
the general public. 'Many times', wrote F. G. Ross in his *Memories of an Old
Theatrical Man*,[3] 'a train would be so crowded that many of the company
had to stand a long time without a place to sit.'

The hotels were rarely first class. Ross noted that 'We always went to a
cheap hotel, and in fact as all the hotels were on the American plan, the most
we would pay was one dollar and a half for room and dining.'[4] Nevertheless,
the hotel was home. Ross found it not so bad when the company stayed a
week or longer in one city,

> but when it came to one night stands, and a new hotel almost every day,
> then one became at times something of a gypsy. Imagine if you will –
> arriving at a town at five or six in the morning; or even if it be as late as
> nine o'clock. This after travelling all night, or perhaps may have left the
> the last town very early with but little rest or sleep the night before. At
> the best hotel in town often one is told, 'We have no vacant room yet;
> but if you wait until later when some check out we can take care of you.'
> Then there is nothing to do but sit around and wait for someone to leave
> the hotel. However, this does not always happen, and rooms may be
> ready on arrival.[5]

Such a consummation as a warm, ready room was evidently not the rule in
the late nineteenth- and early twentieth-century American scene. In Canada
it was worse. Ross recorded that there, often, hotels had no heat in the rooms,
the only source of warmth being a stove in the corridor radiating feebly
through the open bedroom doors.

> There were times when in travelling and [being] forced to play in many
> one night stands, we visited places so dreary, one would feel miserable
> until far from such. Such places as the iron country of north Michigan,
> might well take the heart out of everyone. Ishpenning, Clummet, and
> many other of those northern towns with their dreariness and snow.
> Another section that never appealed to me was the state of Iowa.[6]

[3] Frederick G. Ross, *Memories of an Old Theatrical Man* (unpublished typescript, The
Bancroft Library, University of California, Berkeley, n.d.), Addenda, p. 12. Quoted
by permission of The Director, The Bancroft Library, University of California,
Berkeley. Ross's journal covers, approximately, the period between 1880 and 1920.

[4] Ross, op. cit. p. 56.

[5] Ross, op. cit. pp. 29–30.

[6] Ross, op. cit. p. 34.

Even cleanliness was a problem. Trunks, Ross said, 'are never delivered to individuals on one night stands more than once a week. Transfer companies charged for hauling trunks oft times as high as fifty cents per trunk, never less than twenty five cents. So only the trunks used at the theatre were hauled daily.'[7] Conditions at many theatres approached a definition of squalor. Often there were no facilities for washing backstage. Ross remembered a local theatre manager who commented, 'Hell, they're supposed to be clean when they come here, ain't they?' Taxed with the fact that his theatre provided not even a drinking glass backstage, he was puzzled: 'Why that's funny. There was a glass here a year ago.'[8] It is difficult to avoid the conclusion that on a long tour the odour of stale linen and cheap cologne must have been the actors' perpetual ambiance.

Road companies were preceded then, as now, by an advance man, whose duties Ross once undertook: to lay out the printing and supply copies of advertisements and photographs for the newspapers, to confer with local critics, to fix admission prices, to arrange transit problems and hotel accommodations. If a contract was broken and a playing date cancelled, his was the problem of arranging emergency bookings. Often to do all this he had only a day, for the company followed close on his heels, playing one-night stands no more than a week or ten days behind him.

Receipts were small, salaries for the most part minuscule. In 1809 John Durang, a travelling actor whose territory was generally west and south of Philadelphia, recorded the receipts of forty-eight performances between 12 July and 22 September at five cities. His box-office income totalled $1557.76, his expenses $938.40, leaving him a nightly average profit of $19.57.[9] By the standards of 1809, the sum was adequate, but it did not augur riches. Ross noted as an exceptional gross the $18,000 achieved by Edwin Booth, playing seven performances in St Louis about 1880. Towards the century's end, the actor William Florence, co-starring with the famous Joseph Jefferson and Mrs John Drew, received $2500 per week, while Jefferson took 80 per cent of the gross income.[10] The stars, evidently, were well paid, but in the lower ranks of the touring companies and of the resident stock companies the pay scale was much less.

Ross detailed the structure of a stock company in San Francisco in the

[7] Ross, op. cit. p. 91.
[8] Ross, op. cit. Addenda, pp. 11–12.
[9] John Durang, *The Memoir of John Durang, American Actor, 1785–1816* (Pittsburgh, Pa., 1966), p. 128.
[10] Ross, op. cit. p. 29 (re Booth), p. 51 (re Florence).

1870s and 1880s. At the lowest level were the Supers, recruited from the town and paid fifty cents a night. One night's salary, however, had to be kicked back to the captain of the Supers when he paid off at the week's end. A step up from Super was Utility Man, who was considered a regular member of the company and was paid a salary of $5 weekly. Unlike the mute Supers, he was given one line to speak, and thereby became a candidate for the next step in the hierarchy, the Responsible Utility Man, who had two or more lines of dialogue. Next, with suitable salary advances, came the Walking Gentleman, who played roles such as young lovers that were beneath the dignity of more impressive company members like the Juvenile Man. Next highest in rank, the Juvenile Man played important characters, and an actor of his stature stood at a significant crossroad of his career. If he displayed genuine talent, it was from Juvenile Man that he stepped up to the exalted position of Leading Man, although the move was not usually made in the company that had promoted him thus far. It was generally the case that he would move to a position as Leading Man in a different, more obscure company, where he could perfect his talents, and from which he would ultimately move towards better engagements. The alternative route from Juvenile Man, should the actor not be possessed of the talent for leading roles, was to character roles, 'such as comedian, character man, heavies [villains] or old men'. Ross remarked that it took years to go from one grade of actor to another, but, he concluded, 'when the round was complete, the actor knew his business.'[11] He was doubtless correct.

The Leading Man was the centre of attraction. On stage, he was expected to thrill with his declamatory voice and often to titillate with a reticent display of his biceps and calves. Edwin Forrest was known for his physique, which he displayed discreetly but vividly in roles such as Spartacus in *The Gladiator* by Robert Montgomery Bird. Suggesting something of the style of these actors, Eugene O'Neill described them affectionately as 'those big-chested, chiseled-mug romantic old boys, who could walk onto the stage with all the aplomb and regal splendor with which they walked into the old Hoffman House bar, drunk or sober.'[12]

The women stars were less 'grand' in their manner, the chief exception being Charlotte Cushman, whose speciality, in addition to such strong tragic roles as Lady Macbeth, were men's roles – Hamlet, Romeo, Cardinal Wolsey and others – a phenomenon that in the mid-nineteenth century delighted her public and made her an exceptionally successful actress and

[11] Ross, op. cit. pp. 5–6.
[12] Quoted in Arthur and Barbara Gelb, *O'Neill* (New York, 1960), p. 885.

manager. More orthodox, relying on energy and charm, were Laura Keene and Anna Cora Mowatt, both actresses of skill and managers of repute. Mrs Mowatt, in addition, became skilled as a playwright.[13]

It is difficult to know what drove these men and women into the barely civilized regions of the new nation, carrying their own costumes and props, and ready to play at any time and under any circumstances. Certainly theirs could not by any stretch of the meaning of the words be called a life in art, nor were the rewards by other standards great. Yet perhaps there was something in being admired. The famous description of the voice of Edwin Forrest suggests something of the adulation he was able to command, and upon which he undoubtedly fed:

> His voice surged and roared like the angry sea; as it reached its boiling, seething climax, in which the serpent hiss of hate was heard, at intervals amidst its louder, deeper, hoarser tones, it was like the falls of Niagara, in its tremendous down-sweeping cadence; it was a whirl-wind, a tornado, a cataract of illimitable rage.[14]

Yet praise, however fulsome, was not likely to motivate men to endure the genuine hardships of the life of the touring actor in nineteenth-century America. Some other reason than the adulation of primitive audiences must be sought, in order to know, for example, what drove Edwin Booth into the wilderness.

From 1852 to 1856, Booth, who was to become the greatest actor in the nineteenth-century United States, lived in the west, playing in San Francisco and making short tours into the mountainous gold country, north and east of the city. Occasionally there were theatres to receive him and his fellows, but equally often there were only quickly rigged trestle stages in a saloon or barn, where the troupe performed before the labourers from the mines. They were rough audiences, but not unlettered. Many who attended knew the classical texts by heart, and they could be exacting in their demands. Such crude theatre no doubt provided an excellent training ground where an actor could learn his business. For a young artist like Booth, it was also a stage on which he could take risks and experiment with ways of exciting and holding an audience. His Iago, which became known for its imaginative conception

---

[13] Cf. Garff B. Wilson, *History of American Acting* (Bloomington, Ind., 1966), for an incisive and revealing account of the major American players. See also his survey history, *Three Hundred Years of American Drama and Theatre* (Englewood Cliffs, N.J., 1973).

[14] Quoted in Richard Moody, *Edwin Forrest, First Star of the American Stage* (New York, 1960), p. 96.

and daring execution, was first evolved before the miners. From accounts of his later acting style, Booth was one who sought to put his audiences under an almost hypnotic pressure, to see how much of his quiet domination they could bear. The style may in part have been developed as a way of commanding attention from the miners.[15]

Yet Booth was not alone, nor were tyros only on tour. The celebrated tour of Mrs Minnie Maddern Fiske in Langdon Mitchell's *The New York Idea* is a legendary example of an established star touring into the back country for reasons that were not entirely clear. She was at war with the theatrical Syndicate that controlled bookings into most of the first-class theatres in the country. Her apostasy caused her to be barred from appearances in established theatres west of the Missouri River, but she defiantly fought back with a tour that went irrationally far into the wilderness.

Mitchell's play was a witty, outspoken commentary on the divorce laws. First produced by Mrs Fiske in the autumn of 1906, it seemed to its audiences sophisticated and daring in its suggestion that marriage was not necessarily a sacrosanct institution. The production was elegant and lavish: the press releases detailed the information that to handle the furniture the stage hands were required to wear white gloves. The play was superbly cast with George Arliss and Dudley Digges in important roles.

Following the successful New York run, which closed in January 1907, Mrs Fiske took the play on a tour that ended six months and 18,000 miles later. From February until May she toured the eastern seaboard, moving gradually westward, finally breaking into the forbidden territory west of St Joseph, Missouri. Following the river northward, the company played at Yanktown, South Dakota, worked west to Denver, Colorado, and thence south into Texas and the New Mexico Territory. With the exception of Denver, where the audiences could muster a degree of sophistication, *The New York Idea* was presented to ranch hands, cowboys, farmers and their wives. At Rayon, in what was to become the state of New Mexico, the audience arrived out of the surrounding desert in wagons and surreys to see the play staged in a skating rink. The company continued through the southwest, Las Vegas, Albuquerque and El Paso, where the company's car became disconnected from the train and was left stranded for hours in the desert.

The tour wound on in the heat of the summer, along the line of the Mexican border, into small towns like Bisbee, to Tucson, and north to a copper-mining town, Globe. The journey from Albuquerque to Globe, a matter of perhaps

---

[15] On Booth's tour in the gold country, cf. Eleanor Ruggles, *Prince of Players: Edwin Booth* (New York, 1953), pp. 58–60.

150 miles, was a slow trip by narrow-gauge railroad, made even slower by the train's stopping at every possible point to take on passengers bound for Globe to see the play. Dragging under its load, the train arrived hours late, but the stage was set in full view of the patient audience, and the final curtain fell about 2.00 a.m.

The tour stretched west to Los Angeles, north to San Francisco, a city just recovering from the great earthquake and fire, thence to Seattle and on into Canada. Performances were given in churches and community halls, wherein stages had to be fabricated, and in old theatres so long disused that, in one, bats caused a short-circuit in the electrical wiring. The tour ended in July, in Winnipeg, Canada.[16]

The thought of an actress of Mrs Fiske's quality – she had pioneered productions in the United States of *A Doll's House*, *Hedda Gabler* and *Rosmersholm* – to say nothing of her distinguished company, travelling in the hot, sooty cars to the limits of the civilized world is not today entirely comprehensible. To say that she did it to fight an oppressive system of theatrical control is not really to the point. Battle could be joined only in the major cities, as it was in San Francisco, where Charles Frohman, a producer and organizer of the Syndicate, sent his greatest star, Maude Adams, to play *Peter Pan* opposite her appearance there. Yet the battle was only part of the motive. For Mrs Fiske, for Booth and for all of the nomads who made the long railroad jumps from one provincial theatre to another to tour was to serve.

'Serve' is a word to be used with caution. These actors were members of no priesthood. Like the Hallams in the eighteenth century, they were making a living, and, like actors everywhere, they were gratifying their vanities. Some of them had justifiable claims to be called artists; some had pretensions to the name; some had none. A few became rich, most remained poor, and many careers dwindled to more workaday occupations, as companies were stranded by absconding managers, as engagements were summarily ended by a temperamental star or a selfish producer, or as the wearisome round of uninspired plays took its toll of the actor through unallayed boredom.

Yet service, or something like it, was an element in what these actors did. One reads and dismisses as sentimental public relations accounts of audiences that corporately feel love for the actors who perform for them and of actors who admit to a deep obligation to give of their best in order to requite that love and its attendant adulation. Nevertheless, the phenomenon has some reality. Today, in the demonstrations of almost pathological affection for the

[16] The full story of the tour is told in Archie Binns, *Mrs Fiske and the American Theatre* (New York, 1955), pp. 173 ff.

rock singer in concert or in the fervid acclaim of the cultists for their favourite film star, the special public devotion of audience and star can be seen in grotesque manifestation. There is no reason to deny the reality of such affection because it is sentimental.

Essentially, the emotion that audiences felt was one of gratitude to the star and his company for coming. 'You are welcome to Elsinore ...' and to Denver and El Paso and San Francisco and Seattle. The players were welcomed with surprise that they had come and with gratitude for what they had brought. The image of the stars clasping audiences to their hearts, though developed by the publicity mills, had a reality that formed an important part of the theatrical context. Lesser actors basked in the adulation given the star, the superflux shaken to them. 'How should I fare with a strange audience to whom my personality was unknown, my temperament strange, and my methods an experiment?' wrote the young Frederick Warde when he appeared for the first time with Edwin Booth in Baltimore in 1876. He found out quickly:

> What an audience it was! ... What a glorious reception they gave Mr Booth! The entire audience rose in their places and cheered. It was a spontaneous tribute of love and esteem for the man. Then, they sat down to appreciate the actor. ... How modestly he received the applause of his audience. How generously he insisted on his comrades sharing it with him. ... Mr Booth was recalled again and again, and each time insisted on my accompanying him before the curtain.[17]

Such demonstrations from mature audiences are no longer comprehensible. Certainly they are no longer given to actors of *Hamlet* or *Richelieu*. Yet the testimony to their recurrence is too extensive in the annals of the American theatre to deny that this adulation was real and passionate. Warde is right in calling it a form of love. Men even killed for it, as they did in 1849 at Astor Place in New York City.

There, one of the darkest scenes in the American theatre was played out – a civic riot arising from the personal and managerial rivalry of Edwin Forrest and the English tragedian, William Macready. The antagonism between the two actors had begun in 1836, when Forrest made his début before London audiences. Forrest's success in this engagement set poorly with Macready, who was then the lord of the British stage. Forrest's physicality contrasted sharply with Macready's more studied, intellectual style of acting, and – much as in the comparisons of Shakespeare and Jonson – the

[17] Frederick Warde, *Fifty Years of Make-Believe* (Los Angeles, Calif., 1923), pp. 120–2.

American came to represent the rough vitality of Nature, while Macready was cast, somewhat pejoratively, as the representative of Art, in the studied tradition of the British theatre.

Upon his return to the United States, Forrest found that news of his success abroad had made him the darling of American patriots, and when Macready crossed the Atlantic in 1843 the rivalry, although it was masked by seeming cordiality, became even more nationalistic. In such a theatrical opposition, there is always a box-office potential, and Forrest made the most of it, following hard on Macready's heels and inviting comparison by playing many of Macready's roles. Matters came to a preliminary climax in New York City in 1844, when the two played the same role on the same night in rival theatres, thus leaving the judgement of Nature versus Art and America versus Great Britain to the final arbiter, the gate receipts.

In 1845 Forrest returned to London, where his reception was cooler than it had been nine years earlier. Now, and apparently at Macready's instigation, Forrest's performances were heckled and hissed by gallery rowdies. Leaving London, Forrest toured Scotland, only to find that his path again crossed Macready's. Early in 1846, in Edinburgh, he saw Macready play Hamlet, and, at a point in the action where Macready's stage business appeared to him impossibly effete and precious, he yielded to what must have been overwhelming temptation and hissed his rival derisively.

Like the biting of the thumb at the beginning of *Romeo and Juliet* the hiss led to tragedy – to the deaths of at least thirty-one persons, to the wounding of many more, and to extensive civil disorder. When Macready returned to the United States in 1849 fulminating against Forrest's discourtesy and playing the game of rival performances, the affair came to its violent conclusion outside Macready's theatre, the Opera House in Astor Place, where his *Macbeth* was scheduled opposite Forrest in the same role at a nearby theatre. Earlier in the week, Macready's *Macbeth* had been stopped midway by tumultuous demonstrations and by missiles – vegetables, eggs, theatre chairs. Although Forrest was innocent of contrivance, the mob had made him its hero and it ruled the theatre. When Macready announced that he would repeat *Macbeth* on Thursday, 10 May, he was made the subject of a barrage of inflammatory handbills prepared by a jingoistic group, calling itself 'The American Committee', which urged the American 'workingmen' to unite and prevent 'English rule' in the city.

New York officials had martialled the police and, in reserve, a large troop of soldiers to keep order. In vain. The riot inside the Opera House silenced the performers and developed such a degree of physical violence that the audience was forced to huddle in the foyer as the auditorium was wrecked. Outside the storm was worse. The mob attacked the theatre with bricks and stones, storming protective barricades and forcing the police to summon military reinforcements. Inevitably then, with the mob's temper at fever pitch, the command to fire was given. As the mob counter-attacked, control of the militia was lost, and firing became self-defensive and random. Although Macready left the city immediately, New York remained under martial law for a week as the full toll of the riot was taken.[18]

Normally, the rivalry between players was not lethal. Relying on the admiration of their audiences, competing leading men in rival stock companies would often try to outdo one another with practical 'in-jokes' their audiences would be sure to appreciate. Ross related occasions in San Francisco when James O'Neill and Tom Keene, stars of the Baldwin and California theatres respectively, would plague one another during performances. O'Neill, being offstage in his own production, would walk over to Keene's theatre, wearing whatever costume his role required. There he would simply walk on and interrupt the play being performed by Keene. The two actors then would improvise an encounter, which ended only when the visitor was forced to return to his own theatre in time for his entrance. Such visits were invariably returned a few nights later.[19]

Informality sometimes led to disaster. There were productions like *The Ace of Clubs*, in which Ross had a hand. At the end of the rehearsal period, 'it was discovered that the hero and heroine were still in prison; and it had been forgotten to release [them] and give the play a happy ending. . . . It was too late to write a scene to take them out. So the play was one big failure.'[20]

The experienced actor learned to stay away from the wings, for if any mechanical failure took place – perhaps a curtain failed to fall on cue, or a drop could not be flown out – whoever was handy was seized by the stage manager and thrust on stage to fill in until the problem could be remedied. The wings, with a good view of the action, was, of course, the favoured spot of the untutored supers who were often pressed into service and forced into a desperate improvisation. Ross told of one unhappy novice who was dressed as a Chinese coolie, complete with pigtail and straw slippers. Thrust on stage with the command 'For God's sake, *do something*!' he found himself before a

---

[18] This account is based on that by Richard Moody in *Edwin Forrest, First Star of the American Stage*.
[19] Ross, op. cit. Addenda, p. 11.
[20] Ross, op. cit. p. 39.

raucous audience, and apparently alone in mid-ocean, for painted on the backdrop was a billowing ocean with no land in sight. Quickly shuffling towards the safety of the opposite wing, he promoted himself from super to utility man by improvising a line in pidgin dialect to match his costume: 'Me walkee on wattah, all samee Jesus Clist.' The local critics, believing that this remark was in the script, damned the play.[21]

The hardships, the jokes and the informality combined to create a theatre that was without pretensions to art, and yet one that demanded, were an actor to survive in it, complete professionalism. One area where no compromise was permitted was in language and voice. Backstage at the Baldwin in James O'Neill's time there were two dictionaries, Webster's and Worcester's, on the prompt table. No actor was permitted a pronunciation for which one or the other dictionary did not give authority, and the seasoned actors were always alive to the errors of the young. New actors were taught how to train their voices, to 'trick' them so that they could be heard in every corner of the house, even with their backs to the audience.

Similar assistance was sometimes offered to rivals. At one time, Thomas Keene, playing in California, was engaged to go to Boston to perform the role of Copeau in David Belasco's adaptation of Zola's *L'Assommoir*, a role in which James O'Neill had had substantial success. It was a new role for Keene, and O'Neill set to work to teach him all the business of the part. Keene went to Boston and enthusiastically wired back news of his success: 'eleven curtain calls at end of delirium tremens scene.'[22]

One senses that there was in resident companies such as those in San Francisco a familial *esprit de corps*, in which rivalries and jealousies existed but did not flourish, and in which the consistent training of the novice and a professional respect for discipline led to the development of style.

These actors were highly disciplined. For example, they were called upon to perform prodigious feats of memory. Memorization was, of course, a favourite form of academic instruction in American schools well into the twentieth century, and such a teaching method may have prepared the stock actors for what was required of them – a continual shifting from role to role, with no time to luxuriate in preparation. Ross noted that, in one stock engagement, he was required to learn three leading roles a week, and that he learned Romeo in two days. Several times he was forced to appear in leading parts without even a day's notice: 'I did not study more than an hour. In the morning a short rehearsal; a little more study, and I played the part that

[21] Ross, op. cit. p. 14.
[22] Ross, op. cit. p. 32.

afternoon as though I had always played it. Had a long solo scene too, which means no help from the rest of the cast.'[23]

As the anecdote of Keene's appearance in Boston suggests, there was a formality to the proceedings of rehearsal and production that must have shaped a general style of performance. Frederick Warde described his first rehearsals with Booth in such a way as to suggest the security of a prevalent playing style. Engaged by Booth to play ten roles in what he called a 'congenial repertoire' of Shakespearian and classic plays, Warde knew the lines and traditional business of all but three. He met Booth first at a morning's rehearsal of *Hamlet* in which he was cast as Laertes. The rest of the cast was drawn from the local stock company, and all, Warde said, 'were perfect in the words, familiar with the business of the play, and only one rehearsal was necessary.'[24] Booth did not rehearse. His role was taken by Henry Flohr, his dresser, who knew all Booth's roles and business. Booth watched the rehearsal, made a few suggestions and practised briefly with Warde in the duel scene. The play was a substantial success.

It was followed by *Othello*, Warde playing the title role to Booth's Iago. The rehearsal again was low key. Warde wrote:

> It is usual for the star to tell his supporting actors the positions he desires them to take, the crosses to make, the tempo and inflections of their lines and business he wishes them to do. I was anxious to receive these instructions, but Mr Booth gave none. At last I asked, 'Have you no instructions to give me, sir?' He replied, 'No, you seem quite familiar with the play.'

Warde persisted in asking for instructions:

> 'Are my positions satisfactory to you, Mr Booth?' 'Don't be nervous, my boy,' he answered. 'I'll find you wherever you are.'[25]

Secure in style, and in the relatively simple traditions of blocking and business, the stars and their retainers moved through the land like kings and dukes, satisfying a hunger in themselves and their audiences in a way that somehow justified all hardship and absurdity. Judging from the respect paid to actors like O'Neill, Booth and Forrest, there was even room for artistry that transcended the traditional performances in conventional repertory.

Edwin Booth's qualities, both as an actor and as a man, are praised in all

[23] Ross, op. cit. p. 61.
[24] Warde, op. cit. p. 119.
[25] Warde, op. cit. pp. 122–3.

accounts. In the beginning of his career he had little competition.[26] The dynamic Edwin Forrest was the reigning star. Forrest had come to the front by what amounted to brute force. A man of boundless energy, a patriot, a physical-culture addict, he anticipated the type of muscular American typified by President Theodore Roosevelt. The beefcake photographs of the actor as Metamora, 'the last of the Wampanoags', or as Spartacus, the gladiator, give very little evidence of what his presence in the theatre must have been. Paintings of Forrest as a youth show a man with Byronic beauty, sensitivity and charm, and, although the features coarsened, there is no reason to doubt that Forrest's personality remained winning to the end. Yet his was a style that attacked audiences frontally, dominating and subduing them by the voice, the physique, the animal magnetism. In the end, as his strength faded and his body thickened, the ageing Forrest must have seemed feeble and foolish beside the new sophistication of Booth's style. His devotees stayed with him, but many deserted, enchanted by the new star, whom Forrest surveyed with wonder. Booth's quiet and natural manner was not, to him, acting at all.

Booth's power came from within. Unlike Forrest, he made the audience come to him. He cracked no verbal whips. Ross called him 'the most colloquial tragedian of his day', and phonograph recordings he made late in his life bear this out, revealing him to have understated his readings, with a surprisingly naturalistic but mellifluous style of delivery. Ross recalled a typical moment in Booth's production of *Richard III*. Booth had revived Shakespeare's original text after playing for several seasons in the popular Colley Cibber acting version. According to Ross, who timed the display, Booth at the battle of Bosworth Field was seated at stage left on a stump, his chin cupped in his hand. There were a few offstage sounds of battle, but Booth did not move. Only his eyes turned, right or left, as a bugle or drum would sound. He held the moment, acting, as Ross said, 'with his eyes only', for more than a minute. Then, as a special bugle call sounded, he jumped to his feet and took command. By any definition of performance, to hold an audience, keyed to the final moments of *Richard III*, for a full minute of silence was a remarkable *tour de force*.[27]

There are many tales of his kindness to fellow players – of his insistence that they precede him and share his curtain calls and of his compliments by

[26] Booth made his stage début in 1849 in the theatrical company of his father, the actor Junius Brutus Booth. He accompanied his father on a tour of the far-western America in 1852, remaining in California for four years, learning his craft. He made his eastern début in 1856 and remained a star until he died in 1893.

[27] Ross, op. cit. Addenda, p. 7.

telling them that they played certain roles better than he could do. Eugene O'Neill's father received such an accolade.[28] Equally remarkable are the stories of his power over an audience which at times approached that of a hypnotist. A remarkable example is to be found in Ross's account:

> I have never seen [Macbeth] done better. A little incident occurred one night as he was playing Macbeth which convinced me of his greatness. My part in this play at the time was the minor role of Seyton. During the banquet scene, it was the duty of Seyton to stand at the back of the stage as a guard. The Ghost of Banquo (which Booth only pictured in imagination) had appeared to him. Booth rose from the chair at the table, in act three. He sees Banquo; then comes the long speech, beginning with 'Avaunt and quit my sight –' He follows his pictured ghost down towards the front of the stage, waving it away from his sight, and ending with 'Hence, horrible shadow! Unreal mockery, hence.' The Ghost being gone by now, Macbeth wipes his brow with his hand, saying at the same time, 'Why so; – being gone I am a man again.' It was only then as he turned to go back to his seat, I realized I was standing alongside of him looking at his face. The man had drawn me down stage from my position away back. And I had followed him all the way down to the end of the speech. Quickly realising what I had done, I drew my sword and saluted him and went back to my original position. I do not know if he mesmerized me or what it was or how it was I ever got there. Booth took it as a compliment he said. But I knew the rest of the cast wondered at the time.[29]

As well they might. Yet the lore of the American theatre contains other similar anecdotes, testifying both to the acting skills and to the kindness of the stars. Ross related the story of a super playing in the crowd in *Virginius*, starring James O'Neill. After O'Neill played the dramatic curtain scene, the super dropped to the floor in a faint. When he was revived, O'Neill asked him what the trouble was. As Ross told it:

> The super replied, 'Mr O'Neill, I just couldn't help it. Your acting at the end was so terrific I could not stand it and I fainted away.' This O'Neill considered quite a compliment, and later [he] handed the super a five dollar bill. The next night and at the same place all the supers dropped to the stage, but they did not get any five from Jim.[30]

[28] See O'Neill, *Long Day's Journey Into Night*, Act IV, p. 150.
[29] Ross, op. cit. Addenda, p. 7.
[30] Ross, op. cit. p. 33.

The business of satisfying the hunger of a scattered nation for entertainment would come to be extraordinarily profitable. At first, in the nineteenth century, resident stock companies under the direction of a theatre manager who leased the building, cast and directed his plays, and retained artistic control proved sufficient. Occasionally such companies were joined by touring stars, but for the most part the drama was a community affair. By 1870, as the network of railroads spread west of the Mississippi to the Pacific, the increasingly sophisticated tastes of middle-class America for better drama, together with an insatiate demand for novelty, made the resident stock companies insufficient. Touring stars objected to their quality and to the makeshift productions. As the century came to its end, the stars began to travel with full companies and complete productions. These shows, called 'combinations', put an end to the local stock companies. The managers turned from art to commerce, and became the landlords of the theatres they rented to the travellers. The phrase 'direct from New York' became an important advertisement as more and more combinations were assembled there, played for a period and then went on the road. By 1890 the combinations dominated the legitimate theatre in America.[31]

To ship a major production around the nation involved financial risk, but there were fortunes to be made. In his book, *Trouping*, Philip C. Lewis records a growth in the actor population between 1880 and 1905 from 5000 to 21,000, according to government census figures.[32] By 1905, he estimates, there were 311 productions touring out of New York City and between 100 and 200 out of Chicago. In that year even small towns could expect to see as many as 228 different performances through the touring season. As the twentieth century began, there were upwards of 3000 theatres, of which at least 1000 could accommodate large-scale productions.[33] Inevitably, in the wake of such expansion, more efficient and formal control of booking than the improvisations of an advance man became essential. The landlords, who were to end the easy, joyful days of the nineteenth-century theatre, moved in.

The Syndicates were trusts which controlled the booking of legitimate drama and vaudeville by controlling the physical space, the theatres, in which the presentations would play. Syndicate directors – among them Charles Frohman and Al Hayman, Marc Klaw and Abraham Lincoln

[31] Cf. Jack Poggi, *Theater in America: The Impact of Economic Forces, 1870–1967* (Ithaca, NY, 1968). Poggi gives a detailed account of the centralization and decline of the commercial theatre in the United States.

[32] Philip C. Lewis, *Trouping: How the Show Came to Town* (New York, 1973), p. 18.

[33] Lewis, op. cit. pp. 7–9.

Erlanger, the three Shubert brothers, E. F. Albee, and minor entrants into the fields such as William Morris, Martin Beck and Marcus Lowe – began by persuading local theatre owners to grant them exclusive rights to book events on their stages, promising them in return stellar attractions, lavishly produced and in continuous supply. It was not long, of course, before the Syndicates purchased theatres outright, thus assuring themselves not only of a substantial part of the gross of each attraction, but substantial rentals from independent producers who needed Syndicate theatres to tour. Poggi estimates that, in 1904, 500 theatres including 'all but two or three first-class houses in New York City and all but one each in Boston and Chicago were under syndicate control. Other cities – Philadelphia, Baltimore, Washington, St Louis, San Francisco, not to speak of hundreds of smaller communities – were completely in its hands.'[34]

The Syndicate directors argued plausibly that they could evolve tours which were coherent, eliminating long jumps by railroad cars, moving back and forth across the country in 'pendulum swings', and that they could eliminate needless destructive competition for audiences. In fact, they obtained an all but complete monopoly on theatrical production, legitimate and vaudeville, making it impossible for a star or a production not controlled by them or paying liberally into their coffers to appear anywhere.

The first Syndicate agreement was signed in August 1896, between Frohman, Hayman, Klaw and Erlanger and two other theatre owners, S. F. Nixon and J. F. Zimmerman. The agreement organized the theatres controlled by one or more of the partners into a booking circuit built on a principle of exclusiveness: any attraction that played in 'opposition' theatres was thenceforth barred from appearing in Syndicate houses. The techniques of the blacklist and of blackmail conjoined, for it soon became evident that no attraction was permitted into Syndicate theatres unless the Syndicate owned a large percentage of the show. For example, David Belasco was forced to pay Klaw and Erlanger fifty per cent of the gross profits of his production, *The Auctioneer*, in order to tour it beyond New York City. Although at that time he had four other productions available for touring, and although touring profits were an essential element in the budgets for his plays, all were bottled up in New York City by the Syndicate.[35]

The rival to the Klaw and Erlanger Syndicate was formed by the Shubert

---

[34] Poggi, op. cit. p. 13.
[35] Cf. Craig Timberlake, *The Bishop of Broadway* (New York, 1954). Chapters 19 and 20 contain an account of the development of the Syndicate and of the courtroom encounter between the Syndicate and David Belasco.

Brothers, producers and theatre owners, between 1900 and 1905. A long war between the two ended about 1924 when the Shuberts clearly emerged as the controllers of theatrical America. At that time, they produced one-quarter of the plays offered in the United States. They controlled 75 per cent of the theatre tickets sold annually. Their circuit consisted of eighty-six theatres in major cities, in which they could seat 130,000 customers nightly. They had a potential gross business of $1,000,000 weekly. In addition, they booked attractions into 750 theatres for one-night stands. It has been estimated that in that year they controlled about 60 per cent of the major American theatrical productions.[36]

The Syndicates were, as Lewis calls them, 'formulas for making money'. Although some actors rebelled – James O'Neill, Minnie Maddern Fiske, James A. Herne, Richard Mansfield and, on an international tour, Sarah Bernhardt – refusing to play in Syndicate theatres and fighting even to be seen in small towns and miserable theatres, the control of theatrical productions passed from actors and from local managers of goodwill to financial entrepreneurs, with predictable results: productions were scaled entirely to commercial returns, artistry declined, and New York City became the unquestioned theatrical centre of the country.

The producer-director, Arthur Hopkins, wrote that, with the advent of the Shubert Brothers to a position of power, the days of the 'easy-going theatre' ended and the process of centralization of the theatre in New York was complete. Thereafter, managers eager for the returns from the road sent out duplicate productions of successes still drawing in New York City. At the same time, the stars, however eager for recognition, proved reluctant to go on the road for fear of losing an opportunity in Manhattan. 'The important objective was New York success,' Hopkins said. 'Outside of New York there was only Hollywood.'[37]

A taste of the quality of the theatre prepared for national consumption by the Syndicates can be had from an examination of the repertory of plays and musicals produced or sponsored in New York City by the brothers Shubert during the lifetime of their enterprise.[38] Many of the productions played only briefly in Manhattan, moving quickly on tour once they had earned the accolade 'Direct from New York City'.

[36] Cf. Jerry Stagg, *The Brothers Shubert* (New York, 1968), pp. 217, 222.
[37] Arthur Hopkins, *Reference Point* (New York, 1948), p. 4. Jack Poggi marks the beginning of the centralization of theatrical activity in New York at about 1880 and points to a sharp decline in the late 1920s. Cf. Poggi, op. cit. Chapters 1 and 2.
[38] The repertory is given in full in Stagg, op. cit. pp. 405 ff.

In all, the Shubert name appeared on 520 productions between 1901 and 1954 when their empire was finally dissolved. On the list are several repertory appearances by established and reputable stars, for instance Sir Johnston Forbes-Robertson in Shakespeare, E. H. Sothern and Julia Marlowe in repertory, and an appearance by the Abbey Theatre from Dublin which then went on a national, Shubert-sponsored tour. There was even a short-lived attempt to establish an 'art theatre', in association with the producer Winthrop Ames. Yet 'art' was clearly not their province. In fifty-three years of activity that averaged almost ten productions a year, they offered three plays by Shakespeare (*The Taming of the Shrew*, *The Merry Wives of Windsor*, *Twelfth Night*), two plays by Ibsen (*The Master Builder* and, surprisingly, *Little Eyolf*), two by Shaw (*Widowers' Houses* and *Fanny's First Play*), several productions of *The School for Scandal*, including a musical adaptation starring Lillian Russell, and a production of J. M. Barrie's *What Every Woman Knows*. The rest was trash. *Blossom Time*, a dismal operetta based remotely on the life of Franz Schubert – perhaps there was an attraction in the name – was revived six times in New York between 1921 and 1943; cheaply cast, tawdry productions of this sentimental absurdity toured almost continually through the period.[39] Gilbert and Sullivan operettas were a staple commodity, as were elaborate, semi-nude girl shows, bearing the title *Artists and Models*. To read the titles of the legitimate plays is to shudder: *Madame Mosell*, *The Dancing Duchess*, *Wars of the Worlds*, *A Modern Girl*, *What is Love?*, *Consequences*, *Dancing Around*, *The Battle Cry*, *Mary Goes First*, *At the Barn*, *Tonight's the Night* . . . All that can really be said for such an array of the tasteless is that it provided bulk. Actors worked, and on this tide a few playwrights, managers and directors of quality managed to swim to the surface and create a theatre of distinction. But they did not work for the Shuberts.

In the end, the Syndicates died of their own weight, as much as from any opposition taken against them. At the time of the First World War freight rates rose quickly and substantially; costs soared. Taxes on corporate profits were imposed and 'trust-busting' became a continuing government activity. In 1919 the great Actors' Equity strike brought the labour unions firmly into the theatre. Most crucial was the advent of the motion picture, which was to spell death for the touring road. The invention by Thomas Alva Edison in 1889 of the kinetoscope, a peepshow device in which pictures moved, was the start of an industry whose expansion was immediate and phenomenal. By 1896 Edison had formed a company to control the projec-

[39] Cf. Stagg, op. cit. pp. 187 ff.

tion of films in theatres called 'Nickelodeons', after their admission price. By 1907 there were between 4000 and 5000 Nickelodeons in the country. In Chicago, where one-fifth of the world's films were being made, the number of theatres – often no more than converted stores – jumped from 100 in 1906 to more than 12,000 four years later.[40] Projected on wrinkled sheets in trumpery surroundings, the handwriting was clear: theatre on a large-scale, national, commercial basis was finished.

Between the two World Wars, touring theatre survived through the valour of actors and managers. During the period of the Depression, major cities saw handsomely mounted productions of good plays with important stars. Katharine Cornell toured frequently, her roles including Elizabeth Barrett, Candida, Juliet and St Joan. Important actors worked in her companies – Laurence Olivier, Brian Aherne, Arthur Byron, Maurice Evans, Basil Rathbone – and the plays were elegantly staged. A tour of twenty-nine weeks in 1933–4 of *Barretts*, *Candida* and *Romeo* covered the country, travelling 16,853 miles. She played 225 performances to an estimated 500,000 persons and grossed about $650,000.[41] Such extensive tours were the exception in the 1930s. More often performances would be scheduled in certain key cities – Boston, Philadelphia, Chicago, Los Angeles, San Francisco – but these were insufficient to maintain any general theatrical momentum through the rest of the country. The lavish production of Laurence Housman's *Victoria Regina* was only one of several that Helen Hayes undertook. Alfred Lunt and Lynn Fontanne toured repeatedly in productions sponsored by the Theatre Guild, including a memorable *The Taming of the Shrew*, Robert Sherwood's *Idiot's Delight* and *There Shall Be No Night*, and Jean Giraudoux's *Amphitryon*, translated by S. N. Behrman. Important too were Margaret Webster's productions of *Richard II* and *Hamlet*, both starring Maurice Evans. Cleanlined in design, eloquently spoken, rapid in tempo, they obliterated nineteenth-century conceptions and set a new standard for Shakespearian stage production which lasted through the first half of the century.

Yet these valiant tours of the stars of the 1930s and 1940s were insufficient to revive the once wide-flung touring network. However stylish, they could not alone breathe life into a theatre that was threatened by trusts, by motion pictures, by unimagined costs. Their work was only part of a larger revolution that had sprung from a new conception of theatre: that of the little theatres and of the sometimes precious notions of 'Theatre Art'.

[40] Abel Green and Joe Laurie, Jr, *Show Biz: From Vaud to Video* (New York, 1951), p. 50.
[41] Katharine Cornell, *I Wanted to be an Actress* (New York, 1939), p. 129. A map of the tour is included.

2 Art and politics

As in theatres of other countries during the greater part of the nineteenth century, the genius of the actor was the only legitimate claim to art that the American theatre could make.[42] There were, of course, pretensions to

[42] Stage production was by no means lacking in ingenuity. In his remarkable account of the early days of motion pictures, *Adventures with D. W. Griffith* (New York, 1973), Karl Brown describes a thrilling and ingenious stage effect, wherein a lifesize locomotive appeared to rush down the tracks, from rear stage to the front, stopping just before it crushed the hapless heroine. Brown writes (p. 105):

> The headlight of that train became brighter and brighter and more dazzling as the train roared out of the background, heading for our heroine and the audience as well. The locomotive was now in plain sight, headlight blindingly bright, smoke pouring from the stack in great noisy puffs, drivers turning, rods clanking, the very theatre itself rumbling and shaking under the great weight of the onrushing monster.

In a letter to me, Mr Brown disclosed the secret of the effect:

> You know how an accordion works? Squeeze it together and you have little more than a framework. Pull it out and it goes to full arm's length. Well, that's exactly the way the locomotive worked. Sections were made to full scale, squeezed together, using the accordion pleats, and nestled against the backdrop of the stage, with the whole thing being covered by a scrim, lightly painted to represent tracks receding to the vanishing point. The big secret was in the headlight itself. Controlled by a rheostat, it began as a distant pinpoint, then grew to dazzling intensity as the accor-

artistry in other areas. Edwin Forrest's awards to American playwrights who wrote on American themes was an attempt to develop a native drama within the province of 'art'. The care with which Booth cast and staged his plays – he was using the box set by 1870 – reveals a serious concern for the art of stage production, and the theatre he opened in New York in 1869 was hailed as a temple of theatrical art. The actor-manager and playwright, Steele MacKaye, during the latter years of his life, developed a number of stage machines to produce effects of clouds, the sun and moon, rainbows, and to bathe the stage and scenery with colour. From 1880 to 1893 he worked diligently to create a more flexible scene, with moving stages and an adjustable proscenium, in a theatre house that was comfortable and well ventilated. Sketches of his later work, exhibited in what he called a 'Scenitorium', bring to mind the designs of Appia and Craig, while the production itself, a 'Spectatorio' called *The World Finder*, anticipated the work of Max Reinhardt.[43]

Different in its effect, but equally dedicated to the art of the theatre, were the technical innovations and the careful, if excessive, realism of David Belasco, who began staging plays in New York City in 1882. Belasco was to become the *bête noire* of young Turks like Eugene O'Neill and Robert Edmond Jones, yet the care with which he mounted the trivial plays, the painstaking, detailed accuracy of his stage productions, and the important technical innovations in stage lighting must be viewed as a step forward in the development of the arts of the theatre in the United States. Yet in the early twentieth century, despite glimpses of the future by such men as MacKaye and Belasco, there was little that could lay claim to being of substantial artistic merit, in practice or in theory.

There were some indications of change, however. As early as 1891, the author Hamlin Garland, impressed by the serious realism of the plays of James A. Herne, attempted to found a new kind of theatre which he called 'The First Independent Theater Association'. His prospectus, dated from Boston in 1891, states that the objectives of the association are to 'encourage truth and progress in American Dramatic Art, . . . to secure and maintain a stage whereon the best and most unconventional studies of modern life,

---

dion pleat fake locomotive was thrust forward by stagehands working inside. The headlight was so dazzling that nobody could possibly see the formerly concealing scrim pulled away. All that steam and smoke was supplied by a donkey-engine located in the alley (fire regulations), and that hissing and clanking and various other assorted noises were supplied by our backstage effects men.

43 Cf. Percy MacKaye, *Epoch, The Life of Steele MacKaye* (New York, 1927).

and distinctively American life, may get a proper hearing, . . . [and] to remove as far as possible, the commercial consideration and give the Dramatist the artistic atmosphere for his work. . .' He added that the kinds of plays of interest to the society included social dramas and comedies on contemporary American subjects, studies in American history from colonial times to the Civil War, and 'Famous Modern Plays by the Best Dramatists of Europe', by whom he meant Ibsen and his followers. Garland notes that the Freie Bühne of Berlin, the Théâtre Libre of Paris and the Independent Theatre of London are organizations from which his association will take 'helpful hints'. The pamphlet ends with 'A Plea for Art' that stresses the great influence Boston has had on the arts in America and appeals to the 'art-loving population of Boston' to aid in the development of 'a genuine, truthful, buoyant American Drama'.[44]

In the United States, however, Boston is not the equivalent of Paris, London or Berlin, and no drama was to flourish there. Garland's plea was unheard and his pamphlet forgotten, although his arguments were to be reinvented often in the next three decades. They are remarkable only because they are so early. André Antoine's Théâtre Libre had been founded as recently as 1887, Otto Brahm's Freie Bühne in 1889 and J. T. Grein's Independent Theatre in 1891. Garland was a pioneer in vision, if not action. Other groups like the Criterion Independent Theatre in New York in 1897 and the New Theatre, directed by Winthrop Ames and sponsored partly by the Shuberts in 1909, tried and failed to develop standards of reputable

[44] The Garland pamphlet is among the Hamlin Garland papers in the library of the University of Southern California. Mr Gilbert Bunday, Curator of the American Literature Collection, has called my attention to a related letter in the same collection by a Boston publisher, B. O. Flower, to Garland, dated 5 May 1890, which reads in part,

> We must make the people acquainted with the world's miserables. I have often wished that there could be a society formed in Boston where each Sunday morning splendid music would make the entertainment very attractive for the people in the poorer walks of life, where a short fifteen or twenty minutes' address could be delivered by some earnest, sympathetic orator and where in the evening a play such as I take your 'Under the Wheel' to be could be produced and the poor people, young and old could have the pleasure of seeing it without having to pay for it. That is, that each member of the society would be able to distribute tickets to five or ten more persons that they have been able to find who are too poor to enjoy the theatre and such amusements and who could in this way be made happy while they were being stimulated to think and also brought in touch with the best sentiments of the day. It may be that this is Utopian, yet I firmly believe as Victor Hugo believed that nothing can educate the masses like the drama.

A theatre that sets out to make the miserable miserable would appear to have small chance of success.

theatre art that could survive in the cut-throat world. A second attempt by Ames, the Little Theatre, in New York in 1912 went the way of the first.

When the new theatre appeared, it was not in New York City, nor did it build itself according to the models developed by Antoine, Grein or Brahm. Rather it turned to Gordon Craig for leadership, and emerged first as a theatre of stage designers. The earliest hint of the part the visual arts were to play came from Boston, where in 1911 an aptly named 'Toy Theatre' was founded by Mrs Lyman Gale in an old stable. Her director, Livingston Platt, created productions that were noted for their new, unusual designs, and the theatre held on for three reputable seasons before it failed.

The real impetus towards an art theatre came from Chicago. In a survey of the little-theatre movement in the United States,[45] Kenneth Macgowan recorded the establishment there of a 'New Theatre' under the direction of Victor Mapes in 1906, and in 1907 a theatre directed by Donald Robertson which staged Molière, Ibsen, Browning, Calderón and Goldoni. The Hull House Players, formed in Jane Addams's settlement house in 1899, emerged as a well-recognized theatrical group in 1907 under the direction of Laura Dainty Pelham. Most important, however, was the creation in November 1912 of the Chicago Little Theatre, under the direction of the British playwright and producer Maurice Browne and his wife, the actress Ellen Van Volkenberg.

As the second decade of the century began, Browne's theatre was caught up in the literary ferment that characterized early twentieth-century Chicago, where poets, novelists, essayists and critics all caught hold of a new spirit in the arts. It was a climate in which Browne's troupe could flourish. Emphasizing the union of drama and dance, responsive to Celtic mythology (concerts on the Irish harp were a feature), taking its lobby décor from Japanese prints, the Chicago Little Theatre introduced its meagre audiences to a wide range of important plays, including in its first season Yeats's *On Baile's Strand* and *The Shadowy Waters*, Schnitzler's *Anatol*, a double bill of *Creditors* and *The Stronger*, which Browne thought was the first professional production of Strindberg in the United States, and for the opening production Euripides' *The Trojan Women*.[46] To prepare the Euripidean tragedy, Browne rehearsed the amateur players nine hours a day, seven days a week for eleven months in a euphoric condition of creativity that arose partly

[45] Kenneth Macgowan, *Footlights Across America* (New York, 1929).
[46] Maurice Browne, *Too Late to Lament* (Bloomington, Ind., 1956). See also Bernard F. Dukore, *Maurice Browne and the Chicago Little Theatre* (University Microfilms, Ann Arbor, Mich., 1958).

from ignorance of objectives and of the techniques appropriate to the staging of Greek drama, and partly from the dedication that any new idea involving struggle and insight can evoke from the human animal. It was an experimental theatre, working with no budget to develop new and subtle lighting effects and to create aesthetically pleasing scenic pictures in the tradition of *art nouveau*. Their success with *The Trojan Women* ultimately caused them to become a touring theatre, revitalizing in a small way something of the dying tradition of the road. The tragedy, suddenly appropriate to the cries for peace in a world heading for war, was taken throughout the middle west, then south through Colorado and out to the Pacific coast, for a total run on tour of forty-two performances before audiences totalling 33,000 persons.[47]

Browne's work developed simultaneously with that of two young men whose devotion to the art theatre was complete – Samuel J. Hume and Sheldon Cheney. Hume was educated at the University of California in Berkeley and began his theatrical work on the campus in amateur productions of Greek drama and Shakespeare in the newly built William Randolph Hearst Greek Theatre in 1905–6. Upon his graduation, he went abroad to explore theatrical possibilities in Europe. A letter of introduction to Ellen Terry brought him to the attention of her son, Edward Gordon Craig, who invited Hume to study with him in Florence. Hume stayed with Craig from 1909 until 1912, when he returned to the United States. In Florence he built models for Craig, including one for the famous production of *Hamlet* for the Moscow Art Theatre and for a set of screens used by William Butler Yeats at the Abbey Theatre. Clearly he learned much from his teacher. Back in the United States, he attended Harvard University and began working with George Pierce Baker's new class in playwriting, 'The 47 Workshop', from which many of the new playwrights would emerge. Baker was not personally responsive to the new stagecraft, and Hume left his classes to work alone. In 1915, at his studio in Cambridge, he prepared one of the first exhibitions of contemporary European and American stage design. Included were designs for settings and costumes, together with three-dimensional models of work by Craig, Leon Bakst, Adolf Appia and Joseph Urban, as well as the Americans Livingston Platt, Robert Edmond Jones and Hume himself. A working model of a sky dome, sliding stages and demonstrations of new lighting methods from Germany were also included. The exhibition toured from Cambridge to New York and Chicago, where Maurice Browne called it a display that 'revolutionized American stage

47 Browne, op. cit. p. 188.

design'. It closed in Detroit, where, in 1916, Hume was invited to put into practice his theories of the theatre by assuming the directorship of the Detroit Arts and Crafts Theatre, a tenure that was to prove of signal influence in forming the tastes of the small art theatres throughout the country.

Influenced by Craig, but combining with the aesthetic principles a sense of the practical that Craig entirely lacked, Hume created a flexible setting of screens and unit pieces that was adaptable to almost any requirement placed on it, even in the most constricted area. The setting was strongly reminiscent of some of Craig's abstract work, notably the designs for *Scene*, on which Craig was working when Hume was with him in Florence.[48] The setting, however, has a beauty and character of its own, and Hume stands as a direct link between the work of Craig and Appia and the later designs of Robert Edmond Jones.

Although, throughout his life, Hume worked out of the mainstream of the professional theatres, returning from Detroit to Berkeley, California, where he directed productions in the Greek Theatre, his theories on theatre art were well publicized. Always devoted to educational theatre, he wrote a book entitled *Twentieth Century Stage Decoration*, a standard history of scenography, and *Theater and School*, in which he discusses the uses of his screen setting for amateur players. He was also instrumental in the development of a new publication, *Theatre Arts Magazine*, whose early issues gave close attention to his work in Detroit.

The development of the art theatre under such tutors as Hume and Browne spread wildly. Little theatres, community theatres, semi-professional art theatres sprang up in Ohio, Wisconsin, Utah (where the University of Utah shortly was to offer the first bachelor's degree in drama), in Michigan and along both seaboards. In 1912 Platt's and Browne's theatres were unique phenomena, to be differentiated from the run-of-the-mill amateur acting groups by their total dedication to a concept of theatre art, however vaguely the concept was defined. Browne estimated that by 1917 the influence of the two theatres and of Hume had been sufficient to call into being nearly thirty similar companies in and around New York City, and, elsewhere in the country, about 300. By 1920 there were thousands. The influence of the new movement extended not only to the formation of professionally committed groups such as the Washington Square Players which was to become the Theatre Guild, or the Provincetown Players, in whose *atelier* Eugene

[48] Cf. John Seelye Bolin, *Samuel Hume: Artist and Exponent of the American Art Theatre* (University Microfilms, Ann Arbor, Mich., 1970), p. 54.

O'Neill found his first directions. It was also felt abroad. Browne claims that Jacques Copeau told him he had found inspiration for the Théâtre du Vieux Colombier from accounts of the Chicago experiment.[49]

The first editor of *Theatre Arts Magazine*, which quickly became the bible of the new movement, was Sheldon Cheney. Cheney, like Hume, had been a student at the University of California in Berkeley, and had published in 1914 one of the first book-length accounts of the new European theatre, entitled *The New Movement in Theatre*. He was to follow this in 1916 with another work, *The Art Theatre*, which like its predecessor was partly a history of the movement and partly an attempt to formulate the aesthetic principles of the movement and to identify its gods and their priests. *Theatre Arts Magazine* began publication from Detroit in 1914, with Cheney keeping up a running commentary on all that was worthwhile in the new theatre.

The first issue of the magazine is an interesting index to the enthusiasms of the period. It contains a long account of the staging of a 'masque' at Cranbrook, near Detroit, by Samuel Hume, with a text by another Californian, Sidney Howard, who was shortly to emerge as one of the country's leading dramatists. Cheney himself supplied two signed articles, one on a poetic drama, *Grotesques*, as staged by Maurice Browne, and one on the stage designs of A. A. Andries, an associate of Hume's in Detroit. The issue contains notes and drawings for costumes and settings by Robert Edmond Jones, an account of William Poel's American visit, and an article on the relation between arts and crafts societies and the young art theatres – an alliance of particular interest since such a society had sponsored Hume's work in Detroit.

An article on 'Acting and the New Stagecraft' by Walter Prichard Eaton takes a jaundiced view of the enthusiasms of the amateur actor, but Cheney provides ample evidence that the enthusiasm was spreading infectiously by granting considerable space to news items about the progress of theatre arts and the offerings of little theatres throughout the country. New books on theatre are reviewed, as are newly published plays suitable for performance by theatres of the movement. The magazine is lavishly illustrated with plates by leading professional and amateur designers, including Joseph Urban, Herman Rosse and Raymond Johnson.

In his essay, Eaton issued a sour warning: 'We must, I fear, face the fact that the experimental spirit in America is still an amateur spirit, . . . flowering

[49] Browne, op. cit. p. 165.

... in the various "little theatres" and other refuges of the dissatisfied and the dilettantes.' In an editorial, Cheney took a similar view, writing:

> At least the established order has been shaken to the extent of a recognition of new forces bearing in, and a struggle to come. Oftener and oftener the purely commercial producer has to grasp the weapons of art to meet the competition. Outside the old structure, moreover, the independents have built up an organization of their own. Little theatres and art theatres have been established, not on a basis which assures permanence, but with the result that American drama is provided with laboratories for experiment. Playwrights have been encouraged to explore new fields. Decorators have been discovered and trained, and have gone into the regular theatre to leaven the mass there. A few playhouses which are worthy of the theatre as an art have been built. In that there is at least preliminary progress.
>
> On the other hand: The artists have failed to conquer any appreciable proportion of the professional theatres, or to win over any number of the men in power. They have failed to develop a single director or playwright or decorator who can be said to be a great creative figure – an artist of world-measure. The art of acting, in both the professional and the little theatres, continues to suffer alarming relapses. The promised 'new art of the theatre' is hardly nearer realization than five years ago. No American Shaw or Barker or Yeats has been born of the struggle against the established order.
>
> The disarrangement of the old order, the starting of forces that *may* revolutionize the theatre of the great public, the development of *promising* artists, a little shifting from the old inartistic basis toward the imaginative and the poetic – that is all. The struggle is only started. It is not a time to begin crowing – only a time for setting the teeth harder, for resolving that the next five years shall be infinitely more fruitful than the last.
>
> But we have faith.[50]

Cheney has remained a man of faith. Although he relinquished his post as editor of *Theatre Arts Magazine* in 1922, he has stayed in the forefront of theatre theorists, and served importantly as an aesthetician who defined the principles of the new order. In *The New Movement in Theatre*, he set a pattern of argument that most later writers on the art theatre were to follow. He extolled the revival of theatre in Europe, likening it to the theatrical

[50] Sheldon Cheney, untitled editorial, *Theatre Arts Magazine* (1914), 1.

renaissance in Elizabethan England. Ibsen, Hauptmann and Wedekind had fathered a race of important new playwrights, among whom were Galsworthy, Shaw, Barrie, Maeterlinck, Schnitzler, Rostand and Brieux. From an examination of their work, he defined three major modes of the new theatre: drama he called 'aesthetic', typified by Maeterlinck's symbolism; the 'psychologic', like that of Galsworthy, which while adhering to a visible realism sought to plunge deeply beneath the seemingly photographic surfaces to reveal the inner spiritual realities of life; finally, he designated the 're-theatralized' drama which was an attempt to bring 'all the arts of the theatre into more perfect relation with the limitations of the playhouse; and to invent a stagecraft that will serve to mount beautifully written plays of either the aesthetic or psychologic type.'[51] The model for the third mode was not a playwright but an 'artist-director' like Max Reinhardt, whose wordless 'mimo-drama', *Sumurūn*, an Oriental fantasy, had been seen in New York in 1912, the same year that the Manchester Repertory Company had come from England to tour with dramas by Galsworthy, Shaw, John Masefield and Arnold Bennett.

To Cheney, as to the theorists who immediately followed him, the theatre's potential was great, and belief in its future was an article of almost religious faith. That theatre was like a church was a repeated assertion: 'In theatre and in the church, the deeper chords of spirituality are touched as nowhere in life,'[52] he wrote, and exhorted the artist, whether he be realist or idealist, to seek the essence of life in imaginative experience and ennobling interpretation. There was perhaps a reason why Max Reinhardt's religious mimo-drama *The Miracle* was shortly to dazzle American audiences.

The gospel according to Cheney was preached by others, who made their individual variations on his themes. The most notable of his successors was the critic Kenneth Macgowan, who assumed the editorship of *Theatre Arts Magazine* in 1922. Macgowan's initial considerations are to be found in two books, *The Theatre of Tomorrow* (1921) and *Continental Stagecraft* (1922), the latter written in collaboration with Robert Edmond Jones. Like Cheney, Macgowan predicted that drama would move away from mere realism towards depiction of 'spiritual abstractions', especially when it could be aided by new scenic and lighting methods of the European theatres. He was interested both in the spiritual qualities that stirred Cheney and in the 'illumination of the deep and vigorous processes of the human soul which the psychology of Freud and Jung have given us through the study of the un-

[51] Sheldon Cheney, *The New Movement in Theatre* (New York, 1914), p. 16.
[52] Cheney, *The New Movement*, p. 213.

conscious.'[53] Macgowan set dead against realism and advocated presentational or expressionistic drama as the means of approaching important inner truths. Like Cheney, he expressed his faith in the 'artist-director', or in the collaboration of *régisseur* and playwright to ensure clarity and beauty of design.

By the time Macgowan had established himself as an arbiter of theatrical taste and style, two theatres had emerged which were to develop the directors, designers and actors so lacking at the time when Cheney wrote his first editorial. From their group at least one playwright would emerge to become 'a great creative figure – an artist of world-measure'. And, although the seeds for both had been sown by Browne in Chicago and Hume in Detroit, inevitably both were located in New York City.[54]

The two theatres, the Washington Square Players and the Provincetown Players, were founded by men who had known the work of the Chicago Little Theatre at first hand. Lawrence Langner, the guiding spirit of the Washington Square Players, was a patent attorney with an amateur's enthusiasm for the drama. He met Browne in 1914 and was impressed by the fact that such a theatre could exist in the middle-western city. 'If an Art Theatre of this kind was possible in Chicago, it would be even more possible in New York,' he was to write.[55] By the end of the year, his enthusiasm bolstered by the tour of the Diaghilev Ballet Russe and the productions by Harley Granville-Barker, seen for the first time that year in America,[56] Langner assembled a group of writers, artists and a few professional theatre people to discuss the establishment of an art theatre. The group took its name from its location, and in February 1915 opened as the Washington Square Players with a bill of four one-act plays. To a meagre subscription audience and respectful press notices that held them up as a white hope, the Players eked out an existence until the entry of the United States into the First World War decimated the ranks both of players and audiences. Between 1915 and the last bill in April 1918, the Players offered seventy-five one-act plays by a range of authors, American and European, and seven

[53] Kenneth Macgowan, *The Theatre of Tomorrow* (New York, 1921), p. 248.
[54] Several noteworthy small theatres were organized at about this time. The most important was the Neighborhood Playhouse, founded in 1915 at the Henry Street Settlement by Alice and Irene Lewisohn. It produced an interesting repertory until 1927, but it had not the seminal force of other, less successful groups.
[55] Lawrence Langner, *The Magic Curtain* (New York, 1951), p. 83.
[56] The repertory of Barker's company included *Androcles and the Lion*, *The Man Who Married a Dumb Wife* and *A Midsummer Night's Dream*. Later, perhaps taking a leaf from Maurice Browne's book, he presented *The Trojan Women* and *Iphigenia in Taurus*.

full-length plays, including Andreyev's *The Life of Man*, *Ghosts* and *Mrs Warren's Profession*.

In Massachusetts at the summer colony of Provincetown, shortly after the Washington Square Players opened their first bill, a similar group of writers and painters came together in an amiably amateur fashion to play at theatre. Leading the group was a writer and sometime philosopher, George Cram Cook, who like Langner had known Browne in Chicago. In Chicago, Cook, writing a column on the arts for the *Evening Post*, had rebuked Browne for not staging plays by American writers. This became his constant theme when the summer games turned serious and the Provincetown Players were organized.

The theatrical amusements of the first summer were sufficient to carry over to the following year, when the amateurs reassembled and created a theatre in a wharf shed jutting out over the water. With a growing vision of what might come, Cook, together with his wife, the novelist Susan Glaspell, began an ardent campaign to get the local artists to write plays. The net was cast wide, and in it fell a reticent young man who had only begun to try to learn the craft of the playwright. The story of the meeting of Eugene O'Neill with Cook and the Provincetown Players has become romantic legend in the American theatre, as has their first production of his short sea play, *Bound East for Cardiff*, on a foggy night, with the water washing beneath the floor of the shed.[57]

Without O'Neill, the Provincetown Players would have faded as quickly as a summer tan, but his presence gave them a direction and a cause which was set forth in a charter they drew up late in the summer of 1916 as they laid plans for a New York season in Greenwich Village. The Players were to become 'The Playwrights' Theatre' and were to seek out new works by American dramatists. It was not the easiest of projects, but, animated by O'Neill's talent and the urgent spirit of George Cram Cook, they made headway. They were – Cook forced them to be – determinedly amateur, as opposed to the semi-professionalism of the Washington Square Players. They refused to invite critics or hire directors and their scenic means were pitiable. But when the Washington Square Players, bound for professional status, received the notices and were even given credit for having 'discovered' O'Neill, the critics were invited and some attention was paid to purely theatrical needs. Nevertheless, Cook held to his central principles. He felt that the Players should in some measure resemble the participants in a primitive Dionysian ritual, engaged in a common religious purpose so that

[57] The story is affectingly told in Susan Glaspell, *The Road to the Temple* (New York, 1927).

the new drama could be born, as had happened in ancient Greece. In the end, such idealism was doomed. O'Neill's *The Emperor Jones*, which the Players produced in 1920, was a success of such magnitude that the amateur, spiritual theatre of Cook's envisioning was swept away by praise, by the clamour for tickets, and by O'Neill's sense of his emergent professional necessities. Shortly thereafter, the Provincetown Players, in their first phase, disbanded, to be reborn under a triumvirate headed by Eugene O'Neill, Kenneth Macgowan and Robert Edmond Jones. Calling the new group 'The Experimental Theatre', the triumvirate produced a repertory between 1923 and 1925 that was designed to exhibit the new art of the theatre at its best.

In a parallel development, the founders of the Washington Square Players reassembled after the Armistice, determined to move forward in a serious way and to found a theatre that would be true to the new principles of theatre art but would no longer be an amateur's enterprise. The Washington Square Players had always pretended to be professional. Langner described the difference between his and Cook's companies, saying that, from the first, his group was attempting to compete with Broadway attractions: 'The Washington Square Group fought the issue of the art theatre *versus* the commercial theatre.'[58] To combine commerce and art became the guiding motive of the new alliance that named itself the Theatre Guild.

The Theatre Guild became the most successful manifestation of the art-theatre movement in the commercial framework. Others, notably the productions staged by Arthur Hopkins with the Barrymore brothers and Pauline Lord, would add a lustre to the commercial scene, but the Guild established the art theatre as a fully professional and commercially successful undertaking. The basic organization was essentially that of the Washington Square Players and other earlier art theatres, centring in a board of directors, including a director, Philip Moeller, a designer, Lee Simonson, an actress, Helen Westley, a banker, Maurice Wertheim, and an attorney, Langner. The composition was to change from time to time, but government by the board remained the rule through the life of the organization. It was somewhat different from Cook's 'Dionysian' band of amateurs, each with a voice in the decision, but it was not under the control of a single director, as were most of the commercial theatres, Belasco's, Hopkins's or those of the Shubert Brothers. A quasi-democracy prevailed.

Audiences were built not through the sale of individual tickets, but by subscription – a method also used by Browne and Cook. The plan had both

[58] Langner, op. cit. p. 102.

virtues and drawbacks. On the one hand, it ensured a minimal audience for all plays, and ultimately enabled the producers to build secure audiences in cities outside New York. On the other hand, the Guild was forced to produce a given number of plays each season, whether they were failures or successes capable of extended runs. Yet the Guild audience was one of its strengths. Langner described the membership as 'A group of kindly disposed theatre lovers . . . who have rejoiced with us in our successful accomplishments and have borne patiently with our failures over the past three decades. They made it possible for us to be independent of the whims of "patrons of the arts" . . . and to build our foundations on the support of the intelligent theatre-going public.'[59]

The Guild's début was not auspicious. It started with a capital of $2150 and subscriptions amounting to $474. Salaries in the beginning were $25 per week. The first play, Jacinto Benavente's *Bonds of Interest*, in April 1919 occasioned little excitement. The second, St John Ervine's *John Ferguson*, became a hit of unusual proportion and ushered in a distinguished series of productions. Playwrights of the early seasons were for the most part European – Tolstoy, Strindberg, Molnar, Andreyev, Kaiser, Claudel, Ibsen, Galsworthy and Shaw. By the seventh season, in 1924, American dramatists were appearing on the bills – Sidney Howard, John Howard Lawson, S. N. Behrman, Robert Sherwood, Maxwell Anderson, Elmer Rice, Philip Barry, William Saroyan and Eugene O'Neill. The Guild became the forum for the best in European and American theatre during the 1930s and 1940s. Their prestige was sealed when they became the American producers for the two most important playwrights in the twentieth-century English-speaking theatre, Shaw and O'Neill.

Their first Shaw production was of *Heartbreak House* in 1920 while the clouds generated by the dramatist's sceptical attitude towards the World War just ended still hung around his head and over his play. They followed this work with the complete *Back to Methuselah* in 1922, and by 1948 had produced in all sixteen of Shaw's plays. They were equally faithful to O'Neill. The 'Experimental Theatre' proved an inadequate stage as his theatrical reach extended and his plays increased in scope, intensity and depth. The satiric *Marco Millions* and the nine-act experimental work, *Strange Interlude*, were without producers when the Guild undertook them, opening them both in the same month, January 1928.[60] *Marco Millions* was

[59] Langner, op. cit. p. 119.
[60] A season that included *Porgy* by Du Bose and Dorothy Heyward, Stefan Zweig's adaptation of *Volpone* and Shaw's *The Doctor's Dilemma*.

only a moderate success, but *Strange Interlude* became one of the most emphatic hits the Guild had yet produced.[61] It sealed between the playwright and the producers an alliance that ended only with O'Neill's death.

Thus, from 1919 to the Second World War, the Guild provided the platform for the major dramatic enterprise in the United States.[62] Langner noted that the Guild's original objective, 'to produce plays of merit not ordinarily produced by commercial managers', became meaningless when other managers followed the Guild's lead. What was at first a theatre of art became, as Langner rightly claimed, 'the most affluent section of the commercial theatre'.[63] For a few years the American theatre, following the Guild's direction, brought art and commerce into heartening alliance.

The aestheticism most readily visible in the new styles of scene design by Robert Edmond Jones, Lee Simonson, Norman bel Geddes, Cleon Throckmorton, Mordecai Gorelik and Donald Oenslager, together with the literary wisdom in the choice of plays and the commercial acumen that created a steady and demanding audience, also brought about a refinement of acting style. In the simplest formulation, the acting style developed in the 1920s by the Theatre Guild and kindred organizations is best thought of as a transitional style, moving between the exaggerated mannerisms of the nineteenth-century actor and the behaviour-oriented styles of the third and fourth decades of the century. The theatre aestheticians all spoke of the need for greater truth in acting. Actors, they foretold, would learn how to project the psychological truth that was to come in the new playwriting. Certainly the kind of design that became standard in the early years of the century necessitated a new manner of performing. An actor entering a box set through a door must behave differently from one who walks on from the wings in front of a drop. An actor encased by a setting must relate to time and space in a different way from an actor playing on an apron in front of a painting. An actor who must pretend to be the occupant of the setting will reach an audience by different means from one whose art is partly that of the rhetorician and who can address the audience directly. An actor who moves in

---

[61] The Guild directors had been considering the formation of a permanent company of actors who could play in repertory, an idea that recurred continually with several actors and directors during the late 1920s and 1930s. Eva Le Gallienne organized the most successful enterprise of this kind, the Civic Repertory Theatre, 1926–32. *Strange Interlude* was too successful to run intermittently in a repertory season and the Guild abandoned the scheme.

[62] By 1950 its energies were dissipated, and it became little more than a name attached to productions in which it had no artistic interest.

[63] Langner, op. cit. p. 118.

a setting in lights that subtly accentuate details will select different values from one who is brightly illuminated and whose wardrobe has come out of his trunk in much the same way as the scenery came out of a warehouse.

The great actors of the Theatre Guild, and those appearing in productions by Hopkins, Gilbert Miller, Guthrie McClintic and other producers who championed the new theatre, were artists who sought to convey human truth in their performances. They succeeded far more than had their predecessors, who set personal display before impersonation. Yet it is also true that the finest actors of the time were thought of and loved as performers in much the same way as their nineteenth-century predecessors had been. Alfred Lunt and Lynn Fontanne, Clare Eames, Ina Claire, Jane Cowl, Alla Nazimova, Helen Hayes, Katharine Cornell, John Barrymore, Tallulah Bankhead were all bravura performers who were hailed as much for themselves as for their characterizations. There was nothing cheap, trivial or meretricious in what they at their best accomplished, but they wore their roles with a high degree of individuation and played in a style that owed much to their predecessors. The goodhumoured, intricately choreographed encounters of Lunt and Fontanne, for example, were delightful in a way that was often quite independent of the play, but remained very much a part of the aesthetics of design and direction that governed the whole. Fontanne's entrance in *The Taming of the Shrew* involved a great burst of offstage shouts and murmurs, punctuated by her raucous brouhaha, whip cracking and other sounds of menace. The effect built to its climax as, clad in Caroline hunting costume, and armed with a Puritan-style blunderbuss, she swept in a large circling cross on to the stage to the down-centre position where she fired the gun into the flies and brought down a large, dead wild-fowl at her feet. It was crass and irresistible and thoroughly characteristic of the design of the production. Similar comment might be made on the effects wrought by Hayes in *Victoria Regina* or Cornell in *Saint Joan* or *The Barretts of Wimpole Street*. They were studied, controlled and governed by an aestheticism that was not entirely concerned with the projection of simple human reality. They played within the frame of a large production design, and their communication with their audiences was as much a product of their star personalities as of the characters they represented.

It was a daring and virtuoso time in the theatre but it did not endure beyond the Second World War. Although the Lunts were to reappear in a production of Dürrenmatt's *The Visit* and Ina Claire was to return to the stage in T. S. Eliot's *The Confidential Clerk*, no one of the pre-war actors was to dominate the theatre whose most impressive dramatists were

Tennessee Williams, Arthur Miller and, unexpectedly resurrected from oblivion, Eugene O'Neill.

What transpired was a turn away from the aestheticism that had produced the Guild towards a theatre that would, in the words of Harold Clurman, one of the chief progenitors of the new theatrical mode, make men 'aware of the presence of the world itself'.[64] The turn from the art theatre began almost simultaneously with the advent of the great Depression in the decade of the 1930s. As with the art-theatre movement, the newer theatre began in many small groups, some associated with labour movements, others concerned more exclusively with the art of the actor as it was being taught in the tradition of Stanislavsky and the Moscow Art Theatre.

The earliest of note was the New Playwrights' Theatre, formed by John Howard Lawson, John Dos Passos, Michael Gold and others in 1927. Modelled after the Washington Square Players and the Provincetown Players, and backed, ironically enough, by the financier Otto Kahn, who acted as lavish patron to many experimental theatre projects, the New Playwrights' Theatre was one which sought above all to project a truthful social realism. It was a theatre of the radical Left, and its short life was beset by many failures and much controversy. Nevertheless its political courage and its responsiveness to social phenomena earned it an honoured place in theatre history. Like other American theatres, it learned much from the European scene, especially from the scenic conceptions of the German theatre and from the avant-garde productions in Russia of Meyerhold and Tairov.

Similar organizations appeared with express political intentions: the Workers' Dramatic Council, a union of twelve proletarian drama groups founded in 1929, and the Workers' Laboratory Theatre, founded three years earlier and by 1930 presenting agit-prop sketches in factories. The new political orientation was also reflected in the Federal Theatre, established as part of the Works Progress Administration to provide jobs for out-of-work theatre personnel. Under the leadership of Hallie Flanagan, the Federal Theatre worked excitedly to create a politically alert drama on a national scale. Political reaction against the Roosevelt New Deal caused the funds to be cut off in 1939 and the government's venture into theatre came to an abrupt end.[65]

[64] Harold Clurman, *The Fervent Years* (New York, 1945), p. 6.

[65] For a detailed discussion of these and similar organizations, see Malcolm Goldstein, *The Political Stage* (New York, 1974). See also Hallie Flanagan, *Arena : The History of the Federal Theatre* (New York, 1940), and Jane DeHart Mathews, *The Federal Theatre 1935–1939 : Plays, Relief and Politics* (Princeton, NJ, 1967).

The socially committed theatre whose effect was most strongly felt on the national scene was the Group Theatre, organized in the 1930s by Lee Strasberg, Harold Clurman and Cheryl Crawford. The Group began as an offshoot of the Theatre Guild, whose board had permitted younger associates to stage experimental studio productions of plays that were under consideration for a subscription run. The young actors produced as a studio offering the first play from the USSR to be seen in the United States, *Red Rust* by Vladimir Kirchon and Andrei Ouspensky. It was successful and was taken into the regular Guild season, but its reception by enthusiastic Soviet supporters gave the performances a radical tinge that the Guild board mistrusted. The studio was deliberately forgotten. Nevertheless, the desire of the young radicals in the organization to strike out on their own persisted, with the result that the Guild permitted the new organization to have for production two plays belonging to the Guild, and, in 1931, helped them to find a summer place where they could rehearse undisturbed.

Working on minimum salaries and free of Actors' Equity restrictions, the young actors spent eighteen weeks preparing Paul Green's *The House of Connelly*. Equally important, that summer, they worked at adjusting themselves to the necessities of group living and to the exploration of a mode of acting that was new to the national scene. The acting style derived from that developed by the Moscow Art Theatre, taught in the United States by two former actors in the Stanislavsky company, the director Richard Boleslavsky and the actress Maria Ouspenskaya. From their work in the American Laboratory Theatre, Lee Strasberg took inspiration and instruction. He had also had some association with Jacques Copeau, whom the Guild had imported to stage an adaptation of *The Brothers Karamazov*. From Copeau's example arose the idea of forming a theatrical company, like that of the Moscow Art Theatre and the Théâtre du Vieux Colombier, whose actors would assemble not only to develop a style of acting and production, but would undertake a communal search for formative social truths.

Certainly in the American theatre, there had been little attention paid to formal actor training. Some schools existed, but by and large an actor was expected to learn his craft on the job by experiment and luck, much as he had in the nineteenth century. Strasberg's insistence that rehearsal periods were a form of schooling was in a measure revolutionary, as was his sense that presentation was less important than strengthening the actor's craft. In company with Strasberg, Clurman felt an emptiness in the Guild productions – a prettiness, a dilettantism which he mistrusted. He sought to find a way to achieve greater homogeneity among all production elements and a more profound human truth than he could see in most commercial presentations. In his words:

> Theatrical experience was, for the greater part, the antithesis of human experience; it bespoke a familiarity with the clichés of stage deportment, rather than experience with direct roots in life. It seemed to us that without such true experience, plays in the theatre were lacking in all creative justification. In short, the [acting] system was not an end in itself, but a means employed for the true interpretation of plays.[66]

The success of the Group Theatre, as the assembly of actors inevitably was named, provided the American theatre with skilled performers, capable of bringing a new kind of realism to the stage and films. The teachings of Strasberg became the dominant force in the development of a new acting style, which lost almost entirely the sense of 'performance' seen in the more established actors of the time. Actors following the Strasberg teaching, the so-called 'Method', did not seek the direct contact with audiences that had marked so many of the stars of the past. That they should be loved or admired for themselves was far from the point. Rather they sought to blend role and self in such a way as to bring elements of their lives to enhance their characterizations, minimizing 'personality', and attempting to find ways in which personal truths, discovered by profound self-analysis, could match the truths of the characters they played. Not many of these actors attempted to build a full new character appropriate to each role, in the studied manner of Paul Muni or Charles Laughton in their films. Rather there developed a tendency to bend character to individual quality, to shape the outer theatrical essence to personal inner elements. At its best, the new actors played with passion and excitement. At their worst, they turned introspective and mournful and a monotony came over the stage. Unlike the style of the actors they succeeded, the psychological accuracy that many of these actors achieved was as good in films as it was on stage, and it was to prove superb on television, where the cameras could record a detailed but small-scale performance with unusual accuracy. The powers of concentration developed in the 'Method' actor held even when the video lenses bored closely in, and enabled the actor to project a vivid impression of life even through the screen of the machinery.

The social realism of the Group Theatre, like the aesthetic theories of the art theatre, was a somewhat selfconscious attempt at definition of aims and

[66] Clurman, op. cit. p. 43.

purposes. The American theatre has been a theatre in search of itself. Even as it matured in its craft and its literacy, it never lost entirely its naïveté or its charming ability to wonder at itself. Its major designers – Oenslager, Gorelik, Simonson, bel Geddes, Mielziner – all wrote books on their art, following in the tradition of Jones and Macgowan. Its directors and its playwrights wrote quasi-Shavian articles in the Sunday edition of *The New York Times*, defining and justifying their intentions. Its reviewers and critics were seen and heard on radio and television. Politicians scrutinized it and persecuted its artists. Everyone, it would seem, wanted to know what the American theatre was and what it was about.

No ready answers emerged from the attempts to formulate theories as to its behaviour, yet as the playwrights worked to increasingly better purpose, the shape of an answer was formed in the reflecting pool that the drama provided for American life in the period between the two World Wars. Better than any other evidence, the drama the theatre called into being reveals the bizarre context in which it was produced.

3 The central reflector

To find the moment when there appeared an unequivocally American drama is impossible. The individualistic, informal theatre of the nineteenth century was, to be sure, congenial to the nation at large, but it produced no playwrights whose work clearly reflected the dominant concerns of the nation. In the first years of the century, the dramatists who followed the attempts of the more conscientious actors and producers to bring the theatre closer to life came, on occasion, to a partial awakening, as did the popular Clyde Fitch in his drama, *The City* (1909). Some were capable of an unaccustomed sophistication, as was Langdon Mitchell in *The New York Idea* (1906). Some were earnest realists like James A. Herne in *Margaret Fleming* (1890) and *Shore Acres* (1892). One playwright before the First World War attained a genuine social vision. Edward Sheldon's studies of race problems in *The Nigger* (1909), of city politics in *The Boss* (1911) and of the career woman in *The High Road* (1912) are each serious attempts to define and clarify important social problems. They are not in all ways successful, and too often insight is confounded with melodrama, but they are more than half hearted attempts to respond to the bewildering, changing face of life in the United States in the early years of the twentieth century.

The plays written in those years tell little about that life, and taken as a whole can hardly be said to comprise a 'national drama'. To create a drama that will serve as a central reflector of the dominant cultural drives of the nation, several conditions must be achieved. There is the obvious need for money, machinery and fully professional talent. There is need of aesthetic principles that will point directions clearly, justify the nature of success and explain failure. Most important, perhaps, there is need of a city. Men speak inaccurately of the British drama or the French or the Greek. They mean the drama of London, of Paris, of Athens. Great drama does not emerge from the provinces. Until a nation has created a city of such wealth and prominence that it is like a city state, an urban centre that holds in its confines a cross-section of the nation's population, a city that is a magnet for the cultural life of the country and that reflects the essence of that life in such a way as to define it and give it artistic and social formulation – until such a city is achieved there will be no national drama. In the United States, until New York City became the unchallenged cultural capital, no truly national drama could be created, even though the city was clearly the centre of theatrical activity from at least 1880.

After the First World War, however, the city dominated American life, and it is then that a group of playwrights appears whose work, taken in aggregate, and divorced as much as may be from individual predilections of style and interpretation, can be read as a drama reflective of American values. The image of American life they create is not entirely to be anticipated.

In her examination of American comic traditions, *American Humor*,[67] Constance Rourke delineates a number of what she calls 'symbolic Americans', who appear repeatedly not only in drama but in all forms of American comic writing. There is the plain-speaking, homespun American, whose sincerity of heart makes him a better man than his antagonist, in the beginning a foppish Englishman. There is the astute, rural 'hick', the Yankee 'Jonathan' who held the stage in many guises after his early appearance in Royall Tyler's play *The Contrast* (1787). There is his ne'er-do-well cousin, typified by Rip Van Winkle in Joseph Jefferson's characterization of Washington Irving's hero. There is the romantic frontiersman, master of the wild, and hero of such melodramas as Frank Murdock's *Davy Crockett*, or *Be Sure You're Right, Then Go Ahead* (1872).

These character types were products of the eighteenth and nineteenth centuries, and they survived in both dramatic and non-dramatic literature, even into the twentieth century, where they were joined by others and

[67] Constance Rourke, *American Humor* (Garden City, NY, 1953).

suffered a sea-change into figures less clear and confident. A distillation of the central themes and typical characters of the American playwrights between the two World Wars can reveal much about the context of belief in which they wrote and serve as a subtext for the nation's pretensions. What appears is unexpected: the American dramatists have not been true believers in the ostensible destiny of their nation.

The American has always thought of himself as an Antaeus, deriving his strength from his contact with the earth. Understandably in the long westering migrations, in the sense of rightful possession and moral rectitude that comes with wrenching a homestead from the wilderness, in the joy at having endured the brute necessities which the cultivation of the great continent enforced, the American came to a relationship with the land that was both possessive and worshipful. His roots are geographic, not historic. Land, not ancestry, is his good. It is his right to own and to cultivate the land, but it is also essential to him to be possessed by it, to gain strength from wilderness by responding physically to a current of life in the land. That such a response is sentimental and vaguely irreligious does not make it less real, even today, when Americans manifest their belief in the land by attempting to protect it from overcultivation and spoilage, setting aside huge preserves as national parks and 'wilderness areas'.

Belief in the spirit and the power of the land was axiomatic to many of the post-war dramatists. One of the most positive formulations of the belief is to be found in Sidney Howard's *They Knew What They Wanted* (1924). The characters, as the title implies, are assured materialists, yet they discover that in the land there is a force over which they have little control. Amy, the mail-order bride of Tony Patucci, a sixty-year-old Italian rancher, becomes pregnant by his foreman, Joe. The resolution of the situation lies in Tony's ability to forgive the girl and the ranch hand. The play's action is framed by the positions of a doctor and a priest, who establish a dialectic between Christian faith and scientific reason, but neither position helps to resolve the ethical dilemma. Resolution is possible only because Tony's humanity is rich and instinctual. His sympathy is associated with the slowly ripening grapes and the wine he presses from them, and his imagery reveals his closeness to nature. Seeing Amy for the first time, he tells her, 'You come in da house like da spring come in da winter. You come in da house like da pink flower dat sit on da window sill. W'en you come da whole world is like da inside da wine cup.'[68] Amy's reaction to the ranch is similarly associated with a receptivity to nature and with the sense that there she has

[68] Sidney Howard, *They Knew What They Wanted* (New York, 1925), p. 110.

come home: 'Coming up I could taste the wind way down inside me. It made me think of where I used to live.'[69] That home, as she continues to describe it, was like the ranch. There fruit grew lavishly and beautifully, and there she belonged. The implication is that, despite the materialism that presses money from the grapes, despite the shallow assurance revealed by Amy and Joe, and despite the ethical positions of doctor and priest, it is the land that influences the benevolent action and makes it possible for Amy and Tony to come into a right relationship.

A second example can be found in the regional comedies of Lynn Riggs, where the land again contains a force that is controlling and benevolent. In *Green Grow the Lilacs* (1931) the hero, Curly, speaks of the life-force to his enemy, the psychotic Jeeter:

> Outside, the sun's jist crazy 'th heat, beatin' on the prairie and the corn stalks. Passed a field in the bottom this mornin' whur the backwater had been. Ground all cracked and blistered and bakin' in the sun. Likin' it, though! Likin' it good. The crawfish put up their pinchers and hustled about, 'cause their holes is all goin' dry. Seen fields of wheat and oats – fine as a fiddle! The crows went to honkin' at me when I rode th'ough the Dog Crick timber, and I could see hundreds of squirrels friskin' in the blackjacks. I could smell them green walnuts, too, whenever ole Dun ud tromp on 'em. Shore the purtiest mornin' in a long time! Felt like hollerin' and shoutin'. I raired away back in my saddle and old Dun stepped out a-prancin' and we come th'ough Claremore like a streak of forked lightnin'! An' it's shore a funny end to a fine purty mornin' to find yerself shet up in a dark hole bent over a table a-fingerin' a pack of cards 's greasy 's a ole tin spoon, ain't it?[70]

The lyrical description of spring in the Oklahoma territory clearly reflects Riggs's sense that the land creates the energy and the morality of those who live deeply in it. Jeeter, who shuts himself away from it, locked in the dark smokehouse where he lives, is an alien, evil and insane, and in forcing the morning to his attention Curly is in part attempting to exorcize the spiritual darkness of his enemy. In the world outside, for the rest who live on the land, health and harmony come from the earth:

> Look at the way the hayfield lays out purty in the moonlight. Next it's the pasture, and over yander's the wheat and the corn, and the cane

69 Howard, op. cit. p. 49.
70 Lynn Riggs, *Green Grow the Lilacs* (New York, 1931), pp. 67–8.

patch next, nen the truck garden and the timber. Ever'thing laid out fine and jim dandy! The country all around it – all Indian Territory – plumb to the Rio Grande, and north to Kansas, and 'way over east to Arkansaw, the same way, with the moon onto it.[71]

It is an image of a blessed and benevolent world.

The positive imagery of Riggs and Howard which depicts men and the earth bound together in harmony is a simple form of the naturalism which was to be found in European novels – Zola's, Hardy's – and dramas – Ibsen's, Shaw's, Becque's. It had its counterpart, too, in American fiction, notably in the work of Jack London, Frank Norris and Theodore Dreiser, who again show men being controlled by forces of which they are not entirely aware. Nowhere, however, has the naturalistic view of man and his world been given such a clear ethical turn as in the American drama. The view is perilously sentimental, even when it takes on a dark coloration, as in Jack Kirkland's adaptation of Erskine Caldwell's novel, *Tobacco Road* (1935). The drama of the southern share-croppers had a record run, and although its success was in part founded on its scandalous subject matter – incest, female lechery, and the like – it is significant that in the middle years of the Depression, when, in America's middle-west, the extraordinarily fertile land became a 'dust bowl', driving many farmers on a fruitless trek across the country, this play which tells of the land turned harsh and sterile and life-denying should find such a popular reception. There is a moment late in the play when Jeeter Lester, the tenant farmer, reaches out for the land, lifts a handful of the dry earth and then lets it run uselessly through his fingers. The gesture was memorable, and it suggested that somehow the land had betrayed its children, that the force for good had wasted itself.

The image of the wasted land recurs in Robert Sherwood's *The Petrified Forest* (1935), whose central symbol, a forest turned to stone in the middle of a desert, is intended to exemplify modern American life. Again the audiences of the Depression years responded to the idea of the dying land, which Sherwood had borrowed from T. S. Eliot, whose 'The Hollow Men' is quoted in the play. Alan Squier, the protagonist, blames the sterility of modern life on man's attempt to control nature.

> They dammed it up, and used its waters to irrigate the wastelands. They built streamlined monstrosities to penetrate its resistance. They wrapped it up in cellophane and sold it in drugstores. They were so certain they had it subdued. And now – do you realize what it is that is

[71] Riggs, op. cit. pp. 119–20.

causing world chaos? . . . It's Nature hitting back. Not with the old
weapons – floods, plagues, holocausts. We can neutralize them. She's
fighting back with strange instruments called neuroses. She's deliberately afflicting mankind with the jitters. Nature is proving she can't be
beaten – not by the likes of us. She's taking the world away from the
intellectuals and giving it back to the apes.[72]

Squier, the intellectual, will die in an encounter with the last of the plains-
men, a gangster named Duke Mantee, and his death will be given a sentimentally heroic coloration, for he provokes his own murder so that a young
waitress in the desert café can inherit his life insurance and go to Paris to
become a painter. With symbols intact to the end, the play closes as Squier
is buried in the petrified forest, while Mantee is gunned down in a desperate
attempt to escape pursuit. Neither man can find the right way, but must
wander restlessly over an unforgiving and hostile earth.

The concern of the American dramatist for the land is sometimes given
a longer view that is neither negative nor sentimentally positive. In Maxwell
Anderson's *High Tor* (1936), for example, the careless attempts of materialistic Americans to destroy nature – symbolized in the cannibalization of a
mountain to make trap-rock – leads to the formulation that 'Nothing is
made by men / but makes in the end, good ruins.' In Thornton Wilder's
comedy, *Our Town* (1938), as in his short play, *Pullman Car Hiawatha*
(published 1931), the American is viewed *sub specie aeternitatis*, and his life
and death are seen as inconsequential when scaled against the large seasonal
cycles of birth-to-death that all nature follows.

In somewhat later formulations, the image of the land as a moral force
emerges in plays like William Inge's *Bus Stop* and Richard Nash's *The
Rainmaker* (both 1954), where, it is suggested, lives can be rightly conducted
if nature's dictates are heeded. In drama to come, the belief, which amounts
to a basic American credo, will no doubt remain alive, as a memory if not as
a reality.

The belief in the land, while it has been simply set forth in its lyrical
manifestations, has not led to an entirely naïve or sentimental view of the
men and women who live on it. To be sure there is an ample number of
rural idiots in the American theatre, wise-cracking country sages, like the
hero of *Lightnin'* (1918) by Frank Bacon and Winchell Smith, ne'er-do-
wells like Rip Van Winkle or his more recent counterpart, Van Van Dorn
in Anderson's *High Tor*. There are country simpletons aspiring towards

[72] Robert Sherwood, *The Petrified Forest* (New York, 1935), pp. 62–3.

success in the big city, and there are those who manifest what Walt Whitman called a 'barbaric yawp', like the hero of Lynn Riggs's *Roadside* (1930). Yet perhaps the most characteristic landsman is a subtler and more confusing character than any of these rural types. He is a man like Joe in *They Knew What They Wanted*, one who is essentially rootless, a wanderer across the surface of the land. Joe is a 'Wobbly', a card-carrying member of the Industrial Workers of the World, whose political commitment is to the organization of the farm workers into a union structure. Joe admits his radical activities may mean nothing: 'Maybe I'm just restless an' rarin' to go,' he says, and it is his restlessness rather than his belief in labour's cause that seems truly to move him. At his most charming, this figure appears as Riggs's cow-puncher hero in *Green Grow the Lilacs*, but his lineaments are also to be seen in both Alan Squier and Duke Mantee in *The Petrified Forest*. He is clearly present in Maxwell Anderson's hobo-hero, Bartolomeo Romagna, in *Winterset* (1935), and he reappears as Biff Loman in Arthur Miller's *Death of a Salesman* (1949) and Tennessee Williams's roving spokesmen: Tom Wingfield in *The Glass Menagerie* (1945), the itinerant Val Xavier of *Battle of Angels* (1940) and its revision *Orpheus Descending* (1955), and the beach boy protagonist, Chance Wayne in *Sweet Bird of Youth* (1959). He is often filled with a vital energy, but his course is most frequently one that leads him to self-destruction or to a bewildering confusion that saps his will. His sexual inclinations are sometimes Oedipal, and he is frequently threatened with psychological or (as happens to Wayne) physical castration.

His comic counterpart is the mild-mannered, often stupid 'mother's boy', who has repeatedly been chosen as the incarnation of the hero of the American success story. A typical example is the farce by Ring Lardner and George S. Kaufman, *June Moon* (1929), in which a country boy comes to the city to succeed as a songwriter. His success at writing a lyric of consummate banality leads him into the temptations of the metropolis – which is to say marriage to a greedy woman. In time, he sees the light and returns to his true love and to his career. Although the play has a satiric element, particularly in its jaundiced view of the American popular song, it is, at its core, a fable dear to the hearts of American audiences: simple purity, naïve endeavour, true love and good luck breed success for mild men and women. In a curious way, it is allied to the fables that put faith in the land, for it is a tale of the meek inheriting the earth. Its simplicity has made it useful as the narrative thread for countless farces. *Once in a Lifetime* (1930), *You Can't Take It With You* (1936) and other comedies by George S. Kaufman and Moss Hart centre on this fable. Such perennials of the American theatre as *Room Service* (1937) by John Murray and Alan Boretz, *Boy Meets Girl* (1935) by Bella and Samuel Spewack, or *Three Men on a Horse* (1935) by John Cecil Holm and George Abbott offer minor variations on the theme. Interestingly, the naïf is often an artist of sorts, a greetings-card poet, a playwright, an actor; and often, as with Erwin, the hero of *Three Men on a Horse*, he reveals a depressing reverence for the wholesome American 'Mom'.

Whether he is a tragic seeker or a comic cissy, the protagonist in search of a mother has returned with astonishing frequency to American stages. The play which set the pattern most indelibly is *The Silver Cord* (1926) by Sidney Howard. In Mrs Phelps, Howard portrays a mother who is little short of monstrous – a predatory, demanding, self-pitying female, who schemes to destroy her sons' marriages and tries to bind the men to her in incestuous dependence for ever. Howard views her with loathing and concentrates on the conflict generated by her daughter-in-law's attempts to thwart her. At the play's end, although one son is freed, the other is 'engulfed forever', not without a certain contentment at having lost his struggle to assert his manhood. Similar struggles have been the focal concern of many later plays – Tom's struggle against Amanda Wingfield in *The Glass Menagerie*, for example, or the surrealistic dismemberment of the son in *The American Dream* (1961) by Edward Albee.

Variations on the theme are many. In Clifford Odets's *Awake and Sing!* (1935) Bessie Burger is depicted as a woman desperately struggling to hold her family together in the midst of the Depression. To do so, she commits many cruelties, and her acts have tragic consequences: her son's engagement is broken, her daughter leaves home, and her father-in-law commits suicide so that his grandson may inherit his life insurance and with the money escape his mother's domination. Yet, as Odets sees her, she is no simple villain like Howard's Mrs Phelps. Rather she is a woman nearly crushed by the obligation of maintaining the life she has fostered. Something of her spirit was rekindled by Arthur Miller in the depiction of Linda Loman in *Death of a Salesman*, and her courage and cruelty are suggested again in Amanda Wingfield in *The Glass Menagerie*.

Although they are more than willing to depict the American Mother as a daughter of Medea, the dramatists, somewhat illogically, do not show her sons in flight from her fearful presence. Rather they reach out to her, and, if she is absent, they seek her surrogate in mistresses, wives or whores. In Sidney Kingsley's study of life in the New York slums, *Dead End* (1935), the gangster 'Baby-Face' Martin returns to his childhood world to find his mother, who has become a slatternly, broken woman. When they meet he calls her 'Mom', and pleads for her to accept him and love him. She has no use for what he has become. She slaps his face and tells him that she wishes she had been cut open, rather than to have carried him into life. In Philip Barry's society comedy, *Holiday* (1928), the second act is laid in the family nursery, where the grown-up children take refuge from their excessive affluence. It is a charming room, created for the children by their long-dead mother. Here, her son, who has become an alcoholic, and her younger daughter, who has found no way to come to terms with her life except by playing the role of farcical spinster, come to summon whatever in memory remains of the warmth of spirit their mother's death has taken from them. As a third example, in S. N. Behrman's comedy, *Biography* (1932), the love of the heroine, a redoubtable bachelor girl, for a hardheaded Marxist journalist is declared when he tells her of the loss of his parents. He breaks down, weeping, and sinks to his knees beside her. She strokes his hair 'with infinite compassion', and, calling him by a baby's name, 'Dickie', asks him why he has been afraid to love her. His broken declaration of his loss and her response suggest the relation of mother to son as much as the relation of two lovers.

As *Biography* reveals, many of the central male characters on the American stage seek to find a mother in the women they love, and, as an ancillary theme, the American playwrights have frequently developed the motif of incest. There is Stanley Kowalski's rape of his sister-in-law Blanche Du Bois in Williams's *A Streetcar Named Desire* (1947). In *They Knew What They Wanted* Joe's seduction of Amy, the bride of the man for whom he feels the dedication of a son, suggests the possibility. The love of the sisters for their brother is clearly incestuous in Lillian Hellman's *Toys in the Attic* (1960), as is Eddie Carbone's desire for his niece in Arthur Miller's *A View from the Bridge* (1955). Incest or incestuous possibility is an oddly dark element in the American theatre, contrasting strangely with the escapist romantic tales of heroic, beautiful Americans in Hollywood's films. On the stage, the American has been introverted, frustrated and weak, as if something in the American milieu is inescapably life-denying.

When the major dramatists have considered their country, almost inevitably they have found it wanting. In the 1920s, at the height of the boom years, Philip Barry reiterated his sense of malaise at the country's direction in a number of society comedies, of which *Holiday* can stand as the prototype. In this play, he causes the sympathetic characters to express their discontent with the amassing of riches. There must be more, he argues vaguely; there must be a way to have 'fun'. To find it, he causes his hero and heroine to run from the pressures of Wall Street, to retire while they are young, to chart a loosely individualistic course of action that passes for freedom. Although the positive course of action is a childish escape, and although the moneyed class is treated superficially, Barry reaches towards the definition of a set of values that are more than materialistic. What is wrong with the country is that it is too rich. In the year before the great stockmarket crash, the only way out was to run away.

A similar solution is to be found in the comedies of S. N. Behrman. In *Biography*, for example, the heroine, Marion Froude, resolves to leave her leftist lover and to renounce the possibilities offered by the amatory advances of his rival, a conservative politican. The political persuasions of her suitors are important, for Marion realizes that to accept either man means that she must accept his commitment at the cost of the neutrality on which she has based her life. In the end, she makes no choice, but, like Barry's hero, walks out. The play's last line, spoken to her personal maid, is 'We travel alone!' In 1932, as a consciousness grew of the need for the United States to take a position on the international stage, and as the country moved slowly from its traditional isolationism, Behrman's comedy of a free spirit caught between the Right and Left took on allegorical suggestions. He knew, at least, that the country could not stand still, but must 'travel'. Yet like Barry's 'fun', the freedom expressed by 'alone' was vaguely defined, and salvation lay in escape. Behrman was to continue to explore the dilemma of commitment in later plays, such as *Rain From Heaven* (1934), wherein the heroine must choose between a Jewish refugee and a demagogic American fascist. Here the dangers of a fascist America are clearly seen, and Behrman argues for committed anti-fascist action.

Stylishly written, comic in tone, Behrman's plays made their point by allegorical suggestion and he did not look closely at the fabric of American life. Others, however, did, and many found it threadbare. An early example was John Howard Lawson's *Roger Bloomer* (1923). Lawson, who is one of the nation's most interesting playwrights, and perhaps its only true expressionist dramatist, depicted the growth towards maturity of his adolescent hero. The view taken of the crassly materialistic Bloomer family is in the tradition of Sinclair Lewis's novels, but Roger is a more poetically conceived hero than any in Lewis's books. He is shy and sensitive, and he finds no place in his family's world. His life is simple and hard. He attempts to find happiness with a shop girl, but the romance ends with her suicide. The play's climax is an elaborate dream sequence centred on a trial that is reminiscent of Georg Kaiser's *From Morn to Midnight*. At the end, as Roger awakens from his nightmare, he is told to listen: 'far off . . . the tread of marching people, singing a new song.' It is a faintly revolutionary hope, but it is not strong enough to over-balance the image of the vulgar, middle-class, middle-western America, where materialistic ambition suppresses, deforms or kills all those who reach for something more sensitive and alive.

Later, in his most successful play, *Processional* (1925), Lawson continued his revolutionary inquiry in a mordant analysis – presented in the style of an American vaudeville – of the situation surrounding a miners' strike. The play is a bewildering pastiche in which the strikers are attacked by police, militia and the Ku Klux Klan. The hero, an embattled revolutionary, is not only compelled to man the barricades, but must cope with a complex personal life centring on his love for a young Jewish girl and his discovery that his mother is a whore. Lawson's play includes outrageous melodrama, tragedy and farce, and he peoples the action with many of the vulgar, racial stereotypes from the vaudeville stage. The components are welded together by an ironic overview that makes the final vision of the combatants coming together in an idealistic and peaceable comradeship, as President Coolidge proclaims 'Mother's Day', both absurd and wistfully hopeful.

Lawson's revolutionary suggestions were not to the taste of most American dramatists. In the same year as *Roger Bloomer*, the Theatre Guild produced a more congenial analysis of the nation's deficiencies in Elmer Rice's *The Adding Machine*. Rice, like Lawson, was apparently influenced by German expressionism,[73] and used the style to portray the dismal destiny of a small man, the all-but-anonymous Mr Zero. Zero is a clerk in revolt against his life's dreary circumstances. He commits a murder, is executed, and in the afterlife discovers that he is doomed to move backwards, down the evolu-

---

[73] The Theatre Guild produced Kaiser's *From Morn to Midnight* in May 1922 and Capek's *R.U.R.* in October of the same year. *Roger Bloomer* opened under non-professional circumstances in March 1923 and *The Adding Machine* was produced in the same month. Earlier, in a sensational run that began in November 1920, O'Neill's *The Emperor Jones* opened the way towards a successful American use of the expressionistic mode, and he had confirmed that success with a second such play, *The Hairy Ape* in March 1922. The impact of the Europeans and of O'Neill's success was greater on Rice than on Lawson. From his earliest work, Lawson had sought to go beneath the surface of the experiences he depicted and was clearly moving towards what came to be known as 'expressionism'. Rice, on the other hand, was a successful commercial dramatist who tried all styles from courtroom melodramas to society comedies. He wrote nothing else of substance in the manner of *The Adding Machine*, which, nevertheless, remains a work of historic importance.

tionary scale, a senseless machine in the mechanized world of modern society. The elements of Rice's indictment are the same as in Lawson's work: there are scenes of mechanical slavery in offices, sterile domestic life, police brutality, unheeding judges in nightmare courtrooms, and the action is hedged about with surreal scenic distortions suggestive of the violent world of the action which crushes the non-conformists.

In the decade of the 1920s, the view of the American as the victim of social pressures was easily, often glibly, set forward. To escape as the charming people in the comedies of Philip Barry were allowed to do, or to succumb to pressure and move downwards to death or defeat, as in *The Adding Machine*, were typical conclusions. Lawson's cry of revolution was faint indeed, but in the succeeding decade, when there emerged during the Depression a sense of national brotherhood that no war, no social policy, no national adventure had ever been able to create, matters changed.

They did not necessarily change for the better. Lawson's analysis of social inequities and his cries for revolution were, with the exception of *Processional*, unsuccessful in the theatre.[74] Others who followed Lawson's lead adopted easy, radical political stances which often led to trouble with the authorities – municipal and national – but which did not produce works of art, or even works that were held in popular esteem. Marc Blitzstein's operetta, *The Cradle Will Rock* (1938), was modelled on *Processional*. It gained a legendary place in American theatre history, when its original production by the government-sponsored Federal Theatre was, by governmental edict, prevented from opening. Receiving notification that they must close the theatre a few hours before curtain time on opening night, the producers hastily moved to another theatre and directed the first-night audience to walk to the new location. The Union orchestra was not permitted to perform, so a piano was commandeered from a passing truck and carried on to the stage, where the composer and actors played a skeletal version of the work to sympathetic ears.[75] In a simplistic, cartoon-like style, the musical play points to the inequities of the American social scene, making all the

---

74 *Processional* was produced by the Theatre Guild with memorable settings by Mordecai Gorelik. The production succeeded in a curious context for so radical a work. It was one of a season of six productions in the Guild's 1924–5 season. The others were Molnar's *The Guardsman*; Howard's *They Knew What They Wanted*; *Ariadne* by A. A. Milne; a revue, *The Garrick Gaieties*, with songs by Richard Rodgers and Lorenz Hart; and two plays by Shaw, *Arms and the Man* and *Caesar and Cleopatra*. It was clearly not a season in which revolutionary voices prophesied change.

75 An engaging account of the production can be found in John Houseman's memoir, *Run-Through* (New York, 1972).

rich villainous or foolish and all the poor sympathetic and heroic. Naïvely prophesying revolution ('When . . . the final wind blows / The cradle will rock'), the operetta moved further towards the Left than had the earlier American theatre, Lawson's work excepted. The main line of American drama in the 1930s was less assertive, and confined itself to general suggestions that something was rotten and to faintly allegorical hints that change was needed.

Lillian Hellman's study of the greed of the capitalistic Hubbard family is a ready example. In *The Little Foxes* (1939) she traced the career of Regina Hubbard Giddens, who, be it noted, is one more in the roster of destroying mothers. Regina moves to an ambiguous victory, having murdered her husband and having outwitted her two brothers in a complicated financial manœuvre. The play is, if taken as an image of a general American condition, a depressing picture of things as they are. Yet its author was not content to present the American scene only in the negative imagery of the Hubbard family portrait. Rather methodically, she closed each of the three acts on a scene involving Regina's young daughter, Alexandra. Each moment is a step in her education, as she grows from a naïve child to a young woman who finally gains the courage to break from her mother's domination. At the end, she stands firm and alone and announces her intention of leaving home and of finding a place where people don't 'just stand around and watch' the world being despoiled. Hers is an escape, but it is also a search for revolutionary companions who will take the necessary stand against the evils presented.

The direct call for revolution sounded clearly in the early work of Clifford Odets. In *Waiting for Lefty* (1935) a young actor is given a dollar by a kindly stenographer, who tells him it will buy ten loaves of bread. Alternatively, she suggests, he can spend it on nine loaves of bread and a copy of the Communist Manifesto. Misquoting the Book of Revelation ('I saw a new earth and a new heaven; for the first earth and the first heaven were passed away'), she counsels him that it is not the meek but the militant who will inherit the earth. The scene was sometimes omitted from published texts and later productions, but there remained at the end of the play an unambiguous exhortation to strike, a call that in the play's context was evidently intended to promote revolution against the unhappy condition of life in the United States.

Odets followed a revolutionary line through the 1930s, but the call to revolt became less explicit and was finally to die away altogether. It is suggested, however, in *Awake and Sing!* when the young son, while accepting the economic facts of his life, refuses to let himself be crushed by

the poverty that threatens all virtue, all love. He tells his mother that there
is more to life than lies and hatred, that he wants no part of a life that is
'printed on dollar bills'. His mother cries to him to change the world if he
does not like it, and he replies:

> I will! And why? 'Cause life's different in my head. Gimme the earth
> in two hands. I'm strong. There . . . hear him? The air mail off to
> Boston. Day or night, he flies away, a job to do. That's us and it's no
> time to die.[76]

The flight of the mail plane, like Alexandra's repudiation of her family,
suggests the search for revolutionary companions, and the effect is repeated
in Odets's *Golden Boy* (1937), where the young Joe Bonaparte, a violinist
turned prize fighter, fleeing the system that has caused him to murder his
opponent in the ring, rides in a fast car through the night to his death. But
he has gone for the ride because his girl has told him that together they
can find a place where 'happy boys and girls' can teach them a new way of
life: 'We'll find some city where poverty's no shame – where music is no
crime – where there's no war in the streets – where a man is glad to be
himself and make his woman herself.'[77] The cry is like Ralph's and Alexandra's, although in the play's context the condemnation of the America
that crushes a creative spirit is more clearly allegorical in style than in either
of the other works. Interestingly, in expressing the sense of a land or a city
or a vaguely defined 'place' where the revolutionary good can be found, both
Odets and Hellman echo with variations the escapist motif of Barry and
Behrman. Somehow, each seems to say, the revolution is not here, not now.
It lies in a utopian future of whose imminence neither the playwrights nor
their characters are entirely convinced.

Allegorical treatment of social evils and suggested revolutionary action
by way of remedy can be found in several plays by Irwin Shaw, notably
Bury the Dead (1936) and *The Gentle People* (1939). Robert Ardrey's *Thunder
Rock* (1939) and Paul Green's musical play *Johnny Johnson* (1936), with a
score by Kurt Weill, are also of the genre. One of the most successful was
Sidney Kingsley's *Dead End* (1935) which took for its symbolic setting the
dead end of a New York street as it stops at the river. On one side is an
expensive, sunlit apartment house; on the other a squalid tenement. Kingsley's view of the fate of the children who live in the shadows is uncompromising. They are doomed by their poverty to a criminal's way of life.

[76] Clifford Odets, *Awake and Sing!*, in *Six Plays of Clifford Odets* (New York, 1939), p. 95.
[77] Odets, *Golden Boy*, op. cit. p. 316.

Here there is no talk of 'happy boys and girls'; rather there is an unrelenting image of the crushing effect of the materialistic world on its victims. In Kingsley's terms, all men are threatened with extinction because they have failed to assert their dignity and to live true to their sense of beauty and the knowledge of God in their hearts. But it is 'evolution' not revolution that will cause the change. His statement is not unlike Sherwood's concept of nature hitting back in *The Petrified Forest* or Anderson's comment in *High Tor* that 'man makes good ruins'. But Kingsley depicts a darker existence than does either of the others. At the play's end, he focuses on the slum children gathered in the night around a small fire. The moment provides an ironic commentary on the utopian dreams of the more revolutionary playwrights of the 1930s, to say nothing of those who took refuge in meaningless escape. As they watch the smoke fly upwards and talk of the criminal skills they have learned in reform school, one of them sings a cheap ballad he learned there, 'The Prisoner's Song':

> If I had de wings of an angel
> Ovuh dese prison walls I wud fly,
> Straight tuh dee yahms a my muddah . . .

But, the mother mentioned, he can remember no more of the words.

During the 1930s there were, of course, many plays that concerned themselves with the problems of American life in ways that were not allegorical. For example, in *Winterset* (1935) Maxwell Anderson attempted a verse tragedy of modern life whose theme was the quest for justice and the vindication of the hero's wrongfully executed father. Although, in developing his characters and the incidents of his narrative, he helps himself liberally to situations and motifs from *King Lear*, *Romeo and Juliet* and *Hamlet*, Anderson does not go beyond the events of his narrative by symbolism to generalize his case. Similarly in such works as Robert Sherwood's *Idiot's Delight* (1936) or Sidney Howard's *The Ghost of Yankee Doodle* (1937), audiences were asked to speculate directly on the causes and consequences of a new World War. The swing in the country was from isolationism and pacifistic preachment to a belief in intervention in European affairs, a move given some intensity among the revolutionary playwrights by the signing at the decade's end of the Hitler–Stalin non-intervention pact.[78]

With the entry of America into the war, the call for revolution died away, and, while the sense of malaise which the quality of life in the United States

---

[78] For a detailed discussion of the effect of the pact on the American theatrical scene, see Goldstein, op. cit. pp. 209 ff.

had created in its playwrights did not disappear, it was no longer voiced in tones of allegorical or direct protest. Instead, the major playwrights began to explore the nature of patriotism, and, for a time, the question of what it meant to be an American replaced the vaguely defined love of the land that had been expressed in earlier plays.

The new mode was announced decisively in 1939 by the production of *The American Way*, a massive play that was an unexpected departure for Moss Hart and George S. Kaufman, the two best writers of farce in the country. Their play detailed the fate of an immigrant couple in an American small town. With a cast that would have equalled the population of many small towns, the authors saluted the concept of the United States as a 'melting pot' of many races and denounced bigotry and racial intolerance. Lillian Hellman in *Watch on the Rhine* (1940) spoke out explicitly against the patrician world that failed to see the extent of the fascist threat to liberty, sentiments echoed the following year in Robert Sherwood's *There Shall Be No Night*, a story of the Finnish resistance to Russian invasion. American history provided a matrix for the examination of the present in Sherwood's *Abe Lincoln in Illinois* (1939), and Kingsley explored the details of the first years of the struggling republic in *The Patriots* (1941). Examples of patriotism were on display in Arthur Laurents's *Home of the Brave* (1945), Paul Osborne's adaptation of John Hersey's novel *A Bell for Adano* (1944) and Joshua Logan's stage version of Thomas Heggen's *Mr Roberts* (1948). The American way was melodramatically explored in Elmer Rice's *Flight to the West* (1941) and was depicted with realism in Anderson's *The Eve of St Mark* (1942), and even presented in comedy by Russel Crouse and Howard Lindsay in *State of the Union* (1945).

The list of such plays could be extended to the vanishing point. In sum, however, it can be held that they were attempts to treat a new and unexpected theme with force and intelligence. For better or for worse, the United States had set its foot on the international scene and deserted its traditional isolationism. The debate as to whether the country should or should not 'travel alone' ended abruptly in 1941 with the attack on Pearl Harbor, and the major playwrights struggled to understand what the new way was to be. To their credit, although none of their plays has survived its time and its contemporary purposes, they undertook their explorations in no facile way. All the plays have a dark and thoughtful cast; there are no quick-flaring propaganda rockets set up to dazzle the eyes of the audience. Rather, the dramatists turned to examine the roots of democracy in which they had believed, and they tried to set forth its meanings in a way that would enlist allegiance to basic principles of the democratic structure. Their attempt was perhaps a reaction to the explicit left-wing tendencies of the drama of the previous decade, but it went beyond this. Kingsley in *The Patriots* turned his considerable theatrical craftsmanship to a dramatization of the debate between Alexander Hamilton and Thomas Jefferson, just as Sherwood in *There Shall Be No Night* wrote a disquisitory drama concerning the dawning of a patriot's conscience in a man whose scientific objectivity had made him a lazy humanitarian, uncommitted to decisive action.

The allegorists were not silent. In 1941 Philip Barry mistakenly presented *Liberty Jones*, a fantasy with music in which Miss Liberty is sick in bed and is beset by the 'Three Shirts', presumably red, brown and black, finally to be rescued by young American manhood in the persons of Tom Smith, Dick Brown and Harry Robinson. The maverick William Saroyan achieved success in 1939 with a dramatization of his short story, *My Heart's in the Highlands*, which resembles the plays of the Depression period in that it conveys a disconsolate and unlocated sense of national failure, expressed succinctly in the curtain line spoken by the play's nine-year-old protagonist: 'I'm not mentioning any names, Pa, but something's wrong somewhere.' Nevertheless, the play, like the work that followed it, *The Time of Your Life* (1940), looks forward to the patriotic analyses of the next decade. In both, Saroyan spoke of the roots of democracy to be found in the simple, humanitarian love that unites all free men. His point was similar to that made by Thornton Wilder, first in *Our Town* and later in the allegorical account of man's struggle for survival against both natural and man-caused disasters, *The Skin of Our Teeth* (1943). Ranging freely in time and space with an unconventional stagecraft, Wilder celebrated the simple movements of men in their life cycles and praised their courage, their humanity – so set round with folly – and their capacity to forgive the evil done them and to forget the hardship they have endured.

In the middle years of the 1940s two works appeared which prophesied the shape of things to come. One, in 1943, was the musical version of Riggs's *Green Grow the Lilacs*, entitled *Oklahoma!*, by Richard Rodgers and Oscar Hammerstein II. The other was an Ibsenesque tragedy, *All My Sons* (1946), by Arthur Miller. Both plays signalled a turn away from the serious explorations of the nature of democracy and announced a movement backward towards investigations like those that had occupied American dramatists in the 1920s and 1930s.

Richard Rodgers, with his first collaborator, the lyricist Lorenz Hart, who died in 1943, had written some of the most brilliant revues and musical comedies in the American theatre. Hart's lyrics are compact, complicated, witty and concerned always with interesting and unconventional subject matter: a sense of *déjà vu*, for example, or the problems of a lady who hates California, or the lament of a woman whose penchant is murdering her husbands, or the inner monologue of an intellectual stripteaser. With Hart, Rodgers wrote music that epitomized the popular American musical comedy, and in *Pal Joey* (1940), whose book was based on short stories by John O'Hara, the two created a coruscating musical portrait of one of the first anti-heroes on the American stage, the greedy, banal night-club performer, Joey.

Hammerstein, Rodgers's second collaborator, had been one of Broadway's most successful writers of books and lyrics for operettas and had been instrumental in developing what seemed to be a new form of musical play. The quasi-operatic *pâtisserie* of the middle-European composers, Sigmund Romberg, Rudolph Friml and their American imitators, had been a staple of the musical stage, competing with the revues, the Ziegfeld Follies, *Artists and Models* and the *Scandals*. Hammerstein was trained in this school, providing lyrics for Friml's *Rose Marie* (1924) and Romberg's *The Desert Song* (1926). The next year, however, he produced a work which appeared to bring new life to the world of operetta by writing book and lyrics for a more serious musical play, adapted from a novel by Edna Ferber. *Showboat*, with music by Jerome Kern, was for 1927 a departure in a new direction, telling a complicated and not entirely happy love story and considering, however superficially, the problems of the blacks along the Mississippi River. Thereafter, although he had some successes, he did not fulfil the promise of *Showboat*, and by the early 1940s his career was at an ebb. *Oklahoma!* restored him decisively to favour.

It is idle to complain that Hammerstein ruined Rodgers's style and deprived Riggs's play of its acidity. This musical play and those that followed – most notably *Carousel* (1945), *South Pacific* (1949), *The King and I* (1951) and *The Sound of Music* (1959) – set a million stereophonographs throbbing and were, until Allan Jay Lerner and Frederic Loewe set Bernard Shaw's *Pygmalion* to music as *My Fair Lady* (1956), the greatest hits of the American stage.

In the Rodgers and Hammerstein canon, simple rusticity, folk humour and country-western musical touches were the order of the day. To be sure, these rural delights are interspersed with inspirational arias ('When you walk through a storm, hold your head up high . . .') and waltz songs for blankly charming ingénues ('Out of my dreams and into your arms I long to fly . . .'). But Hammerstein hugged rural life joyfully. Words like 'cock-eyed', 'corny' and 'knuckleheaded' are sprinkled through his dialogue and lyrics, and he could write without flinching a song that begins 'This was a real nice clambake'. The message that is shouted by the manly chorus at the end of *Oklahoma!* was a coarsened version, simplified and made into an incredible cliché, of what in the 1920s and early 1930s had had more complex meaning: 'We belong to the land and the land we belong to is grand!'

Oklahoma! played over five years in New York City and toured the country for a sixth year. A second company was on the road for ten years, and in Europe, Africa and Australia it set records. Evidently, in the middle of the years of war, the uncomplicated nostalgia, set to lilting tunes, was a necessity for audiences everywhere. Success, of course, bred imitation. Composers and librettists ransacked the playlists of earlier decades for *Oklahoma!*-like subjects, and new musicals emphasizing the nostalgic past in rural or small-town environments appeared frequently. To list only the most successful: Harold Arlen's *Bloomer Girl* (1944), Irving Berlin's *Annie Get Your Gun* (1946), Frank Loesser's *The Most Happy Fella* (1956), based on *They Knew What They Wanted, Paint Your Wagon* (1951) by Lerner and Loewe, Meredith Willson's *The Music Man* (1957) and Harold Rome's *Destry Rides Again* (1959).

The turn towards a sentimentalized view of the American past as it was exemplified in the post-war musical plays was matched in legitimate drama by a swing away from political explorations and the serious analyses of democracy towards a realistic depiction of suburban or rural life, notably in such plays by William Inge as *Come Back, Little Sheba* (1950) and Arthur Miller's *All My Sons*. In the latter play, with high seriousness, Miller wrote of the moral dilemma that comes to a family whose head has committed a crime against humanity. The depiction of the suburban family is an authentic image of middle-class American life, but it is worth observing that as passions rise in his characters Miller's rhetoric begins to echo some of the same thoughts and to resemble in its sound and imagery speeches written by Odets and Hellman a decade earlier. Hellman, for example, had compared the Giddens family to predatory foxes and to locusts. To express his sense of what is wrong with the world, Miller, like Hellman, turns to animal imagery, and has his hero cry 'This is the land of the great big dogs, you don't love a man here, you eat him! . . . This is a zoo, a zoo.'[79]

[79] Arthur Miller, *All My Sons*, in *The Collected Plays of Arthur Miller* (New York, 1957), p. 124.

The return towards the 1930s was again evident in Miller's much-praised tragedy, *Death of a Salesman*, where, complete with allegorical implications, the playwright tells of the death agonies of an anonymous member of the middle class, not different in essence from Elmer Rice's Mr Zero. Willy Loman, Miller's Everyman, undergoes a disintegration of personality which the playwright attributes to the brutalities of the acquisitive American society. 'He had the wrong dreams' is his son's diagnosis of Willy who moves in a state of trauma between a shabby present and a guilt-ridden past. The past is projected in a series of what Miller thinks of as American images: the familiar suburban sights of fathers and sons polishing the family car, the passing of footballs back and forth in the street, the domestic assembly of neighbours and families on hot afternoons. Miller does not summon such imagery, as Hammerstein does, for sentimental reasons. He regards them sternly as aspects of a corrupting culture. Even so, the play suggests a return to pre-war concerns, to the kind of narrative and theme that Odets had made his special province. Both *Death of a Salesman* and *Awake and Sing!* insist that human values are destroyed by crushing financial circumstances and place emphasis on the struggle of a wife to hold her world together. In both plays characters dream of a time when the world was simple and good, and both conclude with an episode wherein an older man kills himself so that, with the insurance money, a younger may escape the miserable present.[80] An interesting critique of Miller's tragedy, discussing it as it was performed by Jewish actors in New York's Yiddish theatre, analyses the family structure as being essentially Jewish, and criticizes Miller for removing it from its ethnic context. If the reviewer is correct, then, as a play about American Jewish life, it comes even closer to Odets's play.[81]

Both Odets and Miller – as had many another playwright who turned to excoriating the American political and social system – concern themselves with an aspect of the national past that gives them a strong emotional lever against the depressing present: the failure of the American dream. The dream is usually associated with the land, which is viewed much in the manner of the folk dramatists of the 1920s. In the past, it is held, the land offered promise and for those who lived in harmony with it there was a happy time, blessed and peaceful, in which men knew they were whole and that life was good. Willy Loman dimly remembers sitting beside a camp fire

---

[80] The conclusion also, it will be remembered, of Sherwood's *The Petrified Forest*.

[81] George Ross, '*Death of a Salesman* in the Original', *Commentary* (Feb. 1951), 11, pp. 184–6.

in the rich wilderness of the undeveloped American middle-west, hearing the music of a flute playing in the night, and he hallucinates about his brother Ben, who prospected in the Alaskan wilderness. In *Awake and Sing!* a similar dream of an Eden-like existence is conveyed by the recording of Caruso singing 'O Paradiso', which the old grandfather plays incessantly in his room. Bessie's breaking of this record drives the old man to his death. In John Steinbeck's *Of Mice and Men* (1937) the dream is of an unattainable farm, where a simple domestic life away from the present miseries can be found. In *The Glass Menagerie* Williams lets Amanda remember as in a dream her life as a girl in the Mississippi Delta, a life full of joy and jonquils and gentlemen callers. In *A Streetcar Named Desire* the memory is of the plantation, Belle Reve, where Blanche and her sister once knew a kind of happiness. For Birdie, the frail sister-in-law of the Giddenses in *The Little Foxes*, the plantation is called Lyonette, but like Belle Reve its memory is a bulwark against the materialism of the present.

The characters cling to their dreams tenaciously. Their dreams are never fulfilled except in the fantasies of nostalgic romances and operettas. The sterner statements insist that the thrust of American materialism has destroyed all such dreams and left man destitute in a soulless world, a wasteland. Even so, the dream survives.

In the 1960s the wasteland became the strongest reality. Many American playwrights then found their imaginations caught by the frightening setting of Samuel Beckett's *Waiting for Godot*, the barren place in which two lost people fumble towards salvation. Beckett's play was a catalyst for reshaping older concepts. The wasteland that Didi and Gogo inhabit seemed entirely familiar to the American playwrights who habitually wrote of a paradise turned desert. An astonishing number of plays in the 1960s are set in such a wasteland. The scene may be an empty city street, a piece of land razed in a slum-clearance project, a decaying Victorian drawing room, an attic cluttered with the relics of a dead life, the deserted lobby of a cheap hotel in the early dawn, a cellar bedroom, a fusty bar. The settings are linked by their common sterility, their ugliness, their lack of horizon and promise. The action that takes place in these dead spaces is, typically, the entrance of two persons, often strangers to one another, lonely, disappointed men and women who are seeking some way of being less alone, a means of touching another and of being touched. Their desire in an unusual number of instances leads towards a climactic moment when, in a long confessional monologue, one character uses the other as a makeshift priest to whom to confess and from whom to receive absolution for a sin. It is not irrelevant that in a large number of plays the sin is the betrayal of a mother or of a woman who has in some degree been like a mother.

Many of the plays are short, with a playing time of an hour or less, and all have small casts.[82] An early example was Edward Albee's *Zoo Story* (1960), set in a deserted space in Central Park and concerned with two characters, Peter and Jerry. The action is developed from Jerry's need to reach another human being. Roughly he forces a confession of weakness from the conventional Peter, and ultimately reveals his despair in a long monologue of confessional import which is climaxed when he forces Peter to kill him. 'I came unto you, and you have comforted me, dear Peter,' are his last words.[83]

To list only a few of the short works which are cut to the same pattern: there is Terrence McNally's *Next* (1969), which takes place in a physical-examination room for army draftees; John Guare's *A Day for Surprises* (1970), whose locale is the 'pasting room' of a very large library; Leonard Melfi's *Birdbath* (1960), set in a shabby New York apartment; Megan Terry's *Ex-Miss Copper Queen on a Set of Pills* (1966), played on the front steps of a tenement; and Michael McClure's *The Beard* (1965), which offers Jean Harlow and Billy the Kid in a hereafter like that of Sartre's in *Huis clos*. The pattern is predictably followed by much of the contemporary black theatre, notably in Leroi Jones's *Dutchman* and *The Toilet* (both 1964). It has also proved capable of comic treatment in such plays as Murray Shisgal's *The Tiger* (1963), which begins with an attempted rape in a dingy basement and moves towards unabashed romance and a happy ending.

In longer form and on-Broadway, in the major works of Albee, *Who's Afraid of Virginia Woolf* (1962) and *Tiny Alice* (1964), the motifs emerged again. They were developed as well in some of the farces of Neil Simon, such as *The Odd Couple* (1965) and the trilogy of one-act plays, *Plaza Suite* (1968). In Simon's work, beneath a popular and skilfully comic treatment, the voices can still be heard, speaking in isolation of their need to reach another human being. It is perhaps no accident that the major play – indeed

---

[82] The diminished size of many of the newer plays is to an extent a return to something like the experimental theatres of the period immediately following the First World War, when many one-act plays were written. It also reflects the astonishing rise in production costs during the 1960s for professional production on Broadway. 'Off-Broadway' (and inevitably, after a time, 'Off-off-Broadway') theatres played in converted lofts, night clubs, garages, free of actors' and technicians' union jurisdiction. In such circumstances, many young playwrights found they could obtain a hearing and learn their craft before committed, small audiences.

[83] Edward Albee, *Zoo Story* (New York, 1960), p. 61.

the only important legitimate play – in the Broadway season of 1973–4 was a splendid revival of Eugene O'Neill's *A Moon for the Misbegotten* (1943) in which a man and a woman, both emotionally crippled, meet in a moon-drenched emptiness – a pig farm – and confess to one another the substance of their loneliness.

4 O'Neill versus Shav

The position of Eugene O'Neill in the thematic context of the American theatre is central. Just as Bernard Shaw proved responsive to the major currents of his theatre and reshaped its uses for his purposes, and as Shakespeare took from and returned to his theatre many motifs, themes, characters and techniques, so O'Neill stood as a lens, a central reflector of the theatre in America in the twentieth century.

As an artist of influence, his life began in 1916, when the Provincetown Players produced his short play, *Bound East for Cardiff*, which he had written two years earlier.[84] With posthumous productions and significant revivals, he has continued to dominate the American stage until the present, sixty years later. In his lifetime he completed drafts of sixty-two plays. Eleven were destroyed, and several exist in unpublished and unproduced typescripts. Some are short plays, but others are dramas of marathon length, such as *Strange Interlude*, *The Iceman Cometh*, *Long Day's Journey into Night* or the trilogy, *Mourning Becomes Electra*. No playwright in English, except Shaw and Shakespeare, has worked so steadily, so long and so seriously. Like the

---

[84] The fullest and best account of O'Neill's life is that in two volumes by Louis Sheaffer, *O'Neill, Son and Playwright* (New York, 1968) and *O'Neill, Son and Artist* (New York, 1973).

two British playwrights, O'Neill began work at a moment when his theatre was taking its characteristic form, and, like them, he defined its shape by showing his contemporaries the potential of the themes and conventions that were the theatre's available materials. Shakespeare's treatment of the revenge formula in *Hamlet*, Shaw's development of the domestic-triangle plot in *Candida* are matched by O'Neill's work with, for example, the American folk play in *Desire Under the Elms*. Shaw and Shakespeare occasionally nodded and at times O'Neill was staggeringly inept. Yet the greatness of which each was capable justified and fulfilled the purposes of his theatre by pulling together into a coherent system of thought and attitude the elements of which lesser writers used only fragments.

O'Neill's first play that can be seen as fully characteristic of the American theatre was a work that emerged more by accident than design. *Bound East for Cardiff* was one of several inexpert, mannered short plays of no value, written at the outset of his career. Unlike its companions, it is authentic O'Neill and a play of a genuinely American stamp. Its scene is the seaman's forecastle on a tramp freighter, sailing from New York to Cardiff. Its action is an encounter between Yank, who is dying of an injury, and his friend Driscoll. For most of the action, the scene is left to the two men, who speak of the friendship that has emerged during their rough life together and of a dream each has held, but of which neither has spoken earlier, of leaving the sea and of finding a farm inland, where they can become something more than the ocean's nomads. At the end of the play Yank dies, and the dream is lost, but the play offers the suggestion that in the shared confessional the men have touched one another and, in so doing, have justified their existence. O'Neill also suggests that the two, like all those who go to sea, become the sea's children and are held by the sea's power as if they were in thrall to a god.[85]

From this small beginning O'Neill moved forward, trying many styles and subjects, but essentially developing the idea that men sought two goals, the truth of their own natures and the special essence of a force to which they could 'belong'. In *Beyond the Horizon* (1918) he defined the nature of that search more fully as he told of Robert Mayo's restless desire to go to sea and of his destruction when he tries to serve the land, to which he does not belong. At the time of its successful first production in 1920, the only play to which it could conveniently be compared was William Vaughn Moody's *The Great*

[85] The play was heavily influenced by Joseph Conrad's *The Nigger of the Narcissus*. Cf. Travis Bogard, *Contour in Time: The Plays of Eugene O'Neill* (New York, 1972), pp. 38–42.

Divide (1907), a play whose conflict centres on the cultural differences between the refined eastern Americans and the roughneck westerners. *Beyond the Horizon* announced firmly the new themes that were to dominate the plays of rural life thereafter. Mayo is the restless, poetic hero, out of place in his surroundings, a prototype that was to prove for O'Neill and for many of his contemporaries a congenial *alter ego*. His dream of going to sea and of finding exotic lands beyond the horizon is the first statement of the dream motif, the search for an earthly paradise that others were to use repeatedly. The inability of Mayo to respond to the force moving in the earth again anticipates the view of the power of the land that will prevail in plays of rural life. O'Neill's implication, more philosophically complete than the ruminations of later dramatists, is that all men belong to a large, elemental force, which they must serve as if they are serving a god. They are possessed by its energy and power, but if for some reason they fall out of harmony, becoming dispossessed as is Mayo, the sea's man, when he tries to serve the land, they are doomed to a waste of their vitality. The right relationship is shown in the comedy '*Anna Christie*' (1921) in the figure of Mat Burke, who is a child of the sea, and in whom the sea's power beats fiercely. The spiritual waste is again demonstrated in Yank in *The Hairy Ape* (1922) and in Brutus in *The Emperor Jones* (1920).

In his tragedy, *Desire Under the Elms* (1924), O'Neill explored the relation of men and the land complexly and with clear philosophical underpinnings derived from Greek myth (Phaedra and Oedipus) and from the writings of Friedrich Nietzsche. In the conflict of Ephraim Cabot with his son Eben, and in the love story of Eben and his stepmother Abby, O'Neill wrote what was perhaps the archetypal American tragedy, the tragedy of men who belong to the land and who desire to be possessed by its power, but who are trapped into a struggle for its ownership.[86] The land, O'Neill implies, cannot be possessed. It demands surrender. Eben desires to sink into its entity in rapture and Dionysian forgetfulness, as a man might love a woman or lie in a warm, ploughed furrow. He desires to serve the land as its priest and its son, for O'Neill, making the connection that other dramatists have only implied, sees that the land is also a mother. Incestuously loving his stepmother is a way of loving the land, but, when he is trapped into trying to own the land, his sense of alienation and dispossession makes him bitter and potentially violent. In right relationship with the land and the woman, he is in harmony with the source of his life and comfort.

[86] The play bears a strong resemblance to Howard's *They Knew What They Wanted*, produced in the same season. Cf. Bogard, op. cit. pp. 199–203.

Desire Under the Elms brought together into a coherent pattern of thought the fragments that other playwrights used, and it was the capstone of the first phase of O'Neill's career. He continued to explore the lives of men searching to belong, and in particular their search for a woman who, like a mother, will possess them and comfort them and remove the stresses of their disoriented lives. In *Strange Interlude* (1928), for example, he created in Nina Leeds the portrait of a possessive woman who feeds on the lives of all the men around her. Their desire, she says, makes her feel 'whole', and she does all she can to keep them in thrall. Viewed coldly, she is as monstrous as Howard's Mrs Phelps, but O'Neill does not look at her objectively. He casts a veil of sympathy over her, and equates her needs with the tides, the deep rhythm of the sea, the nine-month cycle of human pregnancy. She becomes like the earth, a goddess to be served.

The effect is repeated in the trilogy, *Mourning Becomes Electra* (1931), wherein O'Neill, following the legend of Electra, tells of the conflict of Christine Mannon and her daughter Lavinia. Orin, her son, links her as an object of his desire with a dream of a tropical island paradise, and, after he has murdered her and her lover, he goes with his sister on a voyage to such islands. There the sister changes, taking on the mother's coloration and sensuality to become the sister-mother-lover of her brother.

Throughout O'Neill's work, the image of the desired mother sought in a surrogate woman reappears. She is to be found in Abby, the stepmother of *Desire Under the Elms*, she is the prostitute Cybel in *The Great God Brown* (1926), and in *Dynamo* (1929) she is the cow-like May Fife, to whom the embittered hero goes for refuge from his repressive Puritan family. In his later works, the figures of mother, wife and whore are bewilderingly linked together. In Josie Hogan, the giant slut who comforts Jamie Tyrone in *A Moon for the Misbegotten* (1947), and in the mother and daughter-in-law of *More Stately Mansions* (1962), the figure of the mother who is a lover and of the wife who is a mother and whore are woven into patterns of possession and dispossession, which can give men salvation or lead them to their destruction.

In some plays, of course, O'Neill has it otherwise. The simple Irish peasant wife, Nora Melody of *A Touch of the Poet* (1957), and Essie Miller, the fresh-faced guardian of her family's welfare in *Ah, Wilderness!* (1933), are two important variants on the pattern of possessive maternal force. But in the tragic counterpart of *Ah, Wilderness!*, *Long Day's Journey into Night* (1956), Essie Miller becomes Mary Tyrone, a portrait of O'Neill's own mother, whose failure to act as a guardian has plunged her sons and her husband into emotionally crippling loss. Notably, in the later plays of

O'Neill, the failure of the mother sends the sons to find a surrogate in incestuously oriented relationships with maternal whores, or, as with Josie Hogan, a woman who can be whore, lover, mother and goddess in one.

Like the other American dramatists whose work he anticipated and of whom he is an epitome, O'Neill turned to an examination of the failure of the American dream and to an analysis of the destruction of his country by materialistic greed. And, as with his treatment of the themes of the land, the mother and the lost dream, he was able to bring into a coherent pattern of meaning the elements used by others. The themes of possession and dispossession announced early in his career, which gave rise to his concerns for the mother and the land, also prompted a searching look at America's problems, forming the centre of his long cycle of plays on American historical subjects, *A Tale of Possessors, Self-dispossessed*. The cycle was a work-in-progress, which O'Neill began about 1933 and continued until illness forced him to abandon the effort ten years later. He destroyed the scenarios and uncompleted plays in 1953, the year of his death. Two plays survive, *A Touch of the Poet*, which he completed in 1936, and an unrevised draft of the following play, *More Stately Mansions*, which was finished about 1938. When the scheme was fully developed, O'Neill had in plan eleven plays covering the course of American history from the colonial beginnings to the middle years of the Depression. It was a work of extraordinary magnitude, and, as the surviving plays indicate, would have been of the highest quality. That O'Neill could not live to complete it is a major loss to the drama not only of the United States but of the English-speaking world.

O'Neill's view of his country's failure was that greed – one of the lost plays was entitled *Greed of the Meek* – had destroyed the hopeful freedoms which the citizens of the uncharted new nation had once enjoyed. In tracing the lives of the members of an American dynasty from simple beginnings – its forebear was an Irish immigrant in the mid-eighteenth century – through two centuries of acquisitive corruption of the land, O'Neill asserted what he called the 'spiritual undertheme' of the cycle: that those who attempt to possess the earth are in the end dispossessed; that in gaining the whole world they lose their souls. It was, of course, a theme asserted by many Europeans in the years of the Depression and Second World War, but in America the theme gained especial pathos because, in the United States, what has been lost is so fresh in memory, so recent in history. The pure world of Henry David Thoreau still has reality in American minds. The genial, loving life of Tom Sawyer and Huckleberry Finn is a part of the childhood of most Americans. It does not seem to be dead. Yet, as the nation moved on to the international political scene, as labour organized itself in the face of the agonies of the Depression, as the land turned to dust in the great drought, the memory became a dream, a sentimentalized myth, and in its place there came the greedy enslaver, the hog-like, fox-like American who despoiled and enslaved and transformed his free country into a materialistic wilderness. In *More Stately Mansions* the heroine, Sara Harford, speaks for all the possessors when she tells an employee in her office, 'I am good because I am strong. You are evil because you are weak.'[87]

The lament for the dream lost pervades the late plays of O'Neill and proves to be the most poignant theme of America's tragic drama. In *A Touch of the Poet* Deborah Harford speaks of the men in her family and warns her son's fiancée that the Harford men 'never part with their dreams even when they deny them'.[88] In his final works O'Neill drew portraits of those who are haunted by dreams they have sought to deny. He called the dreams the 'lie of the pipe-dream' and made the lie the core of *The Iceman Cometh* (1946), *Hughie* (1964), *A Moon for the Misbegotten* and the autobiographical tragedy, *Long Day's Journey into Night*. In these plays the action is to measure present realities against a vision of what has been lost, and O'Neill held that the vision, even if it is clearly a self-deluding lie, is better than the present which man has created for himself. The down-and-outs of *The Iceman Cometh* dwell amidst the drifting recollections of the past, each withdrawn into a shell of illusion at Harry Hope's saloon which one character calls 'The Bottom-of-the-Sea Rathskeller'. In *Hughie*, the only remaining play of a planned cycle of one-act plays, the two characters deliberately lose themselves in an illusion which proves to be the only way either can survive. In his autobiography, as he images his mother, father and brother, O'Neill shows himself and his parents as being able to live in the present because each has had something in the past to which they can cling. With whiskey and morphine, they try to drift away from the fog-bound cottage, into the past where each had a vision that was like 'a saint's vision of beatitude'.[89] In *A Moon for the Misbegotten*, which continues the story of his brother Jamie, O'Neill created for the character a fictitious moment – a night of remorseful confession that brings forgiveness and love – that can become the memory of beatitude. Otherwise Jamie would have had no dream.

O'Neill's version of the motif of the lost dream is the fullest statement of the nostalgic clinging to the past that occupied so much of the endeavours of

[87] Eugene O'Neill, *More Stately Mansions* (New Haven, Conn., 1964), p. 152.
[88] Eugene O'Neill, *A Touch of the Poet* (New Haven, Conn., 1957), p. 84.
[89] O'Neill, *Long Day's Journey into Night*, p. 153.

the American theatre in the second quarter of the century. It is no accident that his conviction of the necessity of illusion as a way to sustain life led him, well ahead of his American and European contemporaries, into an exploration of the existential world, and to the kind of play that later was to become a characteristic American drama: the two-character confessional.

The Iceman Cometh is such a play, progressing in confessional duologues and leading to Hickey's massive confession of guilt at his inability to love. Hope's saloon is a wasteland in which men huddle together, getting what warmth they can from touching one another with the endless narration of their dreams. *Hughie*, more clearly a formal prototype of what was to come, depicts two characters in a cheap New York hotel lobby, one talking end-lessly to pass the small hours of the pre-dawn vacuum, the other speaking scarcely at all, hardly hearing and rarely responding to what is said. The voices drop into silence and spell out the existential emptiness of modern life. What saves, again, is illusion – fabricated, open illusion – eagerly accepted by both men. Roles are developed, those of the con man and his mark, the eternal sucker, and the play ends with a saving moment of contact, achieved through the medium of a fake dice game that both pretend is real. The play's lyric intensity makes it one of the true poetic dramas of the modern theatre, a work which lies, for all of its difference of subject, in the direct tradition of Synge.

The Iceman Cometh was written in 1939, *Hughie* in 1941, and the dates place O'Neill well in front of the later group of dramatists who seek to inter-pret the plight of men in a world where God was dead. The American's understanding of that plight was, in its resolution, essentially different from the statements of the French philosophical playwrights or of any of the angry outcries of the British playwrights of the 1950s. O'Neill's humanity, the desperate crying-out for blessing, sets him apart from the harder-edged European scene, but this is not to say that he was incapable of clear percep-tion about his world or that he sentimentalized his characters without a sense of irony as he did so.[90] In all of the late plays, the actions are set forth in such a way as to complicate and round out the central search for vision. Although they are deceptive in their length and their deliberately orches-trated repetition, the last plays are as stripped down, as uncompromising as, say, Sartre's *Huis clos* or the plays of Beckett.

---

[90] It should be noted that he did not escape sentimental musical treatment. '*Anna Christie*' was made into a musical comedy, *A New Girl in Town* (1957), and *Ah, Wilderness!* was twice so treated, once as a film, *Summer Holiday* (1948), and once as a stage musical, *Take Me Along* (1960).

Yet, in the last analysis, it is not Beckett or Sartre or Synge whom O'Neill most resembles but, oddly, Bernard Shaw. The bulk and the quality of the work by the two playwrights is sufficient to mark them as pre-eminent in the twentieth-century dramatic pantheon. Both men spoke clearly for their nation and for their time, and, although on the surface they seem as unlike one another as light and dark, the integral relationship between day and night suggests that at the source the two may have more in common than their common language.

Like O'Neill's, Shaw's works are an epitome of the drama of his time and country. He offered highly personalized versions of the Pinero and Jones triangle play in *Candida*, the melodramatic thriller in *The Devil's Disciple*, the Graustarkian romance, the drawing-room comedy, the chronicle history, the farce, and so on. At the same time, he also moved out of the currents of the popular theatre towards a more personalized kind of play that was thin in narrative, disquisitory in content and mythic in intention. In such a play as *The Simpleton of the Unexpected Isles*, Shaw appears to be writing an expressionistic play, as experimental in its way as O'Neill's theatrical experiments.

Departures from realistic dramaturgy led both men to write plays that were exceptionally long and mythic in content. It was perhaps Shaw's *Back to Methuselah*, which the Theatre Guild produced in 1922, that encouraged O'Neill to write dramas of inordinate length. Yet it is not essential to posit a direct connection between Shaw's massive statement of the myth of creative evolution and O'Neill's long choric drama, *Lazarus Laughed*, which he wrote in 1925. The two plays are attempts to frame new religious doctrine, suitable to their nations and their epochs. Both plays emerge from evolutionary conceptions. Like Shaw, O'Neill had responded creatively to conceptions that Darwin and Lamarck had loosed into modern thought. O'Neill, was no reader of scientists or philosophers, Nietzsche excepted, but had absorbed his ideas of evolution from novelists such as Jack London, Stephen Crane and Frank Norris. Both *The Emperor Jones* and *The Hairy Ape* owe much to London's novel *The Call of the Wild*, which shows how a dog released in the Alaskan wilderness returns to the savage condition of a wolf. Like the dog, the Emperor and the Ape move backwards, down the evolutionary scale, towards savagery and – in *The Hairy Ape* – towards ape-like Darwinian origins. The direction is diametrically opposite to that urged by Shaw, and yet the point of departure is the same. Neither playwright, faced with the consequences of evolutionary theory, was willing to exist in a world without God, and both sought to describe the nature of divinity in plays that were essentially religious. The difference in the myths each formulated lies in the direction of the search.

Back to Methuselah, like *Man and Superman* before it, points towards the upward-spiralling movement of man's evolutionary progress. The Nietzschean superman climbs forward to a point where, his Apollonian impulses fulfilled, he can leave behind all flesh and become the 'whirlpool of pure intelligence' of which Lilith, the universal feminine principle, speaks at the drama's conclusion. O'Neill's superman, the risen Lazarus, also speaks of man's goal as an entry into cosmic forces, but the direction to be taken is downwards to the submerging of life in primordial matter. What men call life is death, O'Neill argued. To die is to lose the corrupting, fearful individuation of being that separates men from the cosmic processes of change and eternal growth. Only while man is conscious does he fear death and tyrannize over his fellows. 'As dust', Lazarus preaches, 'you are eternal change, and everlasting growth . . .'[91] The loss of consciousness, the end of thought, the disappearance into the whirlpool of matter are for O'Neill the supreme good.

The differences between the two dramatists in their systems of value, their philosophical vision and their temperament are myriad, yet there is a radical similarity in their work. For example, one sees woman as the creative, life-giving evolutionary force, the pursuing 'Everywoman', 'Lilith', 'St Joan', goading men to higher achievement. To the other, woman is the womb, the centre of quiet, the sought, the betrayer, the source of lost vision and destroyed dream. Yet both dramatists feel that woman stands near the philosophical centre of life, and that men circle around the force she radiates.

In Shaw, the Irish heritage is loquacious, witty, styled with careful, eloquent rhetoric. In O'Neill, the black Irish urge is towards folk poetry, rhapsodic in its repetition. Both playwrights, it has been said, talk too much. Yet, in the theatre, they create a dialogue entirely appropriate to the tone, texture and meaning of what they present, and it is speech that cannot be entirely evaluated on the page. Certainly no other playwrights in English in this century have so consistently fired their audiences. As masters of theatrical techniques, these two, alone since the death of Shakespeare, have continually filled theatres and have had a steady record of successful revivals.

Interestingly, once both playwrights had become established in their countries, they came under the sponsorship of the Theatre Guild, so that they stood, as it were, side by side before American audiences. In the history

[91] Eugene O'Neill, *Lazarus Laughed*, in *The Plays of Eugene O'Neill* (New York, 1954), I, 309.

of the English-speaking theatre, the conjunction of two such major play-wrights, working steadily from season to season under the sign of a single producing organization, cannot be duplicated except in the Globe Theatre, when Shakespeare and Jonson were at the peak of their careers.

To envisage a meeting of the two is not quite possible. Shaw called O'Neill 'a fantee Shakespeare who peoples his isles with Calibans', and no doubt O'Neill appeared something of a monster to the ascetic Irishman. Yet Shaw understood much about O'Neill. Hearing that the American had given up drinking, Shaw commented that he would probably never again write a good play.[92] Happily, he was wrong, and O'Neill's greatest work lay ahead of that moment. Yet Shaw's comment reveals that he understood O'Neill's Irish turn towards darkness and fantee madness. For his part, O'Neill had found much in Shaw's work that was of formative importance. His reading of *The Quintessence of Ibsenism* had led him as a young man to the work of Ibsen and to other masters of late nineteenth-century thought. Like Shaw he was greatly influenced by Nietzsche, although his reading of the German philosopher was highly selective and fed less on the intellectual substance in Nietzschean doctrine than on the emotional coloration of the writing.

Nietzsche's differentiation between the Apollonian and Dionysian modes of perception conveniently points towards the difference between the two playwrights, at the same time as it suggests the radical connection. It may be said that, in the plays of Shaw, the highest, most compelling action is the education of the characters, an education that causes them to move towards a higher, more conscious plane of being. It is an Apollonian motion. In O'Neill, the movement is Dionysian – towards the rapturous immersion of the conscious self into a centre of life-energy that is eternal and unchanging. Shaw is movement; O'Neill is stasis. Shaw is consciousness; O'Neill forget-fulness. Shaw is thought; O'Neill is memory. Shaw is ascetic; O'Neill is drunken. Shaw is visionary; O'Neill dreams. Shaw seeks life; O'Neill seeks to lose it. What is not true is that Shaw is life and O'Neill is death. Both men were myth-makers and both sought God. In the search, both men failed, for their most mythic plays, *Lazarus Laughed* and *Back to Methuselah*, failed to convince. What does convince is not the quest both playwrights made for a twentieth-century divinity, but the life-seeking energy both men heartily espoused. Although O'Neill saw men as pitiable and felt that only in dope-dreams, drunkenness and physical death could they find relief from the squalid present, and although he came to feel that the only good lay in the communion of life-lies or in the memory of beatitude, he did not finally

[92] Quoted in Sheaffer, *O'Neill, Son and Artist*, p. 253.

deny that life has value. In *The Iceman Cometh* Hickey, the salesman, tries and fails to persuade the derelicts to give over the lie to rid themselves of illusion, to face the world and move up the evolutionary ladder from the bottom-of-the-sea Rathskeller in which they drift endlessly. Hickey's failure, the view that Hickey has brought death not life, is, indirectly, O'Neill's comment on Shaw's evolutionary beliefs. Men, the American held, will not change, and only in human sympathy can there be generated warmth and a sense of life. The Calibans who cry to dream again have little love for the Prosperos whose magic urges them out of the mud.

So brief a juxtaposition of the work of the leading playwrights is not sufficient even by implication to bring into comparison the drama of England and America in the twentieth century. Yet it is true that, despite the admiration extended them by theatre-arts advocates, John Galsworthy and Harley Granville-Barker were not imitated by the Americans. In later years there have been no playwrights in this country displaying such 'anger' as John Osborne has in his protests at the way the Shavian life-force expends itself in nothing very much, like a lightning bolt striking the earth. Nor has Pinter's style found American imitators.

Rather what the American dramatists have revealed about the psychological and social context of their country has pointed to an inner darkness. Certainly other forces in the country have called with certitude for fully committed action in the strong light of virtuous purpose. But in the drama there has been a pervading bewilderment at a life that is too large, at matters that are too vast to attempt to control, and the regret for a lost life of value that yet hangs on the edges of memory. As its major dramatist should have done, Eugene O'Neill summarized the endeavour and wrote a kind of epitaph for the American dramatic enterprise here traced. In *Long Day's Journey into Night*, the actor, James Tyrone, tells his son of his career in the nineteenth-century theatre, and how the great Edwin Booth praised him, saying that he played Othello better than Booth ever had. But Tyrone proceeds to describe how he bought a cheap melodrama for the romantic role it contained, and how he became locked in the part for the rest of his life, unacceptable to the public in any other role.

He concludes his account with a rueful, incompleted sentence, that perhaps can be read as the summary of American theatrical endeavour by its greatest playwright: 'What the hell was it I wanted to buy, I wonder, that was worth —'.

II American actors, managers, producers and directors

Richard Moody

Players and plays have enriched American life since the mid-eighteenth century. And players more than plays have drawn audiences to the playhouse. Not until late in the nineteenth century – some would say not until the advent of Eugene O'Neill in the 1920s – had the play exerted any compelling magnetic power. It was the actor, supported by his managers, producers and directors, who had given the American theatre its remarkable vigour and incredible variety.

Only a few minor theatrical events were recorded prior to 1750. In 1665 three young men, brought to trial for presenting *Y^e Bare and Y^e Cubb* at Cowle's Tavern near Punagoteague, Accomac County, Virginia, were found not guilty of fault. In 1690 Harvard students performed Benjamin Coleman's *Gustavus Vasa*, and in 1702 William and Mary scholars a 'Pastoral Colloquy'. Other academies, the College of New Jersey (Princeton) and Dartmouth, found play recitations helpful in preparing young men for the ministry or for public life and also suitable entertainment for commencement programmes. Unsanctioned plays were apparently not tolerated. Yale student actors and spectators were fined for performing and viewing a play at the house of William Lyon in January 1756.

Anthony Aston, the first vagabond actor, arrived from London, via

Jamaica, in 1702. According to his own erratic account[1] he went ashore at 'Charles-Town, full of lice, shame, poverty, nakedness and hunger, turned player and poet and wrote one play on the subject of the country'. The following year he may have acted in New York, though he reports only that he spent the winter 'writing, courting, and fighting'.

The first American theatre opened in Williamsburg in 1718. Built by William Levingston, the first performance probably featured the talents of Charles and Mary Stagg, Levingston's indentured servants who had been conducting dancing classes for him, though Levingston announced that he had sent to England for 'actors and musicians for the better performance of the said plays'. The playhouse offered infrequent performances – only *The Recruiting Officer* and *The Busy Body* are noted – and it was probably often used by amateurs until 1745 when it ceased to be a theatre and became a common hall and court for the city of Williamsburg.

Other early theatrical activity is scantily recorded. Some time between 1699 and 1702, a Richard Hunter requested permission to present plays in New York, insisting that he had 'been at great charge and expense in providing persons and necessarys in order to the acting of plays in the city.' Though his petition was approved, nothing more is known of his activities. In 1723 strolling players acted on the outskirts of Philadelphia. In 1730 an amateur group presented *Romeo and Juliet* at the Revenge Meeting House in New York. In 1732 perhaps the same amateurs acquired a loft in a New York warehouse owned by Rip Van Dam where they played *Cato*, *The Recruiting Officer*, *The Beaux' Stratagem* and *The Busy Body*. In 1735 Otway's *The Orphan* was performed in a Charleston (South Carolina) courtroom and the following year Charleston's Dock Street Theatre was opened.

The first regular group of players, though of questionable professional competence, appeared under the management of Walter Murray and Thomas Kean in William Plumstead's warehouse in Philadelphia in 1749. In February 1750 they moved to New York, refitted another Rip Van Dam warehouse, opened with Colley Cibber's version of *Richard III* on 5 March 1750 and continued to perform until July 1751. Robert Upton, who had been sent from London as advance man for the Hallams, deserted his employers and joined this company in the spring, and when the Murray–Kean group departed for Williamsburg he recruited strays from the original company and tried another New York season (1751–2), apparently with little success.

In Williamsburg a small theatre, boasting no more than the bare essentials,

[1] *Anthony Aston, Stroller and Adventurer*, ed. Watson Nicholson (South Haven, Mich., 1920).

was built for the Murray–Kean autumn season of 1751, but limited patronage forced them to take to the road, to Norfolk, Hobb's-Hole, Fredericksburg, where the young George Washington saw them perform in June 1752, to Upper Marlborough, and to Annapolis, where they disbanded. The Murray–Kean vagabonds survived for three years in a hostile environment, wrote only a brief sketchy chapter in American theatrical history, yet they ploughed the ground that was to be cultivated by the Hallam family.

Adam Hallam and four of his sons had been second-rate actors in and around London, and his son William had managed the New Wells Theatre at the bottom of Lemon Street in Goodman's Fields. When John Moody, an actor who had performed in Jamaica, returned to London and announced that theatrical riches might be mined in the New World, the Hallams quickly responded. William Hallam sent Robert Upton as his emissary to solicit permissions, organized a company, and designated his brother Lewis (1714–56) as manager. Although he heard no more from Upton who had defected to the Murray–Kean company, 'that sett of pretenders', he did not abandon the project, and in early May 1752 the company sailed on the *Charming Sally*. In addition to Mr and Mrs Lewis Hallam and their three children, seven actors and two actresses (actors' wives) rehearsed twenty-four plays and farces as they sailed by way of Barbados bound for Virginia. On 2 June they anchored at the mouth of the York River and went immediately to Williamsburg where the *Virginia Gazette* (12 June 1752) assured the public that they would be 'entertain'd in as polite a manner as in the theatres in London, the company being perfected in all the best plays, operas, farces, and pantomimes.'

They refurbished the Murray–Kean makeshift theatre, opened on 15 September 1752 with *The Merchant of Venice* 'before a numerous and polite audience, with great applause', and for the next ten months, two to three nights a week, gave Williamsburg and the colonies their first full season of theatre with such plays as *The Beaux' Stratagem*, *The Recruiting Officer*, *Jane Shore*, *Richard III*, *Hamlet*, *Othello*, *Tamerlane*, *The Conscious Lovers* and *George Barnwell*.

In June they moved to New York where Lewis Hallam had been told 'the inhabitants were very generous and polite, naturally fond of diversions rational, particularly those of the theatre.' Apparently Hallam had been misinformed and, when permission to play was denied, he pleaded his case in the New York *Mercury* (2 July 1753), insisting that they 'were not cast in the same mold with our theatrical predecessors; or that in private life or public occupation, we have the least affinity to them.' He little imagined 'that in a city, to all appearance so polite as this, the muses would be banished, the works of the immortal Shakespeare and others deny'd admittance ... when, without boasting, we may venture to affirm, that we are capable of supporting [the stage's] dignity with proper decorum and regularity.' His supplication worked; a 'very large and commodious new theatre' was constructed for them, and on 17 September 1753 they opened with *The Conscious Lovers*.

After an extraordinarily successful season in New York, closing on 18 March 1754 with *The Beggar's Opera*, they transferred to Philadelphia where again Hallam was obliged to counter the opposition by pledging to offer 'nothing indecent or immoral', to give one night's receipts to the poor, and to post bond to cover payment of all debts. Plumstead's warehouse was again remodelled and on 15 April 1754 they presented *The Fair Penitent*. The Philadelphia season continued until June; in the autumn they shifted their operations to Charleston; and in January 1755 departed for Jamaica.

Lewis Hallam died in Jamaica. David Douglass (*c.* 1720–86), a British actor who had been performing in Jamaica, married Mrs Hallam, and when the group returned to New York in the autumn of 1758 Douglass became manager. A sail-loft on Cruger's Wharf was refitted for their use, but when they again encountered opposition Douglass announced that he simply proposed to open a 'Histrionic Academy' where he would give 'dissertations on subjects, moral, instructive, and entertaining'. Apparently his dodge worked and on 1 January 1759 they opened with *Jane Shore*. The New York season lasted only into February, when they again went to Philadelphia. Not until June were they able to subdue the new protests and make ready the new theatre on Society Hill, outside the city limits. During this season, which ran until the end of the year, Douglass tried to placate the opposition by announcing that *Douglas*, performed on 13 July, was written by the Rev. John Home and on 28 and 29 December assigned his proceeds to the hospital and to the purchase of an organ for the college hall.

In 1760 and 1761 the company was on the move, playing in Annapolis, Upper Marlborough, Williamsburg and Newport, Rhode Island, before returning to New York. In Newport the opposition was so strong that they were obliged to adopt the subterfuge of announcing their plays as 'Moral Dialogues'. *Othello*, for example: a moral dialogue in five parts 'depicting the Evil Effects of Jealousy and other Bad Passions, and Proving that Happiness can only Spring from the Pursuit of Virtue'.

After another New York season, 1761–2, they again played Newport and then Providence. On one occasion in Providence, when a mob moved on the theatre trying to prevent their playing, John and Nicholas Brown moved up a cannon to protect the players. The next season, under the banner 'The American Company of Comedians', they were in Virginia and the following year in Charleston, before sailing to England for a holiday in May 1764.

When the Douglasses returned in January 1766 with a new company, they performed first in Charleston and then in the new Southwark Theatre in Philadelphia. Although Philadelphia now had a proper theatre, primitive as it was, they still suffered the abuse of those who abhorred their 'school of debauchery'. In April 1767 they announced *The Disappointment*, a new comic opera by an American, but apparently Douglass decided the satirical thrusts at some local citizens were too strong and never allowed it to reach the public. However, on 24 April 1767 they did introduce the first native play to be performed by professional actors, Thomas Godfrey's *The Prince of Parthia*. Another important step in the establishment of an American theatre was taken in the summer when Douglass went to New York to supervise the construction of the new John Street Theatre, the theatre which Jonathan describes so well in *The Contrast*. After an autumn season in Philadelphia the company went to New York to open the new theatre on 7 December 1767, with *The Beaux' Stratagem*. The company continued in New York until the following June, in the autumn returned to Philadelphia, went back to New York in January 1769, to Albany for a month in July, back to Philadelphia for 1769–70, and in the summer of 1770 to Williamsburg.

Another company under the management of William Verling, calling themselves first the Virginia Company of Comedians and then the New American Company, presumably to confuse the public and profit from the reputation of Douglass's American Company, had been playing in Williamsburg, Norfolk and Annapolis from January 1768 until March 1769. When the Douglass group arrived, now rechristened the Old American Company, their competitors had disbanded.

During the next eighteen months the Douglasses played in Williamsburg, Annapolis, Norfolk, Fredericksburg and Dumfries. Washington attended the theatre on four occasions in June 1770, again on 23 January 1771 and on 8 May 1771. When he became President he held a box at the John Street Theatre, and when the capital moved to Washington he became a regular patron at the Chestnut Street Theatre in Philadelphia. No other president, except Lincoln, followed his example.

In October 1772 the company returned to the Southwark in Philadelphia, in April 1773 to the John Street in New York, to Annapolis in September, Philadelphia again in October, and in November to Charleston where they remained for the season. The company disbanded in the summer. Mrs

Douglass died in Philadelphia, but in the autumn David Douglass was in New York recruiting a new company, including Thomas Wignell (1753–1803), a cousin of the young Lewis Hallam (c. 1740–1808), who had played at Drury Lane. The new season never got under way. On 20 October 1774 the Continental Congress meeting in Philadelphia passed the following resolution: 'We will in our several stations, encourage frugality, economy, and industry . . . and will discountenance and discourage every species of extravagance and dissipation, especially all horse-racing, and all kinds of gaming, cock-fighting, exhibition of shews, plays, and other expensive diversions and entertainments.'

Douglass decided to seek the friendlier climate of Jamaica, 'not to return to the continent, until its tranquility is restored', and when they opened in Jamaica on 1 July 1775 two lines of the prologue read: 'The Muse alarm'd at the loud tempest's roar / Seeks an asylum on this peaceful shore.'

In their twenty-two years of barnstorming, a long tenure for any theatrical company, the Hallam–Douglass company[2] had laid the ground for an American theatre. Like so many actors who followed them, even into the twentieth century, they battled with puritanical opposition, constantly sought new audiences, and lived a hand-to-mouth existence from their meagre shares of the profits. Although little is known of their professional competence, they were probably no more than industrious second-raters. Mrs Hallam (Mrs Douglass) was said to possess a respectable matron-like figure. She could be stately or frivolous as required, was admired for her grace of gesture and propriety of elocution, and was particularly effective in pathetic passages. Mr Hallam played the low comedians with delightful vigour. Young Lewis Hallam was faulted for his articulation. One critic said he 'seems to suck in, or at least not to utter the first letters of the words he speaks.' Mr Douglass was labelled a decent rather than a shining actor.

During the war the theatre was kept alive by the armed forces. British soldier-actors commandeered the John Street Theatre and the Southwark for their performances, and American soldiers, though deprived of proper theatres and prohibited from indulging in frivolities, also did plays. Even at Valley Forge in the bitter winter of 1777–8 a performance of Cato was given with General Washington in attendance.

After the war the professionals quickly returned. Hallam with John

[2] For a full account of the Hallam–Douglass group, see Hugh F. Rankin, *The Theater in Colonial America* (Chapel Hill, NC, 1965), pp. 43–188.

Henry (1738–94) as co-manager was back in Philadelphia in 1784 and in New York in 1785, and for the next nine years they virtually controlled the American theatre, playing from New York to Charleston, but not without considerable rivalry and dissension within the company and with a series of changes in management. In 1791 Thomas Wignell, who had the distinction of playing Jonathan in Royall Tyler's *The Contrast* (1787) and thus introducing the Yankee character to the American stage, joined Alexander Reinagle (1756–1809), a musician, in recruiting a new company from England to open the new Chestnut Street Theatre in Philadelphia on 17 February 1794. The new theatre, a copy of the Royal Theatre at Bath, was said to be larger (seating 2000) and incomparably better than any theatre in the New World. And Wignell had recruited actors who were far superior to any yet seen.

Outstanding in the new Chestnut Street company were Eliza Kemble Whitlock (1761–1836), the sister of Sarah Siddons and John Philip Kemble, an expert at producing tears. Mrs Anne Brunton Merry (1768–1808), another emotional actress of high quality, married Thomas Wignell. James Fennell (1766–1816), a tall, robust young man from Covent Garden, was particularly known for his commanding Macbeth and Othello. William Warren (1767–1832) specialized in comic old men. He married Mrs Merry after Wignell's death in 1803, joined her in management of the theatre until her death in 1808, and was thereafter alone until 1827. John Bernard (1756–1828) was an expert at the young men's roles in high comedy. He was also later to become a manager in Philadelphia, Boston and Albany and author of *Retrospections of America* (published in 1887), a lively account of the theatre at the turn of the century. These were all first-rank actors, but Thomas Abthorpe Cooper (1776–1849) became the big name and the model for later American tragedians, although he was only twenty when he arrived. He was particularly praised for his players' scene in *Hamlet*. His Romeo was possessed of 'electrical strokes of irresistible effect and beauty'. His Macbeth was strong; his Damon, painfully tragic, a masterpiece of art. When the spirit was on him and the part of his choosing, his whole body was involved in the role. In roles he regarded as unimportant he plowed through in lackadaisical fashion, often uncertain of his lines. In his later years, when Edwin Forrest had already begun to outrank him, Cooper was condemned for his statue-like attitudes, for his painful precision of enunciation, and for his too frequent mumbling and rumbling and extending syllables until 'scarcely a word would get away in its natural form'.

To combat Wignell's new talents John Henry went to the source of supply in England to recruit for the Old American Company, bringing back John Hodgkinson (*c.* 1765–1808) and his wife, among others. After Hodgkinson's opening performance at the Southwark Theatre on 26 September 1792, it was clear that Henry had acquired a first-rate actor, and after the season in Philadelphia and then in New York Henry began to regret his choice. As Hodgkinson's popularity went up, his went down. Dissension and rivalry within the company which had begun with Wignell's departure now became a way of life for the Old American Company. In 1794 Henry was forced out and Hodgkinson joined Hallam as co-manager. The new arrangement did not restore peace; it simply introduced a new battle. Mrs Hallam had taken to drink, and her unsteady performances became intolerable to Hodgkinson, precipitating constant quarrels with her and with Hallam. And the severe competition from the Chestnut Street Theatre forced them to abandon the Southwark Theatre in the autumn of 1794. In May 1796 William Dunlap (1766–1839), of whom more later, came into the company, purchasing half of Hodgkinson's share. He was to be the active manager and hopefully the mediator between Hallam and Hodgkinson. Peace was shortlived. In the spring of 1797 Mrs Hallam was barred from the stage. Hallam brought her on in spite of the prohibition, after filling the house with her supporters. Hodgkinson was infuriated and took two months' leave, during which time he busied himself with the new New York theatre that was already under construction. Dunlap and Hodgkinson were to be co-managers of the new enterprise, but, when they tried to buy Hallam's scenery and costumes and Hallam threatened to build a new theatre for himself, they agreed to engage the Hallams as actors.

The thirty-one-year-old John Street Theatre had its final night on 13 January 1798. On 29 January the 2000-seat Park Theatre, matching the Chestnut in comfort and elegance, opened with Hodgkinson playing Jaques in *As You Like It*. After the crowded opening night, audiences dwindled away and were not restored until Dunlap persuaded Cooper to desert Wignell. Cooper's *Hamlet* on 28 February and his subsequent performances of Shakespeare not only attracted the public but relegated Hodgkinson to a secondary position. In the autumn of 1798 Hodgkinson joined the Federal Street Theatre in Boston, leaving the Park management to Dunlap. After a year in Boston, he returned to Dunlap as an actor for three years, before playing his final seasons, 1803–5, in Charleston. Though no more than proficient in tragedy, Hodgkinson excelled in comedy, was devoted to his profession and held a lifetime record of some 375 roles.

Dunlap continued as sole manager of the Park until 20 February 1805, when the theatre was closed. He had two good seasons, 1798 and 1799, but in 1803 he was obliged to mortgage his farm to meet operating expenses and in 1805 lost everything except his mother's house at Perth Amboy.

Although William Dunlap was not an astute manager, apparently too good-natured to be hard-headed about business, he was the first to write and manage his own plays, the first to champion the cause of native subject matter and the native dramatist – though also the first to devise and present many of his own translations and adaptations from the French and German, particularly Kotzebue, and the first to write a history of the American theatre (1832). He rightly deserves the title 'the father of American drama'. He began his artistic life as a painter, but, when he studied with Benjamin West in England (1784–7) and saw *The School for Scandal* and *The Critic*, he became fascinated with the theatre, a fascination that was further sparked by *The Contrast* which he saw on his return. Even had he not written or adapted some fifty-six plays, and taken another turn at management at the Park (1806–11) – as manager for Thomas A. Cooper – he would have left his mark on the life of his time with his biographies of the actor Cooke (1813) and of the novelist Charles Brockden Brown (1815), with his large-scale religious canvases such as *Christ Rejected* (1822), as director of the American Academy of Fine Arts (1817), as a founder of the National Academy of Design (1826) and as professor of historical painting at the National Academy (1830–9).

Other theatres enlivened the American theatrical scene in the final decade of the century. Some strays from the Old American Company, under the management of Joseph Harper (d. 1813), tried a few performances in Boston in 1792 before the anti-theatre forces stopped them. Two years later local resistance was subdued when the new Federal Street Theatre, designed by Charles Bulfinch (1763–1844) who later achieved fame as the architect for the Capitol in Washington, was opened under the management of Charles Stuart Powell (d. 1810). In 1796 Powell built another theatre, the Haymarket, and J. B. Williamson (d. 1802) became manager of the Federal Street. In 1793 Thomas Wade West and John Bignall (d. 1794), from the Virginia Company of Comedians in Richmond, opened a theatre in Charleston. Another Charleston theatre, known first as the French Theatre, later the Church Street and finally the City Theatre, was leased by John Sollee in 1794 and placed under the management of Alexander Placide (*c.* 1750–1812), who had opened a theatre in Newport in 1793. In 1794 Wignell and Reinagle branched out from Philadelphia with a theatre in Baltimore and in 1800 built the National Theatre in Washington.

When the nineteenth century began, the American theatre had established a firm footing on the eastern seaboard. The early years have been sketched in some detail. With the expanding population of actors and managers, native-born and from England, and with the theatre quickly moving on to the frontier in step with the western expansion, this brief account of the years from 1800 to date can only touch the major figures.

In the first quarter of the new century English actors continued to dominate the stage, though some native-born actors and managers began their rise to prominence.

Mary Anna Duff (1794–1857), from London, set the pattern for American actresses who chose the road of high tragedy, as Cooke and Cooper did for the actors. From 1810 to 1838 her graceful figure, her soft, musical voice and her 'wild and plaintive ejaculations of distraction and despair' marked her as the first great tragedienne. Junius Brutus Booth, after appearing with her in *Lear* and *Hamlet*, thought she was the greatest actress in the world.

George Frederick Cooke (1756–1812) had a brief but fiery life on the American stage from 1810 to 1812. Already an established star in London, when he opened with *Richard III* at the Park to a capacity crowd, he established the theatrical tradition of stardom, a tradition that still holds its force today. His performances were charged with passion, yet his voice was neatly modulated, and, according to Washington Irving, his characters possessed 'truth and simplicity'. Audiences were fascinated with this wild, hard-drinking creature; they cheered when he challenged and usually subdued his unsteady legs.

The great Edmund Kean (1787–1833) arrived in the autumn of 1820 for a spectacular début at the Anthony Street Theatre (the Park Theatre had burned down the previous May) on 29 November in *Richard III*, exhibiting the flashes of lightning that illuminated his renderings of Shakespeare. As he worked through his principal roles – Othello, Hamlet and Lear – in Philadelphia and Boston, critics and audiences agreed that he brought a new fire and truthfulness to Shakespeare. If any actor was worth the $14,000 he took home with him, he was. Kean returned for another engagement in 1825–6.

Junius Brutus Booth (1796–1852), though now more firmly registered in history as the father of Junius Brutus, Jr, Edwin and John Wilkes, was regarded as Kean's principal rival when he appeared as Richard III at the rebuilt Park Theatre in 1821. Booth could match Kean on his best nights, but his undependability, often resulting from drink, and his periods of severe depression interfered with his career. Booth adopted the new land as his home and continued acting throughout the country until his death in 1852.

William Charles Macready (1793–1873), who made his first appearance at the Park on 2 October 1826 in *Virginius*, returned to tour the country in 1843 and finally in 1848–9, with disastrous results (to be noted later). Macready was more studied and elegant than his predecessors, more refined in his speech, and continually troubled by the uncouth audiences who provided his livelihood.

Other English actors tested the new theatrical territory. Some stayed, others returned. Among those who appeared for limited engagements were the elder Charles Mathews (1776–1835), Charles and Fanny Kemble (1775–1854, 1809–93) and Charles Kean (1811–68). In his 'At Home' evenings in 1822 and 1834 Mathews impersonated a series of eccentric characters, suggesting the pattern for the later Yankee actors. Charles Kemble, though not as famous as his brother John and his sister Sarah Siddons, gave polished and studied performances when he and his daughter Fanny appeared at the Park in 1832. Fanny captured the public with her Juliet. Edmund Kean's son Charles appeared first in 1830, and again in 1839 and 1845. Insisting on playing his father's roles, he suffered by comparison but in his later visits was praised for the historical authenticity of his productions.

James William Wallack (1791–1864), Joe Cowell (1792–1863), Thomas S. Hamblin (1800–53) and Tyrone Power (1795–1841) made their careers in America. Wallack came first in 1818, but made his lasting mark with his own New York theatres in the 1850s and 1860s. Joe Cowell gained his first reputation as a comedian in 1821, and his second as manager of the Walnut Street Theatre in Philadelphia in 1827. Hamblin tried playing *Hamlet* in 1825 before finding his place as manager of the Bowery Theatre in 1830. Tyrone Power, after his début in 1833, became one of America's favourite stage Irishmen, performing throughout the country.

English actors did not arrive by chance. They were lured to the new adventure by Stephen Price (1782–1840) and Edmund Simpson (1783–1848), the managers of the Park Theatre. Price did most of the recruiting, but Simpson's London journals for 1818 and 1843 reveal his day-to-day manœuvring in search of actors.

Price, son of an affluent New York family, went to Columbia College and read law before buying a share of the Park management from T. A. Cooper in 1808. Simpson was born in England, appeared first as an actor at the Park in 1809, was hired by Price as stage manager in 1810, and when Cooper retired from management in 1815 became a fully fledged partner. From then until 1840, when Price died, the two firm friends and faithful partners managed the destinies of New York's principal theatre, though more often than not Simpson conducted the day-to-day affairs while Price recruited talent in England. For three years (1826–9) Price even did double duty as manager of London's Drury Lane Theatre. After Price's death Simpson continued alone, though the theatre was on the down grade. In May 1848 he sold out to Hamblin, in July he died, and on 16 December the Park, for fifty years the major playhouse in the United States, again burned down.

Although Price and Simpson made the Park the principal American theatre until 1840 with their recruits from London and with such notable premières as John Augustus Stone's *Metamora* (1829), Dion Boucicault's *London Assurance* (1841) and Anna Cora Mowatt's *Fashion* (1845), other managers were active.

In Philadelphia William Warren (1767–1832) took over Wignell's Chestnut Street Theatre in 1803 and in 1809 was joined by William B. Wood (1779–1861), his co-manager until 1826. They also managed the Walnut Street Theatre (formerly the Olympic Circus) in 1820 and Wood controlled the Arch Street in 1828. In 1827 the Tremont Street Theatre in Boston offered competition for the Federal Street with William Pelby (1793–1850) as manager. In 1841 Moses Kimball (1809–95) opened the Boston Museum and two years later W. H. Smith (1806–72) became its manager. In 1844 the Museum recorded the spectacular 100-performance run of *The Drunkard* and continued as a Boston institution for fifty years.

Until the 1820s the Park Theatre escaped major competition, but, as New York became the theatrical centre, other playhouses appeared in quick succession, the first being Mr Barrière's Chatham Garden Theatre in 1822. In 1825 the Lafayette under C. W. Sandford boasted gas illumination and the most elaborate stage machinery yet installed in an American theatre. The Lafayette burned down in 1829 and was not rebuilt. In 1826 the Bowery Theatre opened with Charles Gilfert (1787–1829), a former musician at the Park, as manager. Built on the site of an old tavern and cattle market, it seated 3000 and was fully equipped with gas lighting. When Thomas S. Hamblin and James H. Hackett (1800–71) took over the management in 1830, it quickly became a theatre for the lower classes, featuring such blood and thunder that it was frequently called the 'Bowery Slaughter House'. The Bowery burned down and was rebuilt in 1828, 1836, 1838 and 1845. The Richmond Hill Theatre opened in 1831 under Richard Russell. From 1839 to 1850 William Mitchell's (1798–1856) stock company at the Olympic Theatre monopolized the audience for light entertainment. And Alvah Mann and George H. Barrett's Broadway Theatre (1847) and Burton's Theatre

(1848) supplanted the Park, even before it burned, as the proper homes for the élite.

Prior to the great expansion of theatre facilities in the 1820s, only two native-born actors left indelible records, John Howard Payne (1791–1852) and Edwin Forrest (1806–72).

Although American-born, Payne's theatrical life as playwright and actor was largely spent in England. In his début year, 1809, at the Park, playing Young Norval, Romeo and Hamlet, he was acclaimed as the 'American Roscius', and before departing for England in 1813 he had one moment of real glory playing Edgar to Cooke's Lear.

Edwin Forrest, the first native-born star actor, cultivated his talent under the tutelage of Cooper, Booth and Kean. In 1821, when he was fifteen, he sought Cooper's advice. When Edmund Kean appeared in Philadelphia that same year, Forrest studied Kean as he roared through his Shakespearian repertoire. A half-dozen years later he was sharing engagements with Kean in Albany and Cooper in Philadelphia, and the next year alternated with Booth in Iago and Othello – a spectacular apprenticeship for a twenty-one-year-old. From that time forward Forrest was a star on the eastern seaboard, in the south, along the inland waterways, and later in the far west. He was the first American actor to excite the British public, in 1836 and 1845, and his challenge to his principal British rival ended disastrously. The exchange of insults between him and William C. Macready precipitated the Astor Place Theatre riot in 1849 in which thirty-one persons were killed.[3] Forrest's colourful and spectacular life made exciting copy for the press and drew audiences to the theatre. In the 1850s the newspapers were filled with the lurid details of his divorce trial.

Forrest was a super-patriot who cherished his American heritage and waved the flag whenever he could. In 1828 he announced a playwriting con-test for American writers. From the seven annual contests he received some 200 plays and some of the prizewinners became standard items in his reper-toire: most notably the Indian play *Metamora* (1829) by John Augustus Stone, Robert Montgomery Bird's *The Gladiator* (1831) and *The Broker of Bogota* (1834), and Robert T. Conrad's *Jack Cade* (1835).

For the middle fifty years of the century Forrest dominated the American stage. His compelling power derived from his commanding physique, his booming and penetrating voice, from that indefinable 'X' quality, personal

[3] Cf. pp. 12–14. For a full account, see Richard Moody, *The Astor Place Riot* (Blooming-ton, Ind., 1958).

magnetism, his strenuous realism and his choice of characters – Spartacus, Metamora, Jack Cade – whose driving passions paralleled his own. Although only 5 feet 10 inches tall, on stage his bulky, muscular frame seemed to tower like a giant. With all his rugged Gargantuan strength, Forrest was not heavy-footed. He covered the stage with a firm and graceful stride. His actresses often insisted that no man ever bowed and kissed a hand more gently. The power of his voice matched the power of his massive torso. When, as Richelieu, he threatened to launch the ecclesiastical curse, Forrest's bellow made the theatre walls tremble. Lear's delirious prayer to nature reverberated like a thunderstorm.

Unlike most actors who traded on physique and passion, Forrest did not ride the high-wire one night and plod in the dust the next. He was steady and predictable. Of all his roles, Lear was clearly the greatest. Some thought his Coriolanus would have run a close second had the play been more popular. The flag wavers cheered the native plays.

Forrest did not restrict himself to the comforts of New York and Philadelphia. He braved the frontier and played in most of the primitive theatres that had sprung up across the country: in Pittsburgh, Cincinnati, Lexington, Louisville, St Louis, Memphis and New Orleans. He was the first star actor to become known throughout the country.

In 1822 Forrest began his first western journey from Philadelphia to Pittsburgh, Kentucky and New Orleans. Prior to that time Albany had been the jumping-off place.

Strolling players had appeared at the Albany hospital as early as 1769; in 1813 the Green Street Theatre was opened and in 1825 the Pearl Street. John Bernard (1756–1828) had managed the first Albany theatre and Noah Ludlow (1795–1886), Sol Smith (1801–69) and Samuel Drake (1769–1854) had appeared there before seeking their fortunes on the frontier. In 1811 Luke Usher, who had managed a Kentucky company as early as 1809, converted a Lexington brewery into a theatre, then quickly expanded his circuit to include Louisville and Frankfort. In 1815 Samuel Drake and his family, with Noah Ludlow as one of his actors, took over the Kentucky operations. Performances by amateurs were recorded in Cincinnati as early as 1801, and by professionals in 1811. Cincinnati's Columbia Street Theatre, seating 800 and boasting 'commodious lobbies and punch rooms', was opened in 1821, and in 1823 the Globe Theatre, a barn adjoining the Globe Inn converted to a theatre. Forrest appeared there under Sol Smith's management.

By the mid-thirties a full western circuit was thriving with theatres in St Louis, Memphis, Nashville, Mobile, Natchez, and with sumptuous accommodations awaiting the strolling player at the end of the river trail in New Orleans. As early as 1809 three French theatres operated in New Orleans. In 1817 Ludlow brought a company from Lexington to New Orleans; in 1824 James Caldwell (1793–1863), from Charleston, opened his new American Theatre on Camp Street and in 1833 his magnificent St Charles Theatre. Seating some 4000, with a crystal chandelier in its domed ceiling weighing 4000 pounds, its 23,330 cut-glass drops lit by 250 gas lights (Caldwell owned the local gasworks!), this beautiful establishment was said to be equalled only by the opera houses in Naples, Milan and St Petersburg. Theatrical elegance indeed for a city of some 75,000 inhabitants. When the theatre burned down in 1842 and Caldwell retired, the second St Charles (1843) was managed by Ludlow and Smith. It was a more modest structure seating only 1500, but with Caldwell now out of the field the lively partners took control of the western circuit. Fortunately each has left illuminating accounts of his adventures.

In the early years actors stuck to the circuit along the Ohio and Mississippi. By the late thirties primitive theatres became available in Buffalo, Cleveland, Detroit and Chicago, and any actor who ventured out of New York (and most did) scheduled the northern as well as the southern cities, and, with the Gold Rush of 1849, quickly added California to his itinerary. A canvas building called the Eagle Theatre opened in Sacramento in 1849 and Tom Maguire (c. 1816–96) built three Jenny Lind theatres in San Francisco (1850–2), quickly replacing them as they burned down.

As they had from the beginning, actors went wherever they could summon an audience, and as theatres and companies multiplied more native-born aspirants entered the field. By the middle of the century most of the lines of theatrical business that were to carry through to our own time had their popular exponents among actors who had been born on the western side of the Atlantic. And, just as public taste now demands a supermarket range of variety in its actors, so it did then. The range on the living stage was even greater before the theatrical diversification into motion pictures, radio and television.

During the middle years of the century a tribe of robust physical specimens blessed with strong lung-power followed in Edwin Forrest's path: Augustus A. Addams, John R. Scott (1805–56), J. Hudson Kirby (1819–48), McKean Buchanan (1823–72) and John E. McCullough (1832–85). They all played with Forrest before striking out on their own; they adopted his style and his roles, and they all found their chief admirers among the gallery rowdies. John E. McCullough, the chief disciple, had a favoured apprenticeship with Forrest, established his independence with a style of his own, and had a longer professional life than any of the others, from the late forties until the early eighties. Like Forrest he was well built, endowed with spectacular muscles and a strong voice, though in later years he subdued and spaced his emotional outbursts, smoothed and dignified his actions, cultivated the tender feelings, and relied more on his handsome face and body.

Josephine Clifton (1813–47) was not a Forrest follower in the same sense, though she was close to him – too close, according to some who testified at the Forrest divorce trial. This brawny amazon made her New York début in 1831, became Forrest's leading lady, and seems almost to have matched him in muscles and masculinity. This taste for masculinity in female performers persisted, at least through Charlotte Cushman's time. In an age when the stage was still off-limits to well-bred ladies not born to the profession, a virile female was regarded as better equipped to withstand the assaults on her moral character.

Charlotte Cushman (1816–76) was Forrest's contemporary, and her professional life extended over almost the same span of years. She began as a singer in Boston in 1835, but quickly moved to New Orleans; when her voice failed she launched a dramatic career, and by 1843, in support of Macready, she had worked her way up to leading lady. Macready urged her to try London. She did and with great success. Although some objected to her masculinity, one London critic noted that the fault 'was on the right side'. Others spoke of her 'lightning flashes', her 'terrible seething whirlpools of feelings'. When she returned to her native land in 1849 she was a star, and from then until 1875 when she retired – just three years after Forrest's death – she was the commanding tragic actress on the American stage.

Her 'incarnate power' was so irresistible, the critic William Winter noted, that she could have ruled an empire. She specialized in sustained, intense grief, in anger and denunciation. When her square shoulders, her tall, sturdy frame and her husky and hollow voice were employed to full advantage, in Lady Macbeth, for example, no Macbeth could have resisted her commands. With all her physical and emotional strength, she was a superb elocutionist. Syllables and words were always distinct, meanings clear and transparent.

Her excursions into transvestism are now difficult to fathom. Although she never laboured to conceal her broad hips and full bosom, she was called the best breeches figure in America. And the contemporary records are filled with unqualified praise for her Cardinal Wolsey, Hamlet, Claude Melnotte and particularly Romeo. In her forty years on the stage she ranged over 188 roles, with Lady Macbeth, Queen Katherine and Meg Merrilies in the dramatization of Scott's *Guy Mannering* unquestionably her best.

Cushman and Forrest may have been the leading lights in the middle years. They were not the only notable performers. In 1830 James Murdoch (1811–93) played Pythias to Forrest's Damon in Augusta, Georgia. He was also linked with Edwin Booth. He played with him in San Francisco in 1853, and they died within a month of each other in 1893. Murdoch's major performing life extended from 1845 to 1860. In 1856 he commanded London's Haymarket Theatre for 110 consecutive nights. In all of his roles – ranging from Othello, Hamlet and Macbeth to Claude Melnotte, Charles Surface, Benedick and Petruchio he worked for an idealized rendering of reality, faithful to the poet's image. He deplored rant and verbosity, and the ridiculous assumption that an actor could or should drown himself in a role. Although most critics ranked him fourth among our major actors – after Booth, Forrest and Cushman – his greatest impact was made with his lecturing and his books. His *Analytic Elocution* (1884), *A Plea for Spoken Language* (1883) and *The Stage* (1880) became the standard texts for the teaching of elocution.

E. L. Davenport (1815–77) began his career in Providence in 1835, became Anna Cora Mowatt's leading man in 1846 and went with her to England, remained there in support of Macready for seven years, and returned to claim attention for his 'intelligent and impressive' conception of Lanciotto in Boker's poetic tragedy, *Francesca da Rimini* (1855). Versatility was Davenport's strong point. He moved from Bill Sikes to Hamlet, from Sir Lucius O'Trigger to Othello; on a single evening he once played Hamlet, an act of *Black-Eyed Susan* and a farcical Yankee in the afterpiece. His smoothness, polish, good taste, soft, musical voice and gentlemanly manners marked him as a model leading man.

Anna Cora Mowatt (Ritchie) (1819–70) is now remembered as the author of *Fashion* (1845). In her own time she was also known as a public reader and as an actress. She upset tradition by demonstrating that a well-bred, high-society lady could weather the evils of the stage and that an attractive and unrepressed emotional amateur could challenge the well-schooled professionals. Encouraged by Longfellow she began her readings in Boston in 1840, the next year shifted to Stuyvesant Hall in New York, and when *Fashion* achieved its great success at the Park Theatre she became an actress, touring the country for 200 nights the following year as Lady Teazle, as Juliet and as Pauline in Bulwer-Lytton's *The Lady of Lyons*. Personal charm and feminine emotionalism were her distinguishing marks. Poe, one of her admirers, spoke of her grace, her radiantly beautiful smile, her self-possession, her richness of voice, the naturalness of her acting so pleasantly 'removed from the customary rant and cant – the hack conventionality of the stage'. Joseph Jefferson was less kind: shyness and uncertainty could not be concealed – 'once an amateur, always an amateur'. Still she established a tradition that has carried to our own time. The charming amateur with compelling gifts of emotional commitment can and often does outrank the seasoned professional.

Before the Civil War players of many descriptions found favour with the growing audiences. In his twenty years at the Park Theatre, Henry Placide (1799–1870) performed some 500 different roles and Forrest called him 'the best comedian the United States has yet produced'. William Warren II (1812–88), son of the Chestnut Street Theatre manager, became a public institution at the Boston Museum for thirty-six years following his début in the late forties. He was said to have performed 13,500 times in 600 roles, bringing joy whenever he appeared. William E. Burton's (1804–60) theatre in New York City became known as the training school for comedians from 1848 to 1856, and he himself as the chief exemplar of the art. One critic called him the 'funniest man who ever lived'.

John T. Raymond (1836–87), who later devoted himself almost exclusively to Colonel Sellers in *The Gilded Age* (1874), and John Brougham (1810–80) first appeared at Burton's. Brougham was a genial, breezy, jovial Irishman who captivated his audiences with personal magnetism and impromptu curtain speeches. He was also a prolific playwright. His *Po-Ca-Hon-Tas; or, The Gentle Savage* and *Metamora; or, The Last of the Pollywogs* were classics in the burlesque line.

Like Brougham, Dion Boucicault (1820–90) was both playwright and player, and like Brougham he specialized in lovable Irishmen, most of them his own creations. Boucicault was a clever and skilled technician, in his writing and in his playing, and not averse to lifting his plots and his performances from others. His Conn, the Shaughraun, was an Irish copy of Jefferson's Rip. (He had had a hand in adapting the *Rip Van Winkle* for Jefferson.) Boucicault's theatrical activities were not limited to playwriting and acting. In 1859 he managed the Winter Garden Theatre (formerly Burton's) and the following year took the entire company of his *The Colleen Bawn* on tour, thus establishing the 'combination company' practice. Heretofore principal players had filled out their casts from the local stock company. Hereafter the road companies, complete self-contained units, usually presenting one play, followed the paths of the rapidly expanding railroads throughout the country. Boucicault wrote and lectured extensively on theatrical matters, was one of the chief advocates of the first copyright law (1856) protecting playwrights, and at the end of his career was teaching at the Madison Square Theatre's acting school.

Among the favoured actresses who began their careers in the middle years were Clara Fisher (1811–98), Maggie Mitchell (1837–1918), Lotta Crabtree (1847–1924) and Adah Isaacs Mencken (1835–68). The sixteen-year-old Clara Fisher came from England in 1827 and held the stage with her bewitching specimens of sprightly femininity until her retirement in 1880. Maggie Mitchell's animation, vivacity and hoydenish charm, particularly well exhibited in *Fanchon the Cricket* (an adaptation from a George Sand story) brought her an army of admirers from 1851 to 1891.

Lotta Crabtree was also endowed with personal magnetism, though she was rowdier and bawdier. Born in New York, she went to California when she was six, took dancing lessons with Lola Montez, and in the early fifties became the darling of the California miners. When she came back to New York in 1867, she was billed as 'a sunbeam', 'a cataract', 'a doll', 'a kitten', 'a canary-bird', 'a sparkling ingot'. One critic wrote: 'her snowy-white pants, braced with starch, hung just low enough to reveal a very pretty foot, and a neatly-turned ankle. Her mouth constantly twitches with the inward spirit of mischief which pervades her.'

Crabtree's ankle, however well-turned, could not match Adah Isaacs Mencken's Godiva-like bareback ride in *Mazeppa*. The advertisements in the sixties regularly announced that 'Miss Mencken herself will ascend the fearful precipices and fight her own combats, not as hitherto by deputy. She herself will ride to the top of the theatre bound on the horse.' Her tights matched her flesh so well that one reporter noted that the house was regularly filled with drivelling old men with opera glasses.

Among the many personality performers who adopted popular indigenous character types, the Yankee specialists were the most numerous in the early years. Although the theatrical riches of the down-easter were duly signalled in Tyler's *The Contrast*, his potentialities were not realized until the second quarter of the century.

James H. Hackett (1800–71) initiated the Yankee line in 1826 at the Park Theatre with his 'Story of Uncle Ben' and *Sylvester Daggerwood*, an assortment of imitations following the pattern established by the English actor, Charles Mathews. After his initial success, he created the Yankee character of Solomon Swap in *Jonathan in England*, but he did not limit himself to Yankees. He played the western frontier hero, Colonel Nimrod Wildfire, in

The Lion of the West and was known as the greatest Falstaff of his time.

Like Hackett, George Handel Hill (1809–49) began with Yankee stories (Albany, 1829), and in 1832 became a fully fledged Yankee actor, first in Dunlap's *Trip to Niagara* and then in Woodworth's *The Forest Rose*. His natural nasal twang peculiarly and admirably fitted him to the character. In 1840 one critic said he was 'the funniest actor, and the cleverest fellow, in the Yankee signification of the word – in Christendom'. Audiences enjoyed his sleek, plausible cunning, his great industry, and his scanty and pliant honesty.

Other actors followed their lead. Danforth Marble (1810–49) in *Sam Patch* and *The Vermont Wool Dealer* was called 'a Yankee up to the hub, perfectly killing'. Joshua Silsbee (1813–55) began his Yankee career in *The Forest Rose* and later added *The Yankee Pedler* and *The Green Mountain Boy*. Among the many others who adopted the Yankee line were John E. Owens (1823–86), George E. Locke (b. 1817) and Denman Thompson (1833–1911).

Although not so abundant as the Yankees, there were other one-role specialists. In the late forties Frank S. Chanfrau's (1824–84) 'Mose' became the hero of the 'Bowery B'hoys' (the gallery rowdies). Dressed in a ridiculous red shirt and plug hat, Mose was a cocky, warmhearted rogue, always itching for a fight or racing with the volunteers to fight a fire; his life was filled with adventures Bowery B'hoys dreamed of. After Chanfrau struck gold in *A Glance at New York* (1848) at Mitchell's Olympic Theatre, a series of 'Mose' plays followed: *Mose in California, Mose in a Mess, Mose in China*.

While the Yankees and such lovable rogues as 'Mose' held the stage, another group of eccentric solo, duo and ensemble performers matched (some would say outdistanced) them in popularity. These were the ersatz Negro specialists.

Thomas Dartmouth 'Daddy' Rice (1808–61) introduced his famous song and dance of 'Jim Crow' some time between 1829 and 1831, and in 1833 began concocting 'Ethiopian Operas'. Rice composed the music, the dance and the verses for his 'Jim Crow', the refrain of which went:

> First on de heel tap, den on de toe,
> Ebery time I wheel about I jump Jim Crow.
> Wheel about and turn about and do jis so,
> And ebery time I wheel about I jump Jim Crow.

This chorus and the pictures of his eccentric costume and pose – all that we have – leave the essence of his popularity unfathomable, but the fact of his success is clear. He continued 'jumping Jim Crow' until his death in 1861.

When he appeared in London for the full season of 1836–7, one critic complained: 'This disgusting buffoon carries away seventy pounds per week, while many of our charming and lovely young actresses cannot, by unwearied assiduity, earn more than twenty-five to thirty. What an indelible disgrace to our country!'

The long phenomenal history of the minstrel show cannot be recited in detail. After Dan Emmett, Billy Whitlock, Dick Pelham and Frank Bower presented the first evening of black-face entertainment in December 1842, followed by an opening at the Bowery Amphitheatre, on 6 February 1843, and E. P. Christy (1815–62) assembled a minstrel troupe at Mechanics' Hall in 1846, Negro minstrels held the stage, here and in England, until well into the twentieth century. In 1881 a London reporter noted that 'dynasties have fallen, whole empires have been upset, but the minstrels go on for ever.'

Other cork-blackened actors showed a more serious face, particularly in *Uncle Tom's Cabin*. The extraordinary stage history of the play began at the Troy Museum in Troy, New York, on 27 September 1852, when George C. Howard (d. 1887) and his family presented George L. Aiken's (1830–76; Howard's cousin) dramatization of Mrs Stowe's novel, and from then until Howard's death in 1887 the family devoted themselves to 'Tomming'. In 1852–3 eight versions of the play appeared in London, and in 1853–4 five in New York. So overwhelming was the demand for the play throughout the country, even into the twentieth century, that many actors spent their entire professional lives as 'Tommers'. In 1879 the New York *Dramatic Mirror* recorded the routes of forty-nine Tom companies; twenty years later there were at least 500; and as late as 1927 a dozen companies were still on the road – a unique phenomenon in American theatrical history.

The rage for minstrels undoubtedly cultivated the taste for other eccentrics. During the fifties two duo acts had their bright day: Mr and Mrs W. J. Florence and Mr and Mrs Barney Williams. They offered a full gallery of gay character types. For example, in *Mischievous Annie; or, A Lesson for Husbands*, Mrs Florence played Annie Tottle, a young actress; Madame Ankilto Wilhelmina, a French opera singer; Mademoiselle Julie, a Spanish dancer; Hezekiah Slocum, a Yankee boy; Molly Leaf, a child of nature; Frau Sligiterskypipesfunderknickelpopplesox, with her great Dutch organ song; and Tom Taffrail, a sailor boy.

During the same decade Colonel H. L. Bateman (1812–75) presented his precocious daughters, Kate (1843–1917) and Ellen (1844–1936), aged nine and seven respectively. They were serious artists and chose the big roles – Richard III, Richmond, Hamlet, Macbeth, Shylock and Portia. Although it cannot be detailed here, the Bateman story is one of the most fascinating in American theatre history. Kate and her younger sisters Isabel (1854–1934) and Virginia (1853–1940) became mature actresses in England; the Colonel from Louisville managed the Lyceum Theatre in London and brought Henry Irving (1838–1905) to prominence with *Hamlet* in 1874. His name may now be forgotten, but he had famous grandchildren, the actress Fay Compton and the novelist Compton McKenzie.

Phineas T. Barnum (1810–91) was responsible for bringing the Bateman children to London, as he was for introducing many theatrical oddities. In 1835 he attracted his first audiences with Joice Heth, an aged and withered Negress who was said to have been George Washington's nurse. In 1841 he acquired Scudder's Museum of stuffed animals and in 1843 discovered extraordinary riches in the midget General Tom Thumb (1838–83). The General apparently delighted everyone, including Queen Victoria at Buckingham Palace, with his songs, dances and imitations. In 1850 Barnum created a sensation in New York when he brought Jenny Lind (1820–87), 'the Swedish nightingale', to Castle Garden. He was the great impresario of the nineteenth century, though since 1871 his name has been identified with the circus.

If eccentric entertainers found a wide audience during the middle years of the century, they were never in complete command. New stars and new managements found an eager audience. Four strong actresses came to power in the third quarter of the century: Laura Keene (*c.* 1820–73), Fanny Davenport (1850–98), Matilda Heron (1830–77) and Clara Morris (1846–1925).

As an actress Laura Keene was gentle, graceful, emotional and pleasingly endowed with feminine charm. As a manageress she was firm, self-confident, efficient and often dictatorial. Her actors called her 'the Duchess'. She received her early training with Madame Vestris in London, was brought here by Wallack in 1852, and had a triumphant opening season as Lady Teazle, Lydia Languish, Portia and Rosalind. She was established as a star immediately, and after two years of playing in San Francisco and Australia she returned to New York as leading lady and manager of her own theatre, first with Laura Keene's Varieties (1855), and then her own new establishment, Laura Keene's Theatre (1856–63). Her productions were greatly admired for their splendour and novelty. During the last ten years of her life she toured and had the unfortunate distinction of luring Lincoln to Ford's Theatre on 14 April 1865, and of identifying John Wilkes Booth as the assassin. Critics admired her ability to simulate the appropriate physical qualities of a character, and most agreed that she exhibited her best comic style with Florence Trenchard in *Our American Cousin*. Like the other three ladies then on stage, she attempted *Camille*. Unlike them, she tried to subdue the indiscretions by pretending that they transpired in a dream.

Fanny Davenport, E. L. Davenport's eldest child, began her career capitalizing on high-spirited femininity and then shifted to power and passion. For the seven years after Augustin Daly introduced her as Lady Gay Spanker in *London Assurance* (in 1869) she was known for her comic coquettishness and her stunning beauty. With Daly's *Pique* (1875) she began a new stage life, specializing in the 'dramatic explosions', and 'simulated frenzies', demanded by Sardou melodramas and by *Camille*. Her Camille was not as fastidious as Laura Keene's, though even she seems to have glossed over the immoralities.

Matilda Heron was not squeamish about *Camille*; she made a life's work of exploiting the sad lady's agonies. When she brought her own translation to Wallack's in 1857, after trying it out in New Orleans, her clinically detailed rendering of the suffering heroine made her the rage of New York. Here was a new kind of 'elemental power' and animal vivacity, an uninhibited exploitation of the visceral emotions, an undisguised recognition of a woman's sexual life. Some critics remarked on her lifelike naturalness. She came on stage unaware of the audience, as if she were entering a real room; she even turned her back on them. If these innovations escaped attention, the painful agony of Camille's final hour did not. As she coughed her way to the grave, tears flowed throughout the house.

Clara Morris did not limit herself to *Camille*; she did stick to tearjerkers. She was *the* weeper of the nineteenth century. She once wrote: 'I have cried steadily through all the years of my dramatic life. Tears gentle, regretful; tears petulant, fretful; tears stormy, passionate; tears slow, despairing.' Although she began as a ballet girl in 1862, her dramatic talents were quickly recognized. She played Emilia to Davenport's Othello, Gertrude to Booth's Hamlet, and became a comedienne with Daly until he discovered that domestic distress, overpowering grief and tumultuous passions were more in her line and plays like *Article 47*, *Alixe* and *Miss Multon* (a version of *East Lynne*) more suitable to her talents. Her death scenes were so ghastly and terrible in realistic detail that they produced visible shudders in the audience. According to her own account, she developed her naturalistic rendering of a heart attack with a gruesome bit of observation. A physician friend of hers paid a heart patient to run up a long flight of stairs. Miss Morris was waiting at the top to study the symptoms.

These players, and others, owed part of their success to the solid and enduring managements that emerged in the third quarter of the century, particularly those of Wallack, Palmer and Daly.

James William Wallack (1791–1864) had divided his acting career between England and America since his first appearance under Simpson's management in 1818. His name was indelibly imprinted on American theatre history when he took over Brougham's Lyceum in 1852 and renamed it Wallack's. In 1861 he opened his own new theatre, and at his death his son Lester (1820–88) assumed the management. Wallack's Theatre was noted for its highly disciplined and superior company – including such actors as Laura Keene, John Gilbert, E. L. Davenport, Maurice Barrymore, Dion Boucicault and Steele MacKaye – for its expert staging of old and new comedies, and for such significant premières as Boucicault's *Poor of New York* (1857), T. W. Robertson's 'cup and saucer' dramas, *Society* and *Ours* in 1866, and Boucicault's *The Shaughraun* (1874). Wallack set the pattern for what was to be expected of a first-class manager.

Albert Marshall Palmer (1838–1905) emulated Wallack. Although he had no previous experience as actor or playwright – he was a lawyer and for a short period librarian of the New York Mercantile Library – he was an expert manager endowed with an extraordinary discriminating taste. Many notable productions were brought out under his banner, first at the Union Square Theatre (1872–83), then at the Madison Square Theatre (1884–91) and finally at Palmer's Theatre (formerly Wallack's, 1891–6): Sardou's *Agnes* (1872), Steele MacKaye's *Rose Michel* (1875), Bronson Howard's *The Banker's Daughter* (1878), Clyde Fitch's *Beau Brummell* (1890) starring Richard Mansfield, and Augustus Thomas's *Alabama* (1891).

Augustin Daly (1838–99) was America's first *régisseur*. His stage-carpenter once said of him: 'That man thinks theatre, talks theatre, dreams theatre, and would eat theatre if he could.' He ran the entire establishment from the ticket office to the stage door, wrote (or adapted from the German and French) many of the plays he produced, and conducted his own rehearsals, instructing his actors in every detail and injecting a life-giving pace into all of his productions. No manager before him taught his actors so much, nor controlled their lives so completely. One of them said: 'I believe he could teach a broomstick to act; he shows everyone just how to move, to speak, to look; he seems to know instinctively just how everything should go to get the best effect.'

Daly was born in Plymouth, North Carolina, in 1838, and took his first step into the theatre in 1856 when he and some fellow amateurs presented scenes from *Julius Caesar* and *Macbeth* in a Brooklyn theatre. This was his first and only attempt at acting. From 1859 to 1868, while he worked as a journalist on various New York papers, he began to adapt and write plays. His first was *Leah, The Forsaken*, from von Mosenthal's *Deborah*, adapted for Kate Bateman. After four more adaptations, in 1867 he wrote his first original play, *Under the Gaslight*, and leased the New York Theatre for its production. Its realistic local-colour scenes such as Delmonico's, the Tombs Police Court, a Villa at Long Branch, and the Shrewsbury Railroad Station and the 10.30 Express Train made it a 'stage-carpenter's dream'. Encouraged by his first success as playwright and manager, Daly acquired the Fifth Avenue Theatre in 1869, formed his own stock company of thirty-two actors and announced his policy: 'Production of whatever is novel, original, entertaining, and unobjectionable, and the revival of whatever is rare and worthy in legitimate drama.' With T. W. Robertson's *Play* for the opening and with his meticulous production of Bronson Howard's *Saratoga* in his second season and Howard's *Diamonds* in his fourth, Daly was securely established as the top manager in the field, a rank he was to hold for the next thirty years.

When the theatre burned down on New Year's Day 1873, he moved to the New York Theatre, renaming it the Broadway, while he waited for his new Fifth Avenue Theatre to be built. It was ready in December 1873, and continued as his home until 1879 when he took over the Broadway Theatre and renamed it Daly's. In 1884 he began transporting his company to London for summer seasons, and after his own theatre, just off Leicester Square, opened in London in 1893 – the first English theatre to bear the name of an American manager – he divided his career between London and New York.

Daly productions were invariably noted for their 'thoroughness and taste', and his audiences for their refinement and elegance. His stage rooms were often 'richer in effect than the actual rooms in many of the fine homes of the city'. 'Contemporaneous' was the recurring description in Daly advertising copy. And audiences were invariably delighted by what they saw at Daly's. As late as 1897 the New York *Herald* found a Daly opening night much like a family party, 'with those behind the footlights as hosts and those before them as guests, only the usual roles are exchanged and the guests welcome the hosts. . . . Daly has established what all managers aim at, a regular clientele. He has the battle already half won before the curtain rises on the first act.'

His principal actor-hosts were John Drew (1853–1927), Ada Rehan (1860–1916), James Lewis (1840–96) and Mrs G. H. Gilbert (1822–1904), all of whom were with him from the late seventies until the end of his career. One critic wrote of his famous quartet: 'They know the heights and depths of each other's power, and one helps the other like a generous comrade; indeed, one seems to inspire the other to better things.' And when Daly's company appeared in London many critics found their ensemble-playing superior to that of the Meiningen troupe. Above all else Daly demanded actors who would submit to his orchestration. He once wrote: 'I don't want individual success in my theatre! I want my company kept at a level. Put them all in a line and then I watch, and if one head begins to bob above the others, I give it a crack and send it down again.' He could tolerate his quartet because their heads rose together.

No nineteenth-century manager held such a firm hand on his theatre; no manager so firmly set the style for his successors; yet even Daly and Daly's actors did not dominate the theatre. Other actors and managers found an audience.

Just as the Yankee actors and the minstrel performers discovered an enduring speciality, other actors depended largely on single roles. Two of these came from the cast of *Our American Cousin*: E. A. Sothern (1826–81) and Joseph Jefferson III (1829–1905). Sothern enlarged and exploited the part of the eccentric Lord Dundreary in the play and made a career out of it. Jefferson abandoned his part, Asa Trenchard, and found his lifetime companion in Rip.

Jefferson came from a line of actors stretching back to his great-grandfather, made his début as a child with 'Jim Crow' Rice, worked through many roles during a fifteen-year apprenticeship, and finally hit his stride with *Rip Van Winkle* at the Olympic in 1866. In 1881 Jefferson reported that he had played the role 2500 times, and he continued with it until his retirement in 1904. During his early years Jefferson searched for a part in which 'humor would be so closely allied with pathos that smiles and tears should mingle with each other.' In Rip he found it. No actor, no character, was more dearly loved than Jefferson and Rip. And no part was so completely the property of one actor.

Frank Mayo (1839–96) found his life's work in Frank Murdock's *Davy Crockett*. From 1874 he was identified with this rough, rude, honest and tender backwoodsman. Mayo once said: 'Damn it, when I first produced it they called it a bad dramatization of a half-dime novel. Five years later they got round to calling it an "idyll of the backwoods". And now, damn 'em, they call it a classic.'

James O'Neill (1847–1920), the father of Eugene O'Neill, had been on his way to becoming a first-rate versatile actor when he was caught with *The*

Count of Monte Cristo. Ironically, he had just a week's rehearsal and was unsteady in the part when it opened in 1883, but his success with the dashing, romantic Count was so overwhelming that he was burdened with the role for the rest of his life. The effects of that burden are movingly chronicled in Eugene O'Neill's *Long Day's Journey Into Night*.

Edward Harrigan (1844–1911) and Tony Hart (1855–91) were gay, brash, eccentric performers, though Harrigan's plays were more than simple vaudeville sketches. They revealed the colourful, humorous and boisterous life of the Irish, Germans, Italians and Negroes on New York's Lower East Side. When they began their partnership in 1871, Harrigan's talents as singer, comedian, sketch writer and manager and Hart's as singer, comedian and female impersonator produced a winning combination. By the time Harrigan's full-length plays began to appear in 1875, 'Harriganandhart' was already becoming a household word. Many thought it was one word. For the next ten years Harrigan's busy pen gave the 'merry partners' rich characters, lively comic dialogue, minstrel-like routines, and uproarious knockdown and slambang adventures. Almost every scene ended with a 'melee' or 'general melee'. Harrigan usually played the gay rogues and Hart the foolish females. Whether in *The Mulligan Guard Ball*, *The Mulligan Guard Chowder*, *Dan's Tribulations*, *Cordelia's Aspirations* or *Old Lavender*, Harrigan and Hart drew their loving public into the theatre. After the partnership dissolved at the close of the 1884 season, Hart faded rapidly, but Harrigan held the stage with his plays and his playing until the end of the century.

Before any of these performers had reached his peak, another star of the first magnitude had been rising, Edwin Booth. The two Edwins were the giant figures of the century. When Forrest was going downhill, Booth was reaching his prime, and, as they passed, comparisons were the order of the day. Now only two simple comparisons can be safely supported: physically and psychically the two men were differently constituted; Forrest rose to his full stature in the age of Jackson and Booth in the age of Lincoln.

Edwin Booth (1833–93) was named after Forrest, made his first acquaintance with the theatre travelling as guardian and valet for his father, Junius Brutus, played his first bit part in *Richard III* in 1849 and when his father died in 1852 began his serious apprenticeship in San Francisco. For four years he played everything in comedy and tragedy. Booth never regretted his time with the light parts. In 1873 he wrote: 'When I was learning to act tragedy, I had frequently to perform comic parts in order to acquire a certain ease of manner that my serious parts might not appear stilted.'

When he went east in 1856, he scored immediately and held his star position until his death in 1893. Even in his early appearances Winter noted his 'extraordinary grace, robust yet refined vigor, and his spontaneous passion'. He had a rough month with the critics on his first visit to London in 1861, and even during his triumphant English engagement in 1881–2, when he alternated Iago and Othello with Irving, some found him too cold, correct and formal, 'too prone to exhibit the whites of his eyes'. The following year he created a sensation at the Residenz Theater in Berlin. Although he was the only actor speaking English, most critics thought he was the best Hamlet they had ever seen.

Events forced a kind of manic-depressive existence on Booth. In 1863 he was stricken by the loss of his wife. The following year he triumphed with his famous 100-performance run of *Hamlet*. When his brother assassinated Lincoln, he retired from the stage for almost a year. In 1869 he opened his dazzling and stately new theatre at 23rd Street and 6th Avenue, the best of its time, with a spectacular production of *Romeo and Juliet*.

Booth's Theatre, 'a great national temple of art', as it was called, was the first theatre in which the stage had been given first consideration. Its elaborate mechanism could lower scenery into the basement or raise it into the stage house, and Booth's productions employed the machinery to its fullest capacity. But successful plays could not compensate for the staggering initial outlay for the building, and Booth's partner, Richard A. Robertson, who had shared equally in the initial million-dollar investment, had manipulated the funds so that the financial burden rested on Booth. Four years after its opening Booth was forced to abandon his theatre and go into bankruptcy.

Thereafter he stuck to acting in New York and throughout the country, constantly perfecting his Othello, Iago, Richelieu and Hamlet, constantly endeavouring to 'reveal the soul of masterpieces', as he described his task. His slight, slender body, his graceful manner and his musical voice with its great range and remarkable carrying power became most strikingly identified with the melancholy Dane, and for two generations of Americans Booth was Hamlet and Hamlet Booth. Of the final scene one critic wrote: 'His voice thrills with an unearthly sweetness and when silence falls we look as on our own dead in a sadness too deep for tears.' Booth's home at 16 Gramercy Park was bequeathed to the Players' Club and still stands as a gracious monument to his memory.

Lawrence Barrett (1838–91) followed in Booth's path, played with Booth, yet always remained in his shadow. Sheer drive, hard work and scholarly study could never compensate for what he lacked in natural talent, yet his persistence brought him into partnership and equal billing with Booth in 1880. If his acting was too mannered and mechanical, his readings too deliberate and pedantic, he was frequently called America's leading actor-scholar. Cassius in *Julius Caesar* was probably his best role, and his production of *Francesca da Rimini* (1882), playing Lanciotto to Otis Skinner's Paolo and finally giving Boker the hearing he deserved, assures his place in the historical record.

Steele MacKaye (1842–94) was also a studied actor, though of a slightly different breed. He concentrated on the science of bodily expression. He introduced the Delsarte system[4] to America in 1871 and founded the Lyceum Theatre School in 1884, later to become the American Academy of Dramatic Art.

MacKaye had a rich and varied career in the theatre, as actor, teacher, playwright, designer, director, manager and, most of all, as inventor and innovator. No theatre man before or after him was so versatile and touched so many aspects of the theatre. In his Madison Square Theatre, opened in 1880, eleven years after Booth's, an entire setting could be moved on its huge stage elevator and replaced by another scene in two minutes. The electric lighting had been installed under the personal supervision of Thomas A. Edison and audience comfort improved with folding seats and the latest in ventilating equipment. *Hazel Kirke* opened the theatre and became a sensation, but MacKaye was bilked out of his share by the Mallory brothers.[5] The evil demon of financial disaster which seemed always to be pursuing MacKaye did not restrain him. In 1885 he built the Lyceum Theatre, again incorporating elaborate stage machinery, the newest in fire-fighting equipment, and an orchestra pit that could be lowered into the basement. In the early nineties he began planning his gigantic Spectatorium for the Chicago World's Fair (the Columbian Exposition). It was to be 480 feet long, 380 feet wide and 270 feet high. According to MacKaye: 'There were to be twenty-five telescopic stages, all of which were to be furnished with scenery of an entirely new species devised by myself.' The project was never completed. When the financial panic of 1893 wrecked the Columbian Celebration Company, MacKaye devised a scaled-down version, the Scenitorium, which was opened on 5 February 1895 (after MacKaye's death) with his *The World Finder*, a

---

[4] François Delsarte (1811–71), the French inventor of calisthenics, invented also a system of attitudes and gestures based (he maintained) on nature rather than on the acting conventions of his time.

[5] When I talked with MacKaye's son Percy shortly before his death some seventy years after this financial fiasco, he was still burning with resentment.

dramatic spectacle depicting the story of Columbus. MacKaye was unquestionably the most unsuccessful successful theatre man of the century. No one matched his magnificent and lofty conceptions, his genius for creating theatrical wonders.

Although not a major actor, he was the chief exponent of the Delsartian system and apparently demonstrated its efficacy, mostly in his own plays. He was praised for his simple and natural movements and gestures, the quiet intensity and absence of rant in his speaking.

James A. Herne (1839–1901) is now known mainly for his plays: *Hearts of Oak* (1879), *Shore Acres* (1892) and particularly *Margaret Fleming* (1891). In his time he was equally known as an actor-manager. He enlarged his written portraits with his own sweet, homely and truthful representations, conducted his own rehearsals and managed his extensive tours. Before his first undistinguished attempts at playwriting in 1879, he performed in Albany, Baltimore and Washington, supported E. A. Sothern, E. L. Davenport, Edwin Booth and even Forrest, played Armand to Lucille Western's (1843–77) Camille, toured California, and in 1878 married Katherine Corcoran (1856–1943). Her magic changed his life. The next year with *Hearts of Oak* he became a major dramatist and a major player, and for the next seven years the Hernes toured the country. A few years ago their son John wrote to me: 'It was their great adoration for each other that made them the great team in American dramatic literature. James A. Herne was a great actor, all by himself, drunk or sober, but it was his leading lady, Katy Corcoran, who made him into a great dramatist.'

Herne was no matinee-idol, yet his round Irish face exuded warmth and charm, and his meticulously drawn portraits were rich in pathos and humour. Undoubtedly he was at his best in Uncle Nat's final scene in *Shore Acres*. For a full five minutes Uncle Nat was alone on stage, slowly making sure that everything was safe and sound for the night. (Some twelve years later Chekhov was to discover the magic of a similar scene in *The Cherry Orchard*.) One night in Boston, as the curtain was closing, Herne heard a voice speaking for the audience: 'Good night, old man, God bless you!'

During the last quarter of the century other actors and managers came to power, and often their careers were intertwined.

The taste for female emotionalism had not vanished, as Mrs Leslie Carter (1862–1937) discovered. She and Belasco also found that striking beauty and a sensational divorce trial could contribute to the making of an actress. For two years Belasco coached her in some forty roles and in 1895 introduced her

1 Mrs Lewis Hallam the younger (Eliza Tuke), New York, 1793.

2 Sol Smith.

3 Scene from *The Contrast*
by Royall Tyler, 1787.

4 Interior of the Park
Theatre, New York, 1821.

5 Scene from *The Forest Rose* by Samuel Woodworth, 1825.

6 Edwin Forrest in John Augustus Stone's *Metamora: or The Last of the Wampanoags*.

7 Edwin Forrest as King Lear.

8 Edwin Booth, still
accounted by many to be
America's greatest actor.

9 Lithograph poster
advertising *Uncle Tom's
Cabin*.

10 Joseph Jefferson III
as Rip Van Winkle.

11 Frank Mayo as Davy Crockett, 1874.

12 A Harrigan and Hart Poster, c. 1880.

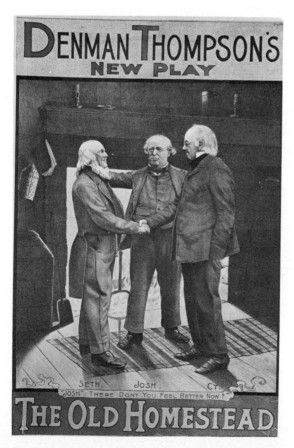

13 Lithograph poster advertising *The Old Homestead*. Denman Thompson is seen at centre as Josh Whitcomb.

14 James O'Neill about the age of 35.

15 Eugene O'Neill about
the age of 35.

16 Scene from *Secret Service* by William Gillette.

17 Blanche Bates and Robert Hilliard in David
Belasco's *The Girl of the Golden West*, 1905.

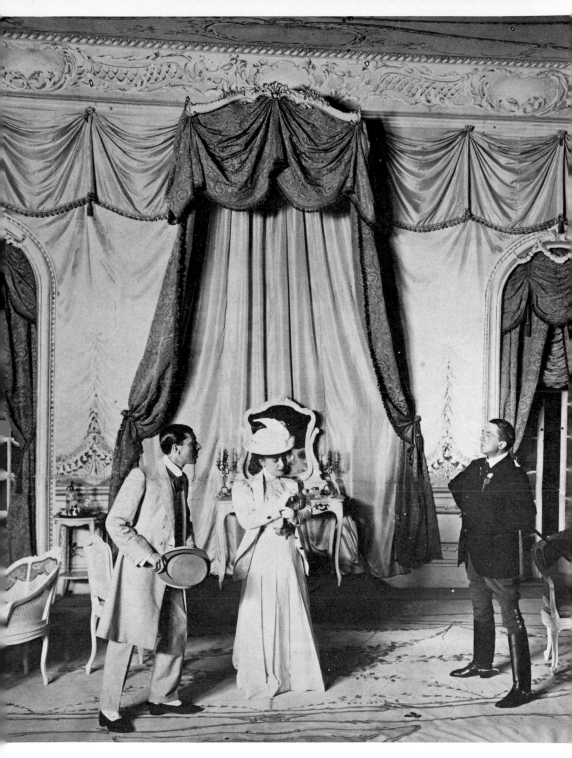

18 Mrs Minnie Maddern Fiske in Langdon Mitchell's *The New York Idea* (1906) supported by George Arliss (*left*) and John Mason.

19 Mrs Fiske in Edward Sheldon's *Salvation Nell* (1908): the bar
room in Act 1.

20 The Wharf Shed at Provincetown, Mass., Eugene O'Neill's first
stage, 1916.

21 Design by C. Raymond Johnson for the Chicago Little Theatre
production of Oliphant Downs' *The Maker of Dreams*. The frame
within the proscenium suggests a window through which the action
is viewed.

22 (above and below) Two arrangements of a multi-purpose setting, designed by Samuel B. Hume for productions at the Detroit Arts and Crafts Theatre.

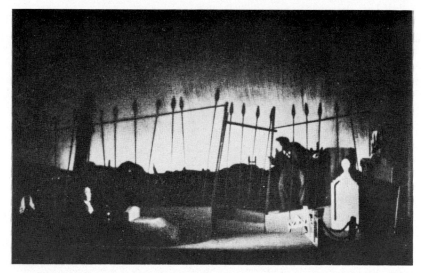

23 Scene from *The Adding Machine* by Elmer Rice, 1923.

24 Norman Bel Geddes's setting from Sidney Kingsley's
Dead End, 1935.

25 The Group Theatre production of Clifford Odet's
Awake and Sing!, 1935.

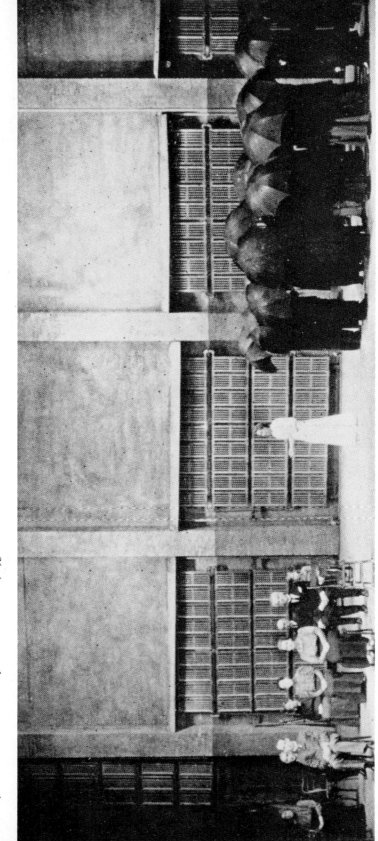

26 Lynn Fontanne and Alfred Lunt in The Theatre Guild production of Shakespeare's *The Taming of the Shrew*, 1935.

27 Scene from *Our Town* by Thornton Wilder, 1938.

28 Katharine Cornell, Tom Powers, Gertrude Musgrove, Ruth Gordon and Judith Anderson in Chekhov's *The Three Sisters*, 1942.

29 Scene from *Oklahoma!* by Rodgers and Hammerstein, 1943.

30 Robert Edmond Jones's setting for the bar room in The Theatre Guild production of Eugene O'Neill's *The Iceman Cometh*, 1946.

31 Jason Robards and Colleen Dewhurst in Eugene O'Neill's *A Moon for the Misbegotten*, 1974.

to the public in *The Heart of Maryland*. Her emotional pyrotechnics and gymnastic swing on the clapper of the bell so thrilled the audience that she had a three-year run. After this initial triumph, she shifted to *Zaza*, *Du Barry* and *Adrea*. Their stories were slightly lurid and discreetly immoral, proper material for her emotional exhibitions. Mrs Carter invariably won her audience at her first entrance with her mass of fiery red hair, her trim shapely figure, her soft blue eyes and her mellifluous voice; later she entranced them with her hysterics. According to Winter, 'her method was to work herself into a state of violent excitement, to weep, vociferate, shriek, rant, become hoarse with passion, and finally to flop and beat the floor.' After she broke with Belasco in 1906, she continued to perform, but never with the same success.

Three ladies traded on their extraordinary personal charm: Ada Rehan (1855–1916), Maude Adams (1872–1953) and Julia Marlowe (1870–1950). None stood above the others; each had her own army of devotees.

Ada Rehan came to Brooklyn from Limerick in 1860, in 1870 began her apprenticeship in Philadelphia with the Arch Street Theatre stock company which Mrs Drew managed from 1861 to 1892, later played Ophelia to Booth's Hamlet and finally, in 1879, found her proper niche as leading comedienne with Daly. She remained with Daly until his death in 1899, performing some 200 different parts. Her vivacious humour, her bewitching beauty and her roguish charms were exhibited to best advantage as Katherine, Rosalind, Viola, Lady Teazle, or as one of the pixieish hoydens in Daly's adaptations. If any actress ever filled a career with rave notices, it was Ada Rehan. Critics called her 'sweetly reckless', 'ardently impetuous' and 'piquantly alluring'. In England critics classed her with Ellen Terry, and Shaw wrote: 'When she is at her best, the music of her voice melts in the caress of the emotion it expresses.' After Daly's death she never adjusted to life in a new company; she retired in 1905 and died eleven years later.

Maude Adams was born into a theatrical family, though one could not have guessed at her heritage. With the assistance of Charles Frohman, she scrupulously avoided publicity and refused roles that explored the seamy or passionate side of man's nature. She dealt only with joy, goodness, optimism and heart-warming sentiment, largely in the plays of J. M. Barrie, particularly *Peter Pan* and *What Every Woman Knows*. One reporter called her 'the most conspicuous figure upon the English speaking stage, the most notable woman in a nation of a hundred million'. This 'little home-like woman, with gentle intimate graces, and fanciful elfin humor', drew the top money because so many people never went to the theatre except to see her.

For most of the first quarter of this century, Shakespeare meant Sothern and Marlowe. They were a Shakespearian team even before their marriage in 1911. By the turn of the century, the roles of Rosalind, Viola and Juliet had become Julia Marlowe's exclusive property, and feminine loveliness, warm magnetism and admirable grace the standard descriptions of her performances. According to Arthur Symons, 'no actor on the British stage could speak English or English verse so beautifully.'

Mrs Minnie Maddern Fiske (1865–1932) is *the* transitional actress. Her acting style evolved in the nineteenth century but belongs to the twentieth. She began as a child actress, made her début in 1882, ranged over the standard roles, and in the mid-nineties found her real place with Tess, Becky Sharp, Salvation Nell, and the troubled ladies in Ibsen's domestic dramas. The critics quickly perceived that she was of a new breed. They spoke of her mental capacity to analyse a character to its core, of her repose, reserve and silent moments, of the absence of theatrical trickery and display, of the painstaking and revealing detail, and of the sense of an 'intense repressed force'. When young actors sought her advice, she told them: 'Keep it true – keep it true.' Her Salvation Nell was her crowning achievement in natural acting, particularly the scene in which she sat for ten minutes on the floor, her drunken lover's head in her lap and with no words to utter. She kept the audience 'absorbed in the silent pathos of that dumb, sitting figure'. Here was 'an intensity that is absolutely true to life, as true to life as is possible on the stage.'

Mrs Fiske's contributions to the theatre were not limited to her acting. Along with her husband, Harrison Grey Fiske (1861–1942), editor of the *Dramatic Mirror*, she championed the new drama, particularly Ibsen. The homely, unsettled, degraded and psychologically troubled characters from real life fascinated her. With her Manhattan Theatre Company she trained her actors for ensemble playing, and in her battle against the Syndicate she fought to free the American theatre from greedy commercial exploitation.

Some members of the male contingent who held the stage in the last years of the century have already been mentioned. There were others who came into prominence and adopted lines of business that had already been established. Nat Goodwin (1857–1919) and Francis Wilson (1854–1935) carried on the comic tradition. Goodwin was a natural comic; everything he did drew a laugh, whether in Gilbert and Sullivan or in Shakespeare. And because of his early training with Tony Pastor, his performances invariably retained a vaudeville-like quality. Wilson, the first president of Actors' Equity, also began as a song-and-dance man and relied on his comic personality. Audiences delighted in his 'mugging', and his talent for 'hamming-up' a scene.

John Drew (1853–1927), William Faversham (1868–1940) and James K. Hackett (1869–1926) followed the romantic matinee-idol line established by Lester Wallack. Drew began with his mother's Arch Street Theatre Company in the early seventies and in 1879 achieved his matinee-idol rank as leading man for Ada Rehan in Daly's company, a rank he held well into the twentieth century. Faversham came to New York from London in 1887. Although his muscularity and vigour were admired in Romeo and Mark Antony, he achieved his greatest popularity – 'hero of a thousand matinees' – in *Under the Red Robe*, *The Squaw Man* and *The Prince and the Pauper*. In his last role he departed radically from the dashing hero line: he played Jeeter Lester in *Tobacco Road*. Hackett, the son of James H., was tall, handsome and possessed of remarkable athletic agility. After beginning in Shakespearian roles for Daly in the nineties, he became leading man in Daniel Frohman's company, specializing in swashbuckling, in *The Prisoner of Zenda* and *Rupert of Hentzau*.

Otis Skinner (1858–1942) belongs partly with this group, though his range was greater, his repertoire more extensive, and he carried his dash, flash and commanding presence with undiminished force into the second quarter of the new century. He began in Philadelphia in 1877, supported Booth, Barrett and McCullough, had two seasons as Helen Modjeska's leading man, and hit his peak as a member of Daly's troupe. In his sixty-year career he ranged over 325 parts and appeared in sixteen plays of Shakespeare. He was richly endowed with a resonant and flexible voice, a handsome and athletic body, a strong masculine face and a 'fine hardy brain'. The box office judged him at his best in *Prince Otto*, *Mister Antonio*, *Blood and Sand* and *Kismet*.

E. H. Sothern (1859–1933) began with contemporary comedy, shifted to romantic drama, and finally became a tragedian and Shakespearian specialist. Apprenticing with his father, E. A. Sothern, in 1878, his personal charm, his adroitness and his 'unusual finesse' marked him as a light comedian. With Daniel Frohman's Lyceum company from 1885 to 1899 he specialized in adventurous heroes like François Villon and D'Artagnan. At the turn of the century, after appearing in Hauptmann's poetic tragedy, *The Sunken Bell*, and as Hamlet, he spent the rest of his career with Shakespeare and Julia Marlowe. His Romeo, Macbeth, Shylock, Petruchio and Benedick were admired for their liveliness and for their studied understanding. His Malvolio, probably his best role, was called a 'fantastic, tragically comic thing'.

William Gillette (1855–1937) and Richard Mansfield (1854–1907) signalled the changing taste of the new century. Gillette, son of a United States senator, made his début in 1877, then quickly found the proper roles for his wit and charm and his tall, slender figure in his own plays, most notably in *Secret Service* and *Sherlock Holmes*. With his resourceful and imperturbable heroes, seemingly rendered without effort, he achieved an illusion of great naturalness.

Mansfield had a wider range with romantic heroes – Beau Brummell, Monsieur Beaucaire and Cyrano; grotesque creations – Dr Jekyll and Mr Hyde; and with his attention to the new dramatists, Ibsen and Shaw, as Captain Bluntschli in *Arms and the Man* and as Peer Gynt. Mansfield was adored and hated, praised and ridiculed. Actors abhored his vile temper, his egotistical manner and his capitulation to the Syndicate. His friends spoke of his charm, his courtesy, his magnetism. One critic wrote: 'There are good actors, bad actors, and Richard Mansfield.' None could deny his strong individuality, his artistic instinct and his burning ambition. He had a sharp mind, an athletically trained body and a consuming passion for public adulation.

Born in Berlin, Mansfield received his first vocal training from his opera-singer mother, and made his American début in 1882 as the doddering old lecher, Baron Chevrial, in *A Parisian Romance*. By 1886 he was an established star and manager, and from then until his death he kept his dual career going at fever pitch, alternating between long runs and seasons of repertory.

Among the managers who became Daly's competitors during the last quarter of the century, David Belasco was the only one who followed the Daly line as playwright and trainer of actors. The Frohmans and the members of the Theatrical Syndicate were theatre businessmen like Palmer.

David Belasco (1854–1931) began in California, came east to join Charles Frohman, became stage manager for Daniel Frohman at the Lyceum Theatre in 1887, and in 1890 struck out on his own as an independent producer-director. In San Francisco in 1869 he played the newsboy in *Under the Gaslight*, in 1877 wrote and directed eight short plays at Egyptian Hall, experimenting for the first time with the optical illusions to be achieved with lighting, and in 1879 presented a spectacular Passion Play at the Grand Opera House with James O'Neill as Christus and employing the services of some 400 extras. He began writing plays when he was twelve, in 1880 collaborated with Herne on the first version of *Hearts of Oak*, and while he was still with the Frohmans wrote or adapted ten plays, four of them with Henry C. DeMille. He collaborated with Franklyn Fyles on *The Girl I Left Behind Me*, the opening attraction at Charles Frohman's Empire Theatre in 1893, in 1895 had his first great independent success at the Herald Square Theatre with *The Heart of Maryland*, and in 1900, at the same theatre, presented *Madame Butterfly* with its fourteen-minute dusk-to-dawn lighting display while Butterfly sat at the window in silence.

In 1902 Belasco acquired the Republic Theatre, renaming it the Belasco, and in 1907 built his own theatre, first called the Stuyvesant and then the Belasco, the name it still bears. Belasco was fascinated with detailed realism in his settings and with ingenious lighting effects. *Rose of the Rancho* had a six-minute lighting prelude creating the heat of a tropical day before a word was spoken, and *Girl of the Golden West* featured a tremendous blizzard. For *The Governor's Lady* he installed an actual Child's restaurant, and for *The Easiest Way* he stripped a room from a dingy theatrical boarding house and transferred it to the stage. 'Never fake,' Belasco once said. 'The public will always catch you and never forgive you.'

But Belasco did not restrict himself to endowing romantic materials with detailed realistic effects. Like Daly he cultivated his actors and controlled their lives, developing such stars as Mrs Leslie Carter, Blanche Bates, Frances Starr, Lenore Ulric and Ina Claire. He once told a reporter: 'In everything connected with my theatre, from the water-boys in the smoking room to the star on the stage; from the carpets to be laid on the floors to the plays that are produced, I am the master, and my word is the absolute and final law.' He maintained a stock of dollar watches he could crush on the floor when required, though such extremes were not often necessary. The collar and dress of a priest in which he dramatized himself was usually sufficient to establish his autocracy. Throughout his producing career he maintained his absolute independence, and he became the bitter enemy of the Frohmans and the chief opponent of the Theatrical Syndicate.

The Frohman brothers were principally businessmen. Gustave Frohman (1855–1930) began as advance man for Callender Minstrels, managed MacKaye's road companies and was associated with MacKaye's acting school at the Lyceum. Gustave never achieved the managerial status of his two brothers. Daniel Frohman (1851–1940) started as business manager with MacKaye at the Madison Square Theatre, then at the Lyceum, and in 1886 took control of the Lyceum. In 1902 he opened his new Lyceum Theatre on 45th Street, and at Charles's death assumed control of his theatrical enterprises. Charles Frohman (1854–1915) began as manager of one of the road companies of MacKaye's *Hazel Kirke*, became a booking agent, and in 1889 brought out Howard's *Shenandoah*. In 1890 he leased

Proctor's Theatre and in 1893 opened his new Empire Theatre. Although he preferred to call his troupe a stock company, he was devoted to the star system. He fostered the talents of Maude Adams, particularly in the plays of J. M. Barrie, and those of Ethel Barrymore, May Robson, Margaret Anglin, William Gillette and Henry Miller. He was frequently called the 'Napoleon of the American stage', and with good reason. Just after the turn of the century he owned five theatres in New York and one in London, valued at $5 million. He had 10,000 employees and an annual advertising budget of a million and a half. Frohman was on the *Lusitania* when it sank in 1915.

Part of the theatrical power of Charles Frohman derived from his association with the Theatrical Syndicate. The Syndicate reportedly originated at a chance luncheon at the Holland House in New York and was legally established on 31 August 1896 by A. L. Erlanger (1860–1930), Marc Klaw (1858–1936), Samuel F. Nixon (Samuel F. Nirdlinger, 1848–1918), Frederick Zimmerman, Al Hayman (1883–1917) and Charles Frohman. Between them they owned over thirty-three theatres across the country and controlled the bookings in 500 others. If monopoly control and astute management could create fortunes from oil, they believed that the same system could work in the theatre, and for some ten years they held almost absolute control over the American theatre, taking from 5 to 50 per cent of the gross not only on the attractions originated by them but on those they booked. Until its dissolution in 1916 the Syndicate produced, booked or leased theatres to over 600 legitimate productions, over 50 per cent of the theatrical offerings of the period. And, whatever may be said of their 'greedy money-grubbing methods', the theatre expanded remarkably during their reign. In 1889, seven years before they came to power, 300 combinations were on the road, employing some 5000 people, and with gross annual receipts of $15 million. In 1911, 700 companies were travelling with over 30,000 on the payroll, and with an annual gross of over $100 million, $22 million from the seventy-one theatres in New York. They were sharp businessmen, and under the leadership of 'Honest Abe' Erlanger their eyes centred on the almighty dollar.

Not until the Shubert brothers deserted Syracuse and invaded New York was their stranglehold broken, and the Shuberts finally beat them at their own game. The Shubert triumvirate – Sam (1875–1905), Lee (1873–1954) and Jacob J. (1879–1963) – in some ways duplicated the Frohmans. Like Gustave Frohman, J. J., particularly in the early years, was less conspicuous than his brothers; when Sam was killed in a train wreck near Harrisburg, Pennsylvania, in 1905, Lee, like Daniel Frohman, assumed control of their theatrical empire. The Shuberts, of course, outdistanced both the Frohmans and the Syndicate. Even today the Shubert estate retains vast theatre holdings throughout the country.

The Shuberts came to New York in 1900, leased the Herald Square Theatre and opened with a production of Augustus Thomas's *Arizona*. In 1903 they attempted a brief alliance with the Syndicate, hoping to further their own interests by infiltrating the Trust, but, when they discovered that Erlanger and his associates were still out to destroy them, they broke the contract. By 1904 the Shuberts controlled ten theatres, when Sam was killed they had thirteen, a year later their chain had quadrupled, and by 1913 they had broken the Syndicate's grip and taken command. From 1901 until 1954 over 500 attractions carried their banner, ranging over the entire theatrical spectrum. Although known principally for their commercial attractions, they sponsored such controversial productions as Synge's *Playboy of the Western World*, Shaw's *Fanny's First Play*, Fitch's *The City* and Thomas's *As A Man Thinks*. They introduced Al Jolson to Broadway, competed with Ziegfeld's Follies with their *Passing Shows*, blanketed the country with revivals of *Blossom Time*, managed the tours of Sothern and Marlowe and Forbes-Robertson, and even presented Reinhardt's landmark production of *Sumurūn* in 1912. No management before or after them owned and controlled so many theatres and produced so many diverse theatrical attractions.

With the early twentieth-century theatre dominated so completely by big-businessmen, a revolt was to be expected. That Lee Shubert should share in the revolt as business director of the ill-fated New Theatre may now seem incredible, yet not so incredible. America's version of a European art theatre inescapably bore an American mark. Twenty-three wealthy patrons, contributing $35,000 each, built a massive theatre in the Italian Renaissance style on Central Park West at 62nd Street (just a stone's throw from the present Lincoln Center theatres), provided appropriately spacious boxes for themselves and almost 3000 places for the general public, and hired Heinrich Conreid from the Metropolitan Opera as artistic director. When Conreid died before the theatre's completion, they offered the post to Harley Granville-Barker. Distressed at the size of this 'millionaire's playhouse', he refused, and they engaged Winthrop Ames, a young idealistic producer who had made his reputation at Boston's Castle Square Theatre. The gloom and disaster that hung over the New Theatre's short life was apparent at the opening performance on 6 November 1909. Although the theatre's artistic credo had deplored the evils of the star system, the first production starred

Sothern and Marlowe in *Antony and Cleopatra*, roles for which they were manifestly unfitted, and though the stage settings were impressive too often the actors could not be heard, sometimes not seen, and when they were heard could not be understood. In the first season of eleven productions, only Galsworthy's *Strife* and Sheldon's *The Nigger*, the single American play, seemed worthy of the artistic aims to which the theatre was dedicated, and in the second and final season Maeterlinck's *The Blue Bird* was the only notable production. The brief life of the New Theatre ended in May 1911, with a deficit of $400,000.

No single explanation can account for the failure of this noble experiment. A variety of reasons were given then and later: the house was too cavernous and ornate, too much the exclusive property of high society, the acoustics were bad, no good new plays were available, too many British actors were featured, alternating operas with plays confused the public, the productions were inferior to those readily available on Broadway. Whatever the reasons, clearly big money could not buy an art theatre.

American art theatres did, however, evolve. Their beginnings were even more humble than their European progenitors, and they signalled their total rebellion against theatrical commerce by proclaiming their amateur status. Immediately following the demise of the New Theatre and the first tour of Lady Gregory's Abbey Theatre in 1911, art theatres proliferated with astonishing rapidity: the Hull House Players in Chicago, Maurice Browne's (1881–1954) Chicago Little Theatre, Mrs Lyman Gale's Toy Theatre in Boston, Sam Hume's Arts and Crafts Theatre in Detroit, the Lewisohn sisters' Neighborhood Playhouse in New York, and Stuart Walker's (1880–1941) Portmanteau Theatre in New York and on tour. These were quickly followed by the first 'little theatre' enthusiasts: Samuel A. Eliot, Jr, in Indianapolis, Frederic McConnell (1891–1968) in Cleveland, and Gilmor Brown (1887–1960) in Pasadena. No doubt the drive to establish community theatres had been sparked off by Percy MacKaye's (1875–1956; son of Steele MacKaye) book *The Civic Theatre* (1912), advocating the establishment of theatres throughout the country. In the half-dozen years prior to America's entry into the First World War, a new theatre concept permeated the atmosphere as it never had before or since. The Drama League of America (1910) had study groups everywhere devoted to fostering good drama. Professor George P. Baker (1866–1935) began his famous 47 Workshop at Harvard which was then and later to nurture the talents of such notables as Eugene O'Neill, S. N. Behrman, Sidney Howard, Winthrop Ames, Percy MacKaye, Edward Sheldon, Philip Barry, Theresa Helburn, John Mason Brown,

Robert Edmond Jones, Lee Simonson and Donald Oenslager. Other theatre professors followed Baker's lead: Alexander Drummond (1884–1957) at Cornell, Thomas H. Dickinson (1877–1961) at the University of Wisconsin, Thomas Wood Stevens (1880–1942) at the Carnegie Institute of Technology, and Frederick H. Koch (1877–1944), first at North Dakota and then at the University of North Carolina. And Sheldon Cheney (1886–   ) had started a house organ for the new ideas with *Theatre Arts* magazine in 1916.

Most of this theatrical ferment had been generated outside New York. It did not strike the city until 1915 when a group of Greenwich Village artists and writers, calling themselves the Washington Square Players, rented the Band Box theatre on 57th Street near 3rd Avenue and issued a manifesto:

> We believe that hard work and perseverance, coupled with ability and the absence of purely commercial considerations, may result in the birth and healthy growth of an artistic theatre. . . . We have only one policy in regard to the plays which we will produce – they must have artistic merit. Preference will be given to American plays, but we shall also include in our repertory the works of well-known European authors which have been ignored by the commercial managers.

With performances only on Friday and Saturday nights, forty seats in the house, and ten tickets with a $5 subscription, little revenue could be expected. Little was needed. The actors were unpaid and Robert Edmond Jones reported that his total cost for the settings for the opening bill of one-act plays on 19 February 1915 was $35. The four different programmes offered that spring included one-act plays by Edward Goodman, Maeterlinck, Chekhov, John Reed (the journalist who later gained fame for his *Ten Days That Shook The World*) and Basil Laurence (Lawrence Langner, the founder of the group). When they began their autumn season, they had raised sufficient funds to pay all workers $25 weekly, expanded their schedule to seven performances per week, and advanced the admission price to $1, but they still stuck to one-act plays: by Philip Moeller, Lewis Beach, Zoë Akins and, most notably, Alice Gerstenberg's *Overtones* anticipating the technique O'Neill was to employ in *Strange Interlude*. Near the close of the year, in May 1916, they presented their first long plays: Maeterlinck's *Aglavaine and Selysette* and Chekhov's *The Seagull*, a disastrous production according to most reports.

For their third season they moved to the 600-seat Comedy Theatre on 41st Street, east of Broadway, where they remained until they disbanded in May 1918, presenting such one-act plays as O'Neill's *In the Zone* and Susan

Glaspell's *Trifles*, and full-length plays of Andreyev (*The Life of Man*), Ibsen (*Ghosts*) and Shaw (*Mrs Warren's Profession*). In less than four years they had produced sixty-two one-act and six long plays.

No doubt they lost much of their joyous amateur spirit when they moved to the Comedy, for they were amateurs who aspired to be professionals and many of them did later find full careers in the theatre: Roland Young (1887–1953), Glenn Hunter (1896–1945), Helen Westley (1875–1942) and Katharine Cornell (1898–1974) as actors; two major designers, Lee Simonson (1888–1967) and Robert Edmond Jones (1887–1954); Philip Moeller (1880–1958), director of many later Broadway successes; and, of course, Lawrence Langner (1890–1962), who was to transform the group into the Theatre Guild after the war.

During that spring of 1915, George 'Jig' Cram Cook (1873–1924), a leonine villager from Iowa, had urged the Washington Square Group to commit themselves to native playwrights and to plays with 'true seriousness', his favourite phrase. Cook had other ideas. He wanted to form a 'Dream City, a Beloved Community', and a theatre devoid of commercialism could achieve that end. The following summer in Provincetown, Massachusetts, Cook and his disciples initiated the experiment, presenting *Suppressed Desires* by Susan Glaspell (Cook's wife) and *Constancy* by Neith Boyce in the living room of a Provincetown bungalow, and their second bill of one-act plays, Cook's *Change Your Style* and Wilbur Daniel Steele's *Contemporaries*, on the end of a wharf owned by Mary Heaton Vorse. The next summer they began with another one-act programme, including Glaspell's *Trifles*, before they discovered the playwright who was to give the Provincetown Players their place in theatrical history. When Terry Carlin introduced them to Eugene O'Neill and to his *Bound East for Cardiff*, they recognized the play's unique power and immediately produced it on the small stage (10 feet by 12 feet) of the Wharf Theatre. Susan Glaspell has described the opening performance: 'There was a fog, just as the script demanded, fog bell in the harbor. The tide was in, and it washed under us and around, spraying through holes in the floor, giving us the rhythm and flavor of the sea.' Later that summer they also produced O'Neill's *Thirst*.

When the vacationers returned to Greenwich Village in the autumn of 1916, Cook knew their activities must no longer be restricted to the Provincetown summers. Twenty-nine members of the group signed the constitution Cook had devised and eight of the more prosperous contributed 30 dollars each to rent a remodelled house at 139 MacDougal Street; the parlour would accommodate the audience and the dining room the stage. One paragraph of the constitution read: 'The impelling desire of the group is to establish a stage where playwrights of sincere, poetic, literary and dramatic purpose could see their plays in action and superintend their production without submitting to the commercial manager's interpretation of public taste.' Although they produced plays by other members of the group, O'Neill was their playwright. The first winter season they repeated *Bound East for Cardiff* and introduced *Before Breakfast*. In 1917 and in 1918, when they moved to a former stable at 133 MacDougal, they added *Long Voyage Home*, *Ile* and *Moon of the Caribbees*, in 1920 *The Emperor Jones* with settings by Cleon Throckmorton (1897–1965) and featuring Charles Gilpin (1878–1930), a Negro performer from Harlem, and later in the same season *The Hairy Ape*.

In 1922 Cook abandoned the enterprise and went to Greece. With all their success he felt he had not achieved his 'beloved community of life-givers'. Undoubtedly he was also distressed when O'Neill gave his *Beyond the Horizon* to John Williams for a Broadway production in 1920. For a year the theatre was dark. In 1923 it was reopened under the management of O'Neill, Kenneth Macgowan, a young drama critic, and Robert Edmond Jones, the designer who had created the settings for their first productions. This triumvirate continued with O'Neill plays, *All God's Chillun Got Wings* (1923), *Desire Under the Elms* (1924), and introduced Paul Green's *In Abraham's Bosom* (1926) and E. E. Cummings's *Him* (1928). Their final production, *Winter Bound* by Thomas H. Dickinson, opened in November 1929 and the theatre closed permanently on 14 December 1929. Although the stockmarket crash contributed to its demise, the Provincetown had fulfilled its mission. New playwrights with new ideas were now welcomed on Broadway.

While these Off-Broadway groups had sprung into life in the pre-war years, the commercial theatre had not been idle. Most managers and actors who sought their livelihood in the theatre regarded these enterprises, when they knew of their existence, as the playthings of misguided amateurs; certainly they offered no serious competition. Many actors came to prominence during the first two decades of the century, and producer-managers, in addition to the Shuberts, supplied the expanding theatrical market.

With 100 New York productions per year in 1900 and 150 in 1920, even a listing of the principal players becomes unmanageable. Here, as earlier, only the biggest new names can be included: Henry Miller (1860–1925) and Margaret Anglin (1876–1958) gave the emotional vigour and the honest, down-to-earth credibility that made William Vaughn Moody's *The Great Divide* (1906) a landmark production. Miller became a favoured leading man and had a Broadway theatre named after him. Anglin's high emotional power suited her later renderings of Medea, Antigone and Electra. Laurette Taylor (1884–1946) achieved immediate star status when she appeared in J. Hartley Manners's (her husband) *Peg O' My Heart* in 1912. Her wistful eyes, her sad haunting smile, and her joyous manner charmed audiences for 607 performances. Unfortunately she could not find a role to duplicate this first success. Not until 1938, after long miserable years as an alcoholic, did she recover her full powers. And in 1944, two years before her death, she gave the most inspired and luminous performances of her career as Amanda Wingfield in Tennessee Williams's *The Glass Menagerie*. Frank Bacon (1864–1922) patterned his Lightnin' Bill Jones (Lightnin' because he spoke and moved so slowly) after the stage Yankee and Jefferson's Rip. *Lightnin'*, by Winchell Smith and Bacon, opened in 1918 and ran for 1291 performances.

The Barrymores, with their illustrious grandmother Mrs Drew and with actor parents, could not escape the theatre. Although Lionel (1878–1954) never completely adjusted himself to acting (he preferred painting), his life was in the theatre and the cinema. He began with Herne in *Sag Harbor* in 1900, performed in early motion pictures for D. W. Griffith with Gladys Smith (later Mary Pickford), and achieved his first great success with Milt Shanks in Augustus Thomas's *The Copperhead* in 1918. Heywood Broun called it 'the best piece of acting I ever saw'. Although he followed this triumph with Arthur Hopkins's productions of *Macbeth* and *The Jest*, with his brother John, in the mid-twenties he abandoned Broadway for Hollywood.

Ethel (1879–1959) appeared first with her grandmother, had a season with Henry Irving at the Lyceum in London in 1893, and became an overnight star in Clyde Fitch's *Captain Jinks of the Horse Marines* in 1901. Thereafter her strikingly handsome face and figure, her dark vivacious eyes and her melodious contralto voice commanded a vast army of devotees. They loved her in Barrie's *Alice-Sit-By-The-Fire* (1905), Pinero's *Mid-Channel* (1910) and Maugham's *The Constant Wife* (1925), and a new generation discovered her charm in films and in her inspired rendering of Miss Moffat in Emlyn Williams's *The Corn is Green* (1940) – some said it was her best role. Although her last years were spent in Hollywood, her name was not forgotten on Broadway. In 1928 the Shuberts christened one of their theatres the Ethel Barrymore.

John (1882–1942) took to the theatre casually and naturally, though not seriously until Edward Sheldon, the playwright who influenced the careers of so many actors, goaded him into appearing in Galsworthy's *Justice* (1916).

This was followed by striking performances in *Peter Ibbetson* (1917), Arthur Hopkins's productions of *Redemption* (1918), *Richard III* (1920) and the triumphant *Hamlet* in 1922. One critic called it 'alive with vitality and genius – a great, beautiful rare Hamlet', and when he appeared in London (1925) James Agate found Barrymore's sweet prince 'nearer to Shakespeare's whole creation than any other I have seen'. At the peak of his career he abandoned the stage and went to Hollywood, returning briefly in 1940 for a pitiful farewell in *My Dear Children*, burlesquing himself in nightly drunken improvisations. Lionel once said that John was 'like some comet tugged by both the earth and the sun. He was a man in flight and in pursuit at the same time.'

The Barrymore successes depended greatly on the directorial taste and imagination of Arthur Hopkins (1878–1950) and on the $1000 per week Hopkins paid John Barrymore to fend off the Hollywood vultures. Hopkins's commitment to a serious theatre, a theatre of significant experience and not mere diversion, was not forecast in his early training. He operated a Nickelodeon in 1905, produced and booked vaudeville acts, and had his first Broadway success with Eleanor Gates's *Poor Little Rich Girl* (1912). In 1914 he acquired the first option on Elmer Rice's *On Trial*, brought it to the stage with the financial help of George M. Cohan and Sam Harris, and thereafter his productions were geared to an adult intelligence. As he once said, 'I want people to leave my theatre actually quarrelling about what they have seen.' Audiences never quarrelled about the quality of what they saw. Hopkins's directorial and managerial genius was apparent in Alla Nazimova's Ibsen repertory season (1918), O'Neill's '*Anna Christie*' (1921) with Pauline Lord, Anderson and Stallings's *What PriceGlory?*(1924), Philip Barry's *In a Garden* (1925) and *Paris Bound* (1927), and Sherwood's *The Petrified Forest* (1935) which he directed for Gilbert Miller. He opened a wider theatrical world for the talents of Robert Edmond Jones and established him as America's leading stage designer. He also gave a first opportunity to many future stars: Barbara Stanwyck in *Burlesque* (1927), Katharine Hepburn in *These Days* (1928) and Clark Gable in *Machinal* (1928).

Winthrop Ames (1870–1937), like Hopkins, valued artistic quality above commercial success. After the collapse of the New Theatre, Ames built the Little Theatre (299 seats) in 1912. (Next to Sardi's restaurant, it now houses late-evening TV talk shows.) Ames opened the theatre with Galsworthy's *The Pigeon* (1912) and went on to produce Schnitzler's *The Affairs of Anatol* (1912), Shaw's *The Philanderer* (1913) (both with John Barrymore), Kaufman and Connelly's *Beggar on Horseback* (1924) and Philip Barry's *White Wings*

(1926). All demonstrated Ames's taste, intelligence and independence. None was a commercial success.

Although not a producer in the usual sense, Otto Kahn (1867–1934) contributed to the artistic advance of the American theatre by sponsoring Harley Granville-Barker's productions of *Androcles and the Lion* and *The Man Who Married a Dumb Wife* (with designs by Robert Edmond Jones) at Wallack's Theatre in 1915 and those of Jacques Copeau and his Vieux Colombier company at the Garrick Theatre in 1917.

Even with these gestures towards an art theatre, Broadway was still ruled by the Shuberts and their likeminded commercialists: such men as Oliver Morosco (1875–1945) who introduced *Peg O' My Heart* and who built his own theatre in 1918; A. H. Woods (1870–1951) who began with melodramas, *Nellie, The Beautiful Cloak Model*, presented Jane Cowl in Bayard Veiller's *Within the Law*, and made a fortune with a series of 'Potash and Perlmutter' plays; and, of course, George M. Cohan (1878–1942) and Florenz Ziegfeld (1868–1932). Cohan wrote, acted in, staged and composed the music for almost fifty exuberant flag-waving musical shows, introducing such songs as 'Yankee Doodle Dandy' and 'Give My Regards to Broadway'. He was a brash, noisy performer who taught his actors to speak and sing loudly and dance vigorously. He would 'rather make one man laugh than one thousand cry', as he once said. Not until O'Neill's *Ah, Wilderness!* (1933) and Kaufman and Hart's *I'd Rather Be Right* (1937) did he appear in a play he had not written. From 1907 until the late 1920s Ziegfeld made a career of glorifying the American girl in his Ziegfeld Follies, a glamorous Americanization of the Folies Bergère.

After the Armistice in November 1918, the American theatre moved into a lush decade. In 1900, 100 productions had opened in New York; in 1920, the figure had risen to 150; and in the season of 1927–8, with almost eighty playhouses available, there were 264. On 26 December 1927, eleven plays opened on the same evening. Before the stockmarket crash in 1929 the theatre was riding high.[6] And during the decade of the 1920s the Theatre Guild emerged as the leading producing organization committed to a serious theatre.

In December 1918 Lawrence Langner met with his former Washington Square colleagues, Rollo Peters, Philip Moeller and Helen Westley, and formed the Theatre Guild; Guild because it was to be a cooperative venture employing the talents of skilled theatre artists dedicated to giving worthwhile

[6] For information on the theatre as a business, see Thomas Gale Moore, *The Economics of the American Theater* (Durham, NC, 1968), and Jack Poggi, *Theater in America: the Impact of Economic Forces, 1870–1967* (New York, 1968).

plays first-class productions. Maurice Wertheim (1886–1950), a stagestruck banker who had studied with Professor Baker, Theresa Helburn (1908–59), also a Baker student, and Lee Simonson, an energetic artist, joined them. Otto Kahn leased them the Garrick Theatre for a token rental and on 14 April 1919 they opened with Jacinto Benavente's *Bonds of Interest* directed by Philip Moeller. This was followed in May by St John Ervine's *John Ferguson*, an immediate success, and to reap its full potential the production was moved to the larger Fulton Theatre in July. On 6 August it received a further boost. Actors' Equity called a strike against the Producing Managers' Association.

Equity had been organized in 1913 to achieve a standard contract and to prevent the exploitation of actors. With little muscle at the beginning, it was not until 1917 that the producers had agreed to guarantee salaries for four weeks of rehearsal and two weeks of performance. When the contract was up for renewal in 1919, the actors demanded a limit of eight performances per week and threatened to join the American Federation of Labor. The producers' association balked and the actors struck, and until they won their battle a month later *John Ferguson* was the only play on Broadway. The Guild did not belong to the association and had come to terms with the actors.

With this stroke of fortune the Theatre Guild was firmly established, and it soon became clear that they would not rise and fall with any single offering. No theatre had ever been managed by a sextet, and though they began as amateurs, they were all knowledgeable, college-trained amateurs, distinctly a new breed on the Broadway scene. And no producers had ever matched the theatrical riches of their first five years: Shaw's *Heartbreak House* (1920), in New York before London; Molnar's *Liliom* (1921), with touching performances by Eva Le Gallienne and Joseph Schildkraut; Evreinoff's *He Who Gets Slapped* (1922), starring Margalo Gillmore and Richard Bennett; Shaw's *Back to Methuselah* (1922), performed in three parts, each in successive weeks; Kaiser's *From Morn to Midnight* (1922) and Capek's *R.U.R.* (1922), America's introduction to expressionism; *Peer Gynt* (1923), directed by Theodore Komisarjevksy and with Joseph Schildkraut as Peer; Shaw's *Saint Joan* (1923), the première performance; Elmer Rice's *The Adding Machine* (1923), an expressionistic statement about the quality of American life and hailed by some as the most original American play to date; Molnar's *The Guardsman* (1924), introducing the finely matched geniuses of Alfred Lunt and Lynn Fontanne; Sidney Howard's *They Knew What They Wanted* (1925) and the following year his *Ned McCobb's Daughter* and *The Silver Cord*, alerting the public to a new American dramatist; and John Howard Lawson's

Processional (1925), an American political jazz symphony. An incredible record.

In March 1923 the Guild announced plans for a new theatre, raised $600,000 with a bond issue, laid the cornerstone on 2 December 1924, and on 5 April 1925 opened the Guild Theatre on 52nd Street west of Broadway with Helen Hayes and Lionel Atwill in Shaw's *Caesar and Cleopatra*, one of their less distinguished productions. The new house with its unframed proscenium and its spacious lobby was ideal for their productions and for the comfort of their audience; unfortunately its 1000 seats could not provide enough revenue to retire the bonds and turn a profit. To remain solvent they had to transfer their successful productions to larger theatres, take them on the road, and solicit subscribers outside New York. Their business acumen matched their theatrical artistry. In 1926, they had 20,000 subscribers and, in 1928, 30,000; and, during the 1927–8 season, a company on the road with four productions. When the stock market collapsed in 1929, they had four plays running in New York and seven on the road.

Although they continued with exciting foreign importations, they reached their highwater mark with American drama during the 1927–8 season with Dorothy and Du Bose Heyward's *Porgy*, a massive production of O'Neill's *Marco Millions* on 9 January 1928 and his *Strange Interlude* on 23 January 1928. The board had been reluctant to attempt O'Neill's monumental five-hour play, but Langner insisted that 'It proclaims O'Neill the great dramatic genius of the age. . . . If we fail to do this great experiment, if we lack the courage and the vision, then we should forever hang our heads in shame, for we will have lost one of the greatest opportunities in our history.' Langner prevailed, and for a year and a half its six performances per week drew capacity audiences. Alexander Woollcott called it 'the *Abie's Irish Rose* of the intelligentsia'. It was an appropriate culmination to the Guild's golden years.

The Theatre Guild continued to produce notable plays and is still supplying subscribers on the road, but the attrition of age and death has altered the management, and the remarkable first decade has never been matched. The later record of the Guild must not, however, be ignored: Maxwell Anderson's *Elizabeth the Queen* (1930); O'Neill's *Mourning Becomes Electra* (1931); Giraudoux's *Amphitryon 38* (1937), adapted by S. N. Behrman and starring the Lunts; Philip Barry's *The Philadelphia Story* (1938), with Katharine Hepburn; and *The Time of Your Life* (1940). They introduced the first plays of Tennessee Williams, *Battle of Angels* (1940, tried out in Boston but closed before reaching New York), and William Inge, *Come Back, Little Sheba*

(1950). Near collapse in the early forties, the Guild was rescued from bankruptcy by the phenomenal 2212 performances of *Oklahoma!* (1943), the musical that Richard Rodgers and Oscar Hammerstein had adapted from Lynn Riggs's *Green Grow the Lilacs*.

The Guild must also be credited with spawning two other producing enterprises. Eva Le Gallienne appeared in the Guild's *Liliom* before she formed her Civic Repertory Theatre. The organizers of the Group Theatre had been Guild employees, and when they struck out on their own the Guild encouraged them with financial and artistic support.

In the autumn of 1926 Eva Le Gallienne (1899–   ), daughter of the poet Richard Le Gallienne, assembled a group of actors who were more committed to art than to financial gain, tapped some anonymous patrons to underwrite the costs, rented the old Fourteenth Street Theatre and embarked on a repertory season with an opening production of Chekhov's *Three Sisters*. Le Gallienne devoted herself to the classics – Shakespeare, Molière, Goldoni, Ibsen, Schnitzler and Chekhov, alternated regularly in true repertory fashion and with low-scale box-office prices, 50¢ to $1.50. Although the Civic Rep's productions were not always of notable quality, for six years New Yorkers saw plays they would not otherwise have seen. At the end of the 1932 season her patrons' resources, depleted by the Depression, could no longer provide the $100,000 she needed for another season. Thirteen years later Miss Le Gallienne joined with Margaret Webster (1905–   ) and Cheryl Crawford (1902–   ) to form the American Repertory Theatre. This second attempt at repertory was less successful than the first. The vast barn-like International Theatre in Columbus Circle was too big for their plays, and their ponderous opening production of Shakespeare's *Henry VIII* (1945) with Le Gallienne as Katherine of Aragon and Walter Hampden as Cardinal Wolsey did not encourage the audience to return for Ibsen's *John Gabriel Borkman*, Barrie's *What Every Woman Knows* and Shaw's *Androcles and the Lion*. By the time they mounted a delightful revival of *Alice in Wonderland*, their public had disappeared and their initial investment of $350,000 had been depleted. They closed in February 1947, with a deficit of $100,000.

The Group Theatre had a longer life and its goals were of a different order; they were committed to new plays with social significance. Three theatre fanatics with talent and tenacity, Harold Clurman (1901–   ), Lee Strasberg (1901–   ) and Cheryl Crawford, organized the Group in June 1931, and with the blessings of the Guild plus $1000 and the rights to Paul Green's *The House of Connelly* took their company to Brookfield Center, Connecticut, for a communal summer of actor training and rehearsals. When the play opened on 28 September 1931 audiences and critics immediately recognized their intense spirit and serious devotion to the play, and their remarkable ensemble playing. 'Group' clearly identified their uniqueness. Although their second season with Maxwell Anderson's poetic drama of the Mexican War, *Night Over Taos*, and John Howard Lawson's denunciation of the capitalistic system, *Success Story*, did not command as much attention, in 1933 Sidney Kingsley's *Men In White*, with its Pulitzer Prize, assured them temporary financial security.

The company continued to live together in a tenement on West 57th Street – Clurman called it 'the Group's Poorhouse' – and it was here, on three nights in December 1934, that Clifford Odets, one of their actors, wrote *Waiting For Lefty*. First performed in January at Eva Le Gallienne's former stand in 14th Street, the audience's hysterical calls for 'Strike' at the end of the play testified to its revolutionary, agit-prop power. In March *Lefty*, with Odets's *Till the Day I Die* added to fill the evening, moved to the Longacre Theatre for an extended run. A month earlier, on 19 February, Odets's first long play, *Awake and Sing!*, opened at the Belasco Theatre. The Group had found their playwright, just as the Moscow Art Theatre had with Chekhov. Many critics noted Chekhovian qualities in Odets's compassion for his Jewish family struggling with the loneliness in their lives. And most hailed the actors' portrayals as more honest, tense and human than any yet seen on Broadway, for Clurman, as director, had created a Bronx household that breathed with life. It was a triumphant year for the Group and for Odets. Their playwright continued to supply them with plays, even after he was giving more than half his time to Hollywood: *Paradise Lost* (1936), *Golden Boy* (1937; the Group's biggest commercial success), *Rocket to the Moon* (1938), *Night Music* (1940) and *Clash by Night* (1941; the final Group production).

The Group did not limit themselves to Odets. During their evangelical ten years they produced Paul Green's *Johnny Johnson* (1936), Erwin Piscator's rendering of *Clyde Griffiths* (1936; from Dreiser's *An American Tragedy*), Irwin Shaw's *The Gentle People* (1939), Robert Ardrey's *Thunder Rock* (1939) and William Saroyan's *My Heart's in the Highlands* (1939). Most of the productions were not great box-office successes, but they were never routine and hackneyed, invariably their playwrights had significant comments on the human condition, and they were always expertly performed by the Group ensemble.

The Group added Odets to the first-line roster of American playwrights; they also added a substantial list of first-rate actors who were to continue in the theatre and in motion pictures: Luther and Stella Adler (1903– ; 1904–), Morris Carnovsky (1898–), Lee J. Cobb (1911–76), J. Edward Bromberg (1904–51), John (Jules) Garfield (1913–52) and Franchot Tone (1905–68); and two directors: Elia Kazan (1909–) and Robert Lewis (1909–), to mention only those whose names are now best known. And the original triumvirate continued in the theatre: Clurman as critic and director, Strasberg as the master of the Actors' Studio, and Crawford as theatrical producer.

Much of the Group's fervent vitality derived from the social unrest of the Depression. Ironically, the Depression also brought the government into the theatre for the first time. In 1935 the Works Progress Administration created a Federal Theatre to provide employment for needy actors, and on the recommendation of his assistant, Harry Hopkins, President Roosevelt appointed Hallie Flanagan (1890–1969) its director. Roosevelt knew of her experimental theatre work at Vassar College, and she and Harry Hopkins had been fellow students at Grinnell College. In July 1935, when Hopkins and Flanagan met in Iowa City with some fifty playwrights, critics and directors, Hopkins announced that the Federal Theatre should provide the country with 'a free, adult, uncensored theatre'. Unfortunately it never became free and uncensored. With the inescapable government red tape, with 90 per cent of total costs assigned to salaries, and the obligation to draw actors from relief roles, artistic freedom was impossible. It was further inhibited by Washington's watchdogs. When Elmer Rice's New York unit was about to present *Ethiopia*, their first edition of the Living Newspaper, the State Department decided that it might offend Mussolini with its frank documentation of the Italian takeover. The production was cancelled and Elmer Rice resigned.

Later Living Newspapers such as *Triple-A Plowed Under* (1936), *Power* (1937), *One-Third of a Nation* (1938) and *Spirochette* (1939) did reach the stage, though not without painful protests from Washington. And these epic, newspaper-like documentaries exposing social and economic problems, with their multi-media vignettes laced together in cinematic fashion, introduced a new theatrical form that became the trademark of the Federal Theatre.

However, the Federal Theatre sponsored other productions less politically oriented: T. S. Eliot's *Murder in the Cathedral* (1936); Sinclair Lewis's *It Can't Happen Here* (1936), performed simultaneously in theatres across the country; Orson Welles's *Dr Faustus* (1937), on a bare stage and with bizarre lighting, and *Macbeth* (1938), set in Haiti and with an all-Negro company; and the 'swing' *Mikado* (1938), also with a Negro group.

Tension and turmoil behind the scenes perpetually dogged Hallie Flanagan and her associates. A congressional committee forced Miss Flanagan to explain how she had escaped political contamination on her trips to Russia. On one occasion a congressman wanted to know if Christopher Marlowe was a communist. Still the Federal Theatre achieved a remarkable record, provided annual employment of some 10,000 actors, writers and technicians, and with free or minimal prices for admission gave a new public invigorating theatrical experiences. In 1939 Congress refused to make the $10 million appropriation for the next season and the Federal Theatre was terminated.[7]

Just as the Theatre Guild provided apprenticeships for the Group's founders, the Federal Theatre tested the talents of Orson Welles (1915–) and John Houseman (1902–) before they struck out on their own with the Mercury Theatre. They had been associated in the voodoo *Macbeth* and in 1937 were preparing Marc Blitzstein's proletarian music-drama, *The Cradle Will Rock*, for the Federal Theatre, when, just hours before opening-night curtain, Washington decided that all productions should be halted pending a full-scale reorganization of the project. Houseman quickly rented the Venice Theatre; actors and audience moved to the new location, and, with Blitzstein playing the score on a borrowed piano and Welles supplying continuity, the actors improvised a performance on a bare stage. Having out-manœuvred the government, they leased the Comedy Theatre, renamed it the Mercury, continued the opera under their new banner, and began preparing *Julius Caesar* as their first Mercury production. With Welles as director and as Brutus and with the characters costumed as Mussolini henchmen, the play was transformed into an anti-fascist tract. The ideology may have been obscure, but not the suspense and vitality Welles injected into the production. The following season (1938–9) they presented a bawdy *The Shoemaker's Holiday*, a memorable *Heartbreak House* with Welles as Captain Shotover, and finally an anticlimactic, heavy-handed rendering of *Danton's Death*. The final curtain on the Mercury's short life coincided with that of the Federal Theatre. Orson Welles went to a new career in films. Houseman became a Hollywood producer, established the professional theatre programme at the University of California at Los Angeles, became a producer for the Shakespeare Festival at Stratford, Connecticut, an associate with the Phoenix Theatre, the first director of the theatre programme at the Julliard School, and an Oscar-winning film actor (in *The Paper Chase*).

---

[7] In the summer of 1975 a mass of Federal Theatre playscripts, set designs, posters and photographs were discovered in an airport hangar near Baltimore. This collection is now housed at the George Mason University in Washington, DC.

While the Federal and Mercury theatres were in their final seasons, another unique organization began producing plays on Broadway. In November 1937, after a meeting of the Dramatists' Guild, Elmer Rice (1892–1967), Maxwell Anderson (1888–1959) and Robert E. Sherwood (1896–1955) adjourned to the Whaler's Bar in the Midston Hotel and a few hours later had sketched their plans for the Playwrights' Company. They invited Sidney Howard (1891–1939) and S. N. Behrman (1893–1973) to join them, and with $10,000 contributed by each of the five members plus $50,000 from outside sources they could now control their plays completely from typewriter to the stage without outside interference. They would also collect the producers' as well as the playwrights' 50 per cent when their plays were sold to the motion pictures. Broadway's five leading playwrights, thus aligned, made an unbeatable combination as their first season (1938–9) demonstrated: Sherwood's *Abe Lincoln in Illinois*, directed by Rice and with Raymond Massey as Lincoln; Anderson and Weill's *Knickerbocker Holiday* with Walter Huston singing the famous September song; Rice's *American Landscape*; and Behrman's *No Time for Comedy* with Katharine Cornell and Laurence Olivier. Three of the four were hits, only Rice's play had a short run, and *Abe Lincoln in Illinois* won the Pulitzer Prize.

None of their later seasons quite matched this record, though they continued producing until Maxwell Anderson's death in 1959. The original group had a short life together. When Howard was killed in a tractor accident in the summer of 1939, Weill replaced him; two years later John Wharton (1894–   ), a theatrical lawyer, was added. During the war Sherwood turned his talents to politics and to Roosevelt; after the war Behrman resigned; and in 1953, after their success with Robert Anderson's (1917–   ) *Tea and Sympathy*, he became a member. In their twenty years they offered many notable productions: Sherwood's *There Shall Be No Night* (1940); Rice's *Dream Girl* (1945) and Rice and Weill's musical version of *Street Scene* (1947); Behrman's *The Talley Method* (1941); and Maxwell Anderson's *Joan of Lorraine* (1946), *Anne of the Thousand Days* (1948), and Anderson and Weill's *Lost in the Stars* (1949). They also produced plays by non-members: Giraudoux's *Ondine* (1954) and *Tiger at the Gates* (1955); Kingsley's *Darkness at Noon* (1951); Williams's *Cat on a Hot Tin Roof* (1955); and Jan de Hartog's *The Fourposter* (1951), their biggest box-office success.

These producing groups did not monopolize the Broadway scene in the period between the wars, and even with the radical drop in New York's annual output from 264 productions in the 1927–8 season to 72 in 1940–1, other producers and producer-directors found professional pleasure, and sometimes profit, in the theatre. Many, such as Charles Dillingham (1868–1934), Edgar Selwyn (1875–1944), George C. Tyler (1867–1946), William A. Brady (1863–1950), Oscar Serlin (1901–71), Dwight Deere Wiman (1896–1951) and Crosby Gaige (1882–1949), concentrated on end-of-the-day, escapist entertainment, though they also introduced some significant plays. Brady presented Sheldon's *The Boss* (1911) and Rice's *Street Scene* (1929), Serlin produced Lindsay and Crouse's *Life With Father* (1939), and Wiman introduced Sherwood's *Road to Rome* (1927). Brady also had the support of a charming and talented wife, Grace George (1879–1961), whom he starred in such first-class productions as Maugham's *The Circle* (1938).

Other independent producers quickly recognized that the Guild, Arthur Hopkins and Winthrop Ames had sharpened the public's theatrical discrimination. A healthy box office demanded quality productions, and Gilbert Miller, Brock Pemberton, Sam H. Harris, John Golden, Max Gordon, Jed Harris, Herman Shumlin, Guthrie McClintic, George Abbott and George S. Kaufman met the demand.

Gilbert Miller (1884–1969), son of Henry Miller and grandson of Matilda Heron, began his career with Charles Frohman, Inc., and after striking out on his own divided his activities between New York and London. For the Frohmans he produced *The Captive* (1926), a play which so offended police morality that producer and cast were arrested. Under his own banner he presented Molnar's *The Play's the Thing* (1928), Barry's *The Animal Kingdom* (1932), Van Druten's *There's Always Juliet* (1932), Sherwood's *The Petrified Forest* (1935), *The Country Wife* (1936) with Ruth Gordon as Mrs Pinchwife, Laurence Housman's *Victoria Regina* (1936) with Helen Hayes, and T. S. Eliot's *The Cocktail Party* (1950).

Brock Pemberton (1885–1950) came to New York from Emporia, Kansas, as a newspaperman, shifted to the theatre, found the best possible apprenticeship as assistant to Arthur Hopkins, and quickly made a name for himself with Sidney Howard's *Swords* (1921), Pirandello's *Six Characters in Search of an Author* (1922) and Maxwell Anderson's *White Desert* (1923). In later years he had a sharp eye for plays that could fill the theatre with laughter: Clare Boothe's *Kiss the Boys Good-Bye* (1938) and Mary Coyle Chase's *Harvey* (1944).

Sam H. Harris (1872–1941) came up from New York's Lower East Side, joined with George M. Cohan to produce Rice's *On Trial* (1914), presented Jeanne Eagels in her fiery portrayal of Sadie Thompson in *Rain* (1922), sponsored the Kaufman–Ryskind–Gershwin satire on national politics, *Of*

Thee I Sing (1931), and then became identified, almost exclusively, as the producer of George S. Kaufman's plays.

John Golden (1874–1955), an energetic, bombastic showman, wrote songs before he produced Frank Bacon's *Lightnin'* (1918), Austin Strong's *Seventh Heaven* (1922), and in the 1930s the plays of Rachel Crothers, most notably *Susan and God* (1937).

Max Gordon (1892–   ) tried vaudeville before turning producer with Owen Davis's Pulitzer Prize winner, *Icebound* (1923). Most conspicuous among his later productions were Coward's *Design for Living* (1933), Sidney Howard's *Dodsworth* (1934) from Sinclair Lewis's novel, Owen and Donald Davis's dramatization of Edith Wharton's *Ethan Frome* (1935), Kaufman and Marguand's *The Late George Apley* (1944) and Garson Kanin's *Born Yesterday* (1945).

Jed Harris (1900–   ), having known Thornton Wilder at Yale and having established his reputation with Abbott and Dunning's *Broadway* (1926), Abbott and Bridgers's *Coquette* (1927), Hecht and MacArthur's *The Front Page* (1928), and *A Doll's House* (1935) with Ruth Gordon, was given the honour of introducing Wilder to Broadway. He produced and directed *Our Town* (1938). Most noteworthy among his later productions was Miller's *The Crucible* (1953).

Herman Shumlin (1896–   ) trained with Jed Harris before testing his independence as producer and director with John Wexley's *The Last Mile* (1929) and Vicki Baum's *Grand Hotel* (1930). These early successes were followed by Wilder's *The Merchant of Yonkers* (1938; before it became *The Matchmaker* and *Hello, Dolly!*), Emlyn Williams's *The Corn is Green* (1940), Jerome Lawrence and Robert E. Lee's *Inherit the Wind* (1955) and Rolf Hochhuth's *The Deputy* (1964). Shumlin also produced and directed all of the Lillian Hellman plays from *The Children's Hour* (1934) to *The Searching Wind* (1944).

Although the names of MacClintic, Abbott and Kaufman frequently appeared on theatre programmes as producers, they were best known as directors and, in the case of Abbott and Kaufman, also as playwrights.

Guthrie McClintic (1893–1961) received his indoctrination with Winthrop Ames before demonstrating his directing skill with Maxwell Anderson's *Saturday's Children* (1927). Clearly he had a genius for getting to the heart of the play, for selecting actors who could give the right breath of life to the characters, and for moulding text, actors and setting into a tight, precise and vivid theatrical life. Critics repeatedly praised his good taste, the beauty and vigour in his staging of S. N. Behrman's *Brief Moment* (1931), Maxwell

Anderson's *Winterset* (1935), *Hamlet* (1936) with John Gielgud, Judith Anderson (the Queen) and Lillian Gish (Ophelia), and Behrman's *No Time for Comedy* (1939) with Laurence Olivier and Katharine Cornell. From 1921 his professional and private life was linked with Miss Cornell, as her director and her husband. Together they produced, she acted in, and he directed Rudolf Besier's *The Barretts of Wimpole Street* (1931), *Romeo and Juliet* (1933), *Saint Joan* (1936), *Candida* (1937) and *The Doctor's Dilemma* (1941).

George Abbott (1887–   ) studied with Baker at Harvard, acted in *The Adding Machine* and in *Processional*, became a collaborating playwright with *Broadway* and *Coquette* and thereafter shared Broadway's play-doctoring practice with Kaufman, as he also shared top-rank with Kaufman as a director of comedy or farce. A play staged by Abbott invariably raced along at a breakneck pace, crowded with laugh-provoking stage business, and with actors firing their lines with such sharpened precision that no bit of comedy could be missed. Almost every season during the thirties and forties, Abbott-engineered laughs rocked the Broadway theatres. Only a small sample can be listed: John Cecil Holm and Abbott's *Three Men on a Horse* (1934), the Spewacks' *Boy Meets Girl* (1935), Rodgers and Hart's *Boys from Syracuse* (1938) and *Pal Joey* (1948), and Frank Loesser's *Where's Charley?* (1948).

Like Abbott, George S. Kaufman (1889–1961) hardly missed a season as playwright or director, or as both, and, though his lasting reputation rests with the long list of comedies he wrote in collaboration with Marc Connelly, Moss Hart and others, in his time he was equally known as an expert director. He devised the stage life for *The Front Page* (1928), Steinbeck's *Of Mice and Men* (1937), Burrows, Swerling and Loesser's *Guys and Dolls* (1950), as well as for his own *You Can't Take It With You* (1936) and *The Man Who Came to Dinner* (1939). Naturally self-disciplined and well organized, he easily managed a dual career, and for a brief period even a triple career while he served as drama critic on the *New York Times*. He also had a sharp ear for shaping a comedy line, as critic, playwright and director. As a critic, he once wrote, 'I saw the show under unfortunate circumstances: the curtain was up.' He thought the performance of a new actor, Guido Nadzo, was 'nadzo guido'. Watching a play he had directed from the back of the house, he telegraphed to an actor backstage: 'I'm out front; wish you were here.'

None of these producers and directors could have flourished without the rich supply of talented performers who emerged; and, with more energy and more dollars earmarked for personal promotion, star names blazed more brilliantly, in brighter lights, in bigger and blacker type. Many names must be omitted; none will receive the billing they once had. However, on a composite broadside the names of Lunt, Fontanne, Hayes and Cornell clearly demand the top position.

Alfred Lunt (1893–) and Lynn Fontanne (1887?–), husband and wife, blended their remarkable talents into scintillating duets, sometimes subtly sophisticated, sparkling and festive, sometimes serious, even frightening, but always with their matched geniuses perfectly meshed. Lunt came from Genesee Depot, Wisconsin, where they still make their home, received his first stage training with the Castle Square Theatre in Boston in 1912, toured with Margaret Anglin in 1913, made his Broadway début in *Romance and Arabella* with Laura Hope Crews in 1917, and established himself as a first-rank comedian in Booth Tarkington's *Clarence* (1919). Miss Fontanne made her début with Ellen Terry in London in 1905, came to New York in 1910, played Anna in O'Neill's *Chris Christopherson* (later '*Anna Christie*') in Atlantic City in 1919 (it never reached New York), and found her place as a charming comedienne in Kaufman and Connelly's *Dulcy* (1921). After their marriage in 1922, they performed separately only in 1926, she in *Pygmalion* and he in Werfel's *Juarez and Maximilian*, and in 1928 when she created the role of Nina in *Strange Interlude* and he Marco in *Marco Millions*. And, happily for the American theatre, they toured the country with most of their superb duets: Molnar's *The Guardsman* (1924), Anderson's *Elizabeth the Queen* (1930), Sherwood's *Reunion in Vienna* (1931), Coward's *Design for Living* (1933) with Coward, *The Taming of the Shrew* (1935), Sherwood's *Idiot's Delight* (1936), Behrman's *Amphitryon 38* (1937), *The Seagull* (1938), Sherwood's *There Shall Be No Night* (1940), Behrman's *O Mistress Mine* (1949) and Dürrenmatt's *The Visit* (1958).

Helen Hayes (1900–), since the retirement of Katharine Cornell, holds sole right to the title 'First Lady' of the American theatre. She has literally spent her entire life in the theatre, having begun at the age of five in a school production of *A Midsummer Night's Dream*. In 1967 she appeared in the Phoenix Theatre's *The Show Off*, in 1970 in their *Harvey*, and in 1971 in the film *Airport*. Her professional career began in 1909 when she played in Victor Herbert's operetta *Old Dutch*. She then toured with *Pollyanna*, in 1919 appeared with William Gillette in Barrie's *Dear Brutus* and in the same season joined Alfred Lunt in *Clarence*. In 1922 she played in Connelly's *To the Ladies* and in 1925 was selected to do Cleopatra, a role unsuited to her, at the opening of the Theatre Guild's new house. In the next two seasons she clinched her hold on star billing with Barrie's *What Every Woman Knows* and Abbott's *Coquette*. One night in the spring of 1928 a *Coquette* performance was cancelled to allow her to attend the opening of Hecht and MacArthur's *The Front Page*. She and MacArthur were married the following August and thereafter her friends thought she seemed most at home in their house in Nyack, New York, but she never deserted the theatre. Plain, small, modest and unassuming off the stage, when the curtain was up and the lights glowing she gloried in the magic world and her audiences became charmed by the irresistible warmth of her portraits. She was at her best in her vivid and enchanting portraits of Mary in Anderson's *Mary of Scotland* (1933), of Harriet Beecher Stowe in Ryerson and Clements's *Harriet* (1943), of Victoria, her masterpiece, in Housman's *Victoria Regina* (1935). Her later plays, such as Joshua Logan's *The Wisteria Trees* (1950) and O'Neill's *A Touch of the Poet* (1958), have not given her comparable opportunities. She has never taken her eminence as 'First Lady' too seriously. She once said, 'I don't want always to be the whole cheese. I'm no high priestess. I'm not in the theatre merely to make a living, or just to have long runs. I'm also in it for fun.'

Katharine Cornell (1898–1974), daughter of a Buffalo, New York, doctor turned theatre manager, appeared first with the Washington Square Players in 1917 playing an old Japanese woman in *Bushido*, joined Jessie Bonstelle's stock company in Detroit, toured the country with William A. Brady's production of *The Man Who Came Back*, went to London with *Little Women* in 1920, and jumped into the New York limelight in Clemence Dane's *A Bill of Divorcement* in 1921. Alexander Woollcott shouted 'Bravo' in his *New York Times* column; Heywood Broun proclaimed her the 'American Duse'; and a young director, Guthrie McClintic, married her. From then on she was a star, soon a 'First Lady', and from 1931 she and McClintic produced and he directed most of her plays. Her bewitching charm, though clearly evident in *Candida* (1924) – a role she was to repeat in 1937, 1942 and 1946 – as the decadent lost-lady Iris March in Michael Arlen's *The Green Hat* (1925) and in Maugham's *The Letter* (1927), was most apparent in her triumphant portrayal of Elizabeth Barrett in Rudolf Besier's *The Barretts of Wimpole Street* (1931). And her radiant personality, her deep dark eyes always seeming to hide mysterious inner passion and understanding, fascinated audiences throughout the country when she took the Barrett–Browning romance on the road. In Seattle, when the scenery did not arrive on schedule and the curtain did not go up until midnight, the audience waited patiently. Off the stage, like Miss Hayes, her beauty might not be perceived; on stage her high cheekbones, her expressive mouth, her lithe graceful figure, her warm melodious voice created an incandescent and commanding presence. The tenderness and dignity of her Elizabeth Barrett may never have been matched, but her beauty, her passion, her grace, the aura of human decency that seemed always at the core of her portrayals, is well remembered by those who saw her in André Obey's *Lucrece* (1932), Sidney Howard's *Alien Corn* (1933), *Romeo and Juliet* (1935), *Saint Joan* (1936), Anderson's *The Wingless Victory* (1936), Behrman's *No Time for Comedy* (1939) with Laurence Olivier, *The Doctor's Dilemma* (1941), *The Three Sisters* (1942), Anouilh's *Antigone* (1946), *Antony and Cleopatra* (1948), Maugham's *The Constant Wife* (1951) and Jerome Kilty's *Dear Liar* (1960).

Dropping lower on an all-star broadside for the period between the wars, the billing becomes dangerous. Few actors will approve their places; devotees who have followed their favourites in these years are invited to add and delete, as they wish.

Another husband-and-wife team, Frederic March (1897–1975) and Florence Eldridge (1901–), though not so inseparably bound in duet performances as the Lunts, created memorable portraits together in Wilder's *The Skin of Our Teeth* (1942), Miller's adaptation of *An Enemy of the People* (1950), Hellman's *The Autumn Garden* (1951) and in O'Neill's *Long Day's Journey into Night* (1956). March has, of course, also achieved a distinguished career in the cinema.

Walter Hampden (1879–1956) played with the Bensons in England, with Mrs Fiske in New York, and reached the height of his career from 1925 to 1929 when he managed his own theatre and appeared in a Shakespearian repertoire of *Macbeth*, *The Merchant of Venice*, *Hamlet* and *King Henry V*, in Kennedy's *The Servant in the House*, in *An Enemy of the People*, in *Richelieu*, and in his most notable role, Cyrano. No other actor of his time matched him in speaking verse. In 1946 he joined the shortlived American Repertory Theatre and in 1953 appeared in Miller's *The Crucible*.

Raymond Massey (1896–), though Canadian-born, achieved his greatest triumph with his faithful and moving portrait of Abraham Lincoln in Sherwood's play. Earlier he had appeared in *Ethan Frome* (1936), and later with Cornell in *Candida* (1942) and in Archibald MacLeish's *J.B.* (1958).

Maurice Evans (1901–) was brought from London to play Romeo to Cornell's Juliet in 1936 and thereafter became Shakespeare's chief exponent with his vigorous and clearly spoken renderings of *Richard II* (1937), a full-length *Hamlet* (1938), *Macbeth* (1941) and the shortened 'GI *Hamlet*' performed for soldiers in the Hawaiian command. He also specialized in Shaw: *Saint Joan* (1936) with Cornell, *Man and Superman* (1947) and *The Devil's Disciple* (1950).

The actresses – and I have chosen more of them – are listed roughly in the order of their first major roles; no judgement about relative importance is intended.

Pauline Lord (1890–1950) created the principal roles in O'Neill's '*Anna Christie*' (1921), Howard's *They Knew What They Wanted* (1925) and his *Late Christopher Bean* (1932), and in Owen Davis's *Ethan Frome* (1936). She followed Lynn Fontanne as Nina in *Strange Interlude* and played it throughout the country. Her characters invariably seemed to possess a passionate inner life that was shielded by a tremulous mystical quality.

Jane Cowl (1884–1950) began as a Belasco protégée and achieved her first fame with Juliet in 1923, though tearful audiences had already recognized her sentimental powers in *Smilin' Through* (1919). Her grace, charm and commanding presence supported Coward's *Easy Virtue* (1925), Sherwood's *Road to Rome* (1927), Stephen Phillips's *Paolo and Francesca* (1929) and Behrman's *Rain from Heaven* (1934).

Gertrude Lawrence (1899–1952) first displayed her vivacity and virtuosity when she came from London to New York in *André Charlot's Revue* (1924). Her extraordinary exuberance and joy animated every performance as she sang, danced and acted her way through Coward's *Private Lives* (1931) and *Tonight at 8.30* (1936), Rachel Crothers's *Susan and God* (1937), the Hart–Weill–Gershwin *Lady in the Dark* (1941) and Rodgers and Hammerstein's *The King and I* (1951).

Alice Brady (1892–1939), daughter of the producer William A. Brady, had a long, healthy career beginning with Robert Mantell's Shakespeare company in 1909 and reaching its high point with the tragic splendour of her Lavinia in O'Neill's *Mourning Becomes Electra* (1931).

Ina Claire (1895–   ) was a sparkling comedienne who began in vaudeville, was tutored by Belasco, and appeared in an early Ziegfeld Follies before finding her proper niche in Lonsdale's *The Last Of Mrs Cheyney* (1925), and in Behrman's comedies, *Biography* (1932) and *End of Summer* (1936).

Josephine Hull (1886–1957) had her early training in Jessie Bonstelle's Detroit stock company in 1922, first appeared in New York in Kelly's *Craig's Wife* (1925), and then in Kaufman and Hart's *You Can't Take It with You* (1936), Joseph Kesselring's *Arsenic and Old Lace* (1941), and Kaufman and Howard Teichman's *Solid Gold Cadillac* (1953). Miss Hull was not a stage beauty; she was dumpy, delightful and lovable.

Ruth Gordon (1896–   ) got her start in 1915 with Maude Adams in *Peter Pan* and studied at the American Academy of Dramatic Art until her teachers advised her that she had no talent. She was too stagestruck, too ferociously persistent to accept their judgement. She proved them wrong in Barry's *Hotel Universe* (1930), John Wexley's *They Shall Not Die* (1934), *Ethan Frome* (1936), Cornell's *Three Sisters* (1942), and with her madcap, ebullient portrayal of Dolly Levi in Wilder's *The Matchmaker* (1955).

Judith Anderson (1898–   ) came to New York from Australia in 1918 and appeared in Barrie's *Dear Brutus* (1920) before beginning her reign as queen of tragedy with her fierce and terrifying portraits: Gertrude to Gielgud's Hamlet (1936), Lady Macbeth with Maurice Evans in 1941, and in Robinson Jeffers's version of *Medea* (1949). She later played in Cornell's *Three Sisters* (1942), and in 1970 made an unsuccessful venture into transvestism as Hamlet.

Tallulah Bankhead (1903–68), after an early try at New York in Rachel Crothers's *Nice People* (1921), shifted to London's West End for her early training. In 1939 she found the Broadway role that would properly display her beauty, her brashness and her throaty baritone voice, Regina in Hellman's *The Little Foxes*. Though she played many parts and always with boisterous vigour, only Regina and Sabina in Wilder's *The Skin of Our Teeth* gave full range to her remarkable talents.

In the quarter of a century since the Second World War Broadway has lost much of its command over the American theatre. First nights have decreased from seventy in 1948–9 to fifty-six in 1970–1. Yet, even with exorbitant production costs and ticket prices within range only for the affluent, a few commercial managers have flourished, particularly with musicals, though their names are not as well known by the public as those of the directors who have maintained artistic control over their productions.

Theatrical experimentation and innovation has shifted to Off-Broadway and Off-off-Broadway under the guidance of dedicated, zealous and often fanatic theatrical gurus. Regional professional theatres have sprung up in cities across the country, some augmenting and others replacing the local community theatres, and many have had substantial financial encouragement from the Ford Foundation. In the season of 1970–1 three plays that were later to reach Broadway were premièred in regional theatres: *The Trial of the Catonsville Nine* by Father Daniel Berrigan at the Mark Taper Forum in Los Angeles; *The Effect of Gamma Rays on Man in the Moon Marigolds* by Paul Zindel at the Alley Theatre in Houston; and *The Great White Hope* by Howard Sackler at Washington's Arena Stage.

Most universities and colleges offer extensive courses in drama and theatre and provide their publics with a full season of plays, often performed by professional, or semi-professional, companies. During the 1970–1 season *The Night Thoreau Spent in Jail* by Lawrence and Lee had 111 productions in regional and university theatres throughout the country; it was not seen in New York.

Broadway's fabulous invalid may be ailing, fewer serious plays survive its financial rigours, yet still the market remains healthy for a limited number of 'hits'. David Merrick has been and continues to be the most active producer with such importations as Osborne's *Look Back in Anger* (1957) and *Luther* (1963), Weiss's *Marat-Sade* (1965) and Stoppard's *Rosencrantz and Guildenstern Are Dead* (1967), and such native products as *The Matchmaker* (1955) and its incredibly successful musical version, *Hello, Dolly!* (1964). Roger L. Stevens (1910–) has also drawn on London for Pinter's *The Caretaker* (1961) and Bolt's *A Man for All Seasons* (1961). And, before he began devoting his administrative genius to the John F. Kennedy Center in Washington, he produced Laurents's *A Clearing in the Woods* (1957), Jean Kerr's *Mary, Mary* (1961) and Williams's *The Milk Train Doesn't Stop Here Anymore* (1963).

Leland Hayward (1902–71) and Joshua Logan (1908–) joined forces to present such notable successes as Heggen and Logan's *Mister Roberts* (1948) and Rodgers and Hammerstein's *South Pacific* (1949). Hayward was also co-producer with Rodgers and Hammerstein of their *The Sound of Music* (1959), and Logan directed his own *The Wisteria Tree* (1950), an adaptation of *The Cherry Orchard*, and Inge's *Picnic* (1953). Harold Prince (1928–) was master of the musical: *Fiorello* (1959), *Cabaret* (1966) and the long-running *Fiddler on the Roof* (1964). Arnold Saint-Subber (1916–) has held a monopoly on Neil Simon's sure-fire box-office successes – *Barefoot in the Park* (1963), *Plaza Suite* (1968) – and Kermit Bloomgarden (1904–76) replaced Shumlin as Hellman's producer beginning with *Another Part of the Forest* (1946). He also presented Miller's *Death of a Salesman* (1949) and Goodrich and Hackett's *Diary of Anne Frank* (1955).

Alfred De Liagre, Jr (1904–), and Michael Myerberg (1906–), though less prolific, brought important plays to Broadway. De Liagre produced Giraudoux's *Madwoman of Chaillot* (1948) and MacLeish's *J.B.* (1958); Myerberg, Wilder's *The Skin of Our Teeth* (1942) and Beckett's *Waiting for Godot* (1956).

Jean Dalrymple (1910–) occupies a unique position as a theatrical producer. Since 1944 when the Mecca Temple on 55th Street reverted to the city for unpaid taxes and Mayor La Guardia converted it to the City Center for the performing arts, she has made the best plays and musicals from

Broadway's recent past available at reasonable prices and often with their original performers.

Among the many directors who have held the artistic reins on Broadway productions during the past twenty-five years, three names stand out: Elia Kazan (1909–   ), Harold Clurman (1901–   ) and Alan Schneider (1917–   ). Each in his way has a genius for finding the heart of a play, for discovering the nerve centres of characters and actors and weaving them into a unique stage life, for meticulously theatricalizing the playwright's text, giving it a bold and dynamic new existence. With their sensitivity, their brilliant command of actors, their scrupulous respect for the author's world and their refined perception of the theatre's magic, they have given the substance of life to many important plays.

As already noted, Clurman began directing with the Group Theatre. Kazan acted with the Group, and Schneider's roots trace back to the Group via the Actors' Studio. Kazan and Clurman joined together as producers, with Kazan as director, of Arthur Miller's first Broadway success, *All My Sons* (1947).

High on the list among Clurman-directed plays after his years with the Group are Carson McCullers's *The Member of the Wedding* (1950), Lillian Hellman's *The Autumn Garden* (1951), Inge's *Bus Stop* (1955) and Miller's *Incident at Vichy* (1965). In recent years Clurman has devoted himself to theatre criticism for *The Nation*, to lecturing, teaching and writing (*On Directing*, 1972; *All People Are Famous: Instead of an Autobiography*, 1974).

Kazan's bold personal brand appeared most conspicuously on the Williams plays – *A Streetcar Named Desire* (1947), *Camino Real* (1953), *Cat on a Hot Tin Roof* (1955) – and on Miller's *Death of a Salesman* (1949) and *After the Fall* (1963), though it was also on Wilder's *The Skin of Our Teeth* (1942), Inge's *Dark at the Top of the Stairs* (1957) and MacLeish's *J.B.* (1958).[8]

Schneider has been the chief interpreter of Edward Albee and Samuel Beckett: Albee's *The American Dream* (1961), *Who's Afraid of Virginia Woolf?* (1962), *Tiny Alice* (1964), *A Delicate Balance* (1966), and Beckett's *Waiting for Godot* (1956), *Endgame* (1958) and *Happy Days* (1961). He also directed McCullers's *Ballad of the Sad Café* (1963) and Pinter's *The Birthday Party* (1967). In 1976 Schneider succeeded John Houseman as director of theatre training at the Julliard School.

The names of many actors have lighted the marquees of New York theatres since the 1940s. Only those who shone brightest and the plays in which their

---

[8] Kazan has now made a new career as a novelist.

talents were most conspicuous are included here, and many of them achieved greater fame in films.

No one who has followed the theatre in recent years will forget the performances of Katharine Hepburn (1909–) in Barry's *The Philadelphia Story* (1939), as Rosalind at the Shakespeare Festival in Stratford, Connecticut, in Shaw's *The Millionairess* (1952), and her recent excursion into the musical theatre, *Coco* (1969); Mildred Natwick (1908–) in Coward's *Blithe Spirit* (1941), with Cornell in *Candida* (1942), and in Anouilh's *Waltz of the Toreadors* (1957); Mildred Dunnock in Hellman's *Another Part of the Forest* (1946), *Death of a Salesman* (1948) and *Cat on a Hot Tin Roof* (1955).

Also vividly remembered: Julie Harris (1925–) in *The Member of the Wedding* (1950), Van Druten's *I am a Camera* (1951) and the Anouilh–Hellman *The Lark* (1955); Shirley Booth (1909–) in Inge's *Come Back Little Sheba* (1950) and Arthur Laurents's *Time of the Cuckoo* (1953); Maureen Stapleton (1925–) in Williams's *The Rose Tattoo* (1951), Hellman's *Toys in the Attic* (1960) and the revival of Odets's *The Country Girl* (1972); Uta Hagen (1919–) in *Saint Joan* (1951) and *Who's Afraid of Virginia Woolf?* (1962); Geraldine Page (1924–) in Williams's Off-Broadway *Summer and Smoke* (1952) and his *Sweet Bird of Youth* (1959) on Broadway; and Anne Bancroft (1931–) in William Gibson's *The Miracle Worker* (1959) and in the revival of Hellman's *The Little Foxes* (1967) at Lincoln Center.

Plays invariably require more men than women to complete their casts, but few men have matched the star brightness of the ladies. Some male performers do stand out: José Ferrer (1912–) as Iago to Paul Robeson's Othello and Uta Hagen's Desdemona in 1943, and as Cyrano (1946); Marlon Brando (1924–) with his sullen, muttering Stanley Kowalski in *A Streetcar Named Desire* (1947); Lee J. Cobb (1911–76) as the weary Willy Loman in *Death of a Salesman* (1949); and Jason Robards (1922–) in the Off-Broadway revival of O'Neill's *The Iceman Cometh* (1955), in his *Long Day's Journey into Night* (1956), in *Toys in the Attic* (1960), in Miller's *After the Fall* (1963) and most recently in *A Moon for the Misbegotten* (1973).

Broadway producers, directors and actors have committed their professional expertise to many worthy plays in recent years, but for the most part theatrical innovation and experimentation has been left to the Off-Broadway and Off-off-Broadway messiahs. During the 1950s, and particularly in the 1960s, stage fever reached near-epidemic proportions in Greenwich Village, the East Village, the Lower East Side, even on the Upper East Side, and on the fringes of Broadway. And, as always, length of life for these ventures has depended on the vision, skill and vigour of their leaders.

T. Edward Hambleton (1911–   ) in partnership with Norris Houghton (1909–   ) and with John Houseman as occasional artistic adviser has guided the Phoenix Theatre (Theatre, Inc.) through its several incarnations, and Hambleton's persistence and generosity has kept the Phoenix alive. Not wildly experimental nor committed to avant-garde plays, the Phoenix, not unlike the Theatre Guild, prided itself on quality productions of quality plays. They began in 1953 in the old Jewish Folks Theatre on 2nd Avenue and 12th Street with Sidney Howard's last play *Madam Will You Walk?*; in the season of 1954–5 presented Tyrone Guthrie's productions of Schiller's *Mary Stuart* and Capek's *The Makropoulos Secret*; in 1958 T. S. Eliot's *The Family Reunion*; and in 1959 O'Neill's *Great God Brown*. In 1961 they shifted to a small theatre on East 74th Street where they had their first financial success with Arthur Kopit's *Oh Dad, Poor Dad, Mother's Hung You in the Closet and I'm Feeling So Sad*. In 1964 they brought Ellis Rabb's Association of Producing Artists (APA) under their banner with Pirandello's *Right You Are* (1964), *Man and Superman* (1964) and *You Can't Take It With You* (1965). The Kaufman and Hart play was transferred to the Lyceum Theatre in 1966, and in their new location on Broadway was followed by *The Wild Duck* (1967), Kelly's *The Show Off* (1968) with Helen Hayes, Eliot's *The Cocktail Party* (1968) and Coward's *Private Lives* (1969). The APA disbanded in 1969, but the Phoenix has continued: with *The School for Wives* (1971), in a new translation by Richard Wilbur, and with Houseman's production of Father Daniel Berrigan's *The Trial of the Catonsville Nine* (1971).

Julian Beck (1925–   ) and Judith Malina's (1926–   ) Living Theatre has created more commotion and confusion than any other group, particularly in 1968 after the Becks returned from their barnstorming tour of Europe with *Frankenstein, Mysteries and Small Pieces*, and *Paradise Now* at the Brooklyn Academy of Music, the shock waves even reaching the pages of *Life* magazine. Their eccentric inclinations, if not their political rebellion, were apparent in the Becks' first productions – Picasso's *Desire*, Gertrude Stein's *Ladies' Voices* and Eliot's *Sweeney Agonistes* – at the Cherry Lane Theatre in 1952. With Jack Gelber's *The Connection* (1959), Kenneth Brown's *The Brig* (1963), and with the Becks' imprisonment in 1963 for refusal to pay taxes, they proclaimed their commitment to social justice. Since 1965, and in their 1971 adventure to South America, the Living Theatre tribe has functioned as an anarchistic commune, collectively devising intense theatrical rituals in which, according to Beck, 'the spectator approaches something of a vision of self-understanding, going past the conscious to the unconscious, to an understanding of the nature of all things'.

Joseph Chaikin (1935–   ) deserted the Living Theatre to found the Open Theatre in 1963, an actors' ensemble devoted to improvisational exploration of new visceral relationships between actors and between actor and audience. 'We make up symbols and metaphors of things we care about and we perform them,' according to Chaikin. Jean-Claude van Itallie's *America Hurrah* (1966), his *The Serpent* (1968), Megen Terry's *Viet Rock* (1966) and their own *Terminal* (1970) have evolved from their collective workshop.

Joseph Papp (1921–   ) could have been a leading Broadway entrepreneur. Instead he has committed his inexhaustible energy, his vision and his theatrical taste to Shakespeare in Central Park, to his Public Theatre, four theatres under one roof, in the former Astor Library on Lafayette Street just south of Astor Place, and to the Vivian Beaumont Theatre in Lincoln Center, which in 1973 he added to his theatrical empire. He began his free Shakespeare productions in 1956 in an amphitheatre near the East River. In the summer of 1957 the city provided him with a permanent home in the outdoor Delacorte Theatre in Central Park, where he has presented three Shakespeare plays every summer. In 1964 he augmented his enterprise with a Mobile Theatre in which cut-down productions could be taken to street audiences throughout the five boroughs, and in 1966 added the Public Theatre to give him a year-round operation. Here he has done the original production of *Hair* (1967), Charles Gordone's Pulitzer-Prize-winning *No Place to Be Somebody* (1969) and David Rabe's *Sticks and Bones* (1971). This production and a musical version of *Two Gentlemen of Verona* from the summer of 1971 have had an extended life in Broadway theatres during the 1971–2 season. With his persuasive finesse Papp has pieced together his $2 million annual budget from city, state and federal funds, from private benefactors and from foundation grants. Always possessed of a new theatrical vision, he has recently announced plans for an American National Theatre Service to be funded by government and from private sources to bring significant plays to a new American public throughout the country.

Theodore Mann (1924–   ) and José Quintero (1924–   ) at their Circle-in-the-Square, first located in Sheridan Square (1951) and then in the old Amato Opera Theatre on Bleecker Street (1959), gave new life to plays that Broadway had botched – *Summer and Smoke* (1952) and *The Iceman Cometh* (1955) – and introduced such new players as Jason Robards, Geraldine Page and

George C. Scott (1927–   ). They also produced Behan's *The Quare Fellow* (1958), Dylan Thomas's *Under Milk Wood* (1961), Wilder's *Plays for Bleeker Street* (1962) and *The Trojan Women* (1963).

Ellen Stewart, a beautiful, intense Negro lady, matches Papp in drive and energy, in total commitment to the theatre, though her entrepreneurial inclinations are not so grandiose. Preferring the intimate, small-scale environment of her Off-off-Broadway Café La Mama (1962), successor to Joe Cino's Caffee Cino (1958), she mothers playwrights and plays midwife for their first plays. In the past ten years well over a hundred playwrights, among them Jean-Claude van Itallie, Sam Shepard, Rochelle Owens and Paul Foster, have enjoyed her maternal tenderness. Many plays may have been unworthy of her attention, often her actors either overshadowed the play or were inadequate for its demands, and only one of her directors, Tom O'Horgan, achieved consistent ensemble performances; still Miss Stewart has been steadfast to her purpose: 'I started La Mama so there would be a place where a playwright could write, see and learn. . . . After all the ovum is a tiny egg and if a big hole is punched into it [by the critics] the lifeblood is drained away and the organism dies; in the same way the young artist can die.' Although the La Mama Experimental Theatre Club, as it is now called, continues to offer new plays, almost invariably demonstrating a healthy contempt for conventional theatre practice, La Mama has become known throughout the world with the tours of the La Mama Repertory Troupe and with the outlying La Mama missions Miss Stewart has established in Bogota, Columbia, and in Haiti.

Wynn Handman's (1922–   ) American Place Theatre has also concentrated on new playwrights, if more selectively and principally with established novelists and poets who wished to try the theatre. In the St Clement's Church on West 46th Street, a stone's throw from Broadway, they gave productions to Robert Lowell's *The Old Glory* (1964), William Alfred's *Hogan's Goat* (1965), and to plays by May Swenson, Bruce Jay Friedman, Paul Goodman and Joyce Carol Oates. Handman's object, as he has stated it, is 'to help a writer develop his idea to the fullest, to help him make his work effective as a theatre piece, and without the pressures of a Broadway opening night hanging over him.' Critics do not attend the opening night, and, with admission entirely by subscription, critics and the box office do not determine the success of a play. In 1971 the American Place moved into new quarters at the base of the J. P. Stevens Building at 46th and the Avenue of the Americas where they will pay a nominal rental of $5 per year. The rental subsidy comes indirectly from the city, the commercial builder having been allowed certain construction concessions in exchange for providing a theatre facility.

In the late sixties more than a hundred Off-Broadway and Off-off-Broadway groups experimented with new plays, new theatrical eccentricities and new audiences. Conspicuous among them were Al Carmines's Judson Poets' Theatre at the Judson Memorial Church, Ralph Cook's Theatre Genesis at St Mark's Church-in-the-Bouwerie, Robert Hooks and Douglas Turner Ward's Negro Ensemble at St Mark's Playhouse, Robert Macbeth and Ed Bullins's New Lafayette Theatre in Harlem, Richard Schechner's Performance Group, and Robert Kalfin's Chelsea Theatre Center at the Brooklyn Academy of Music.

The Lincoln Center Repertory Theatre, unlike the other Off-Broadway theatres, did not evolve as the artistic brainchild of a theatrical genius. In December 1956 John D. Rockefeller III, the first president of the Lincoln Center for the Performing Arts, announced that Mrs Vivian Beaumont Allen had donated $3 million to establish a repertory company. The financial wizards who guided the enterprise operated slowly. Six years later they selected Robert Whitehead, a Broadway producer frequently associated with Roger L. Stevens, and Elia Kazan as artistic directors, and with the new theatre structure in Lincoln Center still to be built, gave the company a temporary home in a steel tent erected just east of Washington Square. They opened with Miller's *After the Fall*, directed by Kazan, on 23 January 1964, their only solid success of the season. Among the other five plays, only Miller's *Incident at Vichy* directed by Clurman and *Tartuffe* directed by William Ball were favourably regarded.

In the summer of 1964 Kazan resigned, in December the Board announced a shift in management, and in March 1965 Herbert Blau (1926-   ) and Jules Irving (1925–   ) from the Actors' Workshop in San Francisco were selected as artistic directors of the Vivian Beaumont Theatre. Their first season in the elegant new theatre, beginning on 21 October 1965 with *Danton's Death* directed by Blau, was no better than the Washington Square year. Only Irving's production of The *Caucasian Chalk Circle* seemed worthy of the promise and money invested in the enterprise, and the seasons that followed have boasted only limited artistic achievements: *Galileo* (1967), *The Little Foxes* (1967) and Kipphardt's *In the Matter of J. Robert Oppenheimer* (1969). After Blau's resignation in 1967, Irving struggled alone to give the Vivian Beaumont Theatre its proper identity until he turned the management over to Papp in 1973.

In recent years New York's theatrical monopoly has been disintegrating.

Rich theatre experiences are now available throughout the country, in the universities, the community theatres and particularly in the regional professional theatres. Three of these have been conspicuously successful: the Alley Theatre in Houston, the Arena Stage in Washington and the Tyrone Guthrie in Minneapolis.

Nina Vance (1915–   ) worked with Margo Jones's theatre in Dallas before opening the Alley in 1947 in a rented dance studio that could accommodate an audience of eighty-seven. In 1949 she acquired an old fan factory where her stage arena could be surrounded by 215 spectators, and in 1954 she began replacing her amateurs with professional actors. Her reputation for quality productions, most of them directed by her, became widely known in Houston and around the country, and in 1962 she was awarded a Ford Foundation grant of $2.4 million, to be matched by local contributions of another million, for a new building to include two theatres. This architecturally exciting and lavishly equipped new Alley Theatre in downtown Houston opened in 1968 with a production of *Galileo*.

Zelda Fichandler (1924–   ) has given the nation's capital provocative theatre. In 1950 she opened her first Arena Stage in an abandoned cinema with accommodation for 247; in 1956 moved to the 'Old Vat', a former brewery, increasing her audience capacity to 500; and in 1961 to her present location in south-east Washington. Her intimate and superbly functional new Arena Stage seating 833 was also built with the help of the Ford Foundation. In 1970, with an expanding subscription audience, she added the Kreeger Theatre, adjacent to the main building, where she could experiment with new plays in a more intimate environment. Not only has she applied her enormous energy and artistic acumen to Shakespeare, Pirandello, Molière, Brecht and O'Neill, but she has introduced such new plays as Howard Sackler's *The Great White Hope* (1967) and Arthur Kopit's *Indians* (1967). And for her thousands of subscribers she has clearly demonstrated that the theatre can, in her own words, 'galvanize, hypnotize, inspire, cajole and compel an audience into the recognition that, for exhilaration and delight, the experience of the theatre is second only to that of living.'

Tyrone Guthrie (1900–71) was already recognized as the English-speaking theatre's outstanding director at London's Old Vic, at Stratford in Canada, and in New York, before he came to Minneapolis to supervise the construction of the Tyrone Guthrie Theatre and to assemble his first Minnesota Theatre Company. Oliver Rea and Peter Zeisler joined Guthrie in managing the theatre, the first to be built with an audience wrapped around a thrust stage, and in May 1963 a fanfare of trumpets announced the first performance of Guthrie's *Hamlet* with George Grizzard. This was followed in a rotating repertory by *The Miser*, *The Three Sisters* and *Death of a Salesman*. Guthrie remained in Minneapolis for two seasons, Douglas Campbell succeeded him as artistic director, later Peter Zeisler assumed the management, and now Michael Langham (1919–   ) controls the enterprise and continues to give Minneapolis exciting productions of significant plays from our dramatic heritage.

Since 1955 the American theatre has also had its own summer Shakespeare centre at the American Shakespeare Festival theatre and Academy at Stratford, Connecticut. Conceived by Lawrence Langner of the Theatre Guild, it has been managed by Joseph Verner Reed, John Houseman, Jack Landau and others and has featured such actors as Katharine Hepburn and Morris Carnovsky.

The final quarter of the twentieth century appears bright for the American theatre. Decentralization has become a fact of theatre life; audiences expect and respect artistic quality; a rich supply of skilled artists, directors, actors and designers have committed themselves to the theatre; and the public and their government have been awakened to the financial demands of the theatre and their obligation to support it.

III The dramatists and their plays

Walter J. Meserve

1 Introduction

Two-hundred-odd years after the Pilgrims landed at Plymouth Rock a
New England novelist and dramatist, John Neal, stated with some fervour
that 'the writers of America have no encouragement, whatever, to venture
upon the drama.' That he presented the absolute truth for 1824 might be
questioned, but there is abundant evidence to support his view for America's
colonial period as well as the early years of the struggling Republic. It was
not, in fact, simply a matter of lack of encouragement but a much stronger
and definite discouragement. Illustrative of this Puritan attitude towards
the drama is Cotton Mather's question-and-answer argument in 'A Cloud
of Witnesses'. 'What are the Sins forbidden in the Seventh Command-
ment?' he asked: 'Light Behavior – Unchaste Company – Dancing, Stage-
playes, and all other Provocations to Uncleanness in our selves or others.'
When it became clearly established that one certain pathway to Hell was
through the door of a playhouse, who would undertake to see plays, let
alone write them?

Closely behind the clergy in concern for the preservation of public morals
came the city fathers and the self-appointed protectors of private virtue.
The Governor's Council of New York passed a law in 1709 against the acting
of plays, but it was Boston's 1750 act forbidding plays that became a model

for other legislative assemblies. By 1774 the Continental Congress had passed an interdict against 'exhibitions of shews, plays or other expensive diversions and entertainments'. Quite obviously the writing of drama was not encouraged, while actors received considerable abuse. In a letter to the printers of *The Pennsylvania Journal*, 19 February 1767, David Douglass, a theatre-company manager, complained of the 'torrent of incomprehensible abuse which has been, of late, so plentifully bestowed on the theatre, those who countenance it, and the performers.' Yet the theatre, its performers and those who created for it being what they were, plays were written during the seventeenth and eighteenth centuries in America and some of their creators are remembered.

2 Amusement in the colonies

By all accounts amusement was not generally given a very high priority in colonial America. Those adventurers who penetrated the continent around Jamestown found a varied existence in sustaining themselves. The more solemn-minded individuals who found acceptable patterns of living among the freedom seekers of Plymouth Colony or the Puritans in Massachusetts Bay seemingly shunned a lighter side to life. Their poets and writers, for the most part, were absorbed in a personal destiny which allowed them little concern for that 'veil of tears' through which they were so anxious to pass with as few irregularities as possible.

Yet there are certain aspects in the nature of man which makes a feeling for the dramatic and a sense of the theatrical impossible of complete worldly subjugation. Explorers must dramatize their exploits, and there is some evidence that the first white men to settle north of the Rio Grande near what is now El Paso, Texas, described and goodnaturedly spoofed their adventures in a *comedia* written for the occasion by Marcos Farfán de los Godos and performed, in Spanish, early in 1598. Eight years later and many miles distant, another group of adventurers created a pageant of an event which they considered worthy of celebration – the return of Jean de Biencourt, the Sieur de Poutrincourt, on 14 November 1606 to Port Royal, Acadia, where he had first settled with a band of Frenchmen. Called *Le Théâtre de Neptune en la Nouvelle-France* and written by Marc Lescarbot (*c.* 1590–1630), the verses describe the reception of the Sieur de Poutrincourt by Neptune and his six Tritons as well as by Indians anxious to bring gifts to the Sieur. Welcomed by appropriate speeches from all, de Poutrincourt is then approached by four Indians in a canoe. The first three are prepared with gifts and speeches, but the fourth can only offer excuses and, with harpoon in hand, say that he is 'going to fish'. The finale comes as all prepare for the great feasting. For both the Spanish and the French, however, the evidence of the theatre seems to have been a natural and dramatic overflowing of man's nature.

As the more substantial settlements in the New World – those at Jamestown and in New England – grew in size, it became clear that there were striking agreements as well as differences among the colonial patriarchs. An obvious attitude in the minds of New England leaders and clearly stated in the Letters Patent issued by the King of England in 1606 for the colonizing of Virginia was, for example, a missionary concern for the Christian education of the Indians. Continuing education for the colonists in this new land was, therefore, a logical outcome of their early cooperative efforts. Hence Harvard College was started in 1636, and by 1656 the Indian College was built in Harvard Yard, while Sir Edwin Sandys, Treasurer of the Colony in Virginia, attempted a similar experiment in 1619–22 and failed quite dramatically when the Indians massacred their hopeful benefactors. Although the relationship between education and drama is not always so easily established, there can be no question in the minds of those who have read about life in New England during the seventeenth and eighteenth centuries but that the great preachers from John Eliot, Apostle to the Indians, to Jonathan Edwards possessed a sense of the dramatic that was an essential part of their life patterns. 'Reaching' people was their *raison d'être*, and some of their techniques would have delighted a modern theatre director. It is unfortunate that the Christian's traditionally uncharitable view of the theatre was strongly upheld in New England. But it was. Ministerial arguments against the theatre as a place of sin and against actors and actresses as conspirators of the devil have persisted in a long line of mainly repetitive abuse to the present day in America. That there were those in early New England who rebelled against the church's anti-theatre scruples is, however, equally true, as the activities of Thomas Morton and the Maypole at Merry-mount so well illustrate.

Yet for the real if meagre beginnings of American drama one must look to the south of New England where both a tradition of Cavalier England and a few culture-conscious rebels stimulated some interesting 'firsts'. The first known American play written in English was *Y^e Bare and Y^e Cubb* by William Darby. The history of Accomac County, Virginia, notes a production of this play on 27 August 1665. In his theatrical venture Darby was aided by Cornelius Watkinson and Philip Howard with the result that all three were sued by the King's attorney for immoral or illegal activity. Upon inspection of the play, however, the court found the playwright and players 'not guilty of fault'. Unfortunately, the play is not extant. Nor is the play which Anthony Aston, an English actor, claimed he wrote upon arriving in Charles-Town in 1703.

The first play printed in America and worth any critical attention is Robert Hunter's *Androboros* (1714). Hunter (d. 1734), Governor of New York and New Jersey from 1710 until 1719, found such overwhelming difficulties in his work that he wrote this play to air – though probably only in private – his unbounded frustrations. A good friend of Jonathan Swift, Hunter showed in this bitter, satirical farce that he was a worthy compatriot of the Dean. All characters in the play had their counterparts in Hunter's real world, but he reserved his most acid attack for Lieutenant-Governor Nicholson, the absurd and ridiculous hero of the play, Androborus, a name meaning 'maneater'. Hunter himself is the keeper of the madhouse in which these people reside and with the help of Tom O'Bedlam chastises his political associates with both wit and rancour. In the fashion of the bawdy, physical farce comedies, popular since the time of Aristophanes, Hunter lashed out with considerable effect at the Provincial Council, the church government and his particular enemy, Nicholson.

Before the colonies decided to separate themselves from England through revolution there may have been other plays written and produced, though probably not in the New England area. Certain colleges, it is known, gave theatrical performances: a 'pastoral colloquy', at William and Mary College as early as 1702, *The Masque of Alfred* at the College of Philadelphia in 1756–7, and Philip Freneau and H. H. Brackenridge's dialogue, 'The Rising Glory of America', at the College of New Jersey in 1771. There is also the delightful and anonymous satirical farce entitled *The Trial of Atticus Before Justice Beau for a Rape* (1771). Teasingly risqué, the play builds upon a supposed rape and manages quite cleverly to burlesque the professions with whom the plantiff comes in contact – judge, lawyer, astrologer, tavern keeper, soldier, scholar, parson and gossip. But this was amateur theatre. The professional theatre came to America to stay (except for a brief interval during the Revolutionary War) with Lewis Hallam's Company of Comedians' arrival in Williamsburg, Virginia, in 1752. And with this activity there was more playwriting.

The first play written by an American colonist and performed in America by professional actors was Thomas Godfrey's *The Prince of Parthia*, a verse tragedy in five acts, produced for a single performance in Philadelphia's Southwark Theatre, 24 April 1767. Although Godfrey (1736–63) had shown some promise as a poet, his art is only occasionally revealed in this extremely derivative play. His English models are clearly evident in the excessive sentiment and rhetoric of eighteenth-century heroic tragedy and the conventions of Tudor and Stuart drama. Threads from Shakespeare's work in particular appear in phrase, style and theme. Probably written in 1759, *The Prince of Parthia* tells the story of Arsaces, a virtuous and heroic king's son, who must contend with a wicked stepmother, a prideful and ambitious brother, and a father gulled by the evil of both. Although themes of love and honour as well as political tyranny could have provided a meaningful effect for an eighteenth-century audience, the play is significant only for its place in the chronology of America drama.

3 Drama during the Revolution

During any period of social or political upheaval numerous cultural forces are brought to bear upon the volatile issues. In *Main Currents in American Thought*, for example, Vernon Lewis Parrington discusses what he terms the War of the Belles-Lettres in which essayists such as Freneau and Thomas Payne participated on behalf of the colonists. Although theatre during the Revolution had been outlawed by the Continental Congress, the plays that were printed, whether or not they were ever performed, suggest mainly this strong partisanship which is also typical of the theatre during periods of stress. Either as good theatre or good literature, they offer very little material for discussion.

Mercy Warren (1728–1814) was best known during her lifetime as a member of John and Abigail Adams's social group and as a minor poet and historian of the Revolution. The present interest in her occasional adventures as a dramatist would probably have delighted and surprised her. Although she published two dull, didactic verse tragedies in 1790 – *The Sack of Rome* and *The Ladies of Castile* – which suggest her interest in political freedom, her farces provide the best view of her partisan politics. In *The Adulateur* (1773) she comments satirically on the conditions in Massachusetts under Thomas Hutchinson, the last royal governor, and makes heroes of Samuel

Adams and her brother, James Otis. In this polemical poetic farce, as in *The Group* (1775) in which she attacks the Loyalist Council appointed by the king, she writes of the current activities of her contemporaries for whom she supplies names and actions appropriate to her own patriotic bias and fervour. Truly, the lady had a bitter wit, and it is doubtful whether her plays saw more than drawing-room readings – if that.

Another partisan playwright, Hugh Henry Brackenridge (1748–1816), is known in American literature for his novel, *Modern Chivalry*. Verse and drama were clearly not among his greatest accomplishments, but he nevertheless wrote two patriotic plays to further the colonial cause: *The Battle of Bunker-Hill* (1776) and *The Death of General Montgomery* (1777). Neither one is effective dramatically, but they carry the colonists' sentiments vigorously. A much more ambitious play with similar objectives is J. Leacock's *The Fall of British Tyranny; or, American Liberty Triumphant, The First Campaign* (1776). As usual, the characters in the play are readily identifiable and properly biased, but the scope of this play from a pre-war scene in England's House of Parliament through battles in Boston, Lexington and Bunker Hill attracts some interest.

These plays, however, suggest only half of the drama/belles-lettres war. Loyalist playwrights also expressed their bitter condemnation of the patriot cause. *The Americans Roused in a Cure for the Spleen; or, Amusement for a Winter's Evening* (1775), attributed to Jonathan Sewall (1728–96), is a conversational Tory tract which contrasts the wit and intelligence of the British with the confused ignorance of patriot sympathizers. A much more scurrilous satire is *The Battle of Brooklyn* (1776), an anonymous farce which questions the courage, honour and morals of the colonial generals through the harsh humour of caricature and invective. In none of these plays was there an overabundance of finesse. People held strong opinions, and the ribaldry and blatant propanganda of *The Battle of Brooklyn*, in spite of its weak theatrical effect, probably indicate that other plays of a similar nature were performed.

During the war years professional theatre in America had virtually disappeared, and whatever plays were written as propaganda vehicles were probably viewed mainly by a reading audience, although both armed forces performed plays. Mainly the plays that have been recorded here commented on the war or on social conditions from a partisan view. At least one dramatist and essayist, however, Robert Mumford (*c.* 1730–84), attempted a broader perspective. *The Patriots*, published in 1798 but probably written just prior to the Revolution, attacks the halfhearted and hypocritical patriots and shows the author's condemnation of both Tory and Whig politics. In *The Candidates* (1770) Mumford takes a peacetime election and, with an effective touch encompassing both the farcical and the serious, satirizes some of the methods by which politicians get themselves and others elected to political office. But whether the plays of this brief revolutionary period were or were not partisan, with the possible exception of *The Candidates* with its universal thesis and amusing scenes and characters, there is little to recommend American drama of the Revolution.

4 Drama of a new nation 1787–1820

Few would call the drama of either revolutionary or colonial America very effective as literature or as theatre. *The Trial of Atticus* could be an exception; and perhaps Thomas Forrest's *The Disappointment; or, The Force of Credulity* (1767) (the comedy which but for some 'personal reflections' would have been produced instead of *The Prince of Parthia*) would have been lively theatre entertainment. Generally, however, the plays that were published both before and during the Revolution were meagre attempts, inspired by personal indignation or a *cause célèbre*. Satire and propaganda were prominent. As the war retreated with passing years, however, the American's attention was directed to a new national and cultural identity. There was a character to establish, a literature to define, a political view to be determined. In all of this the drama would now assume a minor but definite and developing role.

When actors and actresses began to return to America after the war, playing in the various theatres built by theatre entrepreneur David Douglass, where they were joined by new recruits from England, it became clear that the theatre was to be a part of the new nation and that a playwright might even elicit some slight fame and fortune. Although it would be almost another hundred years before an American could sustain himself as an original playwright, William Dunlap (1766–1839) is frequently called the first professional dramatist in America. It is true that he supplemented his career by writing biography and theatre history as well as managing the Park Theatre in New York around the turn of the century, but his creation of fifty-three plays (twenty-nine either wholly or partly original with him) makes him a significant figure in American drama. It must also be noted that his *History of American Theatre* (1832) is a valuable source for the student of early American drama.

Dunlap's contribution to early American drama is worthy of considerable thought, for it would be a long time before any dramatist could match his accomplishments. Of course, he managed a theatre and therefore had a ready market for his plays. This was an advantage in a country where an author's creativity would be legally and outrageously abused for almost another hundred years. But Dunlap was also a man of considerable talent, energy and imagination. When the Park Theatre was in difficulty, he sensed the popularity of the work of Germany's August von Kotzebue and adapted an English version of *The Stranger*. Opening on 10 December 1798 the play saved his season. By the end of 1800 he had adapted and produced eighteen of Kotzebue's plays, being particularly successful with *False Shame; or, The American Orphan in Germany* (1799). He also borrowed from the French, adapting, among others, two of Pixérécourt's popular melodramas.

All too frequently Dunlap is remembered slightingly for his adaptations, while his original work is dismissed as either ineffective drama or nationalistic propaganda. Although such observations carry some truth, a few of his plays were popular as well as thought-provoking and innovative. *The Father; or, American Shandyism* (1788), for example, displays reasonably drawn characters and some effective dialogue as a young hero cleverly unmasks the villain, thereby bringing great joy to his father and his sweetheart while saving the marriage of a friend. The moral quality was a period necessity, and critics found the play pleasing. His dramatization of the Kenilworth story, first entitled *The Fatal Deception* (1790) and then published in 1806 as *Leicester*, tells of a young wife's adultery with her absent husband's brother; her villainy, madness and suicide upon discovery; and the husband's forgiveness of the dying sinners. Less serious but better received were Dunlap's patriotic plays, such as *Yankee Chronology; or, Huzza for the Constitution* (1812) which describes the battle between the *Constitution* and the *Guerrière*, or *Darby's Return* (1789), that gentle and popular satire of a 'gallant' soldier who returns home and tells of his experiences in America. Towards the end of his life Dunlap created *A Trip to Niagara* (1828), best known for its spectacular diorama including 25,000 feet of scenery.

Dunlap's greatest play, however, is his historical verse tragedy, *André* (1798), which he drastically revised in 1803 as *The Glory of Columbia – Her Yeomany*. Basic to his plot are Major John André, the British messenger who contacted Benedict Arnold and was then caught and hanged by the Americans, and his American friend Captain Bland, who refuses to believe that his country can hang as good a man as André. But the thesis of the play involved a question of universal significance. How can a country assert its national force and at the same time, and without appearing weak, maintain a sense of individual humanity? The problem posed a difficult decision for General Washington, bombarded as he was by Bland's righteous indignation, André's pleading sweetheart, and Bland's mother whose husband was captured by the British and executed when André was not released. In both thought and structure the drama has strong points, but it was not well received, perhaps because it was too close to the event. When Dunlap bowed to popular demand and created a successful spectacle complete with Yankee and foreign characters and humorous dialogue, he lost the original impact of his play, but *The Glory of Columbia* became a 4th of July favourite.

The only other dramatist of stature in eighteenth-century America is Royall Tyler (1757–1826). Although remembered in the annals of drama and literature as the author of a single play, Tyler wrote a novel, numerous essays and poems, and at least seven additional plays, while following a career in law which eventually rewarded him as Chief Justice of the Supreme Court of Vermont (1807–13). That single play, however, *The Contrast* (1787), has been respected by theatre and drama historians down through the years, mainly for its nationalistic thesis, sprightly dialogue and interesting characters. Patriotism, past and present, has a sustaining appeal, as the initial line in Tyler's Prologue – 'Exult each patriot heart!' – may illustrate. Also the Jonathan character has frequently been considered the first of the stage Yankees. That honour, however, belongs to another New England Yankee named Jonathan in *The Downfall of Justice* (1777), although *The Trial of Atticus* in 1771 had a Downeast parson in it. Contemporary critics of *The Contrast* were more divided in their opinions than later historians who view it as the first comedy of American manners with a genuine representation of the tastes, morals and social attitudes of the period.

The major characters in *The Contrast* are Colonel Manly; his servant Jonathan; his sister Charlotte; an American fop, Dimple, who follows the teachings of Lord Chesterfield; Dimple's servant Jessamy; and Maria. The plot of the play evolves around Manly, that stuffy illustration of American patriotism and honour, who falls in love with Maria, subsequently reveals Dimple's duplicity with Charlotte while betrothed to Maria, and finally wins his girl in an honourable fashion. But the plot alone does not indicate the play's distinctions. For these one observes Tyler's clever caricature of his society, his excellent dialogue and humorous epigrams, and his witty scenes with Jessamy the farcical intriguer who teaches Jonathan, the shrewd but naïve country Yankee, to laugh and to woo. Throughout all there is a contrast which in the final scene becomes a national triumph. There are good reasons why the play is considered an optimistic beginning for American comedy.

With few exceptions American drama developed very slowly and with childlike, tottering steps. Fifty years after the Revolution there was, with the exception of William Dunlap, still no dramatist of importance. When John Neal complained that playwrights were not encouraged, he might have been bitter about his own lack of success in the theatre, but he did not speak lightly of the position of the dramatist in America. There were obviously serious barriers for dramatists and theatre people. Newspaper and magazine editors as well as preachers raged voluminously about the stage as 'the direct School of Vice', while the actual physical conditions of early nineteenth-century theatres with their assorted spectacles of violence, prostitution and rats did little to encourage either audiences or writers. But, in spite of all, many plays were being written, some with serious purpose but most as marketable commodities. Playwrights wrote what managers felt that audiences would pay to see on the stage.

Mainly, it would seem, Americans were interested in seeing themselves – what they had accomplished in the past and what they were presently enenjoying. War plays which oozed nationalism and created the most patriotic of heroes appeared frequently. John Daly Burk's (d. 1808) verse tragedy, *Bunker-Hill; or, The Death of General Warren* (1797), is one of the better examples at this time of a romanticized American history on stage, while David Everett's (1770–1813) *Daranzel; or, The Persian Patriot* (1800) dramatizes a historical situation which could be indirectly related to the recent American fight for freedom. This indirect technique was used by numerous playwrights who wanted to suggest the grandeur of the American struggle in terms of well-known battles and figures from the past. Frances Wright (1795–1852), for example, stated in her Prologue for *Altorf* (1819) that the audience should equate George Washington with William Tell. As

America became involved in other wars, dramatists were quick to place them upon the stage. Susanna H. Rowson's (1762–1824) *Slaves in Algeria; or, A Struggle for Freedom* (1794) anticipated the navy's venture to Tripoli, but shows the proper concern for the numerous Barbary Coast incidents. With the War of 1812 managers were able to support their theatres with immediate spectacles of the many sea victories. Yet the best play relating to that war, probably because it is more romance than history, appeared a few years after the fact: Mordecai Noah's (1785–1851) *She Would Be a Soldier; or, The Plains of Chippewa* (1819).

The national spirit also spilled over into plays concerned with politics and society. There was Samuel Low's (b. 1765) defence of the Constitution in *The Politician Outwitted* (1788) and John Murdock's (1748–1834) plea for national unity in *The Politicians; or, The State of Things* (1798). J. H. Nichols's *Jefferson and Liberty; or, Celebration of the Fourth of March* (1801) praised Jefferson and ridiculed John Adams as the Duke of Braintree. Later, when Jefferson had trouble with the Embargo Act of 1807, James Nelson Barker helped him out with a little play called *The Embargo; or, What News?* (1808). Truly, partisan nationalism could easily become partisan politics, and the drama began to serve a political purpose which it still occasionally recognizes. At the same time, Tyler's minor success with *The Contrast* prompted more playwrights to join society's faults and foibles with the patriot's virtues. An anonymous play, *The Better Sort; or, A Girl of Spirit* (1789), satirized America's naïve acceptance of foreign ideas and created a true American champion. James N. Barker's *Tears and Smiles* (1807) contrasted American and French national traits to the satisfaction of America, while Joseph Hutton satirized America's fashion-minded fools in *Fashionable Follies* (1815).

These varied probings of playwrights for the vein of success, however, are rather general, probably to be expected. A more particular development was the enthusiasm with which dramatists adopted the Yankee character. Both *The Politician Outwitted* and *The Better Sort* had Yankee characters, but by 1807 with *Jonathan Postfree; or, The Honest Yankee* by L. Beach and 1809 with A. B. Lindsley's *Love and Friendship; or, Yankee Notions* the Yankee had achieved the top billing which would be his for the next half-century. To show the significance of this step David Humphreys (1753–1818) included a seven-page glossary of Yankee words with his *Yankey in England* (1815). Here was a particular creation that brought the new country and its drama closer together.

5 A poetic drama: serious theatre in America 1815–1855

Throughout the history of literature some of the best poets have written plays, and some of the most significant plays have been written in poetry. Whether it was Kalidasa, Zeami, Euripides or Shakespeare, tradition has merged the poet and the dramatist. On the American stage in the late eighteenth and early nineteenth centuries Shakespeare's plays and the eighteenth-century heroic tragedies were welcomed. It was perhaps only natural, then, that aspiring dramatists should attempt to express themselves in poetry, for such were their models. Consequently, any dramatist who attempted tragedy or wrote with a high and serious purpose chose poetry as his mode. Those with objectives of a more mundane or transitory nature wrote in prose. At least, this is a generalization which holds true until the latter part of the nineteenth century in America when the Age of Realism dictated that people on the stage speak in the same manner as their neighbours on the street.

The colonial dramatists started the tradition; Dunlap, Burk and innumerable others continued it using the same English models. Although the majority of the best-known dramatists writing before the Civil War composed poetic dramas, it would not be correct to infer that they were distinguished either as poets or dramatists. Far from it; most dramatists, in fact, were poor poets. And among the major poets of this period, only Henry

Wadsworth Longfellow (1807–82) and Edgar Allan Poe (1809–49) tried to write for the stage. Of Longfellow's several poetic dramas, only *The Spanish Student* (1842) was not 'closet' drama and that was not acted. Poe's *Politian* (1835) was never finished, and John Neal (1793–1876), a novelist and poet, was unsuccessful with his gothic verse tragedy, *Otho* (1819). Among the minor poets, Nathaniel Parker Willis achieved some reputation in the theatre with a blank-verse tragedy, *Bianca Visconti* (1837), which involved a mixture of love and politics in Milan, and created one of the few acceptable verse comedies of the period, *Tortesa the Usurer* (1839). Even Poe, a very severe critic of the drama, enjoyed this play about a rich Florentine who cancels a count's debts in exchange for his daughter's hand in marriage only to discover that she loves another. Being unable to write good poetry and yet attempting to create poetic drama, however, did not appear to many playwrights as an insurmountable barrier. Among those who tried with moderate success were Epes Sargent (1813–80), a Boston journalist, with *The Bride of Genoa* (1837); Richard Penn Smith (1799–1854), a lawyer from Philadelphia; John Blake White (1781–1859) and Isaac Harby (1788–1828) from the Charleston area. After the Civil War fewer playwrights attempted poetic drama in deference to the dictates of the Age of Realism, but poets continued to write romantic verse dramas which were generally dull and certainly unsuited to the American theatre of this period.

For the early nineteenth-century theatre, however, whether in England or America, there was a demand for the strong, romantic rhetoric of poetic drama. In America there were at least five dramatists whose poetic dramas were outstanding for the period and the major products of their playwriting efforts. Of these, John Howard Payne (1791–1852) was the earliest to achieve success and the most prolific. Although beginning his career as a promising young actor in America, Payne failed to impress English audiences and in 1816, three years after he arrived in England, he began translating and adapting the latest French successes for the management at Drury Lane. From that time until he returned to America in 1832 he wrote most of the sixty-odd plays that are attributed to him and for one disastrous season managed the Sadler's Wells Theatre. Although his plays were widely praised and produced in America, he received little recompense for his work. Like John Neal, some of his comments on the position of the dramatist in America were quite bitter, and he himself left the theatre, became interested in the plight of the American Indians, and finally became United States Consul at Tunis where he died.

As a dramatist, Payne exhibited skill in writing, adapting and translating comedy, melodrama and romantic tragedy. His particular forte was his ability to recognize dramatic material and create a successful play from whatever sources he found necessary. Like other prolific dramatists of the nineteenth century, his talent was not in writing original plays. For the young country, however, he was the first dramatist to enjoy a substantial reputation abroad. Early in his career this reputation got a tremendous boost when he wrote the poetic tragedy of *Brutus; or, The Fall of Tarquin* (1818) for Edmund Kean. In America Edwin Forrest was attracted by the strong leading role and the artificial elegance of the blank verse which in certain bravura passages allowed him to demonstrate the dignity and power of his acting style. Like most of the poetic dramas in America during the nineteenth century, *Brutus* presented an ancient pageantry and grandeur which allowed a new nation to compare some of its cherished ideals with historical events. In addition, as James N. Barker wrote in the Prologue to James McHenry's *The Usurper* (1827),

> Our poet's pencil paints the moral scene,
> Teaching what ought to be by what has been.

When Sextus Tarquin seizes the throne in Rome, Brutus feigns madness to gain time for revenge. Finally his moment arrives. Using Sextus' rape of Lucretia as a rallying call to arms, he leads the Romans to victory over the Tarquins. But it is also a sad day, for Brutus must condemn his own son who was induced to collaborate with the enemy through his love of Tarquin's daughter. The play, primarily through Forrest's acting, was a favourite for many years.

In modern America most people would recall Payne, if at all, as the author of 'Home Sweet Home', but they would not remember that the song came from *Clari; or, The Maid of Milan* (1823). Nor would they know that the air was not Payne's and that the song was sung by the heroine, once head-strong and romantic, as she remorsefully and sentimentally returned home after being deceived in love. (But this second point audiences familiar with operatic melodrama might well have imagined.) They would, however, recognize the name of Payne's collaborator, Washington Irving, in his most successful comedy, *Charles the Second; or, The Merry Monarch* (1824). Like many Payne plays, this was in prose and a free adaptation (Alexander Deval's *La Jeunesse de Henri V*). Thanks to Irving – whose work was kept secret for many years – the comic dialogue makes the play distinctive in this period. The plot evolves around one of the king's 'nocturnal rambles' in which, disguised as a common sailor, he tries to woo a pretty barmaid named Mary.

In the course of the evening he has trouble with the bill as well as with the tavern owner, a Captain Copp who is Mary's uncle and one of Payne's most successful characters. Finally he leaves the place minus a diamond-studded watch (which he has used as a bribe) and explosively followed by lead pellets from a shotgun. The whole episode, however, is satisfactorily resolved the next morning as Copp and Mary return the watch – and are sworn to secrecy. Among Payne's works, this is the play most likely to keep him in the history books.

Of all American playwrights of this period, writing in either prose or poetry, Robert Montgomery Bird (1806–54) gives the impression of being the most intelligent as well as one of the most talented. Starting his professional life as a medical doctor, he switched careers to become a playwright until Edwin Forrest taught him that no one could make a decent living writing for the theatre. Bird wisely turned to politics, journalism and the writing of novels; and as a novelist achieved a major reputation for adventure stories that are similar to those of James Fenimore Cooper. Forrest's unconscious teaching technique was to sponsor a play contest, pay a dramatist $1000 for his labours, and then proceed to make hundreds of thousands of dollars during the following years. Although Forrest was the first actor to do this and one of the most successful, he was not the only actor to use contests: he simply educated some of the better dramatists. Having written four contest plays for Forrest, two of which – *The Gladiator* and *The Broker of Bogota* – became permanent in Forrest's repertory, Bird complained about this unfair financial arrangement, received no satisfaction, and so stopped writing for the stage. This was, of course, many years before a playwright could retain copyright control of his work. Playwrights were thus the unwilling and unhappy prey of both actors and theatre managers, and Bird's understandable rejection of the American stage and its inhabitants was a loss to American drama.

In a most distinctive manner, both in terms of the history of America and a history of its drama and theatre, Bird was that scholarly and imaginative person who was keenly aware of the forces working upon the culture of his period. As an idealist concerned with a sense of freedom that sparked off much of the writing of early nineteenth-century America, Bird easily joined the writers of historical romances and was a major force in bringing Romanticism to American drama. His theories of dramaturgy also reflected the Romanticism of the period. He believed, for example, in the idealized hero as the central force in the play and around whom all dramatic elements evolved – the plot, the dramatic incidents, the poetic speech, the passions of other characters and the theme of the play. Everything, Bird declared, must lead towards the climax of the play and stimulate interest in the hero. Obviously, this was also the kind of play that Forrest demanded, and the fact that Bird could create a strong hero and provide the necessary rhetorical, poetic speech explains why he won four of Forrest's nine contests.

During his career as a dramatist Bird completed nine plays, including such conventionally imitative comedies as *'Twas All for the Best* as well as his mature tragedies in the classical tradition. But his two best plays, and the most popular during his lifetime, were *The Gladiator* (1831) and *The Broker of Bogota* (1834). The earlier play even impressed a critic of the London *Courier* who acknowledged Bird as 'a dramatist of the highest order' when Forrest performed Spartacus for his London début on 17 October 1836. At this time, during the early stages of that period (which extended far into the twentieth century) when English critics found little in American drama worthy of commendation, the praise was distinctive and should be so recorded to indicate Bird's contemporary superiority. True to Bird's theory of dramatic composition, *The Gladiator* revolves around the character of Spartacus, the Thracian gladiator captured by the Romans, who agrees to fight in the arena to free his family and discovers that his opponent is his brother. Together they lead the gladiators in a victory over the Romans only to disagree upon the treatment of enemies, whereupon Spartacus gains moral stature but loses the military power of their previous unity as well as his family and dies as a soldier-gladiator fighting Pompey's legions. *The Broker of Bogota* tells of a stern but honourable father who disinherits a wayward son and then is victimized by that son's refusal to implicate himself in a crime for which his father is condemned. Love is the major factor which determines the son's confession and the consequent freeing of the father, but the scene changes immediately as the distraught son's suicide causes his father's death. The thesis of a noble man trapped by circumstances created by the villain who controlled his son also provided an acceptable moral for the time. Both plays were imitative in form and manner of classical tragedy, and both achieved the success in the theatre merited by Bird's talent for writing speeches of rhetorical effect and his skill in creating sensitive but forceful major characters.

Even in a young country emerging on the political, social and literary scene, there were identifiable groups of serious playwrights concerned with poetic drama. From the New York/New England area there were Epes Sargent, N. P. Willis, Julia Ward Howe and Henry W. Longfellow. From Charleston and the south where theatre in America had had its start during the previous century there was John Blake White, Isaac Harby, George Washington Parke Custis and James M. Kennicott. But the most active writers came from around Philadelphia – Richard Penn Smith, James McHenry, Robert T. Cade, David Paul Brown, John Augustus Stone, James Nelson Barker and Robert M. Bird. George Henry Baker was a late-comer to this group. Within the original number, however, Bird remains the most significant writer – historically and critically important for his plays, his theories of drama and his novels.

John Augustus Stone's (1800–34) reputation in American drama is closely tied to Edwin Forrest whose initial play contest in 1828 was won by Stone's *Metamora*. Subsequent critics and historians have pointed to Stone's dis-appointment in his career, which in conjunction with financial problems and poor health evidently pressed him towards his suicide six years later, and have seen some irony in the inscription Forrest placed on Stone's monu-ment: 'To the Memory of John Augustus Stone, Author of Metamora, by his Friend Edwin Forrest'. Although it is true that Stone would have been far less important had he not written *Metamora*, he would not have been much poorer. Forrest's contest awarded the winner only 'five hundred dollars, and half of the proceeds of the third presentation'. On the other hand, Forrest's reputation jumped miraculously after his performance as Metamora, and he played the part to great financial advantage for the next forty years. Actually, Forrest was following an accepted actors' tradition in what he did, while Stone suffered poverty and anonymity in the accepted fashion of playwrights.

Stone started his theatre career as an actor by playing character parts, primarily in Boston, New York and Philadelphia, but without distinction. In the ten plays which he is known to have written, there is a concern for the past which was consistent with most of the serious poetic dramatists of this time: *Tancred; or, The Siege of Antioch* (1827) and *The Ancient Briton* (1832). However, Stone was obviously wise to the demands of American theatre and, when the stage Yankee became popular, he provided George H. 'Yankee' Hill with a character, Sy Saco, in *The Knight of the Golden Fleece; or, The Yankee in Spain* (1834), which he performed for fifteen years. He also revised James Kirke Paulding's *The Lion of the West* (1831), which brought a backwoodsman to the stage, another character brought forward for popular audience acceptance after the Civil War.

Metamora; or, The Last of the Wampanoags (1828) remains, however, Stone's major achievement. Modelled on the famous New England Indian Chief, King Philip, who attacked numerous white settlements in 1675–6,

Metamora is not only a noble savage, an honest man and a loving husband, but also a defiant and proud person incapable of accepting unjust defeat. Intruding upon this heroic figure is a conventional English love story, complete with disguises, misunderstandings and a discovered son. Yet Metamora provides the focus for idea and action as he defends himself and his people from the English usurpers of his land.

The play stands as a tremendous vehicle for the bombastic acting of Edwin Forrest. Using both prose and poetry, it is also one of the best examples of the numerous plays on Indian themes performed during the first half of the nineteenth century. James Nelson Barker provided one of the early plays with *The Indian Princess; or, La Belle Sauvage* (1808), the story of Pocahontas whose popularity with dramatists was overwhelming. Again and again her romantic and daring rescue of John Smith was enacted upon America's stages. By the early 1840s, however, the popularity of Pocahontas and her Indian friends had reached its peak and started to decline. For stimulating this change in public taste John Brougham must be allowed the major credit. Characterized by Laurence Hutton as the 'Aristophanes' of the American stage, he so successfully burlesqued the Indian in *Metamora; or, The Last of the Pollywogs* (1847) and *Po-Ca-Hon-Tas; or, The Gentle Savage* (1855) that audiences could never accept him in the old way again. When the Indian next appeared upon the stage, he had lost some of his nobility with the enforced realism brought on by the Civil War, the ideas of Darwin and Herbert Spencer, and the expanding nation; and he had become a 'Redskin' in local-colour and backwoodsman plays.

Another from the Philadelphia group, James Nelson Barker (1784–1854), was one of that large number of American dramatists who simultaneously held major positions outside the theatre. Most of his life Barker was involved in government, either in Philadelphia where he was born or at a national level. Although he wrote some plays with conventional themes, more than half of his limited productivity suggests his strong interest in America. *Marmion; or, The Battle of Flodden Field* (1812) is a romantic tragedy, and *How to Try a Lover* (1817) is a light comedy based on a French novel. On the other hand, *America* (1805) is a one-act masque featuring 'America, Science, Liberty, and attendent spirits'; *Tears and Smiles* (1807) imitated the success of *The Contrast; The Embargo; or, What News?* (1808) was written to help President Jefferson; while *The Indian Princess* (1808) celebrated a romantic American legend.

Barker's major place in America drama is secured by eleven critical essays on 'The Drama' (appearing in the *Democratic Press*, Philadelphia, from December 1816 to February 1817) which revealed a strong sense of dramatic literature as well as theatre, and by his New England tragedy, *Superstition; or, The Fanatic Father* (1824). Fusing plot lines involving a regicide of Charles I and a New England intolerance activated by a superstitious mind, Barker created the best romantic tragedy of the period dealing with a native theme. The story is of Charles who returns home from college and falls in love with Mary the daughter of Ravensworth, the village clergyman. When a stranger who seems to know Charles and his mother leads the village against an Indian attack, Ravensworth fiendishly mistakes his own passion for the voice of God, accuses the mother of sorcery and fabricates a charge of murder and rape against Charles. Enacting a relentless revenge against the mother who had refused to kotow to him, Ravensworth drives himself, like Hawthorne's Chillingworth, to his own destruction, dragging others with him. Although other elements of this play are not noteworthy, the eloquence, the intelligence and the twisted beliefs and passions of this villain-hero make him one of the most interesting characters in nineteenth-century poetic drama.

Throughout this period American theatre audiences thrilled to the excessive rhetoric and emotional crises of romantic tragedies. Every serious and ambitious writer for the stage knew this, as the innumerable examples of their efforts, both those lost in time and those gathering dust in special library collections, persistently remind the historian. During this century, however, only one dramatist in America achieved the dream of the many: a play of both literary and theatrical excellence. The dramatist was George Henry Boker (1823–90) and his play is *Francesca da Rimini* (1855). Unfortunately for him recognition of his achievement came long after his creation. Otherwise, he might be recalled by historians for more than a single play.

Born into wealth and position, Boker should have been a banker or a lawyer. At least this was the idea of his father who provided him with a fine education and the European travel traditionally considered an adjunct of that gentlemanly training. Boker, however, had far more a feeling for poetry and drama than a head for a lawyer's brief or accounts transferable. In 1848 his first play, *Calaynos*, was produced in London, to be repeated in New York the following year. For the next twenty-three years he devoted his energies to poetry and the drama, whereas the final period of his life was spent primarily as a gentleman, partially in service to his country, as Minister first to Turkey and then to Russia.

It was as a poet that Boker saw himself in the history books; and as a minor lyric poet, particularly with his patriotic Civil War poems, and a reasonably good writer of sonnets he achieved some reputation. Certainly, without his gift for poetry he would not be remembered in American drama. His two prose plays, *The World a Mask* (1851) and *The Bankrupt* (1855), were deservedly unsuccessful. Unfortunately, his other plays were also invariably unsuccessful. Writing romantic, blank-verse plays, set in foreign countries (eight during the 1850s), he was at cross-purposes with the direction the American theatre was taking. Local-colour writing was becoming popular, and the rise of realism in American literature was fast approaching. Even such a remarkable play as *Francesca da Rimini* ran only eight nights for its opening in 1855. Presumably, however, this reception did not bother Boker, who wanted mainly to be a poet. Yet when Lawrence Barrett successfully revived the play in 1882 (with some rewriting help from William Winter) Boker wrote to him: 'Why didn't I receive this encouragement years ago? Then I might have done something.'

But in 1882 it was too late. His other plays do not warrant attention. Taking the Paolo–Francesca love story from Dante's *Inferno*, Fifth Canto, Boker fashioned a tragedy of the beautiful soul encased in the deformed body. Lanciotto, the hunchback, was a courageous and noble man and when he sent his brother, Paolo, to bring his wife-to-be, Francesca, from Ravenna, he honestly told him that he should take the girl for himself. The first of several very effective dramatic ironies comes when Francesca, prepared to fall dutifully in love with the man who comes for her, learns too late that he is not to be her husband. Equally dramatic in this carefully written play is Lanciotto's pathetic hope when he sees the beautiful Francesca. Could she really love him? He can steel himself and run away when he discovers that he is fooling himself, but he cannot accept being betrayed or gulled. When Pepe, that most malevolent of jesters, bitter himself at the social position forced upon him, vengefully tells him of Paolo and Francesca's love, he must react with violence. Yet if they would only lie to him, he coaxes so pathetically, he could willingly believe and let them live. But they cannot. It is a dramatic story, well told in frequently eloquent verse, and the four major characters are outstanding creations. Lawrence Barrett had one of his greatest successes in the part of Lanciotto with Otis Skinner as Paolo. By general critical agreement, it is the most powerful verse tragedy in nineteenth-century American drama and the best of plays in English on the Francesca theme.

6 Drama reflects a varied society 1820–1865

Playwrights during most of the nineteenth century were, by and large, men and women of rather average intelligence with a taste for the theatre, a flair for the dramatic, and a desire to make a living. Few had any moral or social insight of more than a surface nature with which to endow their work, and no more had outstanding skill in dramaturgy. Whereas those who wrote in poetry sometimes thought that they had a meaningful statement to make about life, the others had a much more practical objective. They wanted only to write something that would entertain the population, catch the public fancy. Either by preaching an acceptable and obvious moral or creating a spectacle for laughter and wonderment, they hoped to make a dollar or two. To put it bluntly, they were, in the main, hacks. But if this observation seems too painfully derogatory, it must be remembered that this position was forced upon the playwright. Once his play was on the boards he had no control of it. Hence, he must please an actor or a theatre manager, and he must do it often if he was to exist. For men of intelligence, great talent or emotional sensitivity these conditions were intolerable, and generally they stayed out of the theatre. Consequently, America can boast some outstanding poets and novelists as well as essayists and short-story writers of distinction, but the number of such playwrights is very small.

Faced with the problem of pleasing a nation, playwrights in frequent collusion with theatre managers resorted to as many gimmicks as necessary. They took advantage of anything that they thought would help them. When the nation was at war, for example, they put as much of the war on stage as possible so that audiences could enjoy vicariously both the adventure and the danger of the battles and the glory of victory. If a social or political event made the headlines, it also appeared in the theatre. If a novel or poem found favour with reading audiences, the theatre audience was given an opportunity to see the story on stage. Then if a particular character in one play was well received, he was immediately made the hero of innumerable other plays. It was popular to be patriotic; and it was quite acceptable to be heroic, boisterous and odd. Ridiculing the other fellow was also part of the game. In fact, almost anything came to the theatre, which in these days could be almost any place – a stage, a tent, a boat, a bar, a museum or an amphitheatre. The plays of Shakespeare and the poetic dramatists of present and past satisfied some of the people, but there were also those hundreds of farces, comedies and exuberant melodramas which were a steady fare in most American theatres. More than most historical sources, these plays suggest the society of this period.

Young America was anxious to assert its independent existence – intellectually, socially and politically. But unity in a large country and among people of singular diversity is difficult to marshal, and on the political and international front every incident became grist to the playwright's mill. When the election of Andrew Jackson to the presidency in 1828 indicated a major political change, the drama reflected his past as a general in the War of 1812 as well as his political problems. In *The Eighth of January* (1829) Richard Penn Smith celebrated Jackson's election by dramatizing his victory over the British in New Orleans on 8 January 1815. During his tenure in office several other plays on the War of 1812 appeared, and when he angrily decided not to deposit money in Nicholas Biddle's Bank of the United States, Henry J. Finn (1787–1840) came up with a play, *Removing the Deposit* (1835). During Van Buren's administration the Panic of 1837 affected the theatre in all phases of its production, while the border dispute between Maine and Canada was dramatized in Nathaniel H. Bannister's (1813–47) *The Maine Question* (1839). President James Polk's territorial desires in the north-west were argued in Joseph M. Field's (1810–56) *Oregon; or, The Disputed Territory* (1846), while the Mexican War provided the background for several plays. Political arguments invariably appeared in the theatre, either in a substantial fashion such as the anonymous *Major*

Jack Downing; or, The Retired Politician (1839) and J. E. Heath's (1792–1862) *Whigs and Democrats; or, Love of No Politics* (1839) or in minor characters and the dialogue of innumerable plays. John Brougham's burlesques, for example, provided a running commentary on New York politics. Throughout the pre-Civil-War period, too, the few past glories of a young nation frequently appeared on the stage in plays about colonial and revolutionary heroes. They shared billing with plays about emigrants, the Mormons and their trek westward, the discovery of gold in California, and a concern for Negroes and slavery.

One item most necessary for a new country is a banner, symbolic or real, under which men of like mind may gather. For the stage a representative character is needed, and such a character was provided with the Jonathan or Yankee figure of the revolutionary period. There are several explanations as to how the word 'Yankee' came into being. Some say it came from a fierce Indian tribe called Yankoos; others say it approximated the Indians' attempt to pronounce English – 'Yengeese'. Whatever its origin, it first designated the New Englander, then spread outwards through Pennsylvania and New York. On the stage the Yankee immediately acquired particular characteristics. John Bernard, in *Retrospections of America, 1797–1811*, divided him into three classes – 'the swapper, the jobber, and the pedler, all agreeing in one grand characteristic – love of prey – but varying in many striking particulars'. Dramatically, the Yankee developed from Royall Tyler's Jonathan, and he was, as David Humphreys stated in the 1815 Preface to *The Yankey in England*, 'made up of contrarities – simplicity and cunning', and so on. But whatever his nature, he was the most frequent single character on the American stage during the nineteenth century.

Although the Yankee was familiar to theatregoers long before the 1820s, it was during this decade that he became a dominant figure on the stage and in literature. Seba Smith had created something of a model with his Major Jack Downing essays in the Portland, Maine, *Courier*, and within a few years Judge Haliburton's Sam Slick, Frances Witcher's Widow Bedott and James Russell Lowell's Hosea Biglow had attracted audiences. Another stimulus for the active promotion of the Yankee in the theatre was the 1822–3 American tour of Charles Mathews, the English actor. Tremendously interested in the Yankee as a vehicle for an actor, he collaborated with Richard B. Peake after his return to England and wrote *Jonathan in England* (1824). Undoubtedly, the financial success of this play inspired American actors and dramatists, and during the next forty years several Americans made fortunes as Yankee actors while 'Jonathan' became involved in innumerable adventures and careers around the world.

The play which is usually credited with creating some mass interest in the Yankee is Samuel Woodworth's (1784–1842) *The Forest Rose* (1825) which held the stage for more than forty years. Although Jonathan Plough-boy is not the main character in this English-American love story, much of the play's comedy derives from his talk, his inability to woo and his naïve simplicity. Equally significant plays in the repertory of the Yankee actor are Cornelius Logan's (1806–53) *Yankee Land* (*c.* 1834), with the delightful Lot Sap Sago, and *The Vermont Wool Dealer* (1840) where Deuteronomy Dutiful controls the farcical action. Joseph S. Jones (1809–77), a medical doctor who also worked in Boston theatres as a playwright, stage manager and actor, probably contributed 150 farce-comedies for audience approval. One of these, *The People's Lawyer* (1839), achieved considerable popularity for its Yankee character, Solon Shingle, whose name eventually became the title of the play. With this play, however, as with others, much of its success depended upon the Yankee actor who would ad-lib and mug his way to popularity. Otherwise, it is difficult to understand the success of these simple sketches. In London in 1852, for example, Josh Silsbee, a Yankee specialist, played Jonathan Ploughboy for ninety-nine performances, following this run with a 125 nights of Hiram Dodge in *The Yankee Pedler*. This second play, which appears in several versions by as many authors (pirating being an ever-popular sport in early nineteenth-century theatre), was subtitled *Old Times in Virginia* (1841) and dramatized the Yankee's colourful and impertinent actions as a pedlar bent on making love along with money.

Although the success of these Yankee plays is difficult to underestimate, there was an end to it – or at least a change. Before that time, however, a Yankee gal was introduced, such as Jedidah in O. E. Durivage's *The Stage Struck Yankee* (1840), but never with Jonathan's success. Even during the 1860s one could still see plays about *The Yankee Jailor*, *Yankee Courtship*, *The Yankee in Cuba* or *The Yankee Inventor*. But by this date, too, the local-colour movement in literature was well under way and the Yankee was disappearing as a popular vehicle only to emerge very soon and somewhat changed as a part of local realism.

There seems always to have been a theory in America that, if one thing or one person was good, two or more of the same would be better. Amount or number was important; therefore, a farmer's worth was judged by the amount of horse manure behind his barn or a rancher's importance by the number of cattle on his land. Audience reaction in the theatre continually promoted this concept. Taste requires an explanation; the position of simple arithmetic or 'I know what I like' is much easier to maintain. When an American audience at a Haydn concert in 1838 shouted to stop the music and play 'Yankee Doodle', a popular attitude was being expressed. If the dramatization of one Uncle Tom and one Simon Legree was good, certainly two Uncle Toms and two Simon Legrees would be better. Reasoning along this line, a French concert manager in America advertised forty pianists playing with five orchestras. America was a big country, and numbers were meaningful. Quantity was important, whether it concerned finances or art.

So the Yankee character multiplied, even attracting English imitation. A number of hack playwrights, such as William Bayle Bernard, made their fortunes adapting American plays (as well as dramatizing American novels) for English audiences. At the same time America was earning its name as a 'melting pot' of all peoples. Beginning about 1844, emigrants came to America in earnest – over 100,000 that year. In 1854 over 400,000 emigrated to America, but that was a peak year, and by 1862 the number had decreased to fewer than 100,000. During these years, however, American society was changed by the steady mass invasion of Irish, Germans, Scandinavians and Chinese, along with lesser numbers of people from other countries. Some of the consequences were the political prejudices that erupted into the Know-Nothing Party of 1856, as well as temperance unions and religious difficulties. For the dramatist, however, the new people with their new ideas provided both characters and plots.

First there were the new characters. If the Yankee had been successful because of his peculiarities, perhaps other peculiarities would be equally successful. Of the immigrants the Irishman with his vivid and boisterous approach to life seemed to offer the most potential. It is true, of course, that the comic Irishman had appeared on the stage long before this period, but he became a more particularized and popular character in America after the great potato famine in Ireland had encouraged him to migrate in considerable numbers. At this time he was known as Ireland's greatest export. Perhaps the great Irish character actor, Tyrone Power, also helped to popularize the Irishman with his tour of America just before his death in 1841 on his return to England. At any rate his plays, such as *The Irish Tutor* with the character of Terry O'Rourke, set a standard which both American playwrights and American-Irish character actors were to imitate. Very quickly a vogue for Irish plays sprang up which was to last about twenty years. Like the Yankee, the Irishman did everything and went everywhere.

Perhaps a sampling of titles, most of the plays being anonymous, will suggest his popularity: *The Irish Attorney*, *The Irish Porter*, *The Irishman in Cuba*, *The Irishman in Greece*, *The Bashful Irishman*, *The Irish Ambassador*, *Ireland As It Is*, *The Irish Lion*. One of the more popular plays was *Shandy McGuire; or, The Bould Boy of the Mountains* (1851) by James Pilgrim (1825–77), a rather prolific writer of farce-comedies. John Brougham (1810–80) acted and wrote some excellent Irish plays – *The Irish Fortune Hunter* (1850) and *Temptation; or, The Irish Immigrant* (1856). As with Yankee plays, a good part of the success depended upon the acting, and Brougham and Barney Williams excelled in these vehicles. Unlike the Yankee plays, however, these plays frequently had no necessary relationship to America; throughout, it was the character which caught the public fancy.

Playwrights also tried to make a commercial product of the German immigrant who rivalled the Irish in numbers, but was far less successful on the stage. Mainly, the Dutchman, as the stage German was called, was an object of ridicule. Although a 'John Schmidt' type did appear, few plays have survived. Perhaps the two farces by S. Barry – *The Persecuted Dutchman* (1845) and *The Dutchman's Ghost* (1857) – are indicative of a more abundant theatre fare. In these plays he was the butt of much farcical humour while his grotesque Anglicized German speech provided an acting vehicle similar to the dialect of the Yankee and the brogue of the Irishman.

The only German-Dutchman play that received any substantial success in the theatre was *Rip Van Winkle*, a distinctive play in American drama for its close association with the acting career of Joseph Jefferson III. It all started with Washington Irving's short story, *Rip Van Winkle*, which first appeared in his *Sketch Book* (1819) but went through several adaptations before it reached Jefferson in 1865. In 1829 John Kerr dramatized the story and added the villainous Derrick Van Slous who had Rip sign a contract whereby his daughter would marry Van Slous's son in twenty years and forfeit her inheritance. Charles Burke's 1850 version added farcical humour with Knickerbocker, who falls in love with Alice Van Winkle. He also made much more of the love episode between Rip's daughter and a young sailor. The final identification scene and trial to establish Rip's legality added to the drama. In a later English version by Thomas H. Lacy, Dame Van Winkle is kept alive in the second act and is married to Nicholas Vedder.

Joseph Jefferson (1829–1905) first became interested in Rip after reading Irving's story in 1859. Leaning heavily on Burke's version, Jefferson had the expert help of Dion Boucicault, and together they fashioned the play which ran for 170 nights when it opened on 4 September 1865 at London's Adelphi

Theatre. For the next forty years Jefferson acted Rip, and for many in the audience the two were one and the same person. The plot is simple. The dreamer, Rip, drinks his life away, nagged by his wife, loved by his children, and threatened by Derrick. But Rip will not sign the document which Derrick urges upon him so that he may get his land. After being browbeaten out of his house and spending a night with the little men in the mountain, he returns to reveal the unsigned paper, foil Derrick, and try to fit into a changed situation.

As with the other character plays in the nineteenth century, Rip Van Winkle in the hands of Jefferson became an idealist with realistic dialect, and the play took on humour and pathos of an intricate design. No doubt the change of attitude in the drama towards the end of the nineteenth century had something to do with the character's success, and its development through the century illustrates that change. It should also be pointed out, however, that the stereotyping of immigrant characters, frequently emphasizing their least appealing peculiarities, was to work to the disadvantage of a national unity by leading Americans to basic misconceptions about people from foreign countries. As time passed, the unfortunate character of these ignorant and innocent impressions would have a serious effect upon society. By the mid-twentieth century, for example, the nineteenth-century stereotypes of the American Indian, the Negro, the Chinese and East European minority groups were beginning to explode in the faces of a passive majority as they began to exercise political, social and economic power. Just as the drama had been a force in creating these stereotypes, it later became a force in breaking them.

Although in the American theatre the spectacle plays of war and history along with the popular vehicles for distinctive characters drew the most headlines (if one omits Shakespeare and English imports), the varied fabric of a more complicated society was also being dramatized. Some of the most popular of these plays built upon many aspects of previously successful works. They would frequently include, for example, as many distinctive characters and their dialects as the plot would hold (Yankee, Irishman, Indian, Negro) plus a nationalistic theme and an idealistic love story with an acceptable moral. During the forty years prior to the Civil War America was a country with many social and philosophical forces working upon it, and little escaped the theatre hack's eye.

The sense of romance, individualism and freedom seemed to be everywhere. Cities boomed as the people moved westward, and new states joined the Union. Minds were at work as McCormack invented his reaper, Howe

the sewing machine, Morse the telegraph, and as Goodyear learned to vul-
canize rubber. Religious idealism and utopianism flowed through the works
of John Humphrey Noyes, Mother Ann, Robert Owen and the faithful of
Brookfarm. Yet there was also chaos, violence, poverty, and a distinct lack
of freedom. The paternal system of labour management in New England
was not yet a problem for labourers, but John Jacob Astor and Stephen
Girard were making their fortunes, and industry would soon meet with
difficulties. The population of San Francisco jumped from 800 in 1848 to
30,000 in 1850; but it was burned six times in 1850–1, and vigilance com-
mittees were quickly created. Temperance was a growing issue on the
social front. In the south lithographs by Currier and Ives and such paintings
as Eastman Johnson's *The Old Kentucky Home* suggested a romantic view.
The poor whites in their single rooms with holes for windows and hand-
to-mouth living as shown by Augustus Longstreet in his rough, humorous
sketches presented another. And there were the Negroes, presumably
proved inferior in Nott and Gliddon's *Types of Mankind* (1854), frequently
menaced by some people while championed by such men as William Lloyd
Garrison. Much of this contrasting romantic and yet violently real life
would reach the theatre in major plays or would be suggested obliquely in
a slight sketch. Whereas the serious dramatist was still convinced that poetry
was his mode, the lesser playwright used melodrama and satire to comment
on the ills or oddities of the world that was moving around him.

The Negro had been a character in plays since revolutionary times, but
he was always a comic stereotype mainly by white actors in blackface,
although as early as 1795 a black actor was cast as Sambo in James Murdock's *The Triumphs of Love*. Thomas Dartmouth Rice only increased the
stage version of the Negro with his 'Jumping Jim Crow' routine which was
followed in the 1830s by innumerable Ethiopian or black operas as well as
other Negro characters such as Gumbo Chaff and Zip Coon who later
became Dandy Jim. They all danced and sang, each with his peculiarities;
and there were sketches such as *Bone Squash*. Bone, a chimneysweep in
love with Junietta Ducklegs, sells himself to a Yankee devil named Sam
Switchell and is forced into extravagant actions to make his escape. Then
came the minstrel show. The first of these was the famous Virginia Minstrels at the Bowery Amphitheatre in New York, 6 February 1843, but they
went on and on, reaching a peak of popularity in the 1870s.

It was a combination of his popularity in entertainment and the increasing
awareness of the slave issue that brought the Negro to centre stage from his
position as corner man or comic. Mrs Anna Cora Mowatt Ritchie in *Fashion*

(1845) gave Zeke a more serious role in her plot, while Aunt Chloe in Mrs Sidney Bateman's *Self* (1856) was a sensitive and stabilizing force in this play. As the Civil War became a darkening inevitability the Negro became a major character in such plays as J. T. Trowbridge's attack on the Fugitive Slave Law, *Neighbor Jackwood* (1857); *The Escape; or, A Leap for Freedom* (1858) by the first Negro playwright, William Wells Brown (*c.* 1816–84); Mrs J. C. Swayze's *Ossawatomie Brown* (1859) which dramatized the efforts of John Brown and his Negro fellow conspirators; and Dion Boucicault's successful melodrama, *The Octoroon* (1859). And there is always the world's greatest theatre hit, *Uncle Tom's Cabin* (1852)!

It is true that Harriet Beecher Stowe refused to allow a dramatization of her best-selling novel because 'the world is not good enough yet for it to succeed'. But this did not stop the playwrights who had long practice in dramatizing the best fiction that appeared. James Fenimore Cooper's novels were particularly well received on the English stage, and the works of Bird, William Gilmore Simms, Hawthorne and even the prolific E.D.E.N. Southworth were brought into the theatre. Five months after *Uncle Tom's Cabin* was published in March of 1852 it was dramatized. By autumn there were at least eight versions playing in London, one of which kept Uncle Tom alive. The stage history of the play and the story of the 'Tommers', those devotees who spent their lives performing this one play, are fascinating as the play grew through at least twelve published versions before 1900, ranging from a single act to a five-hour performance of some fifty scenes. George L. Aiken drafted one of the more successful versions which had thirty-one scenes in six acts. Beginning with George Harris's despair at being born, this adaptation presents Eliza's flight across thin ice with little Harry, shows the St Claire household with Orphelia, Eva and Uncle Tom, and dramatizes the disaster that led to the episode involving Simon Legree and Cassy and the final death of Uncle Tom who joins 'Eva, robed in white . . . discovered on the back of a milk-white dove, with expanded wings, as if just soaring upward.' The spectacle and the sentiment were quite overwhelming.

Slavery was one issue for the playwrights; temperance was another. The mass advent of whiskey-loving Irishmen and beer-guzzling Germans during the huge immigration waves of the 1840s is frequently suggested as a source for the social situation that spawned the temperance plays. In point of fact, the problem existed before this time as the founding of the American Temperance Society in Boston in 1826 clearly suggests. The temperance crusade, however, grew in fervour as the century progressed, and the playwrights jumped on the social-issue bandwagon with such plays as *The Drunkard; or, The Fallen Saved* (1844) by W. H. Smith (1806–72); *The Drunkard's Warning* (1856) by Clifton Tayleure or Taylor (1831–87), a quite prolific hack dramatist of the period; and William W. Pratt's dramatization of *Ten Nights in a Bar Room and What I Saw There* (1858). In every play there was generally the weak man enslaved by drink (and frequently a villain who urged him on) who wrought havoc upon family, friends and himself until he reformed. The rewards for such reform were so great that, as one wag suggested, it was almost enough to make one take to drink just so one could stop and reap the benefits.

Fashionable society or life in the big city was another favourite topic for the dramatists of this mid-century period. In these plays playwrights seemed to have two major objectives: to have as much fun as possible with what they saw, and to emphasize a strong nationalism. Sometimes the two went together as in Anna Cora Mowatt Ritchie's *Fashion; or, Life in New York* (1845). Although Mrs Ritchie (1819–70) wrote other plays and enjoyed some success as an actress, she is remembered chiefly for this play which was a successful combination of several successful aspects of past plays. American society, too, had become very conscious of itself. Thoreau had just explained in *Walden* the weakness that Americans showed by copying the fashions of the French, and Emerson had earlier complained about listening 'too long to the courtly muses of Europe'. Consciously or subconsciously, Mrs Ritchie responded to both writers and explained her comedy as a 'good-natured satire' upon some of the follies of a new country given to imitating the worst from other lands. Her characters include an American hero not unlike Colonel Manly from *The Contrast*; a cantankerous Yankee who distinguishes right from wrong with a cudgel and draws the patriotic moral; a Negro, a boorish poet, a French maid and a fake French count. Fashion, as 'an agreement to substitute etiquette for virtue, decorum for purity, manners for morals', is properly discouraged, and the high-principled heroine is rewarded, albeit with what seems a very dull young man. In the melodramatic side of the plot Mrs Ritchie builds upon the great wealth that an American businessman of this period might accumulate by whatever means. The rich man, Mr Tiffany, is saved from his blackmailing clerk while his daughter is saved from marrying the fake count. Throughout both plots the main object of the ridicule is the social-climbing Mrs Tiffany who apes everything that is foreign. Quite distinct from other plays at this time, *Fashion* has some very witty dialogue in a fast-moving, reasonably well-structured plot.

Numerous playwrights satirized social conditions in such plays as Mrs Sidney F. Bateman's (1823–81) *Self* (1856), which parallels the plot in *Fashion* with the thesis that 'our labors are prompted by that great motive power of human nature – self!' G. P. Wilkins's *Young New York* (1856) ridicules the wealthy, self-made merchant, as well as foreign imitations and the US Congress while extolling young individualism. Anonymous plays such as *New York in Slices* (1854), *The Seamstress of New York* (1851), *Upper Ten and Lower Twenty* (1854) and *Life in New York* (1856) provided temporary entertainment by emphasizing local happenings and stereotype city characters. Comments on slavery, politics, temperance, the foreign element – anything might appear in these plays, and frequently scenes would change as current incidents would be added to a play.

One popular theatre phenomenon resulting from this interest in big-city social life was the Mose play. It all started at the Olympic, that small New York theatre which prospered under the management of William Mitchell. Able to attract both lower- and upper-class New Yorkers to his burlesques of happenings in New York, Mitchell provided good entertainment both on the stage and in the pit. During the early 1840s, when other New York theatres were experiencing financial difficulties, it became fashionable to attend the Olympic. Mitchell's prompter at this time was Benjamin A. Baker (1818–90), and Uncle Ben Baker, like many theatre employees, wrote a play every now and then. For his own benefit on 15 February 1848, Baker wrote and produced *A Glance at New York in 1848* with F. S. Chanfrau playing Mose the fire b'hoy. Subtitled a 'Local Drama', the play shows the greenhorn in New York falling for every big-city gag but helped by Mose who, like most of those in the pit at the Olympic, enjoyed practical jokes and could fight a fire, sing a song or love a girl with equal zest. The play was an immediate success and, with an occasionally added scene, ran for seventy-four performances that year. Chanfrau made his fortune and fame with the part of Mose, and American drama had a new local character. Imitations, of course, immediately appeared. Baker himself recreated his hero in *New York As It Is* (1848), *Mose in China* (1849) and *Mose in California* (c. 1850). Others provided such imitations as *A Glance at Philadelphia*, *Philadelphia As It Is* and *Mose in France*, as the Mose plays multiplied in a fashion similar to the Yankee and Irish plays but did not reach their popularity.

Through its theatre America somewhat haphazardly but quite completely revealed itself. Granted, it was mainly a theatre of entertainment with few dramatists of serious insight, but the wits made their points with effective ridicule while the hacks knew that audiences enjoyed seeing themselves or perhaps their neighbours, near or far. The social plays, therefore, were neither profound nor always particularly well done. Mainly, they were good fun and a bit of an escape for those who found the world 'too much'.

7 Realism and the drama 1865–1900

The Civil War is both a logical and a convenient division in the progress of drama in America. The rapid growth of the country prior to this event had dramatized the conflict of opportunity and idealism along with the confusion of varied social and political approaches to life and the threat of war. Although the opportunity continued, there were a number of new forces working upon man which demanded that he temper his idealism with a strong sense of realism. Spreading to America from France and England, a new concept of realism was becoming a meaningful force in American arts and letters as writers and dramatists reflected the life moving around them. There was, for example, the great westward movement, set off by the Homestead Act of 1862. Although for many this was a time for the romance of western heroes as Walt Whitman chanted 'America . . . the western sea', there were also the plains wars, the tragedy of the Donner Pass party, and the west as portrayed by Ole Rolvag and E. W. Howe. The Civil War itself made Americans look at life more realistically, some bitterly, as scallawags and carpet-baggers plundered the south.

For a great many people Marx's *Manifesto* in 1848, Darwin's publication in 1859 of *The Origin of Species*, and the works of Charles Lyell in geology, Auguste Comte in sociology and Herbert Spencer in biology provided unalterable evidence that life was not a completely optimistic and romantic episode. People throughout America had their beliefs severely shaken, and results were observable in society. For historians the period immediately following the Civil War was the Gilded Age – the age of the robber barons when men like Stanford, Carnegie and Vanderbilt made fortunes that produced, in the phrase of Thorstein Veblen, the 'Age of Conspicuous Waste', the downfall of decency, moderation, gentility. Science, industry and the country itself advanced but at a price. Man was being forced to abandon his romantic view and look around carefully – with an eye to the practical, real world.

All of this the dramatist saw and recorded for the theatre inasmuch as doing so was in accord with his objective of entertaining an audience. If he criticized society, it had to be in so light a manner that an audience would not be forced to think too much, because the playwright was still at the mercy of an actor or manager. Although with the efforts of Dion Boucicault, among others, a copyright law had been passed (18 August 1856) which gave the dramatist the 'sole rights to print and publish' his work as well as to act and perform it, an international copyright agreement was not signed by the United States until 1891. By the late nineteenth century, however, dramatists had gained considerably in stature. At this time a playwright could make a living writing plays, as Bronson Howard illustrated with his career. But he was an exception at this date. The playwright could also claim his work in print and be sure that his name was attached to the play. Until Clyde Fitch became popular at the very end of the century, however, that playwright who wanted to assure his success in America had best be an actor or perhaps own or manage a theatre.

One of the first and most obvious casualties in the new emphasis upon realism in drama was poetic drama. This does not mean, of course, that poetic drama was removed from the stage entirely. Certainly, Shakespeare's plays retained their fascination for American audiences, especially as they were interpreted by Edwin Booth and Lawrence Barrett, and some other poetic dramas were produced. But the influence of the prose plays from Europe was being felt, and W. D. Howells, the major apostle of realism in America, had declared that prose was now the language of the stage. Yet even Howells wrote *Yorick's Love* (1878), a poetic play which Barrett acted off and on until his death in 1891, while Boker's *Francesca da Rimini* enjoyed marked success at Barrett's hands in 1882. But those few new dramatists who tried poetic drama, such as William Young with *Pendragon* (1881), met with little success. There would be a revival of interest in the poetic drama after the turn of the century, but for American dramatists during the rise of realism the mode was prose.

The movement towards realistic drama which seemed to emerge most prominently after the Civil War had already been clearly foreshadowed. Local-colour drama, fiction and poetry had emphasized characters, dialects and customs peculiar to particular sections of America from New England through New York to the south and west. As sectionalism gained strength during the war and an emphasis upon the realistic qualities of man and his surroundings was stressed immediately afterwards, dramatists simply undertook a part in this popular art form that only the theatre could provide. Of the stage characters that had been successful in the past, only the 'noble savage' could not be adapted to this philosophic change. As the backwoodsman gained heroic stature in a national movement westward, the Indian became the natural enemy, to emerge as a semi-hero only in the Wild West shows and such panoramic spectacles as Buffalo Bill's *Scout of the Plains*. With the new emphasis the Yankee became more representative of New England, while the Irishman and German disappeared as major figures in the drama other than in the sketches of Edward Harrigan. New York continued to exercise its unique qualities in plays, while the south remained merely a romantic background for drama. This type of local-colour drama, however, was really a prelude to a few serious dramas at the turn of the century when the realism of Ibsen was more closely imitated.

Western frontier drama might be traced back to James Kirke Paulding's (1778–1860) *The Lion of the West* (1831). The hero of this play was Nimrod Wildfire, but his west was Kentucky, just as the frontier characters dramatized from the novels of Cooper, Bird and Simms did not travel much further west than the Appalachian chain. With the 1870s western frontier drama burst upon an audience anxious to see western spectacle, western customs and western characters. J. J. McCloskey's (1825–1913) *Across the Continent* (1870), for example, is really an impossible mixture of New York melodrama and western scenes. With an Indian raid thwarted at a Union Pacific Station the audience got the excitement it required. Augustin Daly placed his western melodrama *Horizon* (1871) somewhere in the western territories, while Frank Murdock's *Davy Crockett* (1872), played by Frank Mayo until his death in 1896, probably took place in Tennessee. As might be expected, this play's success depended upon 'the strong arm of a backwoodsman', Davy Crockett, the 'natural gentleman' who followed his father's motto – 'Be sure you're right, then go ahead' – and won the girl. Bret Harte and Mark Twain tried unsuccessfully to emphasize the western life with *Ah Sin* (1877), based upon a Harte character, while Bartley Campbell had great popularity with his dramatization of Harte's stcry in *My Partner* (1879). Augustus Thomas (1857–1934) later emphasized the western local in *Arizona* (1899), *In Mizzoura* (1893) and *Colorado* (1901). Joseph Arthur (1848–1906) made the most of an Indiana setting in *Blue Jeans* (1891) but gained fame through his use of the buzz-saw device which the villain employed to intimidate the heroine. And, of course, David Belasco achieved something of a landmark with *The Girl of the Golden West* (1905). Generally, the western drama capitalized on spectacular scenery or on stage machinery which inevitably functioned to save the heroine in the third act.

The best illustration of local-colour drama of New England is Denman Thompson's (1833–1911) *The Old Homestead* (1886). It all started as a thirty-minute sketch produced in 1875 under the title *Joshua Whitcomb* with Thompson playing Uncle Josh. Two years later it was a full-length play which Thompson, with some help from George W. Ryer, then transformed into *The Old Homestead* and presented under this title in April 1886. A tremendous success, the play was toured by Thompson every year until his death in 1911; then other actors took over, and at least five film versions have been made. Not until 1927, however, was the full text of the play published. Swansea, New Hampshire (just outside of Keene), where Thompson spent most of his teenage life, is the scene of the play, and the modern theatregoer may visit the Potash Bowl in July each year and laugh and cry as the Old Homestead Association of Swansea, New Hampshire, produces *The Old Homestead*.

Sentiment filled the theatre as Uncle Josh gave the curtain speech to the audience: 'Come up in June when all natur' is at her best – come on, all of you, and let the scarlet runners chase you back to childhood.' Howells was so impressed that he called it one of the 'sweetest and simplest' of American plays: 'On a wider plane than anyone else has yet attempted, Mr Thompson gives us in this piece a representation of American life.' Be that as it may, the action shows Josh first at his farm in New England worrying about his son who has run away after being falsely accused of stealing; then he visits an old friend in New York, falls for the greenhorn gags, but finds his son a victim of drink. The final act celebrates his son's homecoming in New England. The play is more than a story. It exudes sentiment and morality, but it also exhibits innumerable little New England mannerisms in speech, action and custom – a true example of local colour.

Another area whose local peculiarities excited playwrights was New York City, a point clearly illustrated in drama since the 1840s. In fact, the plays of Edward Harrigan (1844–1911) depended a great deal upon previous New York drama yet added a comic charm and the distinctive atmosphere of an area in New York. His plays, he said, were intended as a 'series of photographs of life today in the Empire City'. For this reason, and because he also believed in the smiling aspects of life which these plays presented, W. D. Howells praised Harrigan's touches of realism and found in his work 'the spring of a true American Comedy'. Other critics were less impressed. A. M. Palmer, manager of the Madison Square Theatre, even found his plays unworthy of serious consideration. Harrigan, however, was most certainly a serious dramatist as well as an excellent comic actor. Commenting on his own playwriting theories in *Harper's Weekly*, on 2 February 1889, he explained that he chose simple and natural plots, worked carefully to present conflicts and create scenes of wit and humour that lead to effective climaxes, and tried always to be realistic, to be 'truthful to the laws which govern society as well as to the types of which it is composed'.

In 1871 Harrigan had started his acting career with Anthony J. Cannon, a young singer and female impersonator who soon changed his name to Hart, and as 'Harriganandhart' they performed together for fourteen years. During this time, Harrigan started writing the sketches that they performed, finally creating the Mulligan plays for which he is best known. The scene of these plays was Mulligan's Alley in New York's Sixth Ward where Dan Mulligan lived. Modelled on the Lower East Side of New York which Harrigan knew so well, his characters, dialogue and scene presented a jumbled population of Germans, Italians, Negroes and Irish as they faced their everyday problems in ward politics, the policy rackets and the battle of the sexes. There was the Wee Drop Saloon run by Walfingham Mc-Sweeny, an Italian junk shop, a Chinese laundry–lodging combination, Lochmuller's butcher's shop, and a Negro social club called the Full Moon Union. Whatever issues bothered the city of New York and its residents – emotional, social, economic or political – Harrigan would create a play about them in record time. And with realistic sets and costumes supported by carefully worked-out 'business' on the stage, he dramatized an international community at Harrigan and Hart's Theatre Comique. The Mulligans, however, seemed to focus his theatrical formula, and *The Mulligan Guard Ball* (1879) was one of his best plays. As usual a situation started the action: Tommy Mulligan and Katy Lochmuller were in love. As the Mulligan Guards celebrated in the Harp and Shamrock Ballroom which was below the Red Man's Hall where a Negro group called the Skidmore Guards were having a dance, Tommy and Katy eloped. There was a great fight when the ceiling collapsed with a 'grand crash' and the two groups unceremoniously merged, and there was another fight when the two sets of parents discovered a marriage which they had both opposed. But it all ended happily as did his other plays featuring the Mulligans as they celebrated such events as *The Mulligan Guard Picnic* (1878) and *The Mulligan Guard Chowder* (1879).

The distinction between realistic drama and local-colour drama is a matter of focus. Whereas the local-colour writer emphasizes the peculiarities of a section of the country in order to give a certain flavour to his play or to make that section distinctive, the realistic writer is concerned with a truthful presentation of life – a focusing of the universe from his particular philosophical position. The local-colour dramatist, then, might also be considered a realist (as Howellls considered Denman Thompson) if the details of his play supported a searching view of life that showed psychological insight and penetrating truths about man.

The critic who commented most fervently on realistic drama in America was, of course, William Dean Howells (1837–1920), the 'Father of American Realism'. As a successful essayist, poet, novelist, critic and journalist, Howells, like other prominent writers in the last part of the nineteenth century, wanted very much to add the drama to his list of accomplishments. He was not distinctive in this desire as the list of those who tried and failed so impressively suggests – Mark Twain, Henry James, Bret Harte, Hamlin Garland, Stephen Crane and Harold Frederic. But only Howells contributed with any degree of success to the realistic development of American drama at this time, and he did so by attempting to adapt to the drama the same principle which he applied to realistic fiction. Prose, he found, was the language of the people, not poetry; and both soliloquies and asides were 'weak crutches' of the dramatist. Morality was the 'soul of all things'; realism, 'a truthful representation of life', was the proper form for literary art. Although he occasionally flouted his theories by writing poetic drama, most of his thirty-six plays emphasized realism in background, scenes, dialogue, characters, incidents and ideas. That he was not a successful dramatist on the commercial stage simply showed that he was out of step with the exciting melodrama that was then popular and that he did not enjoy close ties with the right actors and managers. (Bronson Howard, in fact, felt that Howells's attempt to direct the theatre towards realism was an unwanted intrusion.) One reason for his failure was his obvious insistence that art be based upon the everyday incidents of a man's life, thus eliminating the possibility that he might exploit the tremendous conflicts which provided theatrical excitement during the Age of Melodrama. Lacking that commercial success, Howells's plays, as he later recalled, found 'a very amiable public with the youth who played in drawing rooms and church parlors'.

Although Howells had his greatest commercial success with two full-length plays – *A Counterfeit Presentment* (1877) and *Yorick's Love* (1878), both acted by Lawrence Barrett – the long play was not his forte. *Out of the Question* (1877) was, as he said, a 'middle form' between narrative and drama. *Colonel Sellers as a Scientist* (1883), which he wrote with Mark Twain, never had a fair test on the stage in spite of its extravagant farcical episodes. *A Foregone Conclusion* (1884–5), which he adapted from William Poel's version of Howells's novel, had only a brief stage career under A. M. Palmer's management, and his collaboration with Paul Kester on *The Rise of Silas Lapham* (1898) failed to interest any actor.

Where Howells gained his reputation for realistic drama was in his one-act plays, particularly in those twelve one-act farce-comedies which dramatized incidents in the lives of the Robertses and Campbells (Mr and Mrs Howells and Mr and Mrs Clemens). Following day-to-day problems in a Boston society, Howells dramatized such events as a Christmas dinner delayed when friends of the Robertses are stuck between floors in *The Elevator* (1894), or he explored the problems of a hostess who has two additional guests for dinner in *The Unexpected Guests* (1893). During *Five O'Clock Tea* (1887) Mr Willis Campbell proposed to Amy Somers and the next year became jealous at the seemingly improper attentions of a young man towards his wife in *A Likely Story* (1888). Read as a twelve-act episodic play, the Roberts–Campbell comedies present believable characters in the shrewd Amy Somers Campbell, the scatterbrained but kind and lovable Mrs Roberts, Campbell as a charming wit and intriguer, and Roberts as an absentminded writer incapable of taking affront.

In other one-act plays Howells concerned himself with the problems of young people in love (*An Indian Giver*, 1897; *Self-Sacrifice*, 1911) when through some quirk of feminine psychology a girl must relinquish a man completely before she realizes that she loves him. Throughout, Howells was interested in the ideas and actions of real life from which he could represent the faults, foibles and conventions of a certain level of society. His object was truth, his technique realism, as his carefully written stage directions as well as his scenes and characters illustrated. In these scene descriptions he anticipated the literary quality of J. M. Barrie and G. B. Shaw. With both his criticism of contemporary drama and his plays Howells contributed effectively to the development of the drama in America. Additionally, it should always be noted that Howells was the only significant critic in late nineteenth-century America who saw the value of Ibsen's work.

The only nineteenth-century American dramatist who seriously imitated Ibsen's theories, however, was James A. Herne (1839–1901). As an actor-manager-playwright, Herne felt the impact of the twin forces – science and democracy – that challenged all sensitive life in America. Following the philosophy of Howells and Hamlin Garland, Herne created his own approach in 'Art for Truth's Sake in the Drama' (*Arena* (February 1897), 17, pp. 361–70) when he pronounced *truthfulness* to be the 'supreme quality' of all drama which must 'interest' and 'instruct'. Art for truth's sake, he asserted, emphasizes 'humanity', is 'serious' and works 'to perpetuate the life of its time'. With his most realistic play, *Margaret Fleming*, which was as unacceptable to American audiences as Ibsen's *Ghosts*, Herne truly initiated the period of modern drama in America.

Writing with David Belasco or in the Belasco manner during the first two decades of his theatre career, Herne gave little evidence of his later accomplishments. *Drifting Apart* (1888), which combined a melodramatic plot concerned with temperance with the realistic scene and dialect of a New England fishing village, was his first play to attract the attention of Howells and Garland. Then on 4 May 1891, after a brief try-out at Lynn, Massachusetts, the previous year, *Margaret Fleming* was performed in Boston's Chickering Hall, rented for the occasion by Howells and Garland, among others. Taken to New York after a three weeks' run, it was not successful, undoubtedly because, as more than one critic noted, it did not 'give pleasure'.

The plot of *Margaret Fleming* tells of a sensual and faithless husband, Philip, whose motto 'live and let live' underlines his business activities as well as his personal life with wife and child. The contrasting emotional sensitivity of his wife Margaret is indicated by a disease which may blind her if she receives a great shock. This shock comes when Margaret discovers that the unmarried sister of her own child's nurse has died giving birth to Philip's baby. In the final fourth act Margaret has lost her sight while Philip shamefully returns to a home with two children and a wife whose mysterious smile at the final curtain reveals her own sense of moral superiority as well as hope for the future. The early version did not reconcile husband and wife, but Herne was prevailed upon to write a new final act which combines a traditional stage climax with the smile which suggests an intriguing ambiguity. But the plot does not explain fully the 'epoch-marking' character of this play. Although the moralizing of Margaret's doctor is extremely heavyhanded, the truthfulness of the dialects, scenes and the characters in particular is everywhere emphasized. Symbolism is effective in a song that Margaret sings as well as in the comments on the care of roses. The concept that Margaret reveals through her cry that truth has killed her is a reference to Ibsen's work which appears again in Herne's commentary on the double standard, medical practices, and the scene during which Margaret unbuttons her blouse to nurse the newborn child. This scene was the shocking event for all audiences. A strong emphasis on social determinism also discloses Herne's interest in Darwin and Henry George. Essentially, the play suggests a new objective for the drama and shows the absorption of the dramatist with the ideas that eventually were to shape modern America.

For the historian of American drama *Margaret Fleming* was Herne's most meaningful work. For Herne, *Shore Acres* (1892), which made him a million dollars, was perhaps a more considerable achievement. The central character in this play is Uncle Nat Berry, a kindhearted, tolerant man of selfless character and a spirit of overwhelming sentimental goodness. There was also spectacle in the lighthouse scene and an effective quality of real life in the odds and ends of careworn daily activity which culminate in the play's final scene as Uncle Nat wanders through the house making sure that everything is safe before he goes to bed. Although Herne's final play, *The Reverend Griffith Davenport* (1899), was not a great financial success, it illustrates once again the dramatist's serious objectives in writing plays. When the Civil War began, one Davenport son chose to fight for the north, the other for the south. Davenport himself, with strong anti-slavery theories that are opposed by his neighbours, is finally prevailed upon by Lincoln to lead Union troops to his home where he is captured by his own son and led away to prison. Like Margaret Fleming and Uncle Nat, Davenport is a strong man who faces a crisis and makes a meaningful decision. There is no doubt that, in the main, the work of James A. Herne points to a new emphasis in American drama which, unfortunately, took many years to become fully realized.

Two other dramatists whose works should be seen as contributing to this new realistic approach to writing plays are William Gillette (1855–1937) and Steele MacKaye (1842–94). Actually, Gillette deserves only a brief line because it was due to his acting rather than his playwriting that his plays became realistic. 'The artistic representations of reality': this was his acting objective. Of his twenty full-length plays, only the two concerned with the Civil War – *Held By the Enemy* (1886) and *Secret Service* (1895) – and his dramatization of the exploits of Sherlock Holmes were considered successful on his terms. Steele MacKaye had a more varied career. An intense and artistic genius of the theatre, MacKaye studied with Delsarte in France and lectured on his 'Method' in America, established schools of acting, managed theatres in New York, invented such theatre innovations as the elevator stage and side lighting, designed the fantastic Spectatorium for the Chicago Exposition in 1893, and wrote at least fifteen plays including spectacles such as *The World Finder* (1894) which he created for a Scenitorium production when the finances for the Spectatorium were withdrawn.

Of MacKaye's plays, *Paul Kauvar* (1887) showed his intense concern for the trial of the anarchists after the Haymarket Square riot in Chicago. *Won At Last* (1877) tells of a man who marries for purely cynical reasons and then discovers that he loves his wife. With an interest in realistic character and a social thesis the play might have become a good social comedy had it not evolved into slight melodrama. MacKaye's best and most successful play was *Hazel Kirke* (1879). Dunstan Kirke, a man of iron will, had long ago promised his daughter to Rodney when this man had saved him from bankruptcy. Therefore when she falls in love with Arthur Carringford, his bad temper overcomes him and he curses her: 'May my eyes never more behold thee.' Misfortunes follow Hazel as her marriage to Arthur seems illegal, and she returns home to a blind Dunstan who refuses her forgiveness. Despondent, she tries to drown herself as Dunstan helplessly agonizes, but she is finally saved by Arthur and forgiven by her father. Basically, it is a sentimental melodrama very carefully crafted and made fresh and truthful by the realistic characters of Hazel and Dunstan. Toured successfully for a number of years, it suggests the degree of realism which appealed to American audiences. The more psychologically penetrating realism of Ibsen would have to wait until the twentieth century was well under way before it was acceptable on the American stage.

8 An age of melodrama: sensation and sententia 1850–1912

The 'third form' is difficult to isolate to everyone's satisfaction because it can be approached in quite different yet, depending upon one's interests, equally valid ways. Most critics agree that it is a form that reaches its most satisfying height in theatre production. Hence the structural analyst of drama points out the accumulating series of incidents involving the hero or heroine and the villain, the emphasis upon the manipulation of events to create suspense, the unexpected discoveries which move the plot, and the extreme reversals of fortune which give meaning to the compassion and hate aroused in the audience. For the historian, melodrama is a term presumably invented by Jean-Jacques Rousseau for his play *Pygmalion* (1766) and carried to a degree of overwhelming theatre success by Guilbert de Pixérécourt, the king of French melodrama in 1800, whose creations stimulated innumerable imitations.

Certainly, melodrama has been a serious art form in America. Although Pixérécourt introduced such artificially manipulated characteristics as the flamboyant gesture, the last-minute rescue, providential acts of God, unmotivated surprises and a sense of rigid justice unknown in the real world, he was completely sincere in presenting the thought in the play. Owen Davis, the most successful writer of melodrama in America at the turn of the twentieth century, also emphasized the necessity of believing in his story, of refusing to give in to a cynical mood. Writing of *Nellie, the Beautiful Cloak Model* he said, 'I was honestly moved by the lady's misfortunes.' And so must the audience be moved. Consequently, the emphasis on moral instruction in melodrama has generally been very strong. The numerous temperance plays in America illustrate this point, as does the story of a French mother who discovered that her son was a thief. 'Of what use was it to take you to the plays of Pixérécourt?' she cried. Invariably, the writer of melodrama had a comment to make, whether it was simply the assertion of a wholesome sentiment or an observation about, say, woman's place in a man's world. In America from 1850 to the First World War dramatists were to use melodrama as the chief form of expression for their varied ideas.

The writer of melodrama had one major obligation which he could not refuse: he must excite and thrill his audience. Writers of melodrama in America had no peers in this achievement throughout the late nineteenth-century theatre world. Having learned from Pixérécourt and August von Kotzebue (whom William Dunlap had first adapted in the late eighteenth century), they went on to even more grand stage successes. Probably the culture of nineteenth-century America contributed more than casually to this theatrical phenomenon. Here were an emotionally idealistic and romantic people who believed in that opportunity where the best could be reached if one worked. 'Root, hog, or die!' was a popular sentiment, and there was faith in the individual. As the romantic simplified his world, so did the writer of melodrama who easily divided good from evil and right from wrong. The heroic adventure stories and sentimental novels of the mid-nineteenth century became the great success tales of the late nineteenth-century Horatio Alger. A pragmatic philosophy underscored both the social and scientific advance and helped to reveal a generation of American culture. The reasons are quite complicated, but the lack of popular acceptance of the pessimistic determinism of Theodore Dreiser and the ideas of Zola simply re-emphasized the general enthusiasm for melodrama in America before the First World War.

Shortly after the turn of the century the thought in melodrama began to change noticeably although the form remained basically the same. Clayton Hamilton noted this change in an essay on 'Melodrama, Old and New' (1911), when he found 'a new species of melodrama that is ashamed of itself' as it takes the form of 'a serious study of contemporary social problems'. Although Hamilton was showing an ignorance of the traditional potential of melodrama, he was indicating something quite true about the general character of late nineteenth-century American melodrama. Melodrama, of course, had always enjoyed an eclectic subject matter. The wild west, the city, the historical past, the romantic or realistic present, crime, temperance, war – the writer of melodrama had few restrictions. Obviously he was not primarily concerned with psychological insight into character or catastrophe that accompanies tragedy. Instead, he created characters that were generally one-dimensional, while he relied less on plot than on an abundance of situations to which the characters were sublimated while sensation and sentiment gave a ring of truth to the advertising: 'For every smile a tear, for every tear a smile.' By the First World War one kind of melodrama in America had reached its zenith and passed. Consciously and unhappily, Hamilton noted the fact.

By definition, according to genre, most of the American plays written before the Civil War were either farce-comedy or melodrama. It is also true that most of the plays adapted from the French for American audiences were melodrama. Dunlap adapted several as did Payne. Richard Penn Smith's *The Sentinels; or, The Two Sergeants* (1829), adapted from D'Aubigny's *Les Deux Sergents*, illustrates both his own preference for melodrama and the popularity of adaptations. In this play the villain Morazzi works his evil to prevent the arrival of one of the sergeants in order that he may execute the other and then marry his fiancée. But the hero is 'Saved!' – a watchword of this type of drama – through the careful manipulation of time, thus illustrating another basic factor in melodrama: the artificial contrivance of both time and action. Another very popular melodrama of this early period was *Mazeppa; or, The Wild Horse of Tartary* (1825) in a version by Payne adapted from Byron's poem. The exciting scene in this play was the wild ride by the protagonist tied to the back of a horse. In the large nineteenth-century theatres where equestrian drama was also very popular, the scene was spectacular, made all the more so in the 1860s when Adah Isaacs Mencken took the ride strapped 'naked' to the back of a 'wild' horse.

Among the numerous writers of melodrama in America during the last half of the nineteenth century three names are outstanding: Dion Boucicault, Augustin Daly and David Belasco. The earliest of these, Dion Boucicault (1820–90), is sometimes questioned as an American dramatist because he remained basically Irish both as an actor and as a playwright and because his time was divided between America and England. His influence upon America, however, was considerable, and most of his best work was accomplished in America. Certainly, he effectively illustrates the kind of melodrama that dominated the American theatre during his life-time.

When he first came to America in 1853, Boucicault had already had more than twenty plays produced under his name in London, including the very successful *London Assurance* (1841). Before he returned to England in 1860 he had produced two of his most memorable American melodramas, *The Poor of New York* (1857) and *The Octoroon* (1859), plus the Irish melodrama, *The Colleen Bawn* (1860). The first of these, an adaptation of Édouard Brisebarre and Eugène Nus's *Les Pauvres de Paris*, shows Boucicault at his melodramatic best. Frightened by the financial panic of 1837, Fairweather deposits $100,000 in Bloodgood's bank, then learns that it is about to fail. He dies of apoplexy when he is not allowed to withdraw his money, which Bloodgood then keeps while dumping the body in the street to be found the next morning. But a clerk named Badger has witnessed the event and found the deposit slip. Twenty years later, during the Panic of 1857, Fairweather's widow and children are poverty-stricken, and Bloodgood is still trying to get that deposit slip from Badger. Finally, he sets a house on fire to gain his end but is foiled as all melodramatic villains are. A brief analysis shows that the principal characteristics of melodrama are carefully adhered to in *The Poor of New York*. The four principal stock characters of melodrama are found in Bloodgood as the villain; Mrs Fairweather as the major virtuous heroine with her daughter as the secondary one; Mark Livingstone as the hero, once wealthy but now poor, who helps the Fairweathers; and Badger as the comic relief who helps the hero. Clearly, the action of the play progresses almost completely through the machinations of the villain who is finally arrested and punished while the good people are rewarded. The pathos and sentiment of the play are particularly displayed through the virtuous poverty of the Fairweathers who also suggest the temporary serious-ness of the major action of the play. Finally, the fire provided a sensation very popular with nineteenth-century audiences.

The Octoroon not only employed a socially sensitive and significant thesis – the love of a white man for a Negro – but added the popular characters of Indian, Yankee and Negro, with their dialects, to the established criteria of melodrama. By emphasizing a romantic love and creating the necessary pathos and sentiment around a beautiful and intelligent woman about to be sold as a slave, Boucicault was able to avoid sectional passions and remain discreetly noncommittal. Besides the suspense and sensation of the auction scene and the pursuit of the villain following the spectacular burning of the steamer, Boucicault added the realistic device of the exposed photographic plate by which the villain is identified. Although this device came from one novel and the plot of the play from another, Mayne Reid's *The Quadroon* (1856), Boucicault contributed both original thought and craftsmanship to make a popular play. Unlike many melodramas, however, the play has an un-happy yet sentimental ending with the heroine's death. At this time, of course, it could have had no other final curtain. English audiences, however, were so repulsed by this ending that Boucicault, though very reluctantly, supplied a conventional happy conclusion for certain London performances of his play.

From 1873 until his death in 1890 Boucicault spent the majority of his time in America, but wherever he was he wrote plays, at least 135 either alone or in collaboration. Some of his most successful were *The Shaughraun* (1874), *Belle Lamar* (1874), *Jessie Brown; or, The Relief of Lucknow* (1858) and *Andy Blake* (1854). Melodrama was his forte, and when William Winter, in *Other Days, Being Chronicles and Memories of the Stage* (1900), listed Boucicault's 'supreme achievements', he noted 'the ticking of the telegraph in "The Long Strike"; the midnight farewell of the schoolmaster in "The Parish Clerk"; and the incident of Jessie's concealment of the broken floor in "Jessie Brown"'.

Boucicault also deserves credit for having evolved a meaningful theory of drama which he passed on to readers of the *North American Review* in some thirteen essays from 1877 to 1889. In his 'The Art of Dramatic Com-position' (*N.A.R*, January, February 1878) he shows a debt to Aristotle as well as his own invention. 'A drama is the imitation of a complete action, formed by a sequence of incidents designed to be acted, not narrated, by the person or persons whom such incidents befall. Its object is to give pleasure by exciting in the mind of the spectator a sympathy for fellow creatures suffering their fate.' He also observed that 'the drama is the necessary product of the age in which it lives, and of which it is the moral, social, and physical expression.' Both as playwright and as teacher, he contributed to America's developing melodrama.

It was not just by chance that the best-known dramatists in late nine-teenth-century America were also active and well-known people in the theatre. In fact, it is impossible to write the history of American drama in the nineteenth century without tracing to some extent the history of American activity in the theatre. Although Augustin Daly (1838–99) did not combine acting and theatre management as Boucicault, MacKaye, Belasco and Herne did, he was probably the most powerful man of the theatre during his lifetime: the first stage director in the modern sense. A logical extension of his control over the theatre was his ability to write and adapt plays for his theatre and company. It was, however, clearly in the tradition of the theatre manager that he was concerned with pleasing the public and making money. With this motivation he created (mainly with the help of others, particularly his brother Joseph) local-colour plays (*Horizon*, 1871), business plays (*The Big Bonanza*, 1875), poetic drama (a translation of *Un drama nuevo*, 1874), simple farces (*A Night Off*, 1885), social melodramas and comedies (*Divorce*, 1871; *Pique*, 1875) and sensational melodrama (*Under the Gaslight*, 1867). Aided by an effective system for adapting good foreign plays to American circumstances, Daly provided what he thought the public wanted. As the country advanced and tastes changed, he changed his bills. When certain writers such as Howells and Mark Twain became popular, he tried to get them to write for the theatre but with the limitations which he felt the public dictated. In such instances, therefore, he did not stimulate the writing of good plays, and he should not be considered to be one who encouraged the free expression of original drama in America. Shaw and Ibsen, through similar reasoning, were never produced on his stages. A strongminded impresario, he followed the economic, social and political changes taking place and tried to write or adapt plays that would be acceptable to his audiences.

Daly started out as a drama critic, but after 1862, the date of his first successful play, *Leah the Forsaken*, he became part of the theatre – playwright-adaptor, theatre manager and *régisseur*. As an adaptor of foreign plays, Daly relied upon translators, and in all of his dramatic writing, even as a dramatic critic, his brother Joseph played a significant part and may have been almost totally responsible for some of the plays. Because he understood the requirements of the theatre, Daly was able to inject the right ingredients into his adaptations. Both as an adaptor and as a writer of original plays, however, his reputation is deservedly limited. He was mainly a contriver of effects, a bold and ingenious creator of theatre magic. But in his commercial successes he also suggested something of the society that his sensational melodramas reflected.

From among his excellent melodramas – *A Flash of Lightning* (1868) with its water and fire spectacles; *The Red Scarf* (1868), in which the hero was tied to a log and sent to the sawmill; *The Dark City* (1877); and *Undercurrent* (1888), dealing with the rough side of city life – *Under the Gaslight* (1867) shows his bag of tricks as well as any. In four acts and eleven scenes carefully arranged for sensational effect Daly first shows Laura's fall from social acceptance when the villainous Byke and Old Judas claim her, then her attempt to hide so as not to embarrass Ray who was to marry her before he discovered her past. Snorkey's persistent efforts to help Laura, who is finally able to save him from death when Byke ties him to the railroad tracks, provide excitement, while the final revelation that Laura is indeed well-born and deserving of Ray brings a happy ending. The exposition in Act I is well handled as villainy and comic relief are backed by strong social comment. Laura is beautiful, kind and good; and her acknowledgement of a superior power which she does not question ends the act with an excellent line: 'It is Heaven's own blow!' The affluence of the Blue Room at Delmonico's is dramatically contrasted with the basement room which houses Laura at the beginning of Act II, an act filled with fascinating new city characters such as Peachblossom and Bermudas, as well as a police court scene with the identifying devices of melodrama in the ebony box and the child's clothes, and a pier scene complete with vaudeville acts, a fight and Laura's jump into the river. It is difficult to build on such an act as that, but Daly did it with his famous railroad scene. After that, the scene switches to an elegant boudoir in a Long Branch cottage where the bad are punished and the good rewarded. All happens 'just in time', and there will be hope for tomorrow. In Laura's words, 'We shall have come to bless it, for it will bring the long sought sunlight of our lives.' Perhaps Daly's success did prolong melodrama on the American stage, but there is little doubt that he created excellent examples of that type.

Perhaps because some of his plays were translated into more serious dramatic art and perhaps because he lived into the modern period and was forced to cope with a new drama, the name of David Belasco (1853–1931) is better known among Americans than are the names of his almost equally successful early contemporaries. Like the others, however, he was an actor-manager-playwright as well as an innovator in the theatre. And like the others he could be identified as a dramatist by Ambrose Bierce's definition in his *Devil's Dictionary*: 'one who adapts from the French'. Throughout his career his playwriting (by himself or with his dozen or more collaborators), his theatre management, his heroic opposition to the Theatrical Syndicate and his work as a director were all inextricably entangled. As the 'Bishop of Broadway', so dubbed because of his affinity for reversed collars, he was a man of the theatre. It was unfortunate that he had to experience that awkward situation for any public figure who somehow outlives the era of his greatest popularity and yet remains in the business.

Belasco's theatre education started early as an actor and playwright on the west coast. It was there that he became associated with James Herne and collaborated on *Hearts of Oak* (1879) and other plays. In 1882 he came to

New York and soon showed the kind of play he could create most success-fully, *May Blossom*, a Civil War melodrama with a strong part for an actress. Later, with Henry C. DeMille (1853–93), he wrote four comedies – *Lord Chumley* (1888), for example – but melodrama was his forte both as writer and director. Realism was the vogue in literary art, and Belasco had the quick eye, the imagination and the insight to put an abundance of realistic detail on the stage in a theatrically effective manner. His technique was manipulation of detail, but the effect was a natural appearance that gave him a name among theatre innovators. In plays that he directed and/or wrote, his contrived spectacles and concern for detailed realism pleased audiences – the appearance of the volcano on stage, the bell in the church steeple, the passing of a night in Japan, Child's Restaurant down to the flies on the mince pies, the particular room for the actress down on her luck. He was not a writer in the new realism of Ibsen, and he was not naturalistic in any literary sense of that term involving a pessimistic-deterministic approach to life. Howells never believed in Belasco as he had in Herne because Belasco was not that kind of thoughtful writer.

He was, however, a fine writer of sensational melodrama. *The Girl I Left Behind Me* (1893), with Franklyn Fyles, describes the intense and violent life on a western army post and a conflict between Indians and the US Cavalry complicated by the fact that the chief's daughter and the general's daughter love the same man. *The Heart of Maryland* (1895) showed Mrs Leslie Carter, an actress and Belasco's protégée, as Maryland Calvert risking life and limb for her lover. *Madame Butterfly* (1900), based on a story by John Luther Long and dramatized with him, was a tender and pathetic tale of Cho-Cho-San waiting patiently with her child, Trouble, for Lieutenant B. F. Pinkerton who can never marry her. Two years later Long and Belasco wrote *The Darling of the Gods* which dramatized the Japanese story of Yo-San who falls in love with the outlaw leader, Kara, is tricked into betraying him, and finally commits suicide with him. A thousand years later they meet in the first Celestial Heaven and ascend to the second together. During the period when Oriental fantasies were popular this was a delicate and delightful romantic melodrama. His last play of any signifi-cance was *The Return of Peter Grimm* (1911), an experimental fantasy in which love and sentiment are strong enough to bring Peter back from the dead to be an unseen influence upon the living. At a time when psychical research and hypnotism were gaining importance in America along with New Thought and spiritualism in general, this was a pertinent and effective drama in conception and production.

Belasco was also a resonant voice in American drama and theatre prior to the First World War. In an essay, 'The Playwright and the Box Office' (1912), he emphasized his concern for 'true life' upon the stage and his feeling that a play should not be so 'refined and precise as to make it merely a piece of literature'. Drama is 'the thing done', he wrote. In his plays, his direction and his theories, contemporary critics saw the good and the bad. For the New York *Tribune* in 1895 *The Heart of Maryland* was 'decidedly cheap sensationalism'. In 1902 the *New York Times* thought *The Darling of the Gods* the 'most beautiful stage spectacle we have ever seen'. Much later, critics branded his work as 'hokum', but in Belasco's obituary in 1931 Stark Young made an astute final assessment by praising him as a particular man of his generation who, above all, possessed a 'theatrical sincerity' by seeing theatre everywhere.

Even a quick review of nineteenth-century American melodrama could not be complete without a brief mention of some plays that still fill theatres. The adaptation of Mrs Henry Wood's *East Lynne* (1863) by Clifton W. Tayleur presents a classic picture of a woman, Isabel, who is deceived by the villain and leaves her husband only to repent in scenes of tortuous pathos. 'If all the scalding tears that fell in sympathy for Isabel were gathered up throughout the years, 'twould be an awful lot of tears.' *Rosedale; or, The Rifle Ball* (1863), by the actor Lester Wallack (1820–88), included more mysteries and discoveries than *East Lynne*, but the obligatory sentimental scene had its usual effect. Between 1879 and 1885 the most popular writer of melodrama was Bartley Campbell (1843–88) whose *The White Slave* (1882) contains the line that every heroine needs to spit in the face of the villain: 'Rags are royal raiment when worn for virtue's sake! Rather a hoe in my hands than self-contempt in my heart.' And when the century came to an end, the team of Al Woods and Owen Davis (1874–1956) as theatre manager and playwright produced 'thrillers' at a phenomenal rate. Starting with *Through the Breakers* in 1899, Davis wrote 129 melodramas before switching to comedy in 1913. In a delightful essay entitled 'Why I Quit Writing Melodrama' (1914) he explained the system by which he produced plays that were 70 per cent successful on stage. The title, he felt, was very important – *Convict 999*, *Confessions of a Wife*, *Gambler of the West* – as was the third act where the stage carpenter saved the heroine. After the war Davis tried realistic drama and won a Pulitzer Prize with *Icebound* (1923). Perhaps he also illustrates the loss of popularity with the sensational melodrama: he tired of writing them. But the cinema was also a factor with its greater potential for electrifying suspense and terrifying danger.

9 Comedy and social drama: caricature, comedy and thesis plays 1865–1920

The most distinctive development in American drama from the period of the Civil War up to the end of the First World War was the increasing interest shown in the problems of man. In 1865 man was still primarily a caricature in American drama – either romantically conceived, or burlesqued or a stereotype, but hardly a man, that 'poor, bare, forked animal' struggling to cope with the daily problems of this world and his fears of the next. By 1920 both the United States and man in it had changed drastically, while drama as a faithful reflection of a culture responded in kind. Slowly at first, because the Age of Realism in literature and the Age of Melodrama in theatre coincided to a certain extent, the plays of Howells, Bronson Howard and Clyde Fitch indicated the transition taking place. Complete change, some say, never occurs, but tendencies towards change are constantly intruding upon the status quo. By the early twentieth century dramatists were beginning to consider serious issues but, limited by conservative views and the techniques of the older melodrama, they persisted with the traditional or moralistic dénouement. It was only with the plays of Eugene O'Neill that the concept of a modern drama, first presented by James Herne, was realized in the theatre.

The reasons for the changes in drama may be explained by the new forces operating on society. Quite clearly, during the latter part of the nineteenth century ideas were being introduced and events were taking place that caused the intelligent and sensitive man to look at life more carefully and critically than had previously been his custom. The triumph of industry, for example, which raised capital investments in manufacturing 432.5 per cent between 1850 and 1880, created empires in steel, meat packing, oil and railroads. The monumental wealth of these new rich – Stanford, Vanderbilt, Carnegie, Huntington – was illustrated in 1880 by their move to build the Metropolitan Opera House with its Diamond Horseshoe when the Golden Horseshoe of the New York Music Academy could not accommodate them. This act also dramatized the uncomfortable conflict this new moneyed class presented to a weak social aristocracy – one reflected in such novels as Edith Wharton's *The House of Mirth* which Clyde Fitch dramatized in 1906. With this confrontation of Victorian gentility and Western individuality came the downfall of gentility and moderation along with decency as well. The Age of Conspicuous Waste was the age of scandals and corruption in governmental and financial circles and the age of labour problems and strikes. All was due primarily to an increasing industry which was to man both benefactor and devil. Too often it was the latter, and by the turn of the century novelists and dramatists were beginning to express themselves quite freely and candidly on the issues which arose from the problems inherent in a newly industrialized nation.

The most important single intellectual force upon late nineteenth-century America was social Darwinism. The early reaction to Darwin's 1859 theories of evolution showed the strong division within the social, religious and scientific worlds of man. Theologians had been stunned and were additionally enraged when Darwin's *The Descent of Man* appeared in 1871. No major break came in the religious-scientific argument, however, until the Rev. Henry Ward Beecher was converted to what he called a 'cordial Christian evolutionist'. Beecher acknowledged being impressed by the writings of Herbert Spencer whose unparalleled written commentary in the fields of sociology and philosophy influenced many writers such as Dreiser, Garland, Herne and London, as well as the common man.

In post-Civil-War America there had been rapid expansion, industrially and geographically, and a desperate competition among men as they fought for success. For Spencer it was all a vast human dramatization of the Darwinian struggle for existence, and survival came to the fittest. For the speculator, the financial tycoon or the businessman the philosophy of pragmatism, which was one result of Darwinism and Spencerian philosophy, was a ready explanation for the aggressive capitalistic techniques which had made them successful. As John D. Rockefeller pointed out, 'The growth of a large business is merely the survival of the fittest.' Another consequence of Spencerian thought was a reluctance to support reform. What was the use? Just wait for evolution. In contrast to the philosophic optimism which attracted the businessman, other men became cynical and pessimistic. No one really escaped the social changes, since rural life too felt the impact of the expanding urban areas. The virtuous and the evil, the wealthy and the poor, the survivors and those who failed – all became more truthfully presented by novelists and short-story writers as the century closed, and by the First World War there appeared serious writers of social comedy and thesis drama who treated these same subjects.

The economics of the burgeoning business world which was largely responsible for directing late nineteenth-century America had been briefly suggested by pre-Civil-War dramatists – as in *Fashion*, *Young New York* or *The Poor of New York* – but it had always been a device rather than an issue in a play. With an expanded economy after the war the dramatist had more to work with, but his purpose remained primarily that of entertainment. Both Bartley Campbell in *Bulls and Bears* (1875) and Augustin Daly in *The Big Bonanza* (1875) used Wall Street and financial speculation as the basis for farce. Benjamin E. Woolf's (1834–1901) *The Mighty Dollar* (1875) is concerned with a speculator interested in a railroad land grant. By 9 May 1891 the New York *Dramatic Mirror* mentioned 'the average Wall Street play of which we have had so many'. Generally, they had become dull, and George Broadhurst's (1866–1952) *The Speculators* (1896) was a late theatre speculation that justly failed.

Plays that dealt with the labour side of the industrial world, on the other hand, developed in a definite fashion. Early in the period they are clearly more interesting for particular historical social comments than as drama. *Bertha, The Sewing Machine Girl* (1871) by Charles Foster portrayed a heroine who worked a fourteen-hour day for $8 a week before she was rescued by the hero. The heroine of Leonard Grover's (d. 1926) *Lost in New York* (1887) complained bitterly: 'I work sometimes eighteen hours a day for a bare living. They say slavery is abolished, but there is more slavery among women who sew in New York than was even known among the Negroes.' Then working conditions, which had been bad for years, began to provide the dramatist with his plot. Plays about strikes – *The Strike* (1877), *The Workingmen's Strike* (1881) – had already appeared when Samuel Gompers formed the American Federation of Labor in 1886. Other playwrights carried on the protest for the forces of labour. Hamlin Garland (1860–1940) was bitterly polemical and realistic in *Under the Wheel* (1890) while Augustus Thomas was justly sympathetic to labour in *New Blood* (1894). By the turn of the century dramatists were using labour problems in social-thesis plays. Charles Klein's (1867–1915) *Daughters of Men* (1906), for example, deals with a strike, and Charles Kenyon's (d. 1961) *Kindling* (1911) dramatizes the poverty and desperation that a labour strike can cause. Meanwhile, plays about businessmen and money were generally farces such as Winchell Smith (1871–1933) and Byron Ongley's *Brewster's Millions* (1906) or George M. Cohan's (1878–1942) *Get-Rich-Quick Wallingford* (1910). Eugene Walter's *Fine Feathers* (1913) provides the exception to the rule by showing the power of money to corrupt man and drag him to ruin.

The only dramatist of this period to emphasize the businessman in his plays in any systematic fashion was Bronson Howard (1842–1908), a man of several distinctions in American drama. Although during the last dozen years of his life he seemed to lessen his stature as a man of independent thought and creativity by writing for the Theatrical Syndicate, he is generally considered a good craftsman who brought some new ideas to American drama. The fact that he was the first American to make a professional career of playwriting says something about his approach to drama as well as his abilities – yet not completely complimentary, of course. He was obviously limited by his adherence to some of the commercially oriented conventions and requirements of the late nineteenth-century theatre. No one would seriously question this. At the same time, he saw playwriting as a profession and in 1891 founded the American Dramatists' Club which was to help force theatre managers to acknowledge the importance of the dramatist. Interestingly enough, his principles of dramaturgy which he called 'The Laws of Dramatic Composition' suggest his individuality as well as his subjugation to conventions. A play, for example, must be 'satisfactory' to the audience. Accordingly, he reasoned that no audience would accept the death of a heroine in a play, and he changed the ending of *The Banker's Daughter* (1878). 'So far as possible,' he also noted, the playwright should deal 'with subjects of universal interest.' Generally, however, the laws of dramatic composition demanded 'merely the art of using your common sense in the study of your own and other people's emotions'. Yet in his essay he showed some contemporary distinction which was revealed in his thought and characters. At a time when only Howells and Henry James were emphasizing the international aspect of social life, Howard dramatized similar themes. Also his use of the American businessman as a central figure in social comedy suggested his alertness to the socio-economic conditions that were moving around him. Although for the most part no one could call his plays particularly outstanding as either drama or theatre, through his own personal force and his commercially successful plays he suggested a direction that drama would take and made the way for younger dramatists in America a little more secure.

During the last quarter of the nineteenth century the businessman was no stranger to the stage, and Howard showed not only the business problems of man but the broader problems of the businessman. Taking its name from the railroad which was the issue of a financial rivalry between a father known as 'the Napoleon of Wall Street' and his son, *The Henrietta* (1887) was a successful satire of life on the stock exchange. The contemporary critic, John Corbin, hailed it as a new kind of play – the business play. A much more noteworthy play, however, was *Young Mrs Winthrop* (1882). Although one need not agree with a contemporary critic (quoted in Odell, *Annals of the New York Stage*, XII, p. 19) who saw it as 'the great American drama so long and so ardently awaited', it was solidly written, and it emphasized a very modern idea. There is in the necessary complexity of the business and social worlds something dangerous to married happiness as the husband, thoroughly immersed in his business, neglects his wife. Howard, of course, could not tolerate an unhappy ending, and he appropriately patched up the marital difficulties. The problem he saw, however, was a real one. So was his concern for wealth, old and new, in *Aristocracy* (1892). New millionaires, Howard realized, are seldom acceptable in an old society. The way to enter New York society, therefore, was through London society. Mainly, Howard ridiculed and caricatured his people in this play, but in these and other plays he pointed out to future dramatists an awareness of a new social class in America.

Although Howard's comic technique was more towards caricature than developed characters, society with its manners and morals was his basic concern as a dramatist. *Saratoga* (1870), written early in Howard's career, is an average farce involving one man and four women, but the scene of the play at one of America's favourite resorts gave it a distinctive flavour. When Frank Marshall adapted it to English circumstances under the title *Brighton* (1870), it clearly showed more of a current popularity than a universal appeal, but the transatlantic move indicated the relevance of Howard's social perception. Two years later, in *Diamond* (1872), which Brander Matthews called a 'comedy of contemporaneous manners', he dealt with society in New York City and Staten Island. *One of Our Girls* (1885) was Howard's first play to dramatize the international contrast. With its scene in France, the play shows the conflicting marriage customs of the French and the Americans while emphasizing the superiority of American independence and freedom. Two other Howard plays are generally mentioned by critics, though for their contemporary popularity rather than their social comment. *The Banker's Daughter* (1878) was written first as *Lillian's Last Love* (1873) and dramatized the marriage of an older man with a young woman who years later rediscovers an earlier love and is destroyed by her revealed passions. Howard himself gave this play importance through a lecture, 'Autobiography of a Play' (given in 1886) in which he detailed the rewriting through which he changed his final curtain from unhappiness to happiness. *Shenandoah* (1888) is a sentimental Civil War play involving lovers who are on opposite sides of the conflict. Some of Roosevelt's Rough Riders once added to the spectacle by appearing in a Boston production, but the play offers mainly a romantic tale of love and war.

Although progress seemed slow, the number of plays that attempted to depict aspects of social life with a degree of seriousness multiplied during the late nineteenth century, until playwrights such as Clyde Fitch and Rachel Crothers took over the obligations of the social commentator that Bronson Howard helped make a legitimate concern of the drama. The early plays of this period are interesting mainly because they reveal a certain seriousness on the part of the dramatist which he was unable to follow through fear that his theatre audience would not accept his ideas. In Augustin Daly's *Divorce* (1871), for example, three couples dramatized some possible marriage problems – poverty and marriage, excessive freedom and indifference in marriage, and a marriage involving youth and old age. After a first act indicating potentially serious treatment, however, the play evolves into a light satire on divorce lawyers and accompanying farcical and melodramatic action. The same is true of Daly's *Pique* (1875), concerning a girl who marries out of pique. The play begins as a good social comedy and then disappears into contrived melodrama.

William Dean Howells was only partially successful in putting his social consciousness into plays. The scenes against which his characters operated, however – dinners, teas, receptions, summer residences – added to the social awareness he showed in his Roberts–Campbell plays. He knew society and its conventions, and he commented on these at first with considerable wit in *A Letter of Introduction* (1892) or *The Unexpected Guests* (1893). Later, he showed a bitterness, quite like Mark Twain's late gloom, in *The Night*

Before Christmas (1910) and *The Impossible* (1910), both of which make one
ponder the meanings that organized society holds for man. Mainly, however,
Howells was interested in the ever-present struggle between man and
woman and the relationship between women – believing as he did that
women dislike other women and tolerate them only for the emotional
stimulation they provide. Such plays as *A Previous Engagement* (1895) and
An Indian Giver (1897) illustrate this point along with the Roberts–Campbell
farce-comedies. Although he was not successful in the commercial theatre,
Howells was unquestionably the best writer of comic dialogue of the period
and the playwright most sensitive to nuances of character in social situations.
That he did treat the more dramatic social issues (divorce, miscegenation,
psychic problems) in his novels rather than in his plays may only suggest
the realistic attitude he held towards his contemporary theatre.

Plays on marriage and divorce and women in modern society began to
hold the theatre audience's attention by the turn of the century. As dramatists continued to treat these subjects, however, a dramatic change of attitude took place. At first, the marriage scene of struggle, separation and reunion was commonplace as dramatized in Henry C. DeMille and David
Belasco's *The Wife* (1887) and Julia C. Fletcher's (b. 1853) *A Man and His
Wife* (1900). If there was a problem of immorality, it was easily solved by
Bronson Howard's dictum: 'The wife who has once taken the step from
purity to impurity can never reinstate herself in the world of art this side of
the grave' (*Autobiography of a Play*, 1910). Even with social changes brought
by the new century some dramatists such as A. E. Thomas (1872–1947)
with *Her Husband's Wife* (1910) and Augustus Thomas with *As A Man
Thinks* (1911) continued to support the conservative view. Others, Rachel
Crothers in particular, objected to the double standard regarding immorality
but always provided a conventional dénouement in their social comedies.
More realistic plays about man and woman came from Eugene Walter
(1874–1941), probably the most skilful writer of social melodrama before
the First World War. *Paid in Full* (1908) contrasts weak and strong humanity
in an unusual plot in which an embezzling husband urges his wife to use
herself to bargain for his freedom, while *The Easiest Way* (1908) demon-
strates the concern for disagreeable truths that Herne had foreshadowed.
In this psychological drama the money-loving, easygoing heroine is defeated
by her basic desires. A final step before the First World War in the drama's
progress towards a realistic presentation of society might be illustrated by a
concern with prostitution in such plays as Bayard Veiller's (1869–1943)
The Fight (1913) and Charles Rann Kennedy's *The Necessary Evil* (1913).

Witter Bynner's (b. 1881) *Tiger* (1913) showed how a girl is lured into a house of prostitution thinking that she would marry the man who took her there – only to be saved by her first customer, her father.

The contribution of Clyde Fitch (1865–1909) to the development of social comedy in America is generally acknowledged to be that of a theatre craftsman who combined excellent powers of observation with skill in drawing character to produce faithful representations of American society. Much more a man of the commercial theatre than a literary figure, he wrote easily and rapidly, turning out thirty-four original plays and twenty-two adaptations of foreign works or dramatizations of novels during a twenty-year period. Undoubtedly, his membership in the 'Syndicate School' of dramatists helped assure him the success which made him the first millionaire dramatist in America, but his 1901 record of four plays in New York theatres at one point in the season indicates something more than a favoured position. By this time, of course, America's 1891 acceptance of the international copyright agreement had completely changed the playwright's situation in America. He now had some stature, and Fitch's considerable success in England added to that stature, besides giving Fitch an international reputation as his plays were translated into other languages. Although a very colourful figure in the theatre world, Fitch was far from being a fraud. He had a sensitivity for life and tried to reflect 'absolutely and truthfully the life and environment about us; every class, every kind, every emotion, every motive, every occupation, every business, every idleness!' (Fitch is quoted by Barrett H. Clark, *A Study of the Modern Drama*, p. 376). With realistic and truthful detail he was at his best, but he lacked the larger perspective of life and the meaningful ideas that might have distinguished his work. When he carried his enthusiasms for realistic detail to excess, as he sometimes did, the result was either a caricature or an overabundance of what was termed 'Fitchian detail'.

Very much a man-about-town, Fitch enjoyed picturing the social scene in and around New York or the favourite 'watering holes' of New York society. The problems of married life, the peculiarities of individuals, the faults and foibles of a fast-changing society – these were the aspects of life that interested Fitch. His first attempt at a full-length social drama was *A Modern Match* (1892), a thin play which tells of a flippant and selfish wife who refuses to assume the responsibilities of marriage. Here he followed one of Bronson Howard's 'Laws of Dramatic Construction': 'The wife who has once taken the step from purity to impurity can never reinstate herself in the world of art on this side of the grave.' Fitch's satire on aspects of

New York social life, *The Climbers* (1901), is a better play with an opening scene that shocked many theatregoers as it ridiculed the hypocrisy and unfeeling materialism of a family immediately after the funeral of the father. *The Stubbornness of Geraldine* (1902) and *Her Great Match* (1905) showed Fitch's interest in the international scene, particularly the problem of an American and English marriage. Although in these plays and others he wrote some fine scenes about society, such as the dinner scene at the beginning of *A Happy Marriage* (1909), he never wrote a complete and effective comedy either on society in general or on the theme of marriage.

Instead, he seemed more comfortable with melodrama and farce. In these genres he was in the mainstream of American drama of the period. The ever-popular farce had been produced by every late nineteenth-century dramatist from Daly through Howells and Gillette to George Ade with a· high point appearing in the works of Charles Hoyt (1859/60–1900) in such satires as *A Temperance Town* (1892), which dealt with prohibition, and *A Texas Steer* (1890), which explored politics. Although Fitch's *A Blue Mouse* (1908) was an adaptation from the German, it provided excellent farcical intrigue about a young man who hires a chorus girl to pose as his wife because his boss is susceptible to pretty women. Melodrama, however – social melodrama – was Fitch's great strength. Two of his historical melodramas – *Nathan Hale* (1898) and *Barbara Frietchie* (1899) – were stage successes along with *Captain Jinks of the Horse Marines* (1901), a period piece about an opera singer in New York in the early seventies which gave Ethel Barrymore her first major role in the theatre. In his best social melodramas he concerned himself with character idiosyncrasies and resulting conflicts and struggles within a sophisticated society. The individual social vice that overwhelmed *The Girl with the Green Eyes* (1902) was, of course, jealousy. Jenny Tillman seems to have inherited her weakness and nearly ruins her marriage when she misunderstands her husband's concern for another woman. Actually, he was trying to help Jenny's brother out of a marital mess, but circumstances cloud the truth for Jenny, who attempts suicide. Fortunately, however, she is saved by Fitch's manipulation of time and the happy ending required by the 'Syndicate School'.

The Truth (1906) dramatizes the problem of a pathological liar married to a man who is as naïvely honest as Jenny Tillman's husband was incapable of understanding a jealous person. Although Barrett Clark, American critic and drama historian, called it 'one of the few genuine American comedies of manners', he abused the genre. Fitch worked with contrived opposites in each play and limited his character development to his heroines. Consequently, the artificiality of his plays detracts from his few good characters as well as from the wit of his dialogue and his effective use of dramatic irony. Only in his final play, *The City* (1909), did Fitch attempt to combine a contemporary issue with a larger view of society. With the death of the father, the Rand family move from their small-town home to New York City where the son develops political aspirations only to have them thwarted by scandals within the family. Presumably there is a certain solution in the family's decision to leave the 'evils' of the city and return to their small town, but the issue is clouded by the fact that the major source of corruption is a blackmailing, degenerate, illegitimate son spawned in that same small town. Produced after Fitch's death, it showed his typical melodramatic techniques and platitudinous moral assertions but with the added strength that can be provided by a realistic presentation of an advancing society's problems. Never a profound thinker, Fitch was a craftsman of the theatre whose particular insight allowed him to create works that appealed to his contemporaries, but there is no doubt that his concern for external facts in everyday existence made him lose sight of the inner forces that direct social man.

A contemporary of Fitch's, Langdon Mitchell (1862–1935), wrote one play which serves as a kind of landmark in the progress of social comedy in America. Basically, *The New York Idea* (1906) is a drama which mixes farce and comedy very effectively while proclaiming Mitchell's psychological insight through his witty and satirical comments. As a satire on marriage in New York society, the play defines marriage as 'three parts love and seven parts forgiveness of sin'. Two divorced women are planning marriages to each other's ex-husband until one of them decides what she really wants and reflects that the man she had first married is the one she loves. That is the plot. The dialogue is generally fast-moving and clever while the humour, particularly at the expense of the clergy, is quite pungent. Most of the characters are one-dimensional foils for the author's quick wit – the stuffy husband, the insipid clergyman, the English fop intriguer – while the farcical situations such as the contrived wedding and the club-house scene are carefully set up and executed. With humour emanating from language, incongruities, situations, ironies and material devices, the play treats a serious issue with a modern touch that provides some distinction at this period of American drama.

As divorce and the position of women became more dominant issues in society, they provided the dramatist with material which he might either consider seriously or exploit with his wit. There is no doubt that Eugène

Brieux's *Les Avariés* (1902), a study of venereal disease, caused a sensation in America when it was produced under the title of *Damaged Goods*. Audience reactions were quite diverse, while in the *New York Times*, 19 October 1913, Brieux was quoted as wanting to defend woman whom he considered 'mistreated and maltreated', deserving of 'a better position in life'. At this date in America, however, most theatre attempts to gain the suffragist's support, such as Anne Crawford Flexner's (1874–1955) *The Marriage Game* (1913) and C. W. Bell's *Her First Divorce* (1913), were so slight and lacking in insight as to insult the object of their adoration. On the other hand, there was a seriously concerned advocate of American women already on the stage, Rachel Crothers (1878–1958), whose productivity far into the modern period would seem to contradict her obscurity in the history of American drama.

Although it sounds like a platitude, critics generally agree that Rachel Crothers's plays present a reasonable study of the manners of the American woman during the first quarter of the twentieth century. In *A Man's World* (1909) she wrote of the double standard and continued her discussion in *He and She* (1911). Typical of her point of view as well as of her dramatic technique, *He and She* presents contrasting views of the career woman and the homemaker in both major and secondary plots. In the main plot Tom and Ann Herford, husband and wife sculptors, compete for a commission which Ann wins but eventually relinquishes when Tom's attitude dramatizes an old conflict and their daughter needs her. In theory, Tom and Ann agreed that it was a woman's world as well as a man's, but the dramatist made it perfectly clear that a woman has responsibilities as well as rights. In a careful if controlled study she contrasted the rather romantically conceived attitudes towards man (bold, strong, controlled, a craftsman) and woman (emotional, full of abandon, pure inspiration) as suggested by their sculpting. Obviously, she made a point which satisfied some and irritated others. When *Young Wisdom* (1914), her play about an attempt at trial marriage which ends in conventional matrimony, appeared, it was endorsed by the New York State Association Opposed to Women's Suffrage. Although an eager spokeswoman for women and for truth in modern society, she also had a conservative view of rights and responsibilities.

Throughout her long career Rachel Crothers wrote about the position of women in America. *Nice People* (1920) describes the rich young generation after the war and defends the fun-loving heroine who refuses to avert scandal and marry a man who spent a night with her alone in the same house (albeit on different floors). In the final act, however, the heroine is changed to the homespun romantic who has found the man she wants to marry. *Mary the Third* (1923) shows three generations of Marys living in the same house, each with a different set of values. Young Mary shocks her mother by declaring that she is going on a two-week camping trip with two boys to find out which she loves by seeing both at their best or worst. She doesn't do this, however, because she overhears her father and mother discussing the unhappiness of their own marriage and is deeply shocked. To establish a truthful basis for living, she insists that her parents get divorced. Finally, her mother explains that marriage is not wrong. It is only what one does with marriage that can be considered wrong. Essentially, Rachel Crothers followed her thesis to a point and then evaded the issue. Young Mary is an independent woman who will live with a man only as long as she loves him; she must be true to herself, which is quite different from indulging herself. This is also the thesis of *Expressing Willie* (1924). Striking at the fad of existentialism during the 1920s, the play satirizes the excessive selfishness in 'the expression of oneself'. *Susan and God* (1938) dramatizes the plight of the alcoholic husband and the wife who hides behind a religious movement, understanding nothing until she thinks of God '*here in us*'. Like other Crothers heroines she discovers the falseness of self-assertion without responsibility.

Rachel Crothers remains a careful craftswoman of the theatre and a thoughtful dramatist who tried to treat the social problems of her time honestly and clearly. Showing insight into certain conditions, she occasionally penetrated beyond problems of moral propensities to those of personal values. The freshness and force with which she presented some social issues, however, are marred mainly at the end of her plays where her Victorian attitudes dominate and a conventionally acceptable dénouement closes the evening. For a modern audience some of the values that she observed have become more standard than stimulating: self-expression doesn't always mean freedom; parents can disillusion their children; love and honesty are important. Yet the issues which she raises are not without meaning in any society. In a pre-O'Neill drama she was a definite force, both in her ideas and in her language, towards a better and more sophisticated social drama in America.

William Vaughn Moody (1869–1910), Percy MacKaye (1875–1956) and Charles Rann Kennedy (1871–1950) were also outstanding among those new dramatists after the turn of the century who were trying to view life clearly and seriously. Each had a different approach to the drama and a distinct bias. What they shared was a belief in being honest. MacKaye was a true son of Steele MacKaye with a primary interest in pageant drama and community theatre, but his dramatization of Nathaniel Hawthorne's 'Feathertop', *The Scarecrow* (1908), is a play which still carries a meaningful comment for man. Created before the audience's eyes with a display of imagination and theatrical skill, the scarecrow comes to life as Lord Ravensbane and achieves a considerable sense of humanity before it succumbs to the wiles of mankind and its own artificial construction.

Moody, a poet and teacher-scholar, was an outraged idealist who tried to discover a common ground on which to express the Victorian sense of humanity which was his heritage as well as an acquired sympathy for the Social Darwinists' views of present society. His objective was to create a belief in the potential greatness of man. As a critic of society, he wrote such strong humanitarian poems as 'Gloucester Moors', while his plays also dramatized the conflicting ideologies and individual problems for which he suggested humanitarian consequences. *The Great Divide* (1906) contrasts the freedom of the American west with the inhibiting tradition of New England as they become an integral struggle within a New England girl whose basic desires war against her heritage. Moody's evaluation of his age also included the humanitarian's concern for science and religion as shown in his poem 'Menagerie'. He was always the idealist, the believer in man 'the radiant and loving, yet to be'. His other prose play, *The Faith Healer* (1909), dramatizes the necessary union of man's earthly love and divine mission. Scorned by the medical doctor and the clergyman, the faith healer loses his mystical powers until he recognizes the individual force of his own love for a woman and is able to triumph over his opposition.

Throughout most of the nineteenth century religion and religious figures had been presented in orthodox and undistinguished ways. There were exceptions, of course. James Nelson Barker's Rev. Ravensworth in *Superstition* (1824) was a thoughtful portrayal of the misguided cleric who mistook his own visions of power for the Word of God. Mainly, however, the clergyman was a conservative figure working for 'good'. Later poetic and religious dramas such as G. H. Hollister's *Thomas à Becket* (1866) simply removed everything from a real world, while those prose dramatists who suggested reality in their plays began to place religion in a social context. The Rev. Hardman in Charles Hoyt's *A Temperance Town* (1892) is a limited but good man who works for his beliefs. Augustus Thomas discusses the Washington lobbying practices of the Catholic church in *The Capital* (1895). Herne, in *The Reverend Griffith Davenport* (1899), focuses upon a humanitarian rather than a religious issue. Howells condemns current religiosity in *The Night before Christmas* (1910). Meanwhile, historical spectacles emphasized the traditional values as in William Young's (1847–1920) *Ben Hur* (1899) and the two adaptations of *Quo Vadis* in 1901.

The activity of the drama at the turn of the century reflected the new upsurge in religion. Much more popular than the bitter comments by Stephen Crane and Theodore Dreiser were the poems of Edward Rowland Sill and the stories of Sarah Orne Jewett which suggested man's faith in his God. Sentimental novels also emphasized the goodness of man, but not even the Horatio Alger stories could top the contemporary enthusiasm for *In His Steps* (1896), the Rev. Charles Sheldon's story of a minister who tried to follow the example of Christ in his daily life. This book framed the message of a movement back to the simple teachings of Jesus, and the drama took up the cause. The question which bothered the mid-nineteenth-century man – 'May a Christian go to the theatre?' – had changed to 'Shall the church use the theatre?' and been resolved to the satisfaction of some on both sides of the Atlantic by Jerome K. Jerome's *The Passing of the Third Floor Back* (1908) and Charles Rann Kennedy's *The Servant in the House* (1907). The Christ image as a reformer, either personal or social, had come into existence with a strong social-gospel movement. Kennedy believed that 'God does things as a dramatist would' and set out to dramatize Christianity. In *The Servant in the House* he gathered a group of people who illustrate the lost meaning of a church built upon dogma, ritual and a concern for wealth. To convert them Kennedy introduced into his main character's house an expected visitor, the Bishop of Benares, in the unexpected disguise of a butler, Manson (an obvious Christ-figure, 'the son of Man'), who smites the conscience of those present and demands repentance. In this as in other social-gospel plays incidents depicting social vices are presented against the basic assumption of the contagious and redemptive power of good.

Viewing the ills of society in this distinctive fashion, Kennedy declared in all of his gospel plays that man could not remain outside the circle of Christ. In *The Terrible Meek* (1911), a one-act play, he realized that atrocities could occur even while the faithful did their duty, but he clearly noted that change could be accomplished. Against a scene revealing the crucified Christ, Kennedy explored the thesis that 'the real meek are beginning to inherit the earth' and sent copies of his play to all world heads of state. *The Winter Feast* (1908) portrayed the power of hate and falsehood to destroy, while *The Idol Breaker* (1914) dramatized in a somewhat confused but searching fashion, and certainly with intriguing symbolism, the problems of individual freedom in a society where Christianity does not seem to be contagious. *The*

Fool from the Hills (1919) shows man's hunger for bread as food for the body and the spirit after war and revolution. A later trilogy was built around Jesus in *The Chastening* (1922), Columbus as a discoverer in *The Admiral* (1923), and the love of Paolo and Francesca in *The Salutation* (1925). Although many dramatists used social-religious themes in a more realistic attempt to solve problems – such as Joseph M. Patterson's (1879–1946) *Rebellion* (1911) which dramatized the struggle of a Catholic woman who must decide whether or not to divorce a drunken husband and remarry – none equals Kennedy's combination of Christian idealism and effective dramatic technique.

One final dramatist of this period who wrote his best plays around social themes was Edward Sheldon (1886–1946). Although his career bridged the First World War, he was most effective in his early years during which he emphasized a realistic approach to the drama. Later even his play titles suggested the change he experienced. In *Romance* (1913) he created quite a popular play about the love of an American clergyman for an Italian opera singer and the later marriage of the clergyman's grandson with an actress. The same romanticism guided his theme of a search for beauty in *The High Road* (1912). After the war, poor health and failing eyesight largely incapacitated Sheldon. He worked mainly with collaborators, and a number of very prominent dramatists such as Robert Sherwood have acknowledged him as a source of inspiration as well as an enthusiastic helper with particular dramaturgical problems. Unfortunately, those plays for which he has accepted credit of partial authorship are not outstanding. He remains a pre-war dramatist of strong social realism.

Sheldon's first three plays are considered his greatest achievements; yet it is for an attempt rather than a finished product that his reputation exists. His first play, *Salvation Nell* (1908), was a melodrama about a scullery maid who joined the Salvation Army rather then enter a 'profession' that was repulsive to her and in that service persuades the man she loves to adopt her beliefs. The romance of this play suggested one future direction Sheldon was to take; the social realism suggested another. In *The Nigger* (1909) he courageously dramatized the story of a southern governor who discovered that his grandmother was an octoroon slave. Sheldon's resolution, however, in which the governor is able to 'tu'n the bad into the good' through self-disclosure provides a romantic conclusion which destroys any serious social comment. A similar technique for treating social problems is presented in *The Boss* (1911). When a rowdy Irish contractor, Regan, threatens the uptown contractor, Griswald, with tactics that will bring him and many innocent people to ruin, Griswald's social-reforming daughter accepts Regan's proposal of marriage (in name only) in order to curb his abuses. Then, after some violent labour–management conflicts, she is able to persuade him that he should have consideration for the common man and pride in himself. In each play Sheldon takes an interesting issue, creates some realistic scenes and characters, and then provides a conclusion within existing conventions. The insight that the issues in his plays seemed to demand was never satisfactorily dramatized.

During the decade of the First World War when these dramatists were accepted as America's best, the little-theatre movement in America was beginning to reflect European activity. At the same time experimentation in the theatres in New York was increasing, while the commercial dramatist found himself in the enjoyable position of growing importance. Mainly, however, he was still trying to appease his audiences, not always in the themes he chose – for these were frequently controversial – but in his treatment of these themes. This was the beginning of a period of change in American drama, but progress was slow. Few plays demand critical attention. Social comment was a major focus, and the first Pulitzer-Prize-winning play was Jesse Lynch Williams's (1871–1929) *Why Marry?* (1917) which questioned and then carefully defended the institution of marriage as the best society has to offer. In America, Ibsen's Nora stayed safely at home. Fermentation for change, however, was evident. Some of it appeared in the one-act dramas of Lewis Beach whose *Clod* (1914) showed how little things reveal a person, or in Susan Glaspell's chilling *Trifles* (1916) where motive for murder is explored as effectively and as barrenly as Hamlin Garland had described mid-western dregs of humanity tempted to similar action, or in Edna St Vincent Millay's (1892–1950) poetic satire on war, *Aria da Capo* (1919). A major spokesman for American drama, however, was urgently needed. He must know the theatre and be a man of insight, imagination and courage, with the searching mind of modern man and the sensitivity of a poet. Society was ready; the theatre was ready; and that dramatist finally appeared as Eugene O'Neill.

10 Arrival of a master playwright, Eugene O'Neill

More than any other American dramatist Eugene O'Neill (1888–1953) has attracted the attention of critics around the world. And more inconsistent in his dramatic creation than any other American dramatist, reaching as he did from abysmal failure to the most artistic achievement, O'Neill has received the most damning criticism along with extravagant praise. As conflicting agonies tore his soul, he cried out like the sensitive artist he was, 'Why was I born without a skin, O God?', and then travelled a tangled path of artistic experiment, searching – haunted and cursed – for understanding of himself and man. Whether he is the best of American dramatists may be a matter of preference. What is true is that he came into the American scene when a man of his talent was needed. For some critics his work constitutes the beginning of American drama. More accurately, however, he propelled American drama into the modern era more effectively than other dramatists. In that sense he wrote the kind of drama that James A. Herne had foreshadowed, although the hiatus between the two dramatists had been filled by playwrights who provided O'Neill with little if any inspiration. A lone individual when he started writing plays, and a lone individual throughout his career, he was clearly a significant force in a developing American drama.

Yet without O'Neill's plays the change to modernity in American drama would undoubtedly have come – though not as dramatically. Susan Glaspell (1882–1948), for example, wrote for the same Provincetown Players (that group which her husband, George Cram Cook, had organized) that O'Neill did, and was considered the equal of O'Neill by some critics. In *The Verge* (1921), a play about a woman on the verge of insanity struggling but always being eluded in her attempt to understand her own soul, Susan Glaspell shows why critics would have drawn the comparison. But circumstances cut short her career while O'Neill went on to produce more than thirty plays in New York and receive the Nobel Prize for Literature in 1936, although even then condemned by *The Saturday Review* as unworthy of the award.

The youngest son of an actor, James O'Neill, of some status in American theatre, Eugene O'Neill absorbed certain attitudes and experiences which propelled him towards his career. It is also an important aspect of his background that, under the tutelage of a whoring and drunken brother, he lost the faith of his Catholic upbringing: this loss precipitated him into feelings of guilt which never left him. A drifter and sometime sailor, he did not decide to become a playwright until his twenty-fifth year when fate placed him in a TB sanatorium and he began to read plays. In 1914 his father published a collection of five of his one-act plays, melodramatic and vaguely suggestive of the gloom and horror he saw in life. *Thirst*, for example, takes place on a raft at sea as a gentleman, a dancer and a Mulatto fight to survive. At the end of the play only the dancer's necklace remains on the raft as a symbol of their personal and spiritual failure. Continuing his playwriting, O'Neill studied with Professor George Pierce Baker's Harvard playwriting class and finally found his way to Provincetown on Cape Cod in the summer of 1916 where the Players produced his one-act play, *Bound East for Cardiff*. During the winter of 1917 he stayed with the one-act form but showed his concern with the themes that were to be continued in his mature writing: the defeat of the sensitive person, the living hell that man endures, and the forces that drive man in the modern world. These plays included *In the Zone*, *Ile* and *The Moon of the Caribbees*. The following year, 1918, he wrote *Beyond the Horizon*, a full-length play which, when produced in 1920, won O'Neill his first Pulitzer Prize.

Structurally, *Beyond the Horizon* is composed of three one-act plays, each with two scenes. The main character of this play, Robert Mayo, dreamer and poet, is persuaded by one of O'Neill's early dominating women to marry her and to stay on the farm. Consequently, Robert abandons his planned voyage with an uncle to see 'beyond the horizon' and gives the opportunity to his brother Andrew, a practical man who loves both the farm and Ruth, the girl Robert marries. Three years later, the mistake is obvious as Ruth is increasingly bitter about her life even after having a child. When Andrew returns briefly, having travelled all over the world and seen nothing, all three are shown as basically lost in wrong worlds. Five years pass, and the irony of their separate existences is clear. Robert is dying, in debt and misery, defeated by a life in which he was an incompetent contender; Andrew has lost his fortune; Ruth, defeated in all that she ever wanted, cannot even feign love for a dying husband. For the sensitive man encumbered by individual and social forces that worked against him, 'beyond the horizon' is a dream. In future plays O'Neill would deal more thoroughly both with the types of characters that he presented here and with the main idea in this play.

During the fifteen years after his writing of *Beyond the Horizon* O'Neill created a body of drama with which he achieved a major position on the American stage. Although to some he brought only a high degree of melodrama, to many others he brought a thoughtful concern for modern man rendered exciting by his theatrical experimentation. Far from being a writer of simple melodrama, O'Neill was capable of great psychological insight. Not a philosopher yet a thoughtful man who, like all thoughtful men, pondered the seemingly unanswerable questions of life, he was fascinated by ideas. The major problem in this fascination, however, as most critics have observed, was his personal sensitivity which made him overwhelmingly introspective, with the result that his plays invariably turned in upon himself. Objective concern for truth was beyond him. Therefore, the ideas of others appealed to him as a means of expressing and dealing with his own psychological problems. Or perhaps his dramas helped him create a sufficient artistic distance to see life with some clarity. At any rate, as he searched frantically for understanding and relief from his own suffering, he passed quickly from one person's thoughts to those of another, mainly using rather than absorbing. Because he was a modern man, however, his plays have a probing significance for all men.

The place of men in the world has often been revealed by philosophers and thinking men as lonely, alienated, lacking a sense of belonging. It was a place of unexplainable conditions combining hope and hopelessness where the sensitive man, facing extinction in modern society and searching for his identity, must resort to the mystical. 'Men, those haunted heroes,' says O'Neill's Lazarus, 'obsessed, driven, haunted.' And so it was with O'Neill, searching for that understanding, that absolute – like Herman Melville's orphan, like Henry Adams's ego looking for a unity in a twentieth-century multiplicity, like Thomas Wolfe's dream of 'a stone, a leaf, an unfound door'. In his attempt to express the torment and tension of the human mind, searching out the secrets of the self which would explain the predicament of man, O'Neill borrowed ideas in many directions. Freudianism, with its concern for men victimized by subconscious desires and its methods of psychoanalysis, was particularly important to O'Neill during the 1920s as he created his major characters in *Strange Interlude* and *Mourning Becomes Electra*. The introversion–extroversion concept of Jung and Kierkegaard's theories of self were perhaps even more influential. *The Great God Brown* dramatizes these ideas as well as Nietzsche's philosophy which can also be traced through several other plays such as *Lazarus Laughed* or *Marco Millions*. More than most, O'Neill was a lonely man who lamented his destiny (the destiny of all men) in *Long Day's Journey into Night* (1956) as 'a stranger who never feels at home, who does not really want and is not really wanted, who can never belong, who must always be a little in love with death.' Whether there is evidence that O'Neill's obsession may be called a tragic sense of life is debatable in a society which has great difficulty defining the concept of tragedy. He was, however, deeply concerned with the spiritual and with the social forces which both elevated and destroyed man. Although he believed in the basic dignity of man, or tried to, he was too frequently overwhelmed by his own brooding and gloomy thoughts to dramatize satisfying conclusions.

Both by inclination and by the circumstances that surrounded the theatre, O'Neill was forced to experiment with the form of drama. The theatre that he had inherited in America was mainly realistic, and for the dramatist attempting to portray man's inner struggles and the subconscious forces it was not adequate. Having been particularly influenced by the works of August Strindberg during his sanatorium days, O'Neill adopted the techniques of expressionism and added to them further devices which sprang from his interest in Greek drama as well as from the ideas of modern social philosophers. One of his earliest experimental plays is *The Emperor Jones* (1920) which uses drumbeats (recalled from his reading about religious feasts in the Congo) and a long monologue as the hero retrogresses through a Darwinian chronology to a primitive existence in which his own modern destruction is realized. This play is also strongly expressionistic and bears a very close comparison with Georg Kaiser's *From Morn to Midnight*. Trilogies provided other means for experimentation. *Strange Interlude* (1927) was such a play in which he also employed Freudian psychology as

the major approach for revealing his characters. In a more carefully structured trilogy, *Mourning Becomes Electra* (1931), he followed Aeschylus'
Oresteia in character and action by placing the New England Mannon
family in a Civil War setting and motivating his characters in terms of
Freud and Jung. 'A modern tragic interpretation of classic fate', O'Neill
called it, with 'fate springing out of the family'. In *Dynamo* (1929) O'Neill
emphasized the dynamo as the symbol of a science which had failed to
provide man with a religion after 'the death of an old God'. In *Days Without
End* (1934) he used two characters, two people on stage, to represent two
dramatically conflicting qualities within a single person. O'Neill's greatest
experimentation, however, came in his use of masks which at one time he
felt all actors in his plays should wear. One of his most complicated plays
using masks is *Lazarus Laughed* (1928) where members of the chorus wear
masks representing the Seven Ages of Man and several kinds of people.
Yet his best mask play is *The Great God Brown* (1926). To protect his sensitive soul, Dion Anthony (Dionysus and St Anthony) wears a mask of Pan
which changes into a cynical Mephistopheles as he grows older. Hoping to
steal Dion's creativity, Billy Brown steals the mask when Dion dies. Then
Brown must wear another mask to face the world, becoming for O'Neill
that most tragic of men who is unable to be *himself* to anyone. It is a difficult
but fascinating and terribly moving play which shows both O'Neill's experimentation and his brooding sense of man's aloneness.

As O'Neill searched for self-knowledge and used all means at his disposal,
both intellectual and theatrical, to pursue that greatest challenge – to
'justify the ways of God to man' – he dramatized a society where all forces,
both the natural and the supernatural, might be seen at work in man-to-God
as well as man-to-man relations. In *The Hairy Ape* (1922) he explained that
'the struggle used to be with the gods, but is now with himself [man], his
own past, his attempt to belong.' Irritated by the social problems inherent
in an industrial revolution, Yank (the Hairy Ape) tries to 'think', tries to
assert himself, tries finally to regain, as O'Neill puts it, 'the harmony which
he used to have as an animal', and finds that he does not 'belong'. He does
not 'fit in' anywhere.

In this society which betrays men like Yank, in this 'sickness of today', as
O'Neill describes it, the businessman became a target for O'Neill's abuse as
well as for his intense sympathy. In *The Great God Brown*, for example, the
sensitive poet, a combination of 'the creative pagan acceptance of life,
fighting external war with the masochistic, life-denying spirit of Christianity', is destroyed by his inability to be creative in modern society. Brown, on

the other hand, the successful businessman, is reduced to a nonentity –
'Man!' 'How d'yuh spell it?' asks the police captain investigating Brown's
death at the end of the play. In portraying Brown, O'Neill was a dramatist
of intense sympathy. It was with equally intense severity that he castigated
the modern businessman in *Marco Millions* (1928). Bitterly and with great
irony O'Neill indicted that part of society which destroys man by teaching
him to worship materialism. Early in this play the youthful Marco Polo
believes in his immortal soul, as O'Neill once had before he lost his faith.
But he eventually becomes only an 'acquisitive instinct', hardened to love
and a mocker of everything. For O'Neill, whose concern for a man-to-man
relationship was an interpretation of his own man-to-God relationship, the
Polos were the true children of a God who is 'only an infinite, insane energy
which creates and destroys without other purpose than to pass eternity in
avoiding thought'. So says the great Kublai Khan. O'Neill's further Nietz-
schian gloom is revealed by the Cathay sage: 'Life is perhaps most wisely
regarded as a bad dream between two awakenings, and every day is a life in
miniature.'

The best play of O'Neill's early period, *Desire Under the Elms* (1924),
incorporates the present with the timeless, the particular with the universal.
There are the forces of greed and freedom which link this play with modern
society, and there is the satiric burlesque of all popularly accepted virtues
as they were currently being enjoyed in a revival of Denman Thompson's
The Old Homestead (1886). By suggesting the Oedipus legend and the
Hippolytus–Phaedra plot while emphasizing the forces of a deterministic
nature as interpreted by modern psychologists – 'Nature'll beat ye, Eben,'
says Abbie – he attempted an enlarged picture of life as he saw it. Religion
again provides an ironic background for man's loneliness – man, alienated,
hating what he longed for most.

Towards the end of the 1920s the forces of religion became an increasing
concern for O'Neill who was struggling, consciously or subconsciously, to
find an end to the torment of orthodoxy. In *Lazarus Laughed* Lazarus was
brought back from the dead to reveal his knowledge through symbolic
laughter. For those who believe there is laughter, 'God's Eternal Laughter'.
Finally, Lazarus is burned at the stake by Caligula who first laughs with
Lazarus, then boasts that he has killed Lazarus before crying out: 'Fool!
Madman! Forgive me, Lazarus! Men forget!' The ambiguity in the play
suggests O'Neill's clouded vision at the time. Finding man incapable of
learning from the past, he both ridiculed and looked earnestly towards
religion. His next play, *Dynamo*, made his point much more clearly as he

saw 'the death of an Old God and the failure of science and materialism to give a satisfying new one for the surviving primitive religious instinct to find a meaning for life in and to comfort its fears of death with.' In contrasting the religious orientation of Reuben Light with the atheist who lives next door, O'Neill made his hero a surface cynic who desperately needs some source of consolation in the modern world. Rejecting a father-god, he prays to a mother-god – suggestive of the great force of women upon O'Neill and symbolized by the dual commutators of the dynamo which represented modern science for both O'Neill and Henry Adams in 'The Dynamo and the Virgin'. 'I don't want to know the truth!' cries Reuben, 'I only want you to hide me, Mother!' It was only in *Days Without End* (1934) that he was able to dramatize a return to Chrisitianity. The Jungian struggle here is between John and Loving ('a death mask of a John who has died with a sneer of scornful mockery on his lips'), two attitudes of the same man: John Loving. Finally, John becomes conscious of his soul, goes to the church and, as Loving dies at the foot of the cross, shouts 'Life laughs with God's love again.'

None of these plays had been satisfactory on the stage, but it is interesting that at this point in his life O'Neill made his third and most satisfactory marriage and wrote his only comedy, *Ah, Wilderness!* (1933). Not only is this play one of the best comedies written by an American, but it also clearly reveals several of O'Neill's major themes and characters. Picturing a nostalgic family weekend in July at the Miller home, O'Neill dramatized the maturing love of a sensitive young man surrounded by delightfully portrayed domestic scenes which stretch from excellent farce-comedy to a moving awareness of the human comedy. If this was a happy period for O'Neill, it was his last and probably one of very few as physical ill health and a concentration upon a cycle of plays possessed him. For the next dozen years he was silent.

From this point in the 1930s until poor health made it too painful for him to write, O'Neill worked upon the nine-play cycle, *A Tale of Possessors Self-Dispossessed*, and wrote *The Iceman Cometh* (1940, 1946), *A Moon for the Misbegotten* (1952) and *Long Day's Journey into Night* (1956). In *The Iceman Cometh*, O'Neill's first opening in New York (1946) after *Days Without End*, he tested the idea that self-deception rather than self-analysis might be meaningful for man. Into a motley group of has-beens, hiding from life, O'Neill brought Harry Hickey, a convert to truth, who forces each of the men to face life again, only to be completely unnerved at their failure to achieve happiness that way. When he tries to explain by confessing the murder of his wife, he only makes them believe that he is crazy – a fortuitous conclusion through which they can easily return to their old illusions and security. Only one of the group understands the truth, and his attitude has already precipitated one death, as ironic an approach to life as illusions are inadequate. The long cycle of plays which burned up O'Neill's energies during the 1930s dealt with the rise of an Irish family in America and the transmission of pride, greed and the desire of power through that family. With the exception of *A Touch of the Poet* (1957) and *More Stately Mansions* (1962), O'Neill destroyed all of his work on these plays. From these two, however, it would seem that the idea of self-delusion is a central concept. The spiritually desolate life of Con Melody (*A Touch of the Poet*) is enhanced neither by the illusion of aristocracy which is beaten out of him by representatives of that very class nor by the substitute illusion to which he then resorts. On the other hand, his daughter Sara, who seduces the wealthy young Simon Harford and is shocked by her father's change, seems to achieve some happiness through a submission to love (as her mother once did), a kind of sustaining illusion of selflessness. In *More Stately Mansions*, which follows immediately in the cycle, Sara's greed provokes a conflict with both Simon and his mother and brings about their eventual retreat from life that blends insanity and illusion in a life-destroying force. With a gloom that overwhelms any personal satisfaction, possessors are dramatically self-dispossessed.

Long Day's Journey into Night is the portrayal of the O'Neill family – father, mother, brothers – that was supposed to be entombed until 1978 but was released by O'Neill's widow, Carlotta Monterey O'Neill, and became his most successful play ever staged. Painful in its agonizing revelation of ugliness, it becomes an exorcism of dignity and power that shows O'Neill as the master playwright he was, terribly wrought by the guilt and fear of modern man yet driven to express himself in some of America's most profound and moving drama. Certainly he arrived on the American theatrical scene when he was most needed, and he infused into that early twentieth-century theatre a concern for experimentation in form and a sense of meaning and power in dramatic literature which had not previously been presented by an American dramatist.

11 An American drama 1920–1941

With the plays that appeared on the American stage between the two World Wars American drama reached a maturity and an artistic sophistication in both form and content that created a distinct contrast with the contributions of the nineteenth-century dramatists. This revelation, obvious to all who read widely in American drama, has influenced a number of critics to conclude that American drama has its beginning, as William Archer dramatically stated, on the sand dunes of Cape Cod during the summer of 1915. He referred, of course, to the initial meeting of the Provincetown Players and their subsequent work with O'Neill. This generalization, however, should be remembered only in conjunction with Oliver Wendell Holmes's carefully phrased observation that 'no generalization is absolutely true, not even this one'. One might, for example, argue from different assumptions that American drama has had several 'beginnings'. For the historian there is clearly one in the seventeenth century. For a distinctive event in the development of American drama, however, the critic must point to the 1891 production of James A. Herne's *Margaret Fleming*. This theatre failure, which showed the influence of Darwin, Spencer, Howells and Ibsen, at the very least suggested a new direction for American drama. Unfortunately, dramatists were either incapable of following Herne's suggestion or unwilling to do so. But before O'Neill became successful and other dramatists had demonstrated both their abilities and their willingness, a few dramatists such as Walter and Sheldon had been edging into that new realism which burst forth in the 1920s. There was certainly a distinct and dramatic change at this time, a new beginning if you will, but the preparation had been slowly under way for thirty years.

An artist, many critics agree, must express the accumulation of forces that work upon him; and a free theatre may best reflect any society at any time, given the artist with sufficient talent, imagination and insight. The First World War, of course, provided an obvious emotional crisis for many people, but in its wake there was in America both economic and social change of a particular character. Immediately, there was a rise in national and individual prosperity while concern for labour was swallowed up in a fast-moving economy. When this economy crashed so dramatically in 1929, the result was the economic depression that created a depression of mind and spirit no less severe. Before the crash, the flappers of the 1920s well illustrate the restless, questioning, pessimistic temper of the times. There were the exorbitant parties of the rich artistically described by F. Scott Fitzgerald who expressed in his titles – *Taps at Reveille* or *The Beautiful and the Damned* – a philosophy of the decade. From the conventions of the past, the confines of religion and the ugliness of government the young people revolted, caught up in the thought of Freud, Kierkegaard and the behaviourist psychologists. Man must express himself. And indeed he did, through creative work and what was termed beautiful living. Although the religious leaders preached 'moral rearmament', a revolt was evident in personal appearance, free sex, more divorces, greater disillusionment. And the result was not satisfying – a Lost Generation. Yet the thinking person of the 1920s was disturbed about the right things, and he frequently expressed himself, whatever the consequences. He satirized the 'booboisie', pointed to *The Waste Land*, portrayed *An American Tragedy* and was shaken by the Sacco and Vanzetti trial.

Movement into the 1930s was accomplished by shock. As the government changed to meet the crisis, reversing Hoover's concern for individualism, Marxists saw the defeat of the capitalistic system. When Franklin Delano Roosevelt was elected to the presidency and initiated the New Deal, he brought strong government control with his National Recovery Act, the Civilian Conservation Corps and the Works Progress Administration in an attempt to encourage the people and bring economic prosperity. The rising state socialism, however, while bringing a sense of security to some, encouraged others to take part in fascist activities which had intruded from other parts of the world. This period, in particular, produced some of the most varied and distinctive drama America had ever known.

As the two distinct decades are juxtaposed, they present a simple, dramatic contrast that many people experienced. Consequently, most writers became absorbed in social issues that disturbed men at the time rather than being concerned with a broad view of life. Thrust this way and that by social and economic forces, writers found it difficult to gain the philosopher's perspective. Should one see life as a cosmic comedy as one critic has assessed Erskine Caldwell's *Tobacco Road*? Should the inequities of social classes be interpreted in tragedy as Paul Green suggested with *In Abraham's Bosom* (1926) or as Marxist writers viewed aspects of life in the 1930s? Or should there be a middle road for the dramatist who could 'always leave 'em laughing' while dramatizing the destruction of man?

There were a number of very thoughtful dramatists during this period, who were seriously concerned with man's condition both on earth in a man-to-man relationship and in the larger relationship of man and his god, however this might be defined. Such a dramatist was, however, severely restricted by the limitations of the commercial theatre in America. He felt that he could not afford that 'tragic sense of life' which Miguel de Unamuno described in *The Tragic Sense of Life in Men and People* (1920). Although he could understand the philosophic problem of attempting 'to reconcile intellectual necessities with the necessities of the heart and will', he was not of the intellectual temper of St Augustine, Pascal or Rousseau, 'men burdened with wisdom rather than knowledge'. Only occasionally aware of the Hawthornian 'unpardonable sin' of setting intellect over the human heart, the American dramatist more often than not offered a sentimental dénouement. Likewise, he disregarded St Augustine and both presumed and despaired. Probably the plays of Robert Sherwood most effectively illustrate the playwright's agonizing and yet failing attempt to dramatize man's contradictions. Like most of the dramatists of this period, Sherwood saw laughter as a necessary escape for man, not, as Unamuno wrote, 'a preparation for tragedy'. Among those who contended more seriously with man's problems, Maxwell Anderson went through several levels of questioning which eventually swept him into political and social conservatism. Other thoughtful dramatists, such as Philip Barry and Thornton Wilder, must be considered for their own individualistic approaches to 'a sense of life'. These dramatists, however, were a minority. There were always those plays of quick comment, even from the better playwrights, which either suggested a solution to a particular social problem or provided an escape through laughter or sentiment which sometimes passed for thought.

The major trend of the period between the two World Wars, though not always indicative of the best plays of the time, was a continuation in principle of a major trend in American drama since James A. Herne. The difference now showed in the greater freedom of the dramatist to experiment in form and content in consequence of America's emergence into the world scene. Its début became a matter of record during the administration of Theodore Roosevelt and was illustrated in the theatre by the emphasis on New Stagecraft and the influence of European and English dramatists such as Ibsen, Strindberg and Shaw. There was also, of course, the changed position and increased stature of the dramatist in America. Clyde Fitch and James Herne had already demonstrated that a good craftsman with some interesting ideas could save money. Eugene O'Neill was to show that, with the help of the new little theatres and the theatrical agencies, a dramatist of distinctive ideas and experimental techniques could also be successful. Consequently, the theatre now appealed to writers who might have chosen a different genre fifty years back.

There is no doubt that critics of the 1920s were very much aware of a new American drama and theatre. (It should also be pointed out that the position of the drama critic had now changed to something quite respectable in drastic contrast to the dominating 'puffers' of the mid-nineteenth century, although there was a slow line of progress in this discipline, too.) Some years back John Corbin had announced 'The Dawn of American Drama' (*Atlantic Monthly* (May 1907), 99), but more significantly Thomas H. Dickinson now introduced the *Playwrights of the New American Theatre* (1925). 'The Playwright as Pioneer' was Percy MacKaye whose efforts as a pioneer were to suffer considerably when followers did not flock to his banner. On the other hand, 'The Playwright Unbound' was Eugene O'Neill who fulfilled Dickinson's capsule criticism admirably. Other dramatists he discussed either as 'interpreters of the American scene', such as Sheldon, Walter, Rachel Crothers, Susan Glaspell and Zöe Akins, or as creators of 'Our American Comedy' – Langdon Mitchell, J. L. Williams, James Forbes, Clare Kummer, Booth Tarkington, George S. Kaufman and Marc Connelly, among others. The divisions of Dickinson's organization say something about the drama of this period while the plays of the dramatists listed here indicate their differences from a new group of dramatists who were already taking their places on the American stage when Dickinson's volume appeared.

With a few exceptions the dramas of Dickinson's playwrights of the New American Theatre are accorded an analysis in the history of modern American drama only through a gesture of generosity. Although a step beyond their own contemporaries, their work was mostly too slight and conventional to be a part of the movement in drama that had gathered considerable force by the late 1920s. Sheldon, Walter, Mitchell, Williams and Rachel Crothers belong to the pre-war generation. So does James Forbes (1871–1938), whose *The Famous Mrs Fair* (1919) dealt with a woman whose successful wartime career nearly ruined her life until she understood where she belonged. Clare Kummer's (d. 1958) first play, *Good Gracious, Annabelle* (1916), is a witty farce about a girl who catches her millionaire and adequately illustrates the type of play she wrote. Booth Tarkington (1869–1946) and Zöe Akins (1886–1958) may be listed among those romantic playwrights who fill the gap briefly and slightly during every theatre season. Tarkington's *Clarence* (1919) has some satiric intent, but it is mainly a farce about a young soldier-scientist Ph.D. Zöe Akins tried to treat divorce seriously in *Déclassée* (1919) but it never got beyond rather far-fetched melodrama. In 1935 she won a Pulitzer Prize with *The Old Maid* (1935) which ran for 305 performances to those New York audiences who always enjoy sentimental, heartbreaking melodrama. These dramatists, however, were hardly the dramatists of the 1920s who were to transform the American theatre.

Of the dramatists who dominated the two decades between the wars and brought a new vitality to the American theatre Elmer Rice (Reizenstein) (1892–1967), briefly but justly recognized by Dickinson, was the first to gain critical recognition. He indicated his strength as a dramatist – talented, forthright, interested in expressing his views in the most effective ways – in *On Trial* (1914), a melodrama which made use of his earlier legal training by including experimental courtroom flashback scenes in an attempt to explore a crime. More than most American dramatists Rice exploded his opinions in the face of the critics and audiences. He renounced the theatre and declared his retirement from it more than once and pronounced his continuing adoration of it even more frequently. For the historian of American drama he will be known for two or three dramas which effectively show certain developments in American theatre – experimentation in technique, protest, realistic detail, Marxism. He had ideas, and he possessed both a good mind and a sensitive nature, but he was not often able to prove himself upon the stage.

Absorbing as he did the vitality of the European theatre as well as the surge of new ideas that inundated the sensitive post-war man, Rice may be approached as a touchstone dramatist in America. The works of Strindberg and the German expressionists appealed to him, and in America he became an influential interpreter of their techniques. The new realism that Sherwood Anderson and Sinclair Lewis were exploiting in fiction became a basic technique in form and content for one of his most outstanding plays (*Street Scene*) – which was one of the best American plays of its kind. An idealist, Rice reacted to the Depression with an interest in Marxism, but although he found himself a staunch liberal, he would never make the move to communism. During the 1930s his almost yearly plays reflected his own problems and solutions in a society to which he frequently reacted with more temperament than sensitivity. He wanted people to take him seriously, but his observations were, in the majority of his plays, neither moving nor profound. A man of the theatre who judged a play by audience response, he was also extremely concerned with the commercial theatre system in America – as most playwrights were and are. As an exponent of realistic social commentary, he questioned both the validity of the theatre as a means of expressing such ideas as well as the foresight of American producers. When the Federal Theatre Project came into existence in 1935, he was an eager leader until government censorship disillusioned him completely and he resigned his position. Only in the Playwrights' Company did he find a producing situation having some degree of comfort. After the Second World War his playwriting continued at a more moderate pace with even less success. The relevant causes he championed between the wars were abandoned for romantic excursions into personality studies. Although he remained a liberal idealist who believed in speaking his mind, though not in his plays at this date, his place in American drama is still confined to those exciting two decades between the wars to which he contributed with some success.

Rice's first major contribution was *The Adding Machine* (1923). Troubled by the growing victimization and dehumanization of modern man, Rice abandoned the usual descriptive and representative truth and created an intensified, emotional expression of modern man – Mr Zero, a simple clerk, condemned as a 'waste product' and the slave of a society which coolly replaces him with a machine. In scenes of symbolic and subjectively imagined activity, Mr Zero reacts by killing his boss, undergoes trial and execution, enters 'a pleasant place' where he operates an adding machine, and finally – and ironically – chooses to return to earth. A bitter satire on many aspects of society, effectively accomplished by experimental techniques, *The Adding*

Machine is Rice's essay on man. Six years later in *The Subway* (1929) he continued his lecture on man as a cataclysmic oppressor and his own victim. As scientists of the future dig in America, they find 'all that remains of Western Civilization' – false teeth, a glass eye, blackened coins, a key for a safe-deposit box, etc. Rice returned to this technique only once and this time peripherally in *Dream Girl* (1945), a fantasy comedy in which the dreams of the heroine are dramatized in carefully worked-out sequences. *The Adding Machine*, however, remains his most worthy contribution to American drama.

Although the theatrical devices in *The Adding Machine* attracted most of the critical comment, there was a strong social protest in the play which he continued on an entirely different dramaturgical plane in *Street Scene* (1929). Theatrically, he was saying the same thing: 'Everywhere you look', exclaims a character in *Street Scene*, 'oppression and cruelty!' What does life hold for anyone? Portraying a cross-section of life in a New York street scene, Rice presented the hopes, dreams and despair of the sensitive person as they conflict with the insensitive good intentions of the hardworking and law-abiding or the impassive or uncaring. In one sense *Street Scene* presents a concept of modern tragedy in conflicting idealized 'goods', that of love versus law and order. But Rice was not a philosopher. His world involved man's daily struggles where man's inhumanity to man was illustrated by the recognizable oppression of political or governmental forces in city halls. Nature was never a part of this man's struggle. Instead, there was the police system, the charity worker, the love that blossomed on a tenement fire escape. Although he asked meaningful questions, his idea of the life that New York held for its people seemed very limited; but, because he was a forthright person, he was not satisfied unless he expressed an opinion. The practice of law, for example, is the complicating factor in *Counsellor-at-Law* (1931) just as marriage is the issue in *The Left Bank* (1931), but both third acts are resolved in ways that would have pleased Bronson Howard fifty years before. When Marxism appeared to be a real alternative to capitalism, Rice dramatized his personal views in strongly propagandistic plays: *We, the People* (1933), *Judgment Day* (1934) and *Between Two Worlds* (1934). But he found that he was not a radical, and by 1938, after a bitter fight with the commercial theatre, he jumped on the same patriotic bandwagon that entranced Robert Sherwood at this time and wrote *American Landscape* (1938) which found basic values in American tradition. Rice seemed to enjoy expressing himself, but after the war he dropped almost completely out of the current of the developing American drama.

Although Rice, with his protests in form and content, became a good transition figure to span the changes brought about by the First World War, he was not a strong force in a developing American drama after the 1920s. By this time others were providing more thought-provoking and exciting plays. Some of this excitement started in 1924 with the production of two plays – *They Knew What They Wanted* by Sidney Howard and *What Price Glory?* by Maxwell Anderson and Laurence Stallings. More than any other play of this period *They Knew What They Wanted* expressed an attitude of the 1920s quite distinct from the social dramas of the previous years. In contrast to the major characters of Rachel Crothers and Jesse Lynch Williams who succumbed to socially acceptable conventions, Howard's characters knew what they wanted and took it. The repetition of this concept in other plays of the 1920s suggests both its validity and its appeal. S. N. Behrman's hero in *The Second Man* (1927), for example, knew what he wanted and kept it. So did Mary and Jim Hutton in Philip Barry's *Paris Bound* (1927). In an earlier Barry play, *In a Garden* (1924), Lissa made a discovery, forcing her to decide what she wanted. In fact, a character's discovery and decision to do something is basic in Barry's dramaturgy. Maxwell Anderson's *Saturday Children* (1927) discover what they want and are still trying for it at the final curtain. Even Owen Davis's Jane in *Icebound* (1923) knew what she wanted and got it. Exceptions to this thesis can be found, of course, but Sidney Howard (1891–1939) should be credited with putting his artistic finger upon an idea which helps demonstrate the change that the new modern drama brought to America.

In contrast to a few of Howard's contemporaries he was not an innovator, although he did take advantage of new ideas such as the influence of Strindberg and the Freudian concepts that provide motivation for his characters in *The Silver Cord* (1926). Mainly, he used the social realism of Ibsen and Herne along with the approach of Sinclair Lewis and Sherwood Anderson and continued in the established tradition of social melodrama. Viewing the dramatist as a 'vicarious actor', he produced vehicles for actors and actresses and concerned himself with a satisfactory ending consistent with his modern psychology. He liked people, forceful and emotional people, and he wrote about them and their problems, emphasizing their emotions rather than their intellects. This approach was particularly evident in *They Knew What They Wanted*. Tony was an old man who wooed a young girl, Amy, by mail using a photograph of Joe, a young man temporarily living with him. On her wedding day, for the first time, Amy sees Tony who has contributed to the problem by breaking both of his legs in a car accident. The shock for

Amy is severe, and that night she is consoled by Joe. Much later, they all face Amy's pregnancy and decide what they want: Amy, a home and love; Tony, a wife and Amy's baby; Joe, the open road. Everything is all right. 'What you have done', says Tony, 'is mistake in da head, not in da heart. Mistake in the head is no matter.' As a dramatist, Howard realized that emotion was much more important than intellect. Mrs Phelps in *The Silver Cord* fights with the diabolic cunning of Strindberg's Laura to keep her two sons for herself in an emotion-packed drama that remains one of America's best thesis plays. The title character in *Lucky Sam McCarver* (1925) is a hardened, cynical man incapable of love, lucky only in an ironic sense. Carrie, *Ned McCobb's Daughter* (1926), is a determined and superior Yankee woman who fights for what is right, while Doc Haggett in *The Late Christopher Bean* (1932) is tortured by greed to take advantage of a servant girl whose husband created valuable paintings. With these characters Howard created some of the better social dramas of the period.

His technique was neither old hokum nor new experimentation. Starting quite simply with well-thought-out characters and a theory of realism, he built his plays around an effective use of dramatic irony and controlled action employing manipulated time and spectacular scenes. Probably his use of irony is as sophisticated a bit of dramaturgy as he wanted, since he had obtained most of his training from the plays of Eugène Scribe and the writers of social melodrama in America. *The Silver Cord*, for example, is a mass of ironies. As for realism, his choice of Sinclair Lewis's *Dodsworth* for adaptation to the stage in 1934 suggests his interests. If he had any thesis which might be traced in his plays, it would be the concept of 'self' as a motivating force in his characters. Looking at people from a social rather than a philosophical position, he found some people aware both of themselves and of life beyond self. These were people like Tony and Amy, Carrie, and Christina in *The Silver Cord* – those who accepted responsibility with their freedom. Those who saw only themselves – Mrs Phelps, Lucky Sam, Doc Haggett – were trapped by their own machinations. This concern for free expression of self was, of course, part of the new psychology, and Howard was only attacking the kind of moral observations that American writers of social melodrama had been doing for many years. Interestingly enough, although most of Howard's twenty-four plays were either adaptations or collaborations, his best plays were those he wrote by himself. By the mid-thirties, however, he seemed to have nothing more to say.

That other spectacular success of 1924, *What Price Glory?*, was the result of a collaboration, but only Maxwell Anderson (1888–1959) became distinguished in the theatre. Like most of his contemporaries, he was concerned with individual freedom as he saw man victimized in the socio-political state by the institutions of power that surrounded him. Although Anderson is too frequently remembered for his attempts to write historical verse tragedy, he wrote a number of prose dramas that are in the mainstream of social melodrama. In both types of drama he asserted a belief in the basic independence of man and a dislike for authority which eventually became a concern for government. After two more plays with Laurence Stallings – *First Flight* (1925) and *The Buccaneer* (1925), both suggesting opposition to government of any kind – Anderson (with Harold Hickerson) characteristically expounded a faith in the individual and a bitterness towards the biased administration of justice in *Gods of the Lightning* (1928), a liberal interpretation of the Sacco and Vanzetti trial. This was a thesis to which he would return with greater power and skill in *Winterset* (1935), a poetic drama. Two years before this he had received a Pulitzer Prize for *Both Your Houses* (1933) which satirized both houses of Congress. Through the eyes of a young idealistic congressman, Anderson dramatized the growing power of a government that threatens individual freedom, a government whose sole business is 'graft, special privilege, and corruption – with a by-product of order'. But when he revised this play in 1939 he changed his approach in order to defend American democracy and to distinguish between man and his institution of government. His emphasis was still on the freedom of the individual, but he had established a meaningful change in his point of view.

In both his poetic and prose drama written during the 1930s he stressed his thesis that government corrupted through power and destroyed individual freedom. 'It rots a man's brain to be in power,' says a character in *Valley Forge* (1934) which portrays George Washington as a rebel-idealist during that terrible winter of the Revolution. Power is more important than love for the Queen in *Elizabeth the Queen* (1930) who also tolerated cruelty in order to protect her throne in *Mary of Scotland* (1933). Rudolf in *The Masque of Kings* (1937) listens to an explanation about the logic of power and realizes that corruption inevitably falls even upon the most idealistic of revolutionaries.

Again and again Anderson asserted his pessimistic theme: government means power and men cannot unite power and justice. In a world where integrity and individual freedom must eventually contend with socio-political power, sensitive man can either accept defeat, become corrupt, or escape through death. In any event, power corrupts. Sometimes there were mitigating circumstances, however, where power might be tolerated as necessary. As the 1930s came to an end and war became inevitable to men like Anderson and Robert Sherwood whose feelings for justice were outraged by world events, there were obviously other ways to view government than as corrupted power. Anderson's previous unbending condemnation underwent a slight change in *Knickerbocker Holiday* (1938), that raucous satire of life under F.D.R.'s New Deal, with music by Kurt Weill, in which he blasted the philosophy of a benevolent despotism. The alternative was humour: 'Let's keep the government small and funny.' All of this was in keeping with the revisions he was then making in *Both Your Houses*. Man may be considered as distinct from his institutions. Besides, there is the concept of patriotism and the possibility that survival may depend upon manipulating one source of power against another. Although Anderson could still write in his 'Thoughts about the Critics' that 'A tyrant is a tyrant, beneficent or maleficent', his soldiers in *The Eve of St Mark* (1942) die for freedom and a democratic government.

The Second World War clearly made a tremendous impression upon several of America's best dramatists of the 1930s. None of them was effective in writing war plays (with the single exception of Sherwood's *There Shall Be No Night*), and Anderson's *Candle in the Wind* (1941) and *Storm Operation* (1944) did nothing for his reputation and perhaps only slightly more for the American war effort. No play showed his previous impassioned protests about man and his government until *Joan of Lorraine* (1946) in which he showed an actress and her director arguing over the interpretation of a Joan of Arc play. Can beliefs be compromised? Clearly, Anderson had been bothered by what he had been writing, and the answer that both he and Joan framed was that one could not live without belief. Although in *Anne of the Thousand Days* (1948) he returned to his bitter attitude towards mankind and his concern with power, it must not have been satisfying. In his last play of any consequence, *Barefoot in Athens* (1951), he re-emphasized his ideas of the late 1930s and settled two questions that had always bothered him: democracy is the only acceptable form of government; truth is the only guide for the individual who endorses freedom and life.

It was the nature of the best American dramatists of the period between the wars to be rebellious, to level attacks upon existing gods and institutions and to emphasize the necessity of expressing the individual and maintaining his freedom. One dramatist who stands away from his contemporaries in this approach to life and art is George Kelly (1887–1974), a man of sturdy and unbending principles who determined to judge the weaknesses of man rather than his institutions. Starting his professional writing career in 1916, he wrote a variety of one-act plays for the vaudeville circuit with such success that in six years he could abandon this practice and concentrate on full-length dramas. The form and the market for these early works, however, clearly affected his later playwriting in which a single human frailty is ridiculed within a well-made structure involving farcical action and caricature. Among the vaudeville sketches *The Flattering Word* and *The Weak Spot* toured the country on the circuits with enormous success. Then during the 1920s Kelly produced a half-dozen dramas which brought him considerable critical attention on the legitimate stage, including a Pulitzer Prize for *Craig's Wife* in 1925. After 1930 he wrote only seven plays, two of which have never been professionally produced or published; *When All Else Fails* (1951) was his last play.

Following in the tradition of Langdon Mitchell, Rachel Crothers and Bronson Howard, Kelly is a master of deliberate construction. Everything begins with a clear presentation of the background. Action is exact as are his references to properties and his use of realistic, even photographic, details. Everything usually takes place in a single location. Within this deliberate formula construction his characters absorb most of his attention as they reveal the idea that he has for each play. And as a playwright he was always a moralist, a teacher, who dramatized some problem from which a moral lesson could be derived. People, Kelly felt, controlled their own lives, and he judged them for their weaknesses and their failures, blaming neither heredity nor social forces. Logically, then, his plays are based on human problems. But as they also demonstrate the consistency between his restricting form in playwriting and his unbending point of view in discussing man, they give the impression of being very controlled pieces of theatre.

Kelly's first two plays were revisions of one-act successes. *Mrs Ritter Appears* was expanded into *The Torchbearers* (1922), that satire of amateur activity in the little-theatre movement which is easily played by amateur groups. *Poor Aubrey* became *The Show-Off* (1924), one of Kelly's two popular successes. As a portrayal of a sometimes appealing braggart and liar who is blessed far beyond his just deserts, *The Show-Off* is a fast-moving satirical farce which impressed audiences and critics with the Promethean magnificence of human faults. These human weaknesses, however, were Kelly's main interest, and his plays continued to dramatize in a more serious manner his strong Puritan attitude towards such frailties. Those people whom Kelly finds wilfully corrupt he damns with a cool conviction. The main character in *Craig's Wife* (1926), for example, is such a person. A quarrelsome woman who alienates her neighbours, tries to ruin a niece's life and maliciously distrusts a good husband, Mrs Craig is condemned at the end of the play to the independent yet now friendless security that she wanted. His unsympathetic castigation of people who have been wilfully corrupt is revealed again in *Behold the Bridegroom* (1927). Once a weak woman of repeated affairs, Antoinette Lyle finally finds love. But when she feels constrained to reveal her past, she is rejected. In *Philip Goes Forth* (1931) Kelly criticized the weakness of a man who allowed stupid pride to push him into betraying his vocation.

In *The Show-Off* and *Craig's Wife* Kelly shows a discriminating insight into character and a careful attention to truthful detail. For these characteristics and his concern for social ills his plays were enjoyed. As a playwright who dispassionately ridiculed folly and vice, seeing in man a natural disposition toward these ends, Kelly was criticized for the severity with which he defended the few moral truths that he preached. Although it would seem that he was out of the mainstream of American drama of this period with his characters controlled by his own stern convictions, he was simply presenting a point of view that prescribed greater restrictions than people were willing to accept. The individual might be as expressive and free as he wished in the vogue of the time, but Kelly insisted that there were limits.

Just as Kelly ridiculed folly with an extremely heavy hand, two other playwrights whom Dickinson had mentioned as part of the New American Theatre ridiculed much of the same society but with a certain touch of lightness that proved to be even more devastating. George S. Kaufman (1889–1962) and Marc Connelly (1890–   ) first appeared as a team in *Dulcy* (1921), a hilarious farce-comedy about a scatterbrained wife whose stupidities would seem to ruin everyone's plans but somehow turn out all right. These two collaborators continued their efforts in four more plays and ended with *Beggar on Horseback* (1924), not only the pinnacle of their cooperative writing but a poignant satire on the position of the artist in a modern commercial world. Connelly, in *Voices Off Stage* (1968), called it 'a fantasy in which a young musician would go through a maze of kaleidoscopic experiences'. In a hilarious and ridiculing dream sequence Neil, the musician, learns about commercialization and decides that the rich man's daughter is not for him. In the best tradition of expressionism the authors used colour, sound, costume, pantomime, distortion, symbolic mechanical action, grotesque forms, stream of consciousness and exaggeration to present their own version of reality. A vigorous protest against industry and science, it is the only commercially successful expressionist play written by Americans.

Kaufman went on to achieve a considerable reputation as a 'play doctor' who knew how to please the people who came at eight. For forty years and in as many plays he entertained Broadway audiences and at the same time, with the carefully applied touch of the comic satirist, ridiculed man and his institutions. With a single early exception – *The Butter and Egg Man* (1925) – Kaufman worked with collaborators. With Edna Ferber, for example, he poked fun at the Barrymore family of actors in *The Royal Family* (1927); with Morris Ryskind he satirized politics in *Of Thee I Sing* (1932); with Ring Lardner he wrote a spoof of Tin Pan Alley, *June Moon* (1929); with Howard Teichmann he exploited the comic possibility of a little old lady's taking over the leadership of a large corporation in *The Solid Gold Cadillac* (1953) which was his only successful play written after the Second World War. His best work, however, was accomplished with the help of Moss Hart (1904–61), who wrote a number of plays himself, only one of which deserves comment. *Lady in the Dark* (1941) is a penetrating study of a woman trying desperately to find her own place in life. Otherwise, as in *Christopher Blake* (1946) which is concerned with the problem of divorce, Hart had difficulty fusing an appropriate theatrical balance with his serious approach.

Working with Kaufman, Hart's intense attitudes were ameliorated by his own basic warmth and touched by Kaufman's light but frequently stinging wit. In their first play together, *Once in a Lifetime* (1930), they created what will probably remain the outstanding burlesque of Hollywood absurdity. *You Can't Take It With You* (1936) brought them a Pulitzer Prize with its humorously appealing but eccentric New York family whose members write plays, make fireworks, print revolutionary literature, study ballet, and generally exist apart from what might be considered normal apartment living. But when normal life and love intrudes into the scene, the result is chaos and excellent farce. Some discriminating critics felt that it was not worthy of a Pulitzer Prize, but arguments over that award become a particular chapter in the history of American dramatic criticism. Four collaborations later they reached their height in light farce-comedy with *The Man Who Came to Dinner* (1939), a play which ostensibly burlesqued the lecture tours of the drama critic Alexander Woollcott. In a cluttered but fast-moving play the authors created Sheridan Whiteside who torments and entertains his guests and the poor family on whom he is thrust, the victim of a presumed broken hip. Provided with innumerable possibilities for farce humour – from the telephone conversations through a gift of penguins to a riotous Christmas radio programme – the play was clearly a welcome break for a country approaching war.

Kaufman was a highly competent craftsman whose irrepressible wit provided the American theatre with fascinating entertainment. Along with
Connelly, Robert Sherwood, Alexander Woollcott, Dorothy Parker, Robert
Benchley and others, he was a prominent member of the group who met at
the Algonquin Hotel during the 1920s to amuse and dramatize themselves.
Connelly's reputation as a dramatist never rose as high as his collaborator's,
although he remained close to the theatre and to theatre people. In 1926 he
wrote an interesting comedy called *The Wisdom Tooth* in which he employed
a dream device to reveal the submerged character of his hero and help him
to gain self-respect if not success in his present world. In any history of
American drama, however, Marc Connelly will be remembered chiefly for
Green Pastures (1930). Explaining the Bible in terms of Negro life, Connelly
humanized God in the guise of a country Negro preacher who watches over
his people. 'De Lawd', as he was called, attends a fish fry in Heaven and
with a spectacular flourish creates the world and man. After 'De Lawd'
strolls around the earth observing his creations with strong distaste, the first
half of the play ends with the Flood as De Lawd says, 'I only hope it's goin'
to work out all right.' The remainder of the play dramatizes the stories of
Moses and Joshua, shows God's anger ('I repent of dese people I have
made') and ends with the approach of Jesus. It is a warm and delightful
play created for an audience of sufficient belief as well as social and artistic
balance to appreciate it.

The American folk drama, of which *Green Pastures* is one of the best-
known modern examples, might well be traced back to the local-colour
character of the early nineteenth century and the backwoodsmen and
pioneers who appeared in the drama following the Civil War. Inasmuch as
traditions were being created in a new country rather than celebrated as in
an older society, American dramatists fused local-colour peculiarities and
semi-myth characters into a kind of romantic-realistic drama. Frank Murdock's *Davy Crockett* (1872) is an excellent illustration just as Davy Crockett
as both legend and man exemplifies the principle of this fusion. Stories
about truly mythical characters also appeared, such as Mike Fink the
legendary flatboat man of the Mississippi and Paul Bunyan who made his
way along the top of the United States and stamped out the Great Lakes
with his feet in the process. There was also John Henry the steel-driving
man and the Irishman named Pat who worked on the railroad. But it was far
into the twentieth century before the dramatists took advantage of these
myths. In essence America was concerned mainly with its contemporary
issues and problems, and the theatre had to wait for the plays of John M.

Synge and William Butler Yeats based on Ireland's folk past before it built upon its own. Chief among those who exploited American mythical material was E. P. Conkle (1899–   ) whose best work was his dramatization of the young Abraham Lincoln in *Prologue to Glory*, produced by the Federal Theatre in New York in 1938. In the true fashion of folk drama, however, he wrote *Bill and the Widowmaker*, the story of Pecos Bill and his purple stallion; *Paul and the Blue Ox*, the problems that Paul Bunyan had with the logging bosses; and *Johnny Appleseed* (published 1947). Other folk plays, such as Ruark Bradford's (1896–1948) *John Henry* (1940) and Guthrie McClintic's (1893–1961) story of Jesse James, *Missouri Legend* (1938), have appeared infrequently on the stage.

The direction that folk drama has taken in modern America is quite similar to that of the local-colour drama of the late nineteenth century. Different regions of the country have suggested peculiarities of character and custom that dramatists used as the basis of plays. In the best plays these peculiarities have been fused with superstition and naïveté to reveal that mixture of sentiment and realism in America which is the common man. In the least effective plays the folk background has been used merely as a flavouring for melodrama. Generally, plays have represented the many different sections of America, although those about the south have been most abundant. Some of the character of New England, for example, was emphasized in Owen Davis's *Detour* (1921) and *Icebound* (1923). With better effect the south-west has been presented in the works of Lynn Riggs (1899–1954). His *Roadside* (1930), with its tall-tale qualities, its elemental freedom, its fresh and rich speech, and its earthy yet dignified characters, uses excellent folk material to dramatize man's love of liberty. The next year *Green Grow the Lilacs* opened on Broadway. Again the scene was the Indian territory of the early 1900s and again, with the folk language and his sense of rural humanity, Riggs created a truthful portrayal of regional life. From that point on Riggs used his regional background to help dramatize more serious approaches to life – such as *The Cream in the Well* (1941) which some critics called tragedy – but he failed. Then *Green Grow the Lilacs* came back to the stage as a musical comedy *Oklahoma!* (1943), and Riggs was famous – but not for what he wanted to say. Although his strong sense of reality was clear in all of his plays, in his later plays he never quite succeeded in avoiding contrived plots to make his severe commentary on man believable to an audience.

Among those regional plays emphasizing the folk characteristics of the American south, Lula Vollmer's (1898–1955) *Sun-Up* (1923) is a good illustration A melodrama in structure, as these plays tended to be, it tells the story of a North Carolina mountain woman who watches a son go to war, hears of his death and, influenced by a strange force, hides a young army deserter whose father killed her husband. The dialect, the peculiar customs and the supernatural vision – all enhance the folk drama. Hatcher Hughes's (1881–1945) *Hell-Bent for Heaven* (1924) was built around the religious fanaticism of the main character who stirs up an old feud for his own personal gain and (in the ending of the original version) is ironically left to the mercy of the God with whom he boasted an intimacy. Probably the best known of the regional folk plays and one of the most successful in the theatre is Dorothy and Du Bose Heyward's (1885–1940) *Porgy* (1927). This story of Porgy, the crippled beggar, and his love for Crown's Bess has many folk elements – the saucer funeral, the dirges, the bleeding corpse, the ominous bird that brings disaster wherever it lands, the conjuring for Bess.

Part of the impetus for this type of drama came from the academic community – George Pierce Baker at Yale, Brander Matthews at Columbia, Frederick H. Koch at North Carolina. It was Koch who suggested one of the ground rules when he told his students to 'write what you know around you, make use of the soil beneath your feet, of the tradition in your heart, of the struggle in your soul, of the breath of your hills.' One of those who took Professor Koch's advice seriously was Paul Green (1894–   ). Perhaps a cue for understanding him may be found in a letter to Barrett Clark concerning the southern community he knew so well: 'and I was one of them', he wrote, '– neither black nor white, but one of them, children of the moist earth underfoot.' It was this intense feeling for man coupled with his searching insight into human character that compelled him to dramatize his abundant impressions of life around him and then led him to protest against the social injustices he saw before finally sensing his place in the theatre as the creator of outdoor pageants of momentous proportions. Regional folk emphasis, strong opinions of protest, a concern for history through his symphonic drama – all show the idealism and the sensitivity towards man and America that make him a distinctively American dramatist.

Before the production of his symphonic drama, *The Lost Colony* (1937), altered his career, Green had carefully followed Koch's advice and written more than thirty one-act plays and four full-length plays from his own southern experiences, creating poignant sketches of the 'children of the moist earth underfoot'. Although Paul Green deserves critical attention for his strongminded plays of the Depression period, those dramas created from his own experiences and observations provide a more subtle and discriminating view of humanity. These are the plays on which his reputation in American drama will rest: one, *In Abraham's Bosom* (1926), is among the best examples of tragic drama in America. Telling his stories episode by episode, in a manner consciously or subconsciously imitative of the Irish dramatists of the period, he built upon the poetic and rhythmic language of the Negro and the folk characteristics of the south. *The Last of the Lowries* (1920), for example, resembles John Millington Synge's *Riders to the Sea* as it dramatizes a mother's reaction to the killing of her last son. Another one-act play of considerable power and bitter sentiment is *White Dresses* (1926), a pathetic and seemingly fated incident in which a Negro woman burns a white dress given by the landlord's son to her granddaughter along with another dress, presumably given to the girl's mother by her real father, a white man.

Among Green's regional full-length plays, *The Field God* (1927) dramatizes the spiritual disintegration of Hardy Gilchrist, a man proud of his individuality who finally feels himself condemned by a religiosity he rejected. *The House of Connelly* (1931) also presents Green's mistrust of fundamentalist religion and his emphasis upon a need for individual freedom. The play shows (in its later revised form) the hero's change of attitude and final denunciation of the corrupt and corrupting southern plantation aristocracy. It is in his prizewinning *In Abraham's Bosom*, however, that Green reveals his greatest insight and strength as a playwright. Idealistic, stubborn and furiously ambitious, Abraham McCrannie wants to learn and to be a teacher of his people. But when his white father finally gets him a school in which to teach, the Negroes are reluctant to attend, and Abe's own son turns against him along with the white men who taunt him until he is driven to murder and suffers the southern consequences of that act. Here is the tragic struggle of an idealist who is defeated not only by his heredity or the white environment that surrounds him but by his own limitations and the distrust of the very people he is trying to help. Like Cain, he kills his brother, in this instance a half-brother. Like modern man, he searches for an identity and blames society for his failures: 'You know what I am – no, I dunno what I am. Sometimes I think that's the trouble.' In this play Green most effectively expresses the feelings of modern society as well as his own probing concern with the social pressures that frustrate man from fulfilling the promises of his individual spirit.

In 1928 Green received a Guggenheim Foundation grant which allowed him to study and travel abroad. When he returned to North Carolina, he wrote *Potter's Field* (published 1931), his first symphonic 'drama' and a turbulent play of Negro communal life that continued his reflection of folk attitudes but failed as a play. Revised as a musical, *Roll Sweet Chariot* (1934), the symphonic effect was clear in the use of music, dance, pantomime and other stylizing elements combined with the folk rhythms and poetry of the dialogue. But this also failed. In the interim Green had written novels and short stories until he tried the drama again with *Shroud My Body Down* (1934), a fascinating and violent play of religious mania which dealt with the heroine's incestuous feelings for her brother whom she imagines to be Christ. Green called it 'sick', and it does suggest a change coming over his work brought about by the Depression and his enlarged consciousness. *Hymn to the Rising Sun* (1936) is a powerful one-act play bitterly protesting the cruelty of the chain-gang system in the south. The heavy irony which Green employs in the Captain's 4th of July speech and in the general use of the chain-gang as a means of administering justice dramatized a new combination of Green's accumulating anger and pity.

In *Johnny Johnson* (1936), 'A Fable of Ancient and Modern Times', Green demonstrated his concern for universal concepts in America's most imaginative anti-war play. It is a beautiful day somewhere in the American south as the townspeople gather to dedicate a 'monument of peace', carved by Johnny Johnson. But war clouds are gathering over Europe and, much to the amazement of Johnny who exclaims, 'Why – why – I thought we were all for peace', the villagers' attitudes change drastically as 'War is declared!' Later, urged by Minnie Belle, Johnny finally enlists in 'a war to end war', but once in France Johnny first shares a hatred of war with a German sniper and then invades an allied high command meeting with a container of laughing gas, almost stopping the war. Back in America after the war Johnny is placed in 'the house of balm' where doctors diagnose his disease as 'peace monomania'. As a strong protest against war, the play is extremely effective while the experimental techniques provided some spectacular theatre. Unfortunately, at this time in America the play was too serious. It demanded thought and sensitivity from the audience and the critics who at this moment were much more impressed with Robert Sherwood's sugar-coated anti-war play, *Idiot's Delight*, and the Kaufman and Hart farce, *You Can't Take It With You*. After this play Green launched a new career as America's foremost creator of spectacular, outdoor pageants.

Robert E. Sherwood (1896–1955) was a playwright with many of the same attitudes towards life and some of the spiritual irritations that bothered Paul Green, but he possessed quite different talents for the theatre. Although he could write both anti-war plays and war plays that would arouse a theatre population to standing ovations, he could not present the understanding of man that Green created in *In Abraham's Bosom*, in spite of his most serious desire to do so. As a result, he became America's most popular dramatist during the 1930s while Green eased himself out of a theatre he found 'an industry and not an art'.

For theatre audiences between the two World Wars Robert Sherwood provided an emotionally satisfying evening occasionally laced with simple, direct thought appropriate for that moment in history. He was not an experimenter nor an innovator, nor was he an influential dramatist in the developing American theatre. As his friend Maxwell Anderson put it, he had a 'virtuosity of stagecraft', and perhaps that is a sufficient comment. Although careful analysis of his plays reveals serious flaws in his dramaturgy, those flaws are quickly forgotten in a theatre where his hokum (a word he loved) was mixed with thought sufficiently appealing to gain him three Pulitzer Prizes. (He won a fourth for his history, *Roosevelt and Hopkins*, 1948.) With his first contribution to the New York stage, *The Road to Rome* (1927), he was successful, and yet his success might almost have been predicted. Growing up in a society which foreshadowed his enrolment in Milton Academy and Harvard University, he absorbed the proper beliefs in God, freedom, truth, peace. Although at Harvard little interested him other than writing for the *Lampoon* and *The Hasty Pudding*, his contribution to the first got him a post-war job with *Vanity Fair* and his co-authorship of *Barnum Was Right* (1917) for the second taught him the value of hokum. *Vanity Fair* led him to a membership in the Algonquin Club where he met the most witty people of his day and further developed his love for the theatre. It was expected that he would write a play and that his natural sensitivity and wit as well as his training, both formal and informal, would guide him towards success. *The Road to Rome* dramatized Sherwood's answer to a historical question: Why didn't Hannibal destroy Rome when he had the opportunity? In thought it was a potent anti-war play, developing out of Sherwood's wartime service and subsequent hatred of war and stressing the positive value of the 'human equation' which Sherwood described as more beautiful than war. Yet in the play it is not an anti-war or humane argument which deters Hannibal – but a beautiful woman. One frequently repeated observation about Sherwood's work (and one which he presumably confessed) is that he always started his plays with a 'big message and ended up with nothing but good entertainment'. This was a problem which marked his first success and followed him throughout his career, but it did not prevent him from being tremendously popular.

Sherwood's place in American drama is as a part of that group of people –
Anderson, Green, Kelly, Rice, Barry, Howard, Kaufman, Connelly,
Behrman and others – who made the world more aware of American drama.
Except in the brilliance of particular plays, most of which have dated rapidly,
he is difficult to distinguish. He did not, for example, present penetrating
ideas or create unforgettable characters or tell memorable stories. What he
did, however, he did well. He dealt honestly yet superficially with emotions
that Americans wanted to feel: belief in God, freedom, peace and truth, for
example. If he asked his audiences to think, it was only for a moment. Yet
within a fifteen-year period he produced six plays which must be considered
major successes in the American theatre.

It all started with *The Road to Rome*. With *Reunion in Vienna* (1932) he
found the right combination of rollicking, bed-rolling farce for the right
actors: Alfred Lunt and Lynn Fontanne. In this play Sherwood thought he
had satirized modern science in the guise of a presumably intellectual
psychiatrist who is cuckolded, but audiences did not feel the conflict of
humanity versus science. They saw a delightful farce full of excellent gags
and situations. For Sherwood, *The Petrified Forest* (1935), his next play,
expressed the despair of the vanishing intellectual. Where does man go?
To the petrified forest, as 'Homo-Semi-Americanus – a specimen of the
in-between age!' But again the play was simply 'first-rate theatrical entertainment', a romantic melodrama linking the gunman with the poet. *Idiot's
Delight* (1936) takes place in an Italian resort hotel where a song-and-dance
troupe and various guests are stranded as the war breaks out. The horror of
war is expressed with considerable power as the German scientist rages against
the 'obscene maniacs' whom he must join, while the little Frenchman attacks
the 'League of Death' – the munition makers of the world. The romantic
plot line ends as Harry and Irene decide that they really did meet in an
Omaha hotel. As the bombs fall, they burst out with 'Onward, Christian
Soldiers', and the final curtain comes down. Democracy and Christianity
plus the typical Sherwood emphasis on sex in the play's resolution provided
a brilliant theatrical ending.

Not until *Abe Lincoln in Illinois* (1938) did Sherwood avoid hokum and
seriously dramatize a period of decision in Lincoln's life as he accepted the
nomination for the Presidency and was elected. 1861 was a terrible time to be
President, and 1938 was also a time of anguish for Sherwood who was
struggling with contradictory virtues – peace and right. A man of peace
filled with compassion for suffering humanity, he was still unwilling to
yield to the disaster of tyranny which he saw in Hitlerism. Finally, in *There*

Shall Be No Night (1940) he spoke out in an emotionalized editorial which demanded that people 'stand up and fight for their freedom against the forces of atavistic despotism'. It was a brilliant stage success, and for the student of theatre as a propaganda force Sherwood showed clearly why F.D.R. did well to select him as a speech writer during the war years. It is unfortunate, however, that when the war ended Sherwood was never again able to write successfully for the theatre.

Throughout his career as a dramatist Sherwood believed that the theatre had two diametrically opposed but essentially equal functions: to entertain and to bring stern realities to the audience. As a moralist and an idealist, he tried to accomplish both and inevitably failed in his own eyes because critics did not understand the serious purpose within the slight framework of plays so carefully embellished with humour. In only one play did he try to express his thoughts seriously, unadorned by any glittering wit. For *Acropolis* (1933), he chose the fifth century BC as his scene and pitted practical men of war against thoughtful men concerned with life and beauty. But the play was not successful on the stage, and, although Sherwood tried several times to revise it, he was never able to satisfy himself. It would seem that Sherwood's message was in Socrates' confession that he is 'beginning to believe reluctantly that there are no final answers'. But there is a strange light on the top of the Parthenon at the close of the play, vaguely suggesting that Socrates' belief in pessimism as the final optimism was not a sufficient answer. Emotionally and intellectually incapable of resting finally upon paradox or ambiguity, Sherwood found *Acropolis* a constant frustration. He needed a simple and direct motivation. An honest man, he did what he felt was demanded by life and by the theatre. After the war years he found his dramatic talents dulled, and he became a victim of his own idealism. Yet during his period of success in the theatre his contributions showed, not his mixed motivations or frustrations, but an integrity and a sense of responsibility for the 'human equation' and the simple concepts of Christianity and democracy in which he wholeheartedly believed.

Since Eugene O'Neill helped usher American drama into the period of sophisticated modernity that eventually brought it worldwide recognition, dramatists had been exploiting socio-realistic consciousness whereby they had shown their awareness of social problems and attempted to view man in relation to himself, his contemporaries and his God. Their means of expression had been mainly the social melodrama that had bothered Clayton Hamilton at the beginning of the century. Some had occasionally experimented in form. Mainly, they employed the usual techniques of farce, comedy and spectacle that Robert Sherwood fused so successfully in his best works. Generally, all had something to say – a message to deliver or a search to pursue.

Of all the dramatists who started their careers in the 1920s, however, only one at that time seemed capable of separating comic spirit from emotional commitment. That was S. N. Behrman (1893–1973). In a manner which distinguishes him in the development of modern American drama, Behrman maintained the attitudes of detachment and expediency when other dramatists were emphasizing involvement and purpose. The society of sophisticated wit clearly appealed to him. In the spirit of high comedy he was able to create a controlled balance of emotion and intellect, to use whatever ideas he found in society as a background and scene for the exploitation of his wit. Essentially, his plays are the major attempts towards a comedy of manners in America. Yet as time passed even he was not successful in maintaining a comic insight and detachment. Although sophisticated comedy was undeniably his forte, the social upheavals that surrounded him eventually made it virtually impossible for him to keep contact with the issues of his age and still retain the detachment necessary for writing high comedy.

Like several others of his generation of dramatists, Behrman learned a great deal of his trade studying with the Harvard professor George Pierce Baker. In his first Broadway success, *The Second Man* (1927), he showed clearly his potential for fine wit, his talent for clever dialogue and his skill in dramatizing a sophisticated situation. Will a cynical, fourth-rate writer, living in comfort with a woman who enjoys supporting him, marry a beautiful and romantic young girl? Although the play is marred by some melodramatic heroics, the 'second man' is the hero, that 'calm, critical, observant, unmoved, blasé, odious' person who makes the expedient decision. As always in Behrman's comedies, indecision creates the delightful discussion which the dénouement concludes. Within this genre Behrman's best play is *Biography* (1932). Here the heroine has to choose between her love for a sensitive, brash young man and her certain knowledge that they would not be good for one another. In the detached and expedient world of high comedy there is, of course, only one choice; and Marion makes it. Her inescapable wit and her ability to throw people off balance while she remains in complete control of her emotions precipitates a dialogue that is both stimulating and genuinely amusing.

While Behrman treated various aspects of social and political life with considerable urbanity and comic skill, he was frequently touched to the marrow of his emotions. As he moved well into the 1930s, the tyranny of power-mad fanatics became more and more a part of his Jewish world until in *No Time for Comedy* (1939) he questioned the value of high comedy in the theatre. Such a question, of course, never bothered most of his contemporaries who, if successful, answered that the stage was their world, or, if unsuccessful, condemned the commercial interests which saw the drama as a commodity rather than an art. Behrman questioned; but in the meantime he had already made a decision, chosen his enemies, usually fascists or capitalists, and subjugated them to defeat in high comic splendour. Although by doing so Behrman obviously lost much of his comic detachment and began to give his characters social consciousness, he retained his situations of comic indecision, his witty discussions and an occasional detached character. Lady Wyngate is such a comic character in *Rain from Heaven* (1934) although much of the argument of the play evolves around a Jew's place in Nazi Germany. In *End of Summer* (1936) Behrman displays his comic wit in the person of Leonie Frothingham whose charming detachment controls the action of the play. Wilma Doran is the indecisive character in *Wine of Choice* (1938) as the scene shifts from Newport to the 'horsey set' of Long Island. In each play, however, there is an issue relevant to the times, a problem for the writer of the comic spirit until Behrman wrote *No Time for Comedy* (1939) in an attempt to justify the writing of comedy in a world threatened by war.

In that a writer is always the consequence at any moment of all forces that have worked upon him, the events of the late 1930s changed Behrman into a playwright of social issues where detachment and expediency found no home. Interestingly enough, he seemed to work himself into this position in three plays. In *Wine of Choice* he had opposed a proletarian writer whose hatred had warped his sense of humanity with a person who upheld traditional values. And he had shown the radical defeated. Then came the questioning in *No Time For Comedy*. Lastly, he created *The Talley Method* (1941), a method of such complete detachment that any sense of humanity was lost; and he found this intolerable too. Behrman continued to write for the theatre but after the Second World War approached his old skill only in *Jane* (1952), a dramatization of a Somerset Maugham story, and *Lord Pengo* (1962), an appropriately comic portrayal of a monopolist based on his own study of Duveen. Like most of the playwrights whose careers began in the 1920s, Behrman has added nothing to his already established reputation as the major writer of comedies of manners in America during a particular period. Otherwise, he disappears into the mass of modern American social dramatists.

As the conditions in America between the wars seemed to claim the attention of the artist interested in man and his problems while the increased activity in the New York theatres emboldened him to write for the stage, new dramatists appeared, following mainly the successfully tested Ibsen realism in social dramas. Most of them entered the theatre on the wave of an enthusiasm for drama created not only by the combined efforts of exciting dramatists, the New Stagecraft and enlightened dramatic criticism, but by the necessary ingredient of an optimistic economy. The Wall Street Crash and the subsequent Depression changed that situation, but activity in the theatre refused to be discouraged. One of the new dramatists to appear in the 1930s was Lillian Hellman (1906–   ). Again, she fitted into a discernible pattern among American dramatists. She was a moralist, a writer with a message, who employed the structure of melodrama in creating realistic commentary on the social scene. Although her scene was generally the American south, her subject was mankind and her point of view was sharply critical as she exposed humanity in all of its selfishness, cruelties and perversities. Detachment was not her objective; nor did she feel the need to lessen her commentary with Sherwood's hokum. While her plays showed a more universal insight than Rice had achieved, her moral position was considerably broader than George Kelly's. A bit younger than these contemporaries, she was also the only one to shift back from the war melodrama which most of them wrote during the early 1940s and write penetrating social drama for a new generation.

Lillian Hellman's first New York play, *The Children's Hour* (1934), shocked many with its theme but suggested very clearly the bold quality of her approach to drama. The play told of a young schoolgirl's malicious reporting of a teacher for lesbianism and the unfortunate consequences. Here as in subsequent plays Lillian Hellman's interest was not simply in presenting a problem or asking a question but in making a definite critical observation. 'I am a moral writer,' she wrote in the Preface to a collection of her plays, 'often too moral a writer, and I cannot avoid, it seems, that last summing up.' She also acknowledged melodrama and its inherent sensationalism as the appropriate mode for her work.

The Little Foxes (1939) shows these characteristics very well: a study of consuming greed among the members of a southern family who cruelly exploit each other as they try to rise with the new industrial south. Making use of the trappings of melodrama – sensation, suspense, sentimental objects, material devices and a manipulated sense of time – Hellman dramatized the cruelty of the Hubbards as they fight among themselves, abuse the Negroes, steal when necessary, even condone killing. Their hate is a warning, not only to those in similar practices, but for others who 'stand and watch them do it'. They are 'the little foxes, that spoil the vines', so terrifying a prospect in some ways that one critic called the work 'an adult horror play'. Lillian Hellman also seemed to find the concept thoughtful and powerful, and after writing two war plays – *Watch on the Rhine* (1941) and *The Searching Wind* (1944) – returned to the devious conflicts of the Hubbard family in *Another Part of the Forest* (1946) which attempted an explanation of their activities prior to the action of *The Little Foxes*. The effect, however, was not as satisfying as the earlier work, and in her next play, *The Autumn Garden* (1951), she seemed to abandon Ibsen for Chekhov. Capitalizing on her skill in creating characters, she presented a southern boarding-house society in which the atmosphere of decadence is illustrated through the confessions and frustrations of each person. Her only other post-war play of any importance is *Toys in the Attic* (1960). There again, moralist and melodramatist, she is concerned with social evils as well as the destruction which may result from the unfulfilled dreams of the desperately lonely and from the innocent who falls in love with truth.

As a creator of sensational tales in the theatre, Lillian Hellman made her mark with plays concerned with lesbianism, unnatural greed and degeneracy. Throughout she expressed a social censure of gossip, the evils of drink and scandal, boss politics and racial discrimination. For each play there was an obvious moral for the audience: the Hubbards are everywhere; therefore, do something! Watch every moment of your life. Don't fool with human loves! Thus simplified, her insights lose some of the power that melodrama brings or the boldness that her stories sometimes suggested. In the theatre it was a different matter. A traditionalist in form, she was a part of the New American Drama that Sidney Howard helped establish in 1924 – that mainstream of Ibsen-inspired, realistic social drama which provided the bulk of theatre fare between the World Wars. Distinctive approaches to drama were not as much appreciated on Broadway during this period, yet they sometimes provided a penetrating analysis of society as imaginative artists tried to shape the form as well as the content of their plays to the human conditions which absorbed their attention.

12 Distinct approaches for the modern dramatist after 1900

In every art there are the majority who tread the accepted route in an attempt either to capitalize on that acceptability or to achieve a perfection in it that distinguishes the one among the many, until, finally, the worn and well-marked avenue to success becomes only a rutted road to mediocrity as society changes and different forces work upon man, even affecting his likes and dislikes, pleasures and vexations. Then the cycle begins all over again. Throughout this cycle, however, there are always those who consider the usual as being average and therefore shun the security of that mainstream of art for the challenge and superior effect of some distinct approach. The drama is no different from the other arts in this view, but as produced in the theatre it may best illustrate this concept in art.

From the turn of the century up to the Second World War the main-stream of American drama was the realism of social comedy and melodrama. Sometimes those who rejected this mode were involved in psychological and philosophical probings of man which demanded a distinctive dramatic form. O'Neill was one of these, of course, as were Philip Barry and Thornton Wilder. Others found their own way because they were protesting against the establishment point of view which the mainstream suggested. These included Clifford Odets and John Howard Lawson. And there were also those who felt that poetry was the only perfect speech for the theatre of elevated thought. At times, all of these individualistic dramatists existed on the periphery of popular theatre; during other brief periods they might be completely excluded or else happily welcomed. Yet during the decades after American drama began to enjoy an acceptance throughout the world, their plays were considered some of the best being written in America.

From the very earliest of plays written by Americans and produced upon American stages, poetry was considered the language of the serious dramatist. Dunlap, Payne, Bird and Boker used poetry as did innumerable others until the rise of realism in American letters began to convince playwrights that poetry was not the language of the people they were presenting upon the stage. Yet because some poets persisted in writing for the theatre and a few actors such as Lawrence Barrett encouraged their work, there was a scattering of poetic dramas in America during the last half of the nineteenth century. When the new century seemed to make America more aware of the rest of the world in terms of art, music, literature and theatre as well as politics and the economics of international exchange, there was a revival of interest in poetic drama. From this point on there has been an intermittent but steady increase in the acceptance and popularity of poetic drama in America, an interest particularly evident during the years since the Second World War. As clearly suggested during those periods when poetry captured the audiences' attention, the seriousness of drama can be enhanced by a careful attention to language when poetry should be defined as nothing more than perfect speech.

With the new century, America entered the cultural world community with greater enthusiasm than had been exercised previously. As the Ballet Russe appeared in America and Debussy's music achieved some popularity, it became clear that America was becoming more sensitive to the arts of other countries, but in no area was this more evident than in theatre and drama. The influence of the Moscow Art Theatre, the Abbey Theatre and André Antoine's Théâtre Libre created the basis for change in theatre presentation that was further incorporated into American theatre activity by the American performance of Max Reinhardt's *Sumurūn* in 1912 and later visits of Harley Granville-Barker and Jacques Copeau. In the wake of the shock of Ibsen and Strindberg, Americans became aware of considerable activity in Britain and Europe by a number of rising poetic dramatists. William Poel, William Butler Yeats, Maurice Maeterlinck, Edmond Rostand – all sensed a beauty and effect from the past which they wished to incorporate into the present. To some poets and dramatists in America where the chaos and corruption of a very rapidly expanding nation was being exposed by such muckrakers as Ida M. Tarbell and Lincoln Stephans, poetic drama seemed an ideal way to express their views. Continuing a tradition of the late nineteenth century – William Dean Howells's *Yorick's Love* (1877), William Young's *Pendragon* (1881) – these dramatists realized that poetic drama need not mirror contemporary life. It could disappear into the past, into the myths and legends of ancient people, and there reveal a search for truth and beauty rather than reflect the detailed anguish of the present.

During the first decade of the twentieth century the revival of a serious interest in poetic drama was one indication of America's emergence into the modern art world. Even though his own attempts at this genre were never produced on the stage, William Vaughn Moody's (1869–1910) reputation as a poet and a prose dramatist had an effect upon other writers of poetic drama. His only poetic plays, a trilogy, dealt with the revolt of man in *The Firebringer* (1904), the conflict between God and the human beings he created in *The Masque of Judgment* (1900, written earlier than the first play in the trilogy), and the final, and unfinished, reconciliation of God to man through Eve in *The Death of Eve* (1906). More poet than dramatist, George Cabot Lodge (1873–1909) was shunned by the theatre but showed his own rebellious and individualistic nature in two poetic dramas, *Cain* (1904) and *Herakles* (1900). Cain, the arch-individualist, believer in his own destiny – 'Ours is the choice, be ours the will!' – accepts God's curse as the result of his own will and still maintains that he is the guardian of the Spirit of Life.

Percy MacKaye (1875–1956), the son of Steele MacKaye, the dramatist and theatre entrepreneur of the late nineteenth century, was the most prolific poet-dramatist of this decade. Later MacKaye wrote some prose plays and emphasized his interest in community dramas where he built upon his talent for creating pageant spectacles in which poetry was to produce an aesthetic effect. But his early work was in poetic drama. *The Canterbury Pilgrims* (1902) was his first effort, a blank-verse comedy exploring the character of the poet Chaucer, his sentimental attitude towards the Prioress, and his conflict with the Wife of Bath who would like to make him her next husband. His best play in terms of its poetry, *Jeanne d'Arc* (1905), was produced quite widely despite the fact that it is mainly an episodic history with little concern for Jeanne as a developing, positive character. *Sappho and Phaon* (1907) makes use of that historical or legendary material which interested him and all other poetic dramatists of this period.

MacKaye generally got his plays before an audience, even if for only a few performances. Other poet-dramatists of this period were less fortunate, but both the poor calibre of their work and the contemporary theory of realistic drama worked against them. The single outstanding poet-dramatist of this period was Josephine Preston Peabody Marks (1874–1922), a friend of Moody and the author of three poetic dramas of some merit. Her first full-length play, *Marlowe* (1901), dramatizes a view of Marlowe as revealed in his 'passionate shepherd' poem. *The Wolf of Gubbio* (1913) presents a thesis of love versus greed in men's hearts, capitalizing on the Christian influence of St Francis of Assisi.

Her greatest work, and the one poetic play from this period which deserves to be remembered, is *The Piper* (1910) which won the Stratford Prize competition for that year. Writing in verse 'because it is so much easier for me to think more vividly so', she built upon the story of the Pied Piper of Hamelin who rid the town of rats only to be refused payment by the town officials. In the play the Piper, part of a group of strolling players, pipes the children out of the town in anger and revenge. Then, having secreted the children in the 'hollow hills', he realizes his growing inner struggle: a prideful wish to punish the villagers, conflicting with his love for the children and his basic human sympathy. For Josephine Marks, the Piper became a 'fanatical idealist' and the drama one of character and forces for which poetry provided an integrating mode involving both scene and character. Those forces of greed, love and the supernatural within the Piper present a universal struggle of human pride against human sensitivity, a cynical bitterness contrasted with a self-denying love. Pitting himself even against God, the Piper is finally overcome by the Christian force. Although ambiguity and structural inconsistencies mar the general effect of the drama, *The Piper* attempts, with some success, to use a romantic myth to make an important statement about man.

A score of years passed before anyone equalled Mrs Marks's moderate success with *The Piper*, yet a number of poetic dramas were written. One stimulus for this activity, of course, was provided by the greater and more distinctive writing among American poets of the early twentieth century. Edwin Arlington Robinson (1869–1935) achieved his reputation with the new century. Beginning with brief dramatic poems ('Miniver Cheevy', 'Richard Cory', 'Mr Flood's Party'), he later created long dramatic narratives about *Lancelot* (1920) and *Tristan* (1927) as well as a dramatic and introspective tale of *The Man Who Died Twice* (1924). It took the English to discover the pre-First-World-War merit of Robert Frost (1874–1963) whose poetry also frequently suggests a dramatist's view of life. *The Death of the Hired Man*, for example, with its concern for plot, character, conflict and crisis, has been performed on the stage as a play. Much later in his life Frost tried without much success to catch something of the Ben Jonson masque in *A Masque of Reason* (1945) and *A Masque of Mercy* (1947). By the time of the First World War, however, poetry was enjoying a meaningful renascence in America from several points of view – the interest of people like Robinson, Frost and Ridgely Torrence in dramatic poetry being one aspect and the poetic dramatists another. At the same time, Harriet Monroe in 1912 was encouraging poetry with her new magazine while Amy Lowell, Ezra Pound and H.D. (Hilda Doolittle) were following new dictums of freedom and concentration in producing the poetry of *Des Imagistes*, the title of their first volume in 1914.

It did not take long for this new vitality in poetry – where language and emotional intensity seemed to merge – to appeal to dramatists and poets alike. Some who tried met immediate failure: Sidney Howard with *Swords* (1921), Maxwell Anderson with *White Desert* (1923), Eugene O'Neill with *The Ancient Mariner* (1924). Alfred Kreymborg's (1883–1966) free-verse *Rocking Chairs* (1921), a biting satire on small-town life, took advantage of the attitudes stirred up by Sherwood Anderson and Sinclair Lewis, but without their success. Contrary to usual poetic plays with historical themes – Edwin Milton Royle's (1862–1942) *Lancelot and Elaine* (1921), Louis N. Parker's (1852–1944) *A Minuet* (1927) – Arthur Goodrich's (1878–1941) *Caponsacchi* (1923) was well reviewed. Wallace Stevens's (1879–1955) *Three Travelers Watch a Sunrise* (1916), a one-act play in free verse, was produced by the Provincetown Players in 1920. Perhaps simply because of Stevens's subsequent reputation as a poet, the play deserves comment. Unfortunately, there is little action as two Negroes and three Chinese suggest both the human suffering and a philosophical explanation concerning a situation involving an Italian girl whose lover has just hanged himself. The rich and strong symbolism helps create an effective mood, but there is little drama involved.

The only significant poet of this period to write poetic dramas worthy of production was Edna St Vincent Millay (1892–1952), and perhaps her reputation as 'the beautiful young actress of the Provincetown' helped her. Her two full-length plays – *The Lamp and the Bell* (1921) and *The King's Henchman* (1926) for which Deems Taylor supplied the music – substantially followed traditional patterns by using settings from the past and romantic, sentimental themes of love. Her most enduring play, however, is a one-act satire on war called *Aria da Capo* (1919). Harriet Monroe, editor of *Poetry*, called it 'a masterpiece of irony, sharp as Toledo steel', and innumerable performances, particularly by amateurs, suggest its effectiveness in the theatre. Upon a stage set for a harlequinade, two reluctant shepherds are forced by Cothurnus, the Masque of Tragedy, to interrupt the frivolous act of Pierrot and Columbine. As their tragic scene falters, Cothurnus prompts the shepherds to unwanted action in which they finally kill each other. He then tells the harlequins to hide the bodies under the table: 'The audience will forget.' Brief but effective, the play boasts the kind of poetry that made Edna St Vincent Millay the most popular poet of her generation.

The American dramatist who wrote the most poetic dramas and became most controversial as a consequence is Maxwell Anderson (1888–1959). The question for critics has always been his sensitivity to poetry as form and language. Although his seriousness in bringing a traditional form to modern themes and audiences has never been in doubt, his talent as a poet has. In his own mind Anderson believed that 'dramatic poetry is man's greatest achievement' and that the theatre should be 'essentially a cathedral of the spirit' in which the dramatist should express himself as poet, 'prophet, dreamer, and interpreter of the racial dream'. These ideas he set down in an essay entitled 'Poetry in the Theatre'. He considered prose to be 'the language of information and poetry the language of emotion'. Believing that man must be emotionally sensitive in order to endure and to love fully and that such enduring could be created artistically only in the theatre, he determined that the serious dramatist must write in poetry. It was a logical extension of these thoughts and very much in the tradition of American poetic drama that the poetic dramatist should also write tragedy.

Throughout his prose plays before the 1930s, Anderson had been concerned with strong individualists who struggled for the freedom they believed essential within societies which constantly tested their beliefs. In his later poetic dramas he continued this interest in individual man. Becoming a concerned idealist, he tried to dramatize a faith in man as an answer to the struggle between good and evil in which he saw evil predominating; and he created a theory of tragic drama for that theatre which he saw as 'devoted to the exultation of man'. Relying heavily upon Aristotle's *Poetics*, he demanded in 'The Essence of Tragedy' that 'a play should lead up to and away from a central crisis, and this crisis should consist in a discovery by the leading character which has an indelible effect on his thought and emotion and completely alters his course of action.' Additionally, the main character must have a tragic fault and endure an experience which opens his eyes to his errors, causing him to suffer. For Anderson, it was the spiritual awakening or regeneration which was the essence of tragedy and which provided modern man with dignity indicative of Anderson's own idealism. The theatre at its best was a 'religious affirmation' in which man, the freedom-loving individualist, groped towards excellence, underwent a regeneration and finally reached that 'exultation of the human spirit' which provided a dramatic climax for Anderson's faith in man.

It is with his poetic dramas that Anderson made his greatest contribution to American drama. And it was during the 1930s that he most nearly achieved the ideals he held for the theatre and for the serious dramatist. Believing in the power of poetry and the necessity of emotional language, he concentrated on dramas in which he used traditional blank verse to convey his thoughts about man and thus lead a serious revival of interest in poetic drama. The fact that he achieved some popular success with his work added to his effectiveness as a leader.

Following a generally accepted practice in American poetic drama, Anderson built his plays around themes and scenes from the past. *Elizabeth the Queen* (1930) dramatized the love and conflict of Elizabeth and Essex; *Mary of Scotland* (1933) considered Elizabeth's cruel treatment of the Catholic Mary; *Anne of the Thousand Days* (1948) presented Anne Boleyn's brief life with Henry VIII. When he tried to dramatize American history, as he did in *Valley Forge* (1934), he was generally less effective. *The Wingless Victory* (1936), a story of a New England sea captain who brought a Malayan princess home with him as his wife, provided an interesting theme of cruel Puritan intolerance but was poorly accepted on the stage. With *Winterset* (1935), however, it is generally agreed that Anderson created his best verse play – a treatment of the 1920s Sacco–Vanzetti case in which the fear of a witness to a crime, the pessimistic view of justice presented by the man's father, the guilt-ridden judge and the love of a young girl combine to bring the son of that celebrated victim of man's injustice to a decision that there is something greater than revenge. In many respects, in both language and ideas, it is a powerful play which follows Anderson's theory of tragedy very closely; yet it is also weakened by a lack of inevitability and questionable character motivation. Although *Key Largo* (1939) best illustrates Anderson's idea of tragic recognition, it lacks a penetrating psychology as the story of a man who tried to hide from his cowardly past and made his important discovery just before he was killed. Anderson's two excursions into musical drama, both with Kurt Weill – a satire of F.D.R.'s New Deal in *Knickerbocker Holiday* (1938) and the tender and yet strong interpretation of Alan Paton's *Cry, the Beloved Country* in *Lost in the Stars* (1950) – showed his felicity in verse but were removed from his precepts concerning 'poetry in the theatre'.

In the development of poetic drama in America Anderson suggests something of the noble failure. He had the right ideas about the meaning of language in the modern theatre, and perhaps in this way he encouraged others by both his failures and his successes. He also had a certain imagination and eloquence, but both were limited – perhaps affected by his sense of outrage against the injustice of man. He was, for instance, equally disturbed by the events preceding the Second World War as was Robert Sherwood. Consequently, his immediate criticism in his war plays – *Candle in the Wind* (1941), for example – or his satire on business in his poetic drama, *High Tor* (1937), intruded to his disadvantage upon his dramaturgy. At other times he took strong, individualistic idealists and showed them suffering from the alienation that disturbed modern man. Mio (*Winterset*) became an 'outcast of the world'; Mary Stuart (*Mary of Scotland*) was 'alone, always alone', as were Oparre (*The Wingless Victory*) and Elizabeth (*Elizabeth the Queen*): 'The years are long living among strangers.' In such plays he approached the probing concern for modern man that distinguishes the best dramatists, but he was usually hampered by an inability to achieve the kind of poetry and the well-structured play that would show the theatre to be that cathedral of the spirit in which he believed.

Such an achievement, of course, is not attained in most societies, although Anderson's efforts encouraged other poets to attempt that ideal within the American theatre. Delmore Schwartz (1913–66), for example, dealt with the christening of a Jewish baby in *Shenandoah* (1939). As another approach to poetic drama in the theatre, radio verse dramas experienced a certain popularity during the 1930s when the American people depended to a large extent upon the radio for their entertainment as well as their information concerning world conditions. Anderson wrote two poetic dramas for the radio, both on social themes – *The Feast of Ortolans* (1937) and *Second Overture* (1938). Norman Corwin, with *They Fly Through the Air* (1936), and Alfred Kreymborg, with *The Planets* (1938), were other important contributors to this genre, but it was Archibald MacLeish (1892–   ) who was to travel successfully from the radio drama of the 1930s to the legitimate theatre. *The Fall of the City* (1937) carried a pointed warning for its time when 'the city of masterless men' was thrown into confusion. As the conqueror dressed in traditional armour entered the city square, it was revealed that the armour contained nothing at all, but the people had wanted to believe in their oppressors and 'The City has fallen'. *Panic* (1935) and *Air Raid* (1938) show MacLeish's interest in social commentary, and both indicate his potential as well as the problems he would have in the theatre.

There was the strong passion of the humanitarian poet, but there was also an absence of dramatic tension in his work.

MacLeish had shown an early interest in dramatic theory, and after the Second World War he began to write for the theatre. In an introductory statement to *Panic* and in an essay entitled 'A Stage for Poetry' (from *A Time to Speak*, 1941) MacLeish revealed his own ideas about the writing of poetic drama. Rejecting the traditional mode of blank verse, he contended that the 'classical rhythm equivalent to American speech' was the trochee or the dactyl. He also favoured what he called 'the word-excited imagination' which became clear in *This Music Crept by Me Upon the Waters* (1953). Set in the Antilles, the play describes that beautiful moment of happiness when two people communicate with each other. But whereas a mood of exaltation is established by the poetry and, in part, by character, the drama of action and conflict necessary for the theatre was still missing. MacLeish did much better, however, in *J.B.* (1958), a re-enacting of the story of Job under modern conditions. There is a richness in this play both in the diction and verse as well as in MacLeish's ability to maintain the universality of Job's provoking story while adding his own justification of the universe through love rather than an acceptance of God. In *Herakles* (1967) he presented a modern interpretation of that Greek myth concluding, as he did for *J.B.*, that a sense of human compassion is superior to man's most heroic attempts to perfect an imperfect universe. *Scratch* (1971), a retelling of the Stephen Vincent Benet tale of 'The Devil and Daniel Webster', was a dignified failure. With all of his difficulties, however, MacLeish has made the American theatre consider him seriously as a poet-dramatist.

Since the Second World War a significant number of poets have written successfully for the American theatre, and the trend continues. Although few have achieved success in a theatre that defines that term only with reference to box-office returns, audiences have been made increasingly aware of the significance of words and language. E. E. Cummings (1894–1963) confronted Death (knowledge) with Santa Claus (understanding) in a rather discursive play called *Santa Claus* (1946). A better and more profound as well as prolific poetic dramatist, Robinson Jeffers (1887–1962) adapted *Medea* for the stage in 1947, revised an earlier dramatic narrative (his version of the *Oresteia*) called *The Tower Beyond Tragedy* (1950) for Judith Anderson, and wrote *The Cretan Woman* (1954) which proved to be a forceful and stageworthy play on the Phaedra–Hippolytus theme. *The Visionary Farms* (1952) by Richard Eberhart (1904–   ) dramatizes the modern paradox of progress versus commercial corruption. William Carlos

Williams's (1883–1963) *Many Loves* (1959) is a prose–verse experimentation in three rather disconnected episodes about love. Among the younger poets writing for the theatre Robert Lowell (1917–   ) has intrigued a number of critics with *The Old Glory* (1964), a trilogy composed of *Endecott and the Red Cross, My Kinsman, Major Molineux* and *Benito Cereno*. All are about revolution. In Nathaniel Hawthorne's stories, Endecott starts one and the Major joins one. But it is the third play, based on a Herman Melville story, in which Delano stops a revolution, that Lowell has been most successful. A number of other American poet-dramatists have also had their work produced upon the American stage. Although poetic drama could not be considered a major aspect of contemporary theatre, it is certainly a developing element in American drama.

Having a particular *raison d'être*, plays of propaganda, protest and politics may present another distinctive approach in American drama. Yet, in truth, plays built around protest and propaganda attitudes are so plentiful in the history of American drama that they lose any distinction and become simply a very broad and inclusive category for the critic and historian. The dramas of the revolutionary period protested quite noisily from one side or another, and, if one defines propaganda drama as any drama that attempts to persuade an audience to accept a predetermined opinion or point of view, there are an incredible number of plays which either wholly or in part may fit the definition. Dramatists of the nineteenth century, for example, may have wanted to please their audiences, but they were seldom shy about asserting absolutes and certainties in the social, political or moral worlds. Temperance plays were clearly propaganda vehicles, and *Uncle Tom's Cabin* (1852) may be the greatest propaganda play of all times, whether produced in America or in other countries around the world. The stereotyped characters, the emotional language appeals, the contrived climaxes, the obvious opinions of the playwrights – all were combined in many of these earlier plays to assert either pro-American or anti-this-or-that attitudes. Politics became a part of this approach to drama early in the Revolution and will remain a staple of the genre by reason of its close association with propaganda and protest, although these two characteristics are certainly not limited to politics. In American drama, however, politics has a rich tradition from *Androboros* (1714) up to the present day. Pride in or irritation with politics and the social and economic institutions deriving from the poltical state has appealed to many playwrights whose minds are more absorbed in the temporal and seemingly relevant than in the universal and profound.

With the emergence of James Herne and the qualified American recognition of Ibsen, American playwrights began to show their social consciousness in plays that commented on social issues and expressed particular opinions. As this kind of play continued in popularity, opinions became more pointedly expressed in satiric drama, and protest became linked with propaganda. Rice provides a good illustration with *The Adding Machine* (1923). He later made a severe comment on existing conditions in *Street Scene* (1929) and then provided a pro-American propaganda piece with *American Landscape* (1938). George S. Kaufman (with his collaborators) was an effective satirist of many aspects of American life. Maxwell Anderson protested against a government that abused the freedom of its people, and Robert Sherwood created forcible propaganda plays both for and against war.

Some plays combined light entertainment with a serious protest, such as James Thurber (1894–1961) and Elliot Nugent's *The Male Animal* (1940) which presented a compelling indictment of a college administration against a comic background. At the other extreme is such a play as Sidney Kingsley's (1906–   ) *Dead End* (1935). A newcomer to the theatre during the decade of the Depression, Kingsley's forte was a detailed realism by which he created vivid pictures of life. Although he won a Pulitzer Prize with *Men in White* (1933), concerned with a young doctor's agonizing decision between love and medicine, Kingsley's only enduring play is *Dead End*, a dramatic protest which Brooks Atkinson called a 'public social document'. There is the filth-covered East River of New York which is the playground of a gang of young hoodlums learning the wrong things. There are also those people who love them, pathetically impotent to effect a change, and the authorities indifferent to anything but an inhuman concept of law and order. As the playwright's mouthpiece says, 'the place you live is awfully important'. Dead End was just that – a 'dead end' for a certain socio-economic class.

With the Depression in America, there emerged a definite drama of protest with a variety of opportunities for production upon the stage. The communists in America saw the Depression as the failure of democracy and immediately set about dramatizing the opportunities of communism in such agit-prop plays as the anonymous *Vote Communist* or John Bonn's *Fifteen Minute Red Revue* (1932). With the stated objectives of propagandizing the Party's revolutionary ideas, such theatres as the Theatre Collective or the League of Workers' Theatre produced plays like Albert Maltz's (1908–   ) *Private Hicks* (1935) which shows a National Guardsman on strike duty condemned by a court martial for possessing labour leaflets. The Theatre

Union produced George Sklar (1908–   ) and Paul Peters's *Stevedore* (1934). In this play the Negro protagonist, falsely accused of raping a white woman, is hounded by a mob and finally killed as members of the communist union join the Negroes to fight against a common enemy. Another propaganda play praised by the critics of the *Daily Worker* was George Sklar's *Peace on Earth* (1933) which dramatized a liberal professor's conversion from political neutrality to Marxist militancy. Such plays were grist to the communist mill, but a major problem in writing this type of play was the inability of dramatists to follow an ever-changing Party line. Dramatists, for example, could protest against what was happening in America with a passion, but they did not always dramatize what the *Daily Worker* or *New Masses* critics considered the correct answer to their protests: belief in the communist philosophy. Such anti-war plays as Sherwood's *Idiot's Delight* were faulted for this reason. Shorter plays, Irwin Shaw's (1913–   ) *Bury the Dead* (1936), for example, which showed the grotesquely effective rebellion of a corps of dead soldiers, were accepted for limited communist propaganda purposes and produced widely during the 1930s.

One dramatist who worked diligently to satisfy the communist critics was John Howard Lawson (1895–   ). His idealism and his bitterness against certain aspects of humanity as well as his dramaturgical skill were revealed in his first major play, *Roger Bloomer* (1923), and throughout the 1920s he searched for something in which he could believe. In *Processional* (1925) he used a strike to dramatize class war; in *Loud Speaker* (1927) he experimented, theatrically, to show the persecution and injustice he found in America. Although he voiced the popular communist protests in both of these plays, he somehow could not avoid a bourgeois sentiment which appeared again in *Success Story* (1932) where he continued his attack on American capitalism. Reviewing *Gentlewoman* (1934) in which Lawson pictured a dying class while showing some admirable characteristics of that class, Michael Gold, writing for the *Daily Worker*, criticized him severely for being ideologically confused. Consequently, Lawson underwent an intensive self-revaluation, and with his final play, *Marching Song* (1937), he produced a model for revolutionary drama. Certainly, the communist critics could not complain about this play in which the violence of an Auto Workers' Union strike ends when the union men capture the power plant and win their point. Unfortunately, Lawson all but abandoned the theatre after this effort – unfortunate not because more revolutionary plays were needed but because his talents were never fully or freely used in the American theatre. His early works showed the effects of an innovative and imaginative person's search for a truth which he should have been able to express in the theatre far more articulately than his plays suggest. He is now remembered mainly for the experimental *Roger Bloomer*, his revolutionary *Marching Song*, and a fine text on dramatic criticism and theory entitled *Theory and Technique of Playwriting* (1936).

If only one theatre agency and one playwright could be identified with the protest drama of the 1930s, one would have to mention the liberal Group Theatre, which existed from 1931 to 1941, and its leading playwright, Clifford Odets (1906–63). Working with Harold Clurman, a director of the Group Theatre, Odets created his strongest and most dynamic plays. A liberal rather than a communist (and a member of the Communist Party for only a very brief period), he was superior to other protest and Marxist writers because he believed that a play should not only be 'immediately and dynamically useful' but also 'psychologically profound'. In two plays written for the Group he was able to achieve this objective. *Awake and Sing!* (1935), 'a struggle for life amidst petty conditions', was the first. In this play he tells the story of a Jewish family in New York as they argue, deceive, enjoy a moment or two and keep on living. Young Ralph and Jacob, the grandfather, represent the idealists – those who may change the world some day, who will not accept a 'life printed on dollar bills'. One dies so that the other may live, not as Jake had imagined but as an inspired, undefeated person. Writing of people he understood and admired, Odets created rich characters and natural dialogue in a play of proletarian sympathies.

The other play is *Waiting for Lefty* (1935), a strong protest built around a meeting of taxi drivers waiting for Lefty before they vote on a strike. In this setting Odets presented various scenes relating to the conditions of taxi drivers and oppressed people everywhere: the poverty of a taxi driver whose wife is about to leave him, a lab assistant who is asked to spy on his superiors, the prejudice levelled against a Jewish doctor. All of this was very real in the 1930s, and when news is brought that Lefty has been killed the workers vote to strike in an agit-prop climax which was planned to arouse the audience to similar thoughts and action. Of the propaganda and protest plays of the 1930s, Odets best illustrates in this play what he wrote to John Mason Brown in 1935: 'I believe in the vast potentialities of mankind. . . . I want to find out how mankind can be helped out of the animal kingdom into the clear sweet air.'

It was a pretentious statement, but these were heady times for Odets. In 1935, writers as diverse as the columnist George Ross and Archibald MacLeish acknowledged Odets's work as the best in New York. When *Paradise Lost* (1935) came to New York to join *Till the Day I Die* (1935), his anti-Nazi–pro-communist play, Odets had three plays on Broadway. In this last play he tried to take a family, the Gordons, as he had the Bergers in *Awake and Sing!*, and suggest both degradation and rebirth. Both plays were proletarian drama, but whereas James T. Farrell could praise the first as superior revolutionary literature, neither he nor others found value in *Paradise Lost*. After this play Odets left for Hollywood where he wrote the script for *The General Died at Dawn* (1938) which prompted the famous Frank Nugent newspaper headline: 'Odets, Where Is Thy Sting?' His return to the Group Theatre with *Golden Boy* (1937) – the Faustian story of Joe Bonaparte who must choose between 'the fist' and 'the fiddle', between the careers of prize fighter and violinist – was a surprising and necessary success for Odets. In *Rocket to the Moon* (1938) Odets took a standard triangle and tried to penetrate the social and psychological reasons for this affair, but without success. And this was also Odets's fate with both *Night Music* (1940), in which the dramatist invested a raw, quite unreal hero with human impulses about love and patriotism, and *Clash by Night* (1941), another conventional plot of erring wife, jealous husband and the invariable climax. In all of these plays after that most successful year of 1935 Odets had made use of Depression conditions and characters he understood, but somehow he was not able to regain the strength of the earlier work nor dramatize the intense struggles of those characters whose difficulties reflected a generalized people whose dreams were the idealized dreams of the proletariat.

The war years were not difficult for Odets as he lived in some splendour in the 'bon-bon town' he called Hollywood and worked on films. In 1949 he attempted a Broadway comeback with *The Big Knife* in which he ridiculed the Hollywood that fed him, but it failed. *The Country Girl* (1950) took a 'boozy, unreliable ham', as one critic described it, and gave him a second chance. Though it capitalized on what John Gassner called 'a corn-fed madonna', it was good theatre, and Odets knew it. Perhaps this play showed what had been happening to Odets, and its superficialities reflect a certain regret one may have for these changes. In his last play, however, *The Flowering Peach*, Odets showed what he really wanted to do. The play is built around Noah, his family and his problems, while Noah's flood may be symbolic of possible atomic destruction. At the end of the play, Noah says: 'Yes, I hear you, God – Now it's in man's hands to make or destroy the world.' More than any of his post-war plays this one shows a new Odets – a playwright of other decades than the thirties to which most historians relegate his career. Whatever he wrote, he never abandoned his social awareness, his love of people. What disappeared was the brash certainty and the didactic quality. As a protest writer, he belongs back in the mid-1930s, but as a playwright concerned with human dignity he made a considerable point in his final play.

Protest drama in America between the two World Wars cannot be dismissed, however, without reference to the plays produced by the Federal Theatre Project of the WPA. During its brief career, 1935–9, the Federal Theatre produced excellent propaganda plays, some of which got them into considerable difficulty with the United States Congress which began to feel that it was sponsoring its own opposition. Not all productions, of course, gave this impression. Sinclair Lewis (1885–1951) and John Moffit's *It Can't Happen Here* (1936) was a strong anti-fascist play. *The Cradle Will Rock* (1937) by Marc Blitzstein (1905–64), on the other hand, was a bitter attack on capitalism through its paid 'lackeys': the Rev. Salvation, Dr Specialist, Editor Daily, etc. Most important of the Federal Theatre activities, however, were its Living Newspaper productions. Composed by Arthur Arents (1905?–) and a staff of writers, the Living Newspapers presented well-documented liberal views. In *Triple-A Plowed Under* (1936) the Voice of the Living Newspaper traced the agricultural depression in the USA in twenty-six scenes, beginning with farm mortgage foreclosures after the First World War and ending with the creation and termination of the Agriculture Adjustment Administration. Perhaps the most significant of the Living Newspapers was *One-Third of a Nation* (1938) which described the housing problem in New York City and agitated for better housing through government action. Arguing forcefully with vivid particulars about insanitary and unsafe conditions, the play made excellent use of the rhetorical devices of propaganda and persuasion. As the play ends, one-third of a nation speaks: 'You know what we're going to do? We're going to holler. . . . Can you hear me – you in Washington or Albany or wherever you are! Give me a decent place to live in! Give me a home! A home!' These were emotionally powerful plays, imaginatively produced. Within that approach to the theatre which makes particular use of propaganda and protest devices in drama, they are certainly the most individualistic.

A third approach to playwriting which distinguishes the dramas after the First World War from those written previously was that marked by the dramatist's intellectual and imaginative attempt to use theme and form as an expression of his search for and understanding of life. Certain American novelists of the nineteenth century had commanded sufficient genius to use their art for this objective. Hawthorne and Melville are excellent examples. Walt Whitman among the poets is also a good illustration. The dramatists of this period, however, had audience obligations thrust upon them besides generally lacking the qualities necessary for such creative and thought-provoking expression. With O'Neill a change in American drama was most obvious as it began to reach towards the level of literary creativity already expressed in American poetry, essay, short story and novel. But O'Neill was not a lone figure on the skyline of American drama. He had appeared at an opportune moment, but he was almost immediately joined by dramatists whose interests in psychological and philosophical probings of the world were no less than his own. Paul Green showed his potential with *In Abraham's Bosom*. Although Maxwell Anderson wanted to play the philosopher, he generally failed to raise his concern for evil above day-to-day realities. Two or three of their contemporaries, however, did provide American drama of this period with the intellectual penetration and psychological insight necessary for distinctive dramatic literature. Second only to O'Neill in his contribution to modern psychological drama, Philip Barry is of this number. So, too, is Thornton Wilder, whose pervading sense of peace and security belies the depth of his insight. Perhaps William Saroyan may be included because of the epic proportions of his fables, although the simplicity of his faith and fantasy is sometimes disconcerting and unsatisfying.

Philip Barry (1896–1949) projected two such distant images for theatre audiences that one drama critic, Frank Nugent, dubbed him a 'lightning bug – now he lights up, now he doesn't'. In terms of Broadway, where Barry's plays achieved erratic success from 1923 to 1949, the metaphor was apt and clever. A very precise writer who revised each scene of his carefully thought-out plays ten or a dozen times, he could create sparkling social comedy with thoroughly developed characters and witty dialogue. Influenced both by his own substantial environment, which included the society of the Gerald Murpheys and the F. Scott Fitzgeralds, and the Harvard workshop of Professor George Pierce Baker, he took something of the social attitude and the theatrical polish of Clyde Fitch, added his own intellectual substance to the social problems he viewed, and created some high comedy of distinctive quality. *Paris Bound* (1927) considered the significance of infidelity in modern marriage and suggested that the spiritual side of marriage was more important than the physical. In *Holiday* (1928) he contrasted the wealthy who lived for their business accomplishments with those who could see something else in life. Tom Collier, a major character in *The Animal Kingdom* (1932), is forced into a situation where he must choose between a stultifying life within a confining establishment and the freedom that honest individuality presents. *The Philadelphia Story* (1939) was one of

Barry's most successful comedies. Against the sophisticated background of a country house near Philadelphia, Barry provides his heroine with a moment of self-realization which brings both delight and a sense of truth about human nature to the audience.

In all of these plays Barry presented a sophisticated scene of character and social conflict in which decisions are made from a sense of personal freedom. He felt very strongly that man must have the opportunity to find out about himself if he was to achieve some meaning in life. Barry did not moralize – in fact, some critics thought him quite immoral; a view which disturbed him greatly – nor did he try to force solutions. Placed in certain situations, usually involving marriage, his characters invariably make dis-coveries about themselves, become more tolerant of humanity and take that first step – a decision for freedom – towards a discovery of truth.

Although his thoughts were important, in the slight framework of comedy they were obscured. Yet Barry obscured them deliberately. He was a man involved in a most serious spiritual search which he pursued throughout his life and for which he formed an answer only in his final play, *The Second Threshold* (1949). But he was also a dramatist who enjoyed success in the theatre. Thus he interspersed his serious plays, which inevitably failed in the theatre, with successful light comedies, making his points unobtrusively in these witty plays. In *Paris Bound*, for example, one character has written a ballet about an angel and a germ who are lionized and, therefore, controlled by society. The thought is clear that man without freedom will die, and the wife in the play wisely accepts this idea in her own situation. In each play, there was a social problem, but Barry had a distinctive way of looking at such problems. He was, for example, a very religious man who was deeply bothered by those questions concerning man, truth and reality which his Catholicism left unanswered. It is the progress of this personal struggle and searching which his serious plays chart and finally resolve.

He first posed his questions about man and reality in *In A Garden* (1925). Here, an egocentric dramatist feels that he can understand, even control, everything including his wife. But he is forced to discover, as Barry was doing, that there is a mystery to life. There is no guaranteed formula – no guiding idea. *White Wings* (1926) is more a farce-comedy than a search for truth, yet the resolution through love (uniting the opposing families which illustrated the conflicting eras of horse and automobile) was one to which he would finally return years later. In *Hotel Universe* (1930) he faced his ques-tion squarely. In a mysterious place where 'time went sort of funny' he presented a group of people who found no value in life. 'What's the answer to the whole works?' one of the group asks as they each reveal their problems to a mysterious person who is 'supposed to have some kind of power' over people and can 'set the hour-glass on its side'. Even with the help of Freud Barry came to no solution in this play, but he did suggest an optimism and a process of thought which is more meaningful to the person studying his work than it proved to be to audiences in the theatre. A long one-act play, *Hotel Universe* dramatizes man as confined and defeated by society and by lost illusions before Barry (through his spokesman in the play) frees him and shows him man's potential for knowing truth.

Later, Barry questioned both the free will that he had allowed man and the inference that truth provided the answer to man's problems. The play in which he did this was *Here Come the Clowns* (1938). In a complicated plot Clancy, a Job character, searches for God and for the answer to a question: why is there so much misery in the world? At the final curtain Clancy is dying but still searching – yet of his 'own free will'. Curiously, the distinction in the play between God and the Devil is consciously vague, revealing man's confused ideas concerning both truth and God. Although the play is weak theatre, Clancy's search clearly exposes Barry's frame of mind. From the production of this play until his unexpected death, Barry worked on *The Second Threshold* which was posthumously produced with some 'carpentry' writing by Robert Sherwood. As the protagonist of this play at the age of forty-two feels that he has come to the end of 'his soul's rope', he discovers that love makes life worthwhile. It is as simple as that and evidently the only satisfying conclusion that Barry could reach. In a play which seemed to combine more effectively than ever before his witty comedy with a serious statement, he answered the vagueness of *Hotel Universe* and the inconclusiveness of *Here Come the Clowns*. Like any thoughtful artist he was concerned with philosophical questions as well as social problems. He thought, he doubted, he questioned. Obviously, he was least effective as a dramatist when he was most probing intellectually, and this is his weakness in American drama.

Thornton Wilder (1897–1975) was never forced to experience the struggle of uncertainty that bothered Barry and tormented O'Neill. Responding affirmatively to the New Humanists, he submitted to the optimism and forbearance of Christian doctrine. Armed with a strong faith, he saw man in a broad and cyclical view. There is good, and there is evil. Man can reason, and he must also accept. In *Our Town* (1938) the Stage Manager declares that 'whenever you come near to the human race, there's layers and layers of nonsense'. 'We're all just as wicked as we can be, and that's God's truth,' says a character in *The Skin of Our Teeth* (1942). How, then, does one live?

Wilder's answer seems to be: he loves, if he can. In almost all that he wrote, Wilder made this observation. In his novels and his plays, both genres having placed him among the leaders of modern literature, he has shown that strength, that 'whole purport of literature, which is the notation of the heart', that has given his work a worldwide appeal.

In ways that are simple without being sentimental he emphasizes love and beauty. In the final lines of his novel, *The Bridge of San Luis Rey* (1929), for example, 'There is a land of the living and a land of the dead and the bridge is love, the only survival, the only meaning.' And there is Emily in *Our Town* crying out: 'Do human beings ever realize life while they live it? – every, every minute?' Man is such a poor creature, fumbling his way along, trying and failing. As Wilder wrote in *Heaven's My Destination* (1935), 'Of all the forms of genius, goodness has the longest awkward age.' But man must still strive for it, must live fully, and try to see beauty. In the foreword to *The Angel That Troubled the Water and Other Plays in One Act* (1928) he observed that 'in those matters beyond logic, beauty is the only persuasion.' Believing in man and his ability to endure, Wilder works from 'the notation of the heart'.

As a playwright, Wilder rebelled from the realism of the past, was somewhat inspired by German expressionism, but created mainly from his views (expressed in an essay entitled 'Some Thoughts on Playwriting') that the stage is 'fundamental pretense' which thrives on a 'multiplication of additional pretenses'. Thus he abandoned traditional staging and with the help of suggested myth and colloquial speech relied upon imagination. By forcing his audiences' minds from a particular stage setting, he could suggest the implications of 'each tiny occasion in daily life' within 'the vast stretches of time and place'. *Our Town*, Wilder wrote, 'is an attempt to find value above all price for the smallest events in our daily life.' A boy and a girl, living next door to each other, grow up, get married, and the girl dies while life goes on. This is life. As the Stage Manager in the play says, 'The cottage, the go-cart, the Sunday afternoon drives in the Ford, the first rheumatism, the grandchildren, the second rheumatism, the death bed, the reading of the will. – Once in a thousand times it's interesting.' With a disarming, folk simplicity, Wilder tells an epic story in which time and place disintegrate as the audience's thoughts are carefully directed to particular actions.

The Skin of Our Teeth is also concerned with the progression of man as Wilder follows the Antrobus family through the Ice Age, the Flood and man's wartime efforts to destroy himself. Both time and space are manipulated for the audience's better understanding. Although time is always *now* on the stage, it is also historical time in the play as well as a means of measuring events in the progress of the Antrobus family. Space is the stage, too, but, with Wilder's rejection of strict realism, 'abject truth' is meaningless. To clarify the thought in his plays Wilder creates moods with different types of drama – dream play, expressionism, vaudeville, musical comedy. Theatrical devices such as a supposed actor rebellion within the play, audience participation, falling scenery to emphasize disintegration of a world, foreign words and phrases which he knows the audience will not understand – everything supports his ideas. For him the theatre is pretence, but it is also allegory and epic. As he manipulates time and space and mood, he emphasizes the now as well as the forever, the individual unity of the 'I' as well as the tremendous multiplicity of the twentieth century.

Wilder started writing plays at Yale University where he produced his 'three minute pieces' – *The Angel That Troubled the Water* and others. In 1931 he published *The Long Christmas Dinner*, which showed the cyclical and fleeting nature of man, along with other one-act plays. *Our Town* came next and then *The Merchant of Yonkers* (1938) which became *The Matchmaker* (1954) and later *Hello, Dolly!* (1964). Since *The Skin of Our Teeth* he has written little for the theatre. *A Life in the Sun* (1955) is an adaptation of Euripides' *Alcestis*. Three one-act plays, *Infancy*, *Childhood* and *Someone from Assisi*, were produced in 1962. At this date Wilder had some plans for a cycle concerned with the Seven Ages of Man of which *Infancy* and *Childhood* were the first two plays. With his pre-Second-World-War plays, however, his reputation in American drama remains secure. Not verisimilitude but reality was his objective as he shows an awareness of the meaning of life through a world beyond time and space that is still familiar to all people.

Quite different from the dramatist haunted by doubts or the dramatist secure in his own beliefs, William Saroyan (1908–   ) found that fantasy was much more satisfying than reality and that there was no reason to question anything. As he wrote in his preface to *Don't Go Away Mad* (1949), 'I seem to insist that people are good, that living is good, that decency is right, that good is not only achievable but inevitable – and there does not appear to be any justification for this.' With this unbounded faith in the goodness of man and his ability to overcome all evil, Saroyan became something new in modern American drama, almost a throwback to the sentimental optimism of the nineteenth century but with substance, depth of feeling, something of the human myth. As an epic fabler, Saroyan eschewed realism and presented characters which, to be successful, had to stimulate the audience's imagination. He made no pretence to being a thinker; feeling was his forte. Life, he found, was basically sweet and perhaps sad but sadly beautiful throughout his plays in which he insisted that the beauty dominate the sadness. And if he disturbed his audience with this view of life and made them think, he was essentially presenting that part of the 'human comedy' which needs retelling.

Saroyan's attitude towards life may be summed up in a line from one of his plays. 'In the time of your life, live – so that in that good time there shall be no ugliness or death for yourself or for any life your life touches.' He established this point of view with his first plays, those which he wrote before the Second World War and which are considered his best work – *My Heart's in the Highlands* (1939), *The Time of Your Life* (1939), *Love's Old Sweet Song* (1940) and *The Beautiful People* (1941). In all of these plays Saroyan chooses an odd assortment of characters with dreams and problems like everyone else, places them in a plot so sketchy that its insignificance is basic in a Saroyan play, and involves them in happenings as rambling and disconnected as ever appeared on a vaudeville stage. Reviewing *My Heart's in the Highlands*, John Anderson summed up the plot and wrote:

> That is, so help me Heaven, all there is to it, if you want it in so many words, no plot, no elaborate build-up of entrances and exits, no careful analysis of character. Saroyan simply glimpses a few human beings, and evokes the moods and situations of compelling emotion. . . . People seemed to find themselves weeping without knowing what the hell was the matter with them.

It was all very disconcerting.

In *The Time of Your Life* Saroyan places his scene in a San Francisco honky-tonk where a storyteller, a dancer, a pinball-machine addict, a comic monologuist, a prostitute and a free-spending hero come to perform, to complain and to dream. They are all the 'beautiful people' who realize that something may be wrong but 'believe in dreams sooner than statistics'; they want to live now and have faith in each other. As Joe tells his friend in *The Time of Your Life*: 'Go ahead. Correct the errors of the world.' And Saroyan would agree. Why not?

After the Second World War Saroyan continued to experiment with more than thirty, mainly one-act, plays. Some were produced in Europe; only *The Cave Dwellers* (1957) received a Broadway production, and this had the usual unusual assortment of characters and the admonition to live while you are still alive. His strengths are perhaps best described as those of a charming improviser who has the magical ability to create a mood and suggest something of lost innocence in the modern world. He is certainly an individualist in the drama of modern America. Barry worked hard and long to arrive at his conclusions in *The Second Threshold*. Both Wilder and Saroyan believe in the same love and beauty, but whereas Wilder reflects that 'notation of the heart' in ways that suggest his Christian faith as well as his carefully stored wisdom, Saroyan strolls through the immensities of life and reacts with a playful innocence. Together with O'Neill these three dramatists induced a thoughtful, probing quality into the drama of the period which, like the works of those dramatists who created propaganda or poetry, further exemplified the distinctive approaches which American dramatists brought to their art.

13 Intruding on the world: drama of the mid-century

Massive social upheavals such as war provide valid divisions in the history of a drama. In such instances changes take place on most social, economic and political levels. Little of the culture that distinguishes a country remains the same when that country is at war, and the theatre reflects those changes. In America the Second World War was quite different from past wars in terms of theatre reaction. As usual, a number of dramatists geared themselves to war and wrote propaganda melodramas and farces – Sherwood, Barry, Anderson, Rice, Lillian Hellman, John Steinbeck. Other playwrights soon joined them. This was the expected activity. But the difference was to show in the tenor of some of the war plays. During the Revolutionary War, satire and poetic melodrama were the accepted modes of the theatre, and these types continued to be written during the War of 1812 with the addition of spectacular melodrama. By the time of the Civil War slavery was an issue in some plays, but after the war, with theatre managers controlling the kind of plays that were written, the conflict was largely romanticized. The object was theatre entertainment, and it was a long time before a James Herne could treat a serious issue in *The Reverend Griffith Davenport* (1899). The situation did not change much after the First World War although for different reasons. The economic prosperity and the social hilarity of the 1920s did not encourage dramatists to consider the past. With the Second World War the economic and social situation had been changed by the Depression, and the calibre of the American dramatist had also changed. For the first time in American drama serious issues resulting from the war appeared on the stage.

Such plays were not produced, however, to the exclusion of the usual wartime theatre fare. Just as vaudeville and the musical comedy revues of the First World War were interspersed with such war melodramas as James Forbes's (1871–1938) *The Famous Mrs Fair* (1919) and Gilbert Emery's (d. 1945) *The Hero* (1921), the Second World War stimulated propaganda melodramas and light comedies as well as plays with serious theses. John Steinbeck (1902–68), for example, dramatized the heroism of the Norwegians against Nazi occupation in *The Moon is Down* (1942), and Lillian Hellman provided a powerful anti-fascist play in *Watch on the Rhine* (1941). At this stage in America's development the cinema had usurped a good deal of the power of melodrama once possessed by the stage, but William W. Haines's (1908–) *Command Decision* (1947) had all of the ingredients of a successful war melodrama – adventure, conflict, surprise, sentiment, satire on congressmen, humour, patriotic propaganda, and the impression that war exhibits no heroes, just heroic men who win the peace for a grateful nation despite incomprehensible blunders by governmental officials. There were also a good number of farce-comedies with wartime themes: Joseph Fields's (1895–1966) story of military and civilian problems in Washington, *The Doughgirls* (1942); John Patrick's (1910–) sentimental tale of a Scottish soldier dying in an unfriendly hospital atmosphere, *The Hasty Heart* (1945); or Joshua Logan's (1908–) hilarious dramatization of GI complaints and rebellion in *Mr Roberts* (1948).

A few dramatists saw the war and the conditions it provoked from a serious point of view and dramatized the individual psychological and social problems that war brings. *Tomorrow the World* (1943) by James Gow (1907–52) and Arnaud d'Usseau (1916–) is such a play as it pictures a Nazi war orphan in America and the seemingly impossible task of re-educating a people once controlled by Nazi ideals. Another play by d'Usseau, *Deep Are the Roots* (1945), deals with race prejudice and war psychology as a southern white girl, grateful for a Negro friend's efforts in the war, offers to marry him when he returns a hero. Perhaps the most penetrating drama of the war, however, was Arthur Laurents's *Home of the Brave* (1945), a dramatization of the shock treatment necessary to make a Jewish soldier aware of both his ethnic sensitivity and his guilt complex which have rendered him paralysed following his sense of relief when a companion was killed in battle. Although

Maxwell Anderson's *The Eve of Saint Mark* (1942) dealt with a soldier's thoughts of home as he tried to find meaning in his own death, and Philip Barry's *Foolish Notion* (1945) contrasted a soldier's actual homecoming with the expectations of those most concerned with his return, the best plays about war were written by newcomers to the American theatre. And this new life in American drama was the most significant change which the war years helped define.

In *Mid-Century Drama* (1960) the English drama critic, Laurence Kitchin, entitled his essay on drama in America 'The Potent Intruder'. Although this intrusion had been started some 150 years previously, its potency had been seriously questioned during most of those years. With those American dramatists who appeared between the two World Wars, however, American drama began to build upon a popularity initiated by Bronson Howard and Clyde Fitch. By the mid-century mark the stature of American drama in world theatre had been finally established. O'Neill, Wilder, Anderson and Sherwood, among others, set some of the standards, but these dramatists had all passed the peak of their careers by the mid-twentieth century. It took new, younger dramatists to make that worldwide reputation meaningful, and two of the most potent forces in America's developing drama were Arthur Miller and Tennessee Williams. Other dramatists were to appear, but by mid-century both Miller and Williams had written plays that had established them in the community of world dramatists.

Like many of the best writers for the modern theatre, Arthur Miller (1915–) has definite views about drama. A writer of philosophic temperament concerned with the personal dignity of modern man, he has created a body of theory and criticism which provides a fit introduction to his plays. For him, the idea is important in a play, and it is the dramatist's objective to state the truth about the nature of man. 'The social drama', which he views as the mainstream in American drama ('On Social Plays'), 'is the drama of the whole man'. In 'The Family in Modern Drama' he reiterated this idea of accounting for 'the total condition of man', both in society and in the family. Thus, Aristotle notwithstanding, Miller sees the common man as a proper hero. 'Rank in society' is not a major consideration, he wrote in the 'Introduction' to his *Collected Plays* (1957); it is the intensity of human passion and the discovery of a conflict or challenge which man can neither resist nor deny that determines the dramatist's feeling for that 'total condition of man'. Accomplishing this, the dramatist approaches tragedy. 'The tragic feeling is evoked in us', Miller wrote, 'when we are in the presence of a character who is ready to lay down his life, if need be, to secure one thing – his sense of personal dignity.' Ideally, Miller felt, the dramatist should be a man of great wisdom, creating that 'great drama [which] is a great jurisprudence' ('The Shadow of the Gods'). Although these theories make heavy demands upon the dramatist, they also describe Miller's own ambitions and achievements. His challenge is a drama that extends itself to 'ultimate causes', suggesting a 'relevancy for the race' and emphasizing a balance which is 'all' in great drama.

Miller is clearly not a static dramatist. Although his basic theories of drama have remained the same, he has developed different approaches, different feelings, in his dramatization of that total condition of man. Whether or not one agrees with his theories concerning the tragedy of modern man, his plays present a compelling, moving portrayal of man in modern society. There he tries to face life, fight off his animal characteristics, and achieve some dignity as his inherent guilt and pride war with each other to bring him closer to disaster. Not what man *is* but what he *should do* concerns Miller. And it is in man's living, demanding and 'doing' that Miller changed his point of view as he progressed from *All My Sons* (1947) to *The Price* (1968) while providing a substantial reputation for himself as well as for American drama in world theatre.

All My Sons established Miller in the American theatre. Before this he had published a novel, *Focus* (1945), and had written, according to his own account, thirteen unsuccessful plays; the earliest that got to New York, *The Man Who Had All the Luck* (1944), failed. *All My Sons* tells of Joe Keller's misguided attempt to make money for his family during the Second World War by shipping out faulty parts for aeroplanes which crash in battle. Finally, he recognizes his responsibility to all mankind and commits suicide in a failing attempt to atone for his deeds. In his next play Miller created one of the best-known protagonists in modern American drama. Willy Loman of *Death of a Salesman* (1949) became Miller's common-man tragic hero – a man with the wrong dreams who is never able to see the truth or accept the world as it is; a man frustrated by his own weaknesses, desperately disappointed in his sons, victimized by his twisted social and personal values; a man without 'a thing in the ground' who will give up his life before giving up his false ideas. He is a man of unreasonable, bitter contradictions. Yet he means well, tries hard and evokes tremendous sympathy among those who see him as his wife does – 'a little boat looking for a harbor'. Tragic figure or not, Willy's appeal is that of the lost, alienated, guilt-ridden, dream-oriented person endlessly spawned by modern society, and as such he has become an object of pity and fear for a generation. The play's appeal is clearly Willy's appeal. He never understands anything: victim and hero, his suicide is an ironic comment on man's concern for personal dignity. *The Crucible* (1953) carried a much stronger, better statement and is more appropriate to Miller's theory of tragedy. Accused of consorting with the devil at a time when mass hysteria has overwhelmed his village, John Proctor denounces the witchcraft trials and, in the face of death, recants a confession and refuses to allow his name to be used to influence others to a confession he knows to be false. He had found that point at which he could not turn his back and, thereby, secured that 'sense of personal dignity'.

In *A View from the Bridge* (1955, 1956) Miller reiterated his point about man's concern for personal dignity. In this play Eddie Carbone informs the United States authorities of some aliens who had entered the country illegally. He is, therefore, a man of guilt as were Joe Keller, Willy Loman and John Proctor. As he finally faces the vengeful Marco, he half demands, half pleads to be given his 'name', his sense of dignity – just as Proctor withheld his 'name' from false use. But Marco sees him only as an 'animal', the opposite of man, to be killed.

At this point in his career, however, Miller left the stage for eight years. When he returned in 1964 with two plays – *After the Fall* and *Incident at Vichy* – some of his ideas had changed. In his earlier plays a sense of personal dignity coupled with guilt had been a prologue to death. In *After the Fall*, a somewhat autobiographical play, the hero, Quentin, struggles with decisions regarding the women in his life. Finally, he accepts the fact of his guilt and decides to live with it, finding this acceptance a firm basis for living. The same acceptance is true for *Incident at Vichy*. In an essay, 'Guilt for the World's Evil', Miller declared with a certain fervour that man's problem is 'to discover our own relationship to evil, its reflection of ourselves'. As Gerald Weales (*The Jumping-Off Place, American Drama in the 1960s*, 1969) has pointed out, this new commitment perhaps weakens Miller's work by placing him in the guise of a reformer rather than an artist contending with man in an alien world.

Miller's change in attitude suggests that after *A View from the Bridge* human dignity took on a new meaning for him, and he became a commentator on the human condition. Guilt-death became guilt-acceptance. In *The Price* (1968) he continued his discussion as two brothers review their own past guilt and accusations in an attempt to live with the conditions that life has given them. The play gains distinction, however, mainly through a ninety-year-old furniture appraiser, Miller's first real comic character, whose intrusions throughout the brothers' arguments and his sardonic laugh as he sits alone at the end of the play re-emphasize Miller's thesis that, guilty or not, life is all there is for you. No matter what happens, 'you still got to believe it! *That's* hard.' With his plays of the 1960s Miller presented a positive view of life while strongly emphasizing its responsibilities, and with his comic character in *The Price* provided an additional sense of humour and opportunity as man faces those terrifying responsibilities. After all, as he had stated clearly in essays, balance is the essence.

No less admired for his dramas, Thomas Lanier (Tennessee) Williams (1914–   ) presents a strong contrast to Miller's work. Whereas Miller is more intellectually involved with the dignity of man, Williams is compassionately involved with man who has little dignity and is inescapably alone in a world where he must try to fight off the 'earth's obscene, corrupting love'. Williams views the corruption that engulfs all men, and is aware of the dreadful distance that separates romance and reality. In that world that impresses Williams, purity is befouled, youthful beauty becomes old and ugly, and sensitive man is destroyed by the crass and brutal. Yet in all of this dramatized ugliness there is a compassion bordering on hero-worship which Williams feels for those who choose to live and love but only fail or die. Revealing the problems and passions of these people with great sympathy and insight, he provides some of the most poetic symbolism in American drama. But it is clear that his vision of man is without hope. Lonely and sensitive, man cannot stand reality; nor can he escape from it. But although 'the deal is rugged', as Kilroy explains in *Camino Real*, Williams's advice is 'don't-pity-your-self'. Man needs to say 'Brother!' to someone. He needs, as Shannon explains in *Night of the Iguana*, 'to believe in something or in someone – almost anyone – almost anything . . . something.' Yet Williams realizes that all of this is impossible. There is only impending doom, and for man, struggling as he is destroyed, he feels the greatest compassion.

As a dramatist sensitive to beauty and dreams, Williams writes here about people who are trying to live – the recluse, the poet, the faded aristocrat. With them, he creates that sense of loneliness in man which becomes a unifying theme for most of his work. As his people attempt their escapes from this condition through sex, through violence, always in desperation, there is a touch of sentiment, a note of romance, but never an escape. In *The Glass Menagerie* (1944) Tom, a sensitive and poetic soul, is nagged by his mother to bring home a 'gentleman caller' for his shy and crippled sister, Laura. But the young man turns out to be engaged and therefore not eligible for Laura. Unable to tolerate his mother's view of life and frustrated by his job, Tom quietly abandons his sister and mother to their living death, while he in his loneliness is never free. When produced in Austria, *A Streetcar*

Named Desire (1947) was called *Loneliness, the Last Step*. Blanche, lonely and confused, fleeing a sordid past, comes to visit her sister as a last hope. Here she tries desperately but unsuccessfully to win friends while the effect she has upon her sister's shaky marriage with Stanley only adds pathos to her situation. In a brutal attempt to rid his house of Blanche, Stanley destroys her one hope with a young man and rapes her, thus driving her to insanity, an inevitable but unsatisfying escape.

Camino Real (1953) is a fascinating revelation of Williams's 'conception of the time and world that I live in'. In a complicated but carefully structured play of sixteen scenes and a prologue, Don Quixote appears and dreams a pageant of old and new meanings in which Kilroy, the all-American boy with a solid-gold heart, meets the corruptions of life, is seduced by fraud, becomes a patsy and is finally chosen as the fit companion for Don Quixote, the dreamer. The price of admission to the Camino Real is 'desperation' the audience is told, for 'Humankind cannot bear very much reality'. 'Lonely!' is a cry of the people, and the forbidden word is 'Brother!' Escape is available only on an uncharted flight of the Fugitivo, through death as symbolized by the macabre Street Cleaners, or through the archway marked 'Terra Incognita'. Frequently called Williams's testament, *Camino Real* reveals his broadest interpretation of mankind and is considered his most thoughtful and challenging play.

Sex in most of Williams's plays becomes a foil to loneliness and a means by which man may find some salvation. Essentially, it is part of Williams's psychology of a corrupt world – perhaps derived from his admiration of D. H. Lawrence – but far too frequently it becomes a standard dramaturgical device in his plays. In *The Rose Tattoo* (1951), for example, sexuality is used as a solution to the world's problems as Serafina discovers that her dead husband had been unfaithful to her and reawakens to normal patterns of life. The *Cat on a Hot Tin Roof* (1955) is Maggie who finally forces her husband to perform in bed and therefore allay his homosexual fears as well as provide a child which will inherit Big Daddy's millions. The sexuality is much more terrible in *Suddenly Last Summer* (1958) with its conception of a homosexual poet devoured by a group of young boys. In this image, however, Williams pictured the sensitive passion of men in a predatory world where only the fittest survive. It remains one of his most horrific interpretations of man's cruelty and indicates the kind of religious anguish which he felt in an alien world. Real and symbolic castration was the dominating action and image in *Sweet Bird of Youth* (1958), a play of abandoned dreams, frustration and doom. An emphasis upon the relationship of sex and religion supported his theme in *The Night of the Iguana* (1961) as Shannon, the defrocked minister unable to control his appetites, hopes vainly for a second chance by freeing the iguana tied beneath his window which tries 'to go on past the end of its goddam rope. Like *you*! Like *me*!' But there is no escape, nothing but the possibility of facing death with some dignity.

In Williams's latest plays death joins corruption as a prominent part of his dramatic universe. *The Milk Train Doesn't Stop Here Anymore* (1964) shows a woman trying desperately to finish her memoirs before she dies, being ministered to by a young man known as the Angel of Death. The two short plays Williams called *Slapstick Tragedy* (1965) as well as *The Seven Descents of Myrtle* (1968) continue his absorption in death and deterioration. Yet even in these late plays Williams's world is the same wasteland of the 'terra incognita', the world of suffering for those sensitive people who must learn to live with hysteria and horror. Although he has sometimes interpreted life in lyric movements and artistically expressed those movements in ways which have been influential through the world, Williams has consistently emphasized the awful flight of time as man's persistent enemy and dramatized isolated moments of that swift, unceasing passage towards death. Increasingly, he has seen everything as a 'horrifying experience' which he once described poetically in *Orpheus Descending* (1957). There he told the story of a legless bird that remains pure because it can never alight on the earth and become contaminated by its corruption. That is the dream of the romantic, yet, as Williams stated clearly in *Camino Real*, 'a dream is nothing to live in'.

With *A Streetcar Named Desire* and *Death of a Salesman* American drama became not just interesting for its differences which the Yankee and Negro drama of the early nineteenth century had introduced to England and Europe, or tolerable on account of its youth and vitality. Instead it has become exciting and in demand for its excellence in form and content. The way had been prepared by the host of good dramatists who thronged the stage between the two World Wars. Miller and Williams provided particular evidence of a 'potent' American drama, and in their wake came a new contingent of dramatists who belonged to the immediate post-war period. None achieved the stature of Miller or Williams, and most were successful only with a play or two before disappearing from view. In general, the American theatre did not provide very exciting supporting drama for Miller and Williams. There was mainly the usual fare of journeymen plays, some light and successful comedies, and the fresh buoyancy of musical comedy on which producers and the New York real-estate people who owned the theatres began to thrive.

William Inge (1913–73) is the single example of a dramatist during the 1950s whose body of work may be considered a contribution to the developing American drama. His first success, *Come Back, Little Sheba* (1950), told the story of a slovenly romantic woman, her alcoholic husband, and the reality they are made to face. In this play and those that followed Inge showed insight into the raw conditions of man and provided a realistic interpretation of life in which the humour of everyday life is enacted with a touch of melodrama and a generous helping of sentiment. Mankind, he found, might be the object of pity or of anger but should be treated mainly with love. In *Picnic* (1953) he dramatized another view of frustrated men and women, caged by a small-town atmosphere and driven by their passions. In all of his plays he managed to mingle sex and sentiment to good effect in the theatre and present lonely people whose problems, for good or ill, are resolved by love. *Bus Stop* (1955) presented an assorted group of people whose attitudes towards love suggest the scope that this emotion holds for mankind. There is no doubt that Inge is a good craftsman who handles characters with insight and skill, but he impairs his craft by adhering too closely to a certain formula construction in his plays, by tending to use sentiment too lavishly, and by letting something called love solve his dramaturgical problems. All of this detracts from his overall effectiveness and suggests a shallow psychological orientation. Although *The Dark at the Top of the Stairs* (1957) attempted a psychological study of the need for love and understanding within a family and among several people, outworn thinking as well as weak devices tended to mar the effect. Then the fear of the uncertain future dramatized in this play seemed to become even more real to Inge, and his subsequent dramas did not reach the calibre of those written during the 1950s.

Among the new dramatists of this period, Arthur Laurents (1918–) made a brilliant start with *Home of the Brave* (1945) and impressed critics with his honest concern for the individual in society, his insight into his characters, and his imaginative experimentation in form. Later in *The Time of the Cuckoo* (1952) he seemed to overemphasize sentiment in his treatment of a spinster schoolteacher touring Europe and learning about herself, but his work interested the reviewers. Like the majority of American dramatists, Laurents was concerned with man's loneliness. In his Preface to *A Clearing in the Woods* (1957) he described the lonely person as one 'who is lonely with himself because he has not accepted himself for the imperfect being he is'.

The play went on to exploit this situation, experimentally, as the audience viewed the main character as a little girl, as an adolescent, as a young bride and as a woman frightened of middle age. The unconventional form offered him an opportunity for timelessness which was never quite achieved, but the play suggested potential. Unfortunately, the potential was never tested because Laurents became highly successful as a scenario writer for such musical comedies as *West Side Story* (1957) and *Gypsy* (1959).

Another dramatist whose plays were sufficiently promising that the members of the Playwrights' Company – originally composed of Sidney Howard, Elmer Rice, S. N. Behrman, Robert Sherwood and Maxwell Anderson – invited him to join their group was Robert Anderson (1917–   ). His *Tea and Sympathy* (1953) was a box-office hit. Treating a lonely and sensitive student who is innocently involved in a homosexual scandal at a New England boys' school, Anderson solved the boy's problem in proving his manhood through the headmaster's wife whose sympathy knew no limits. But Robert Anderson progressed very little. *Silent Night, Lonely Night* (1959) brought together two lonely people on Christmas Eve – a woman who does not believe in adultery and a man who has abstained from sex for five years – and allowed them to indulge in therapeutic sex to help them meet the future demands of their individual lives. Anderson's *You Know I Can't Hear You When the Water's Running* (1967) is as forced and slight as the title suggests. A moment of comedy, it provides nothing that suggests a meaningful contribution to American drama.

One other playwright of this post-war period, Paddy Chayefsky (1923–   ), combined considerable literary skill with a fine touch of humour in two thought-provoking plays. The first was *The Tenth Man* (1959) in which Chayefsky presented a group of Jews searching for the necessary 'tenth' man in order to exorcize a dybbuk from a demented girl who is finally taken from the synagogue by the 'tenth' man they had such difficulty in finding. The presumption that she will be cured by this man's love is romantic and sentimental, but the humour of the play is delightful. *Gideon* (1961) is a more thoughtful play as Gideon, chosen by God to deliver his people, becomes quite humanly prideful and, when rebuked by God for his brashness, he demands that he at least be allowed to believe in himself. Chayefsky's mixture of humour and insight is effective in these plays, but it has not reappeared. These dramatists who once seemed to have potential have not fulfilled their promise. With the exception of Miller and Williams (and perhaps Inge), no dramatist of the modern period produced a measurable body of work until Edward Albee appeared.

While the commercial theatre forged ahead with its accustomed fare of melodrama, comedy and farce, the newly popular musical comedy reigned inside the theatre and historical pageantry outside. For the traditional forms a few titles and phrases will suggest the tenor of the theatre offerings. Joseph Kramm's (1907–) *The Shrike* (1952) illustrates the modern psychological melodrama. In a hospital mental ward an attempted suicide, separated from his wife, learns that he is a potential criminal, subject to release only if he places himself completely under the control of his unsympathetic wife. *A Hatful of Rain* (1955) by Michael V. Gazzo (1923–) deals with the problems of the drug addict. Among the best of these modern melodramas is Morton Wishengrad's (d. 1963) *The Rope Dancers* (1959) in which a woman regards the birth of a child with six fingers on one hand as a curse. In a kind of Hawthornian morality climax, the mother, forcing the child to wear a mitten, is told by a doctor that 'we all wear a glove over something'. But the child dies when the finger is removed.

In the comedy line, the tired businessmen and the matinee ladies enjoyed Mary Ellen Chase's (1907–) play about Elwood P. Dowd's six-foot rabbit, *Harvey* (1944), John Patrick's (1910–) *The Tea House of the August Moon* (1953) where comic sentimentalism runs free on the romantic island of Okinawa, the modern Cinderella theme in Samuel Taylor's (1912–) *Sabrina Fair* (1953), and the wild exploits of *Auntie Mame* (1956) adapted from Patrick Dennis's novel by Jerome Lawrence (1915–) and Robert E. Lee (1918–). And there were more, many more – all for the moment, not for history.

Musical comedy must be considered one of the American theatre's major contributions to world theatre. What it contributes to American drama is another question. Generally, it has emphasized spectacle with some concern for plot and perhaps dialogue but little interest in character or thought. The object of the musical has always been to please audiences with song and dance and lots of romance and sentiment. Not until very recent times has there been a serious thought in a musical or an attempt to put songs and plot together, and perhaps it should only then be considered a real part of the drama. In the past it was closely associated with revues, follies and romantic operetta, and during these years two or three of the musical plays will suggest its developing history in America.

One of the first musical plays was called an opera but has the characteristics of the modern musical comedy – spectacle, song, romance. This was *The Archers; or, Mountaineers of Switzerland* (1796) by William Dunlap, the 'father of American drama'. For some historians Charles M. Barras's *The*

Black Crook (1866) is the proper ancestor of modern musical comedy. With ballet, song and legs – which were sensationally revealed at the time – *The Black Crook* had an equally sensational run of sixteen months. A contemporary critic wrote: 'The scenery is magnificent; the ballet is beautiful; the drama is – rubbish.' At this same time vaudeville and variety theatres were getting started in ways that suggested some origins for the revues of the early twentieth century. Also prior to the First World War, two major writers – Victor Herbert with *Babes in Toyland* (1903) and *Sweethearts* (1913) and George M. Cohan with such musicals as *Forty-Five Minutes from Broadway* (1906) – added romantic operetta and fast-moving comedy to the developing musical routines. Then came a period of experimentation between the two wars in which writers of the musical tested its potential. Rudolf Friml (*Rose-Marie*, 1924), Sigmund Romberg (*The Desert Song* 1926) and Vincent Youmans (*No, No Nanette*, 1925) emphasized music and romance. Jerome Kern (*Showboat*, 1927) and George and Ira Gershwin (*Strike Up the Band*, 1930; *Of Thee I Sing*, 1931, with Kaufman and Ryskind; *Porgy and Bess*, 1935, with the Heywards) added adventure, a more realistic appreciation of the times, and sometimes a touch of satire. Meanwhile, musical revues grew in popularity with songs by Irving Berlin and Cole Porter. Then in 1943 Richard Rodgers and Oscar Hammerstein II adapted Lynn Riggs's play to the musical stage as *Oklahoma!*, and the modern musical comedy had reached maturity.

Since the Second World War the musical comedy has assumed a major position in theatre entertainment, and awards are given not only for the best play of the year but for the best musical as well. John Whiting once wrote ('From My Diary') that 'the purpose of Art is to raise doubt, the purpose of entertainment is to reassure.' Clearly, and in ways that have helped (along with TV programmes) obscure the real and the true from nearly two generations of Americans, the musical has entertained. Like the old David Belasco 'pastepot and scissors' melodrama, many musical comedies were patchwork productions such as Bob Merrill's *Carnival* (1961) or Betty Comden and Adolph Green's *On the Town* (1944). Yet like Belasco's work these musicals could be very successful.

Mainly, musicals are light and happy with few serious thoughts. Arthur Laurents and Stephen Sondheim's *West Side Story* (1959) and Rodgers and Hammerstein's *South Pacific* (1949) are exceptions, while *Man of La Mancha* (1965) by Mitch Leigh, Joe Darion and Dale Wasserman has thoughtful moments. The general formula for success includes topicality, some spoofing (Richard Adler and Jerry Ross's *Pajama Game*, 1954, spoofs capitalism and labour), a liberal amount of nostalgia (Leonard Bernstein's *Wonderful Town*, 1953), plenty of sentiment (Rodgers and Hammerstein's *The King and I*, 1951), and as much love as the songs and book will bear (Alan Lerner and Frederick Loewe's *Camelot*, 1960). Since the success of *Oklahoma!* and *South Pacific*, the best writers of musicals have tried to tie songs with plot, character and ideas. Although this integration of music, dance, spectacle and drama has not always been achieved, audiences have not been very demanding. Those musical comedies which come near accomplishing these objectives, however, are successful on the stage – Lerner and Loewe's musical version of Shaw's *Pygmalion* in *My Fair Lady* (1956) and *How to Succeed in Business Without Really Trying* (1961) by Frank Loesser, Abe Burrows, Jack Weinstock and Willie Gilbert. Rock musicals such as Gerome Ragni, James Rado and Galt MacDermot's *Hair* (1967), the first 'American Tribal Love-Rock Musical', indicate that the musical is not a stagnant art although even these writers and composers are discovering that 'relevance' is difficult to maintain in the fickle theatrical world.

A brief word about American pageant drama. The developing pattern of American drama has always suggested its obligation to bring entertainment to the people. Society and economics determined that the burden was upon the people to go to the 'temple of Thespis' where their subsequent participation, of course, might be haphazard. But this view does not reflect that idea of theatre and drama which sprang from the re-enactment of myths and the folk rituals. Perhaps the pageant brought the theatregoer closer to the ritual origin of drama, and as America became more aware of itself as a nation with a history and a tradition, pageant drama became more popular. Essentially, the pageant is a healthy expression of a democratic and community spirit and can be loosely defined as a festival, in episodes, of thanksgiving, worship or history. The form varies, but history is important, while dialogue, monologue, pantomime, music, dance, spectacle and sometimes allegory are included in the drama. Among the early practitioners of this type of drama Percy MacKaye was outstanding. *Caliban, By the Yellow Sands* (1916), produced on the 300th anniversary of Shakespeare's death, was one of his most ambitious and successful pageants.

During the first three decades of the twentieth century a number of good pageants sporadically appeared: George Pierce Baker's (1866–1935) celebration of the American musician, Edward MacDowell, in *The Peterborough Pageant* (1910); a propaganda pageant called *The Suffrage Allegory* produced in Washington in 1913; Frederick Koch's (1877–1944) *A Pageant of the Northwest* (1914); Baker's *The Pilgrim*

Spirit (1921), and innumerable amateur pageants by church, school and grange.

Then in 1937 Paul Green created *The Lost Colony* which he called a symphonic drama. Using music, dance, a procession, spectacle, dramatic action and dialogue, he told the story, inasmuch as anyone could, of Sir Walter Raleigh's colony on Roanoke Island – the friendship of the Indian Manteo, the birth of the first child born to white parents in the New World, and the desertion of the fort by the colonists under Indian attack. Led by Governor White, the colonists had landed in 1587. But Governor White soon returned to England for reinforcements and was delayed there by England's war with Spain. When he finally reached Roanoke Island in 1590, he found only the word CROATOAN carved on a tree. Paul Green went on to celebrate other historical events in pageants. Among his fourteen pageants are *The Common Glory* (1947), dramatizing the contribution of Jefferson and the state of Virginia during the period of 1775–82; *The Founders* (1957) which tells the story of the Jamestown colony; and *Texas* (1966) which portrays part of the history of that state. Most of Green's pageants are performed annually in the appropriate geographical setting, and his kind of creativity has been imitated in numerous locales.

As the late spring and summer months come to America, and its vacationing population begins to move, pageants and festivals start to play. *The Lost Colony* is performed at the Waterside Theatre in Manteo, North Carolina. Across the state at the Mountainside Theatre in Cherokee, Kermit Hunter's (1910–   ) *Unto Those Hills* (1950) tells the story of De Soto and the Cherokee Indians. From there one may go to Williamsburg, Virginia, for *The Common Glory*; or to Pipestone, Minnesota, for *The Song of Hiawatha*; and on to pageants in Massachusetts, Tennessee, South Dakota, Utah, Texas or California. Not many pageants, of course, approach the artistry of Green's work, but the participation by dozens and even hundreds of actors and actresses suggests another dimension of American drama.

14 Contemporary trends in American drama

A discussion of 'contemporary trends' is a precarious occupation for any historian and particularly a historian of drama which in its traditional cast reflects the varied moods of society. The more sophisticated or complicating the moods, the more potential attitudes there are for drama. Contemporary American drama presents a diverse society, perhaps no different in some ways from the past but with distinct tensions and anxieties. There are the usual social satires (Jules Feiffer's (1929–) *Little Murders*, 1967; Joseph Heller's (1923–) *We Bombed in New Haven*, 1967), the musicals and the light comedies (Jean Kerr's (1923–) *Mary, Mary*, 1961). The most successful contemporary dramatist in this last category is Neil Simon (1927–). From his first hit of the decade, *Come Blow Your Horn* (1961), about a Jewish manufacturer and his playboy son, through *The Odd Couple* (1965) concerned with two men living together, to *Last of the Red Hot Lovers* (1969), he has shown his ability to write just what most Broadway audiences want to see. For those few interested in serious drama, there are new plays by Miller and Williams. But there have also been new directions established in the American drama and new playwrights who are quite distinct from their older colleagues of previous decades. For the 1960s, however, there is only one new playwright whose name may be remembered a hundred years hence.

That is Edward Albee, whose plays have attracted critical attention in the ways that works by Miller, Williams and O'Neill have appealed to scholars and reviewers. Worthy colleagues of Albee, unfortunately, have been few. Excitement in the theatre of the 1960s has depended more upon the rising number of Negro dramatists, the protest plays from Off-Broadway and Off-off-Broadway, and the new interest in poetic drama – all of which may be treated in a brief paragraph or less when time has placed art in a proper perspective.

Edward Albee (1928–   ) has been the only important dramatist to emerge in America since Miller and Williams. With the popularity of the Theatre of the Absurd, Albee's reputation quickly spread as his experimentation in form seemed to place him among those dramatists who abandoned conceptual thinking and logical behaviour for paradoxes, illogical behaviour and absurd situations. Although critics disagree as to whether he is an innovator or an imitator, there is little disagreement that his insights into the human con-dition are more a bitter attack upon man than a compassionate concern for his dignity. He shows both wit and dramaturgical skill as he dramatizes a hatred for social and personal complacency, as well as for the false, smug values he sees expressed around him, and the situation he describes as 'the American dream'. In his dramas the concise quality of his dialogue has been singled out for particular praise. More generally the obscurity and ambiguity of his work has given pretenders to scholarship major opportunities for indulging their imaginations, but the overall value of his work is still seriously questioned. Are the plays of Albee and the other so-called absurdists in America examples of beautifully contrived showmanship or do they have some meaningful relation to life?

Albee is the only contemporary dramatist with a sufficient body of work to allow an assessment of his psychological insight and his playwriting skill. In the numerous examinations of his plays reservations have come more from theatre critics than from the academic community where Albee's works have been welcomed with some enthusiasm. Yet particular views have affected his reputation in both theatre and classroom. A number of his plays, for example – *The Zoo Story, Who's Afraid of Virginia Woolf?* and *Tiny Alice* – have been interpreted as in-jokes for the homosexual population with the result that some people have tended to dismiss his entire work as fraudulent. Although the onesidedness of this view is patently weak, it is clear that *The Zoo Story* is an obvious homosexual play. Whatever the approach to Albee's plays, however, they must be considered the views of a strongminded person. In one interview he stated that 'the responsibility of a writer is to be a sort of demonic social critic'. It is this approach that he practises with a vigorous, didactic determination. In spite of the fact that he has dismissed American drama of the 1930s as propaganda rather than art, he believes in the utility of art and the possibility of social solutions. If this is a contradiction, the problem is in his own subconscious creative process which he has described as beyond his own comprehension. In one way, of course, this statement could be interpreted as his escape from responsibility, but Albee has a reputation for insisting that his plays are misunderstood. Therefore, he has a purpose which is at least clear to him. Either, then, his ambiguity is pur- poseful and profound in his instructive fables, or it is philosophically gelatinous and the plays remain failing illustrations of his art and thought. Whatever the eventual decision, his use of ambiguity, seeming paradox and a tightly directed language provides his critics with opportunity for thought.

Albee's playwriting career began in Berlin in 1959 with a production of *The Zoo Story*; the following year it came to New York. It dramatizes the meeting of two strangers, one of whom, an aggressive critic of the human condition named Jerry, angrily challenges the complacent Peter to defend his rights and then dies on his own knife held in Peter's hand. Presumably, Jerry's personal sacrifice has shocked and forced Peter to see what life is all about. The pessimistic-optimistic ending, however – the alienation of Jerry versus the awareness of Peter – has seemed more melodramatically preten- tious than seriously ambiguous. Another one-act play, *The Death of Bessie Smith* (1960), uses the motor accident of a blues singer, Bessie Smith, and the refusal of two white hospitals to admit her, to illustrate the racial hate and violence of America and to demand both individual and institutional change. *The Sand Box* (1960) and *The American Dream* (1961) characterize the emptiness of American life – the concern for appearance rather than reality, the vacuous state of conformity, and the falseness of success.

Escape from these conditions may be an illusion, but it seems to be one of Albee's objectives while violence becomes a dramatized means in *Who's Afraid of Virginia Woolf?* (1962), his first full-length play. In this play a man and his wife, with malice and ingenuity, practise a rehearsed destruction of each other. But out of the last act, called 'The Exorcism', a tenderness emerges and, presumably, a new strength and understanding for the major protagonists. This play has been Albee's most successful. Necessity for love and the destruction of illusion are here Albee's message for America as the humanistic wars with the mechanical in contemporary Western civilization. His next play, an adaptation of Carson McCullers's *The Ballad of the Sad Café* (1963), enjoyed a respectable reception, while *Malcolm* (1966), a dramatization of James Purdy's novel, did not even please Albee. In a more complicated and controversial play, *Tiny Alice* (1964), Albee wrote about a man 'dedicated to the reality of things' who is torn between truth and illusion. Guided by evil and seduced by God, the 'hero' fights 'going under' in a struggle doomed to failure. Symbolism (particularly of the Christian myth), allegory and metaphor are blatant throughout the play which has been interpreted in many ways – from the homosexual in-joke to an imitation of O'Neill's concern for man's relationship to God. *A Delicate Balance* (1966), Albee's next play, presented a realistic plot of a family home invaded and threatened by neighbourhood friends. At the end, the delicate balance of the home may be preserved but the emptiness at the centre suggests Albee's vision of the human condition. A love–death symbolism underlies the play while the scene of dawn which ends both *Virginia Woolf* and *A Delicate Balance* reveals Albee's basic irony.

There is little doubt that Albee has tried to use the particular in life to phrase his views of the universal. As he has developed, he has moved away from the political and social structure of modern living to a concern with moral and religious illusion. There is a great deal of difference, for example, between the family in *The American Dream* and that in *A Delicate Balance*, just as there is between Jerry in *The Zoo Story* and Julian in *Tiny Alice*. From a hatred of conventional complacencies Albee concerned himself with man's mortality, but his contention that fear dominates man's actions has not changed. He seems to feel that an attitude of human dignity is not a solution while created illusion fails to bring man happiness.

Among those contemporary dramatists who once seemed to be arguing the more serious issues of society – thoughtful Off-Broadway dramatists – are Arthur Kopit (1938–), Jack Gelber (1932–) and Jack Richardson (1935–). Kopit's first play was the imaginative *Oh Dad, Poor Dad, Mamma's Hung You in the Closet and I'm Feeling So Sad* (1960), a burlesque of a favourite American theme – the emasculation of the male. It would seem to be serious, just as *The Day the Whores Came Out to Play Tennis* (1965) would seem to be a comedy with a serious condemnation of that self-contained life which faces an external menace with complacency. Jack Gelber's continuing dramaturgical device is to deny the illusion of the stage and merge the audience and the actors to a point where pretence is unnecessary. *The Connection* (1959) purports to present real drug addicts who ad-lib a plotless evening in search of a 'fix'. In *The Apple* (1961) a group of actors – a Negro, a Jew, a homosexual, a whore, a spastic – are supposed to improvise a play but are constantly annoyed by a drunk. 'No design' may be 'grand design' in the opinion of one of the actors, but what you see in this play is not very stimulating. *Square in the Eye* (1965) tries again to shatter theatre illusion in a play that emphasizes the modern thesis of alienation through the failure of social contact.

Jack Richardson's concern for the victimization of man by various social forces suggests that he is the most intellectually engaging of the young playwrights. In his retelling of the Orestes legend in *The Prodigal* (1960) he made the hero a modern cynic who wished to remain detached from society but is forced to abandon his position. A debasing, life-denying society permeates the play. *Gallows Humor* (1961) contrasts a condemned man with his executioner and shows the greater freedom of the former. *Lorenzo* (1963), a Broadway failure, uses a troupe of players involved in a meaningless conflict in Renaissance Italy to argue the value of illusion versus reality. *Xmas in Las Vegas* (1965) suggests a more cynical view with its scene in America's gambling city. As one character says, if there is one sign in heaven, it should be 'You can't beat the house.'

None of these playwrights beats the 'Broadway' house nor have they been able to sustain their work at a level once thought their potential. Consequently, other dramatists are immediately placed among 'the best of the Young American Playwrights': Frank Gilroy (1925–) with *The Subject Was Roses* (1964), a simple and sentimental play about the problems in a home, youth and age; Lewis John Carlino (1932–) with a moralizing dramatic collage entitled *Telemachus Clay* (1963); or William Hanley (1931–) with *Slow Dance on the Killing Ground* (1964), the attempt on the part of man to escape the violence of the world. But none of these has produced an enduring play.

During the 1960s Negro drama began a sustained drive to attain a mature position in the American theatre. Although not yet a significant voice, the Negro playwright has made substantial gains during the decade. Just as black actors have gained considerable stature and promise in their profession, the black playwrights have emerged as a force particularly in the Off-Broadway and protest theatres. Those who have attracted the most attention are Lorraine Hansberry, Ossie Davis, Douglas Turner Ward, James Baldwin, Leroi Jones (Imamu Baraka) and Ed Bullins. Lorraine Hansberry (1930–65) contributed two plays to American drama which, though conventionally constructed, show both her fine talent as a dramatist and her commitment to the dignity of man while emphasizing a black position in society. *A Raisin in the Sun* (1959) dramatizes the maturing of a young Negro, as a decision to fight a housing situation in Chicago places the burden of action upon the white community. In her second play, *The Sign in Sidney Brustein's Window* (1964), Sidney undergoes a similar education about his own abilities and the social world surrounding him. But Sidney is a realistic and thinking person, a fine illustration of Lorraine Hansberry's strength in character portrayal and her major creation in making a social statement. Ossie Davis's best work is *Purlie Victorious* (1961) which takes a socio-economic situation with southern stereotype characters and manipulates them for purposes of social satire. Douglas Turner Ward's reputation rests upon two one-act plays, *Happy Ending* and *Day of Absence*, produced in 1965. Written for Negro audiences, both plays are based on anecdotes which provide humour at the expense of the white community. In *Happy Ending*, for example, two Negro domestics are absolutely distraught on hearing the news that the white couple who have supported them, consciously and unconsciously, for so long are on the verge of divorce. The explanation of this situation to a black militant is the focus of the play, showing that, in addition to being a gifted dramatist, Ward is an articulate and intelligent spokesman for black drama.

James Baldwin (1924–   ), as a novelist, short-story writer and dramatist, has the most substantial reputation among these writers, although his association with the theatre has been limited to 1964–5 when his two plays, *Amen Corner* and *Blues for Mister Charlie*, were produced. The first dramatizes the story of a woman evangelistic leader who learns that she must first set her house in order as the problems of her personal world bring confusion to her religious leadership. *Blues for Mister Charlie* is based on the Emmett Till murder and shows both bitterness as the killer is exonerated and justice is denied and a broader suggestion of liberal understanding. Both plays build upon Baldwin's expressed difficulties as an individual and as a black, but beneath the thesis drama in *Blues for Mister Charlie* are also strong humanitarian views. Baldwin's instincts are with man. Black or white, his serious answer for all human problems is love through suffering.

Another avenue of black drama is that of the Black Arts movement, the drama as a weapon in revolutionary culture. The acknowledged leader of this drama is Leroi Jones (1934–   ) (Imanu Baraka) whose militant plays discuss the failure of Christianity, the problem of homosexuality and the inevitability of violence between black and white. With a militant attitude revealed in his essays as well as in his plays (one essay is entitled 'The Last Days of the American Empire, Including Some Instructions for Black People', 1964), Jones, by his own confession, became 'even blacker' as the decade of the 1960s progressed. Equally intensified has been the acceptance of his work as a force in black culture. In *Dutchman* (1964) Jones very effectively presents the black situation as a white woman goads a black man to express his blackness, listens to his violent speech, then kills him before going on, presumably to repeat her act. *The Baptism* (1964), an obscene dramatization of a kind of religious-sexual ritual, was less successful. *The Toilet* (published 1963) takes place in a school toilet where the final confessed homosexual love between a white boy and a black boy provides a comment on human sensitivity as well as social pressure. *The Slave* (produced with *The Toilet* in 1964 but presumably written before *Dutchman*) employs a Negro poet as the leader of a black insurrection and the voice of racial violence. In *Black Mass* (published 1966) Jones mixes occultism and propaganda in an attempt to suggest a 'Holy War'. *Slave Ship* (1969) dramatized his usual thesis and, not surprisingly, won an award for Jones. There is certainly an intensity in Jones's technique and a passion in his comment, but his weakness is in character abstractions which frequently occur in thesis dramas. Ed Bullins (1935–   ), for his work with the Lafayette Theatre group and his growing number of plays (*The Duplex*, 1972), would seem to be the most likely dramatist to assume Jones's militant mantle. At present the black theatre is eminently provincial in attempting to establish a clear identity. Hopefully, it will develop to a cosmopolitan stage where its creativity may emerge as universal art.

More than 300 years have passed since William Darby with the help of two friends performed his *Yᵉ Bare and Yᵉ Cubb* in Virginia. Conditions have changed considerably since then. Of that there is no question. But problems still exist for the dramatist. In both stature and sense of freedom the dramatist in America has now endured several cycles of change until he can write just as he wishes. He may get himself into trouble, of course, as William Darby did, the dramatist's constant problem being to make people recognize and understand his particular concern for the human condition. Many people have thought the dramatist shirked this responsibility until after the First World War, but this is a sadly oversimplified view. True, he did attempt mainly to entertain, but even providing entertainment during the years of hostile reception by various forces in society – from church to government – was an accomplishment. The complete history of dramatic criticism in America has yet to be written, but only when it is will the complete nature of dramatic composition in pre-First-World-War America be revealed.

Since its beginnings, American drama has developed slowly but definitely in ways that reflect the growth of a society. Owing to numerous explainable factors, it reached its maturity only very recently. But neither in its actual contributions nor in people's attitudes towards the drama is its development astounding. From American drama of a hundred-odd years ago *Fashion*, *Francesca da Rimini* and *The Octoroon* are reasonable achievements, indicative of the time. Perhaps American drama of the mid-twentieth century will not have more than three plays that might be revived a hundred years hence. Whereas the accomplishments of fiction and poetry in America have been late in receiving popular literary recognition, American drama is still lagging behind with, of course, a limited body of significant work. A major problem for the literary historian, however, is the very nature of drama – written to be viewed in a theatre at a given moment. It is an artistry of here and now in addition to the everywhere and forever, as the eighteenth-century changes in *King Lear* and the late mid-twentieth-century version of *A Midsummer Night's Dream* clearly illustrate. As America developed nationally and internationally, a culture emerged. More accurately than either the plastic or literary arts could trace its achievements, the theatre reflected its strengths and weaknesses, its wisdom and its follies. At the present point in history American drama is a here-and-now art which is accepted everywhere. Only the future can judge its universal and timeless appeal.

Bibliography

I The American drama: its range of contexts

II American actors, managers, producers and directors

Not all books mentioned in the text are repeated here. Many of the entries in the bibliography of Section III, 'The dramatists and their plays', will relate to this section, for example such books as Hodge's study of the Yankee, Percy MacKaye's biography of his father, *Epoch*, and Craig Timberlake's life of David Belasco. For a more extensive bibliography Richard Moody's *Dramas from the American Theatre, 1762–1909* (New York and Cleveland, Ohio, 1966; Boston, Mass., 1969) may be consulted. A useful checklist is that compiled by Pat M. Ryan, *American Dramatic Bibliography, A Checklist of Publications in English* (Ft Wayne, Ind., 1969).

(i) GENERAL STUDIES

Fortunately, the history of the New York theatre from the beginning to 1894 is fully and accurately recorded in the fifteen volumes of George C. D. Odell's monumental *Annals of the New York Stage* (New York, 1927–49). Readers may also wish to consult George O. Seilhamer, *History of the*

American Theatre (originally published in 3 vols from 1888 to 1891; reissued New York, 1968). Detailed basic information about productions, casts, lengths of runs, producing organizations, actors, directors, etc., is available for the period from 1894 to the present in the yearbooks of 'Best Plays', for which Burns Mantle was the chief editor: John Chapman and Garrison P. Sherwood (eds), *Best Plays of 1894–1899* (New York, 1955); Burns Mantle and Garrison P. Sherwood (eds), *Best Plays of 1899–1909* (New York, 1944); Mantle and Sherwood (eds), *Best Plays of 1909–1919* (New York, 1943); and, from 1920 to date, the annual 'Best Plays' volumes. For concise bibliographical information about theatre personalities, see Walter Rigdon (ed.), *The Biographical Encyclopedia of Who's Who of the American Theatre* (New York, 1966). An updated volume is now in preparation.

Several overviews exist: Garff B. Wilson's narrative account of American actors, *A History of American Acting* (Bloomington, Ind., 1966), and the same author's *Three Hundred Years of American Drama and Theatre* (Englewood Cliffs, NJ, 1973); Arthur Hornblow's sketchy *History of the Theatre in America*, 2 vols (Philadelphia, Pa., 1919); and Barnard Hewitt's *Theatre U.S.A., 1668–1937* (New York, 1959), an excellent source book of contemporary views of performances and players.

Illuminating details on theatres may be found in the following volumes: Brooks MacNamara, *The American Playhouse in the Eighteenth Century* (Cambridge, Mass., 1969); Mary C. Henderson, *The City and the Theatre, a History of New York's Major Playhouses from Bowling Green to Times Square* (Clifton, NJ, 1973); and William C. Young's *Documents of American Theatre History*, 2 vols (Chicago, Ill., 1973). An interesting analysis of the theatrical financing is to be found in *The Business of Theatre* by Alfred L. Bernheim, assisted by Sara Harding (New York, 1932). See also Abel Green and Joe Laurie, Jr, *Show Biz, or From Vaud to Video* (New York, 1951), and Jack Poggi, *Theatre in America, The Impact of Economic Forces* (Ithaca, NY, 1968). Two of the best sources for pictures are Daniel Blum's *A Pictorial History of the American Theatre* (New York, 1950) and Oral Sumner Coad and Edwin Mims, Jr, *The American Stage* (New Haven, Conn., 1929).

Although all the papers delivered at the symposium on American theatre at the Smithsonian Institute in 1969 and published in *The American Theatre: A Sum of Its Parts* (New York, 1971), edited by Henry B. Williams, relate to the present study, the following are of special interest: Ralph G. Allen, 'Our Native Theatre; Honky-Tonk, Minstrel Shows, Burlesque'; James H. Butler, 'The University Theatre Begins to Come of Age: 1925–1969'; Lawrence Carra, 'The Influence of the Director – For Good or Bad'; Helen

Krich Chinoy, 'The Profession and the Art'; Alan Hewitt, 'Repertory to Residuals, Acting, 1900–1969'; Barnard Hewitt, 'The Producer's Many Roles'; Richard Moody, 'American Actors and Acting Before 1900: The Making of a Tradition'.

(ii) BIOGRAPHIES AND AUTOBIOGRAPHIES

In most instances, only a single book is listed for each person, usually the most detailed. Some biographical entries, particularly those dealing with managers and directors, appear in the bibliography of Section III.

(a) *From the beginnings to the Civil War*

Francis Courtney Wemyss, *Theatrical Biography of Eminent Actors and Authors* (New York, 1852), provides brief sketches of the lives of early players. Few of these early actors have received full biographical treatment. Grace Overmyer's *America's First Hamlet* (New York, 1957) includes a good account of John Howard Payne's stage career. Others have been treated in unpublished dissertations at many American universities: for example, Billy J. Harbin, 'The Career of John Hodgkinson in the American Theatre' (Indiana University, 1970). The lives of the leading players in the middle years have received more attention: John Crehan, *The Life of Laura Keene* (Philadelphia, Pa., 1897); Edwin F. Edgett, *Edward Loomis Davenport* (New York, 1901); Lawrence Barrett, *Charlotte Cushman* (New York, 1889); Joseph Leach, *Bright Particular Star, The Life and Times of Charlotte Cushman* (New Haven, Conn., 1970); and Richard Moody, *Edwin Forrest, First Star of the American Stage* (New York, 1960).

(b) *From the Civil War to 1915*

Among the many volumes of brief biographies the best are: John B. Clapp and Edwin F. Edgett, *Players of the Present* (New York, 1900); Lewis C. Strang, *Players and Plays of the Last Quarter Century* (New York, 1903); Brander Matthews and Laurence Hutton, *Actors and Actresses of Great Britain and the United States* (New York, 1886); and Montrose Moses, *Famous Actor Families in America* (New York, 1906). Among the many books devoted to the Booth family, the most up-to-date and accurate is Eleanor Ruggles's *Prince of Players: Edwin Booth* (New York, 1953). Joseph Jefferson's own words in his *Autobiography* (New York, 1889) give the best picture of his famous Rip Van Winkle. For a view of the early San Francisco theatre and two of its leading personalities, see Constance Rourke, *Troupers of the*

Gold Coast: or, the Rise of Lotta Crabtree (New York, 1928), and Helen Holdredge, *The Woman in Black, The Life of the Fabulous Lola Montez* (New York, 1955). The careers of the famous acting team, Sothern and Marlowe, are treated in Charles Edward Russell, *Julia Marlowe, Her Life and Art* (New York, 1927), and E. H. Sothern, *The Melancholy Tale of Me* (New York, 1916). Ada Rehan deserves a more vibrant biography than William Winter's *Ada Rehan* (New York, 1898); two other leading ladies have fared better in Archie Binns's *Mrs Fiske and the American Theatre* (New York, 1955) and Phyllis Robbins's *Maude Adams: An Intimate Portrait* (New York, 1956). John McCabe's *George M. Cohan: The Man Who Owned Broadway* (New York, 1973) not only covers the record of the sensational song-and-dance man but also provides a vivid picture of Broadway in the early twentieth century. William Gillette was one of the few actors who wrote about the actor at work in his *The Illusion of the First Time in Acting* (New York, 1915).

(c) *From 1915 to the present*

Because of the abundance of biographies in recent years, the following selective list is limited to the most revealing about the subject and the theatre of his time. Otis Skinner has written well about his long and illustrious career in *Footlights and Spotlights* (New York, 1924). There are two good accounts of the remarkable John Barrymore: his own, *Confessions of an Actor* (Indianapolis, Ind., 1926), and Gene Fowler's *Goodnight, Sweet Prince* (New York, 1944). The brilliant performances of the Lunt–Fontanne team are well reported in Maurice Zolotow, *Stagestruck, The Romance of Alfred Lunt and Lynn Fontanne* (New York, 1964). Richard S. Aldrich has written a loving story of his wife in *Gertrude Lawrence as Mrs A.* (New York, 1955), and Harold Clurman gives a fascinating account of himself and his friends in *All People are Famous* (New York, 1974). *Laurette*, by Marguerite Courtenay (New York, 1955), is a fascinating record of the career of Laurette Taylor, accounted by many to have been the greatest American actress.

(iii) THEATRES, MANAGERS AND DIRECTORS, THEATRICAL ENTERPRISES

(a) *From the beginnings to the Civil War*

Among the accounts of early theatres and managers the following are especially informative: Francis Courtney Wemyss, *Twenty-Six Years of the Life of an Actor and Manager* (New York, 1847), and the same author's *Chronology of the American Stage, 1752–1852* (New York, 1852); William B. Wood, *Personal Recollections of the Stage* (Philadelphia, Pa., 1855); and

Henry P. Phelps, *Players of a Century : A Record of the Albany Stage* (Albany, NY, 1880). For on-the-spot views of performances, see Joseph N. Ireland, *Fifty Years of a Playgoer's Journal, 1798–1848* (New York, 1860), and Montrose J. Moses and John Mason Brown (eds), *American Theatre as Seen by Its Critics* (New York, 1934). P. T. Barnum's astonishing career is detailed in Irving Wallace's *The Fabulous Showman* (New York, 1959); see also Neil Harris, *Humbug: The Art of P. T. Barnum* (Boston, Toronto, 1973).

There are autobiographical accounts of travelling actors' lives by Noah Ludlow, *Dramatic Life as I Found It* (St Louis, Mo., 1880; New York, 1966); Sol Smith, *Theatrical Apprenticeship* (Philadelphia, Pa., 1856), *The Theatrical Journey* (Philadelphia, Pa., 1854) and *Theatrical Management in the South and West* (New York, 1868); and John Durang, *The Memoirs of John Durang, American Actor, 1785–1816* (Pittsburgh, Pa., 1966). The frontier theatre is also explored in two books by William G. B. Carson, *Managers in Distress* (St Louis, Mo., 1949; New York, 1965) and *The Theatre on the Frontier* (Chicago, Ill., 1932; New York, 1965). Paul T. Nolan (ed.), *Provincial Drama in America, 1870–1916, A Casebook of Primary Materials* (Metuchen, NJ, 1967), and West T. Hill, Jr, *The Theatre in Early Kentucky, 1790–1820* (Lexington, Kentucky, 1971), are of related interest.

(b) *From the Civil War to 1915*

Three important managements are well described in Lester Wallack, *Memories of Fifty Years* (New York, 1889); Daniel Frohman, *Memories of a Manager* (New York, 1911); and David Belasco, *The Theatre Through its Stage Door* (New York, 1919). Walter Pritchard Eaton, one of the best critics of his time, has written two excellent accounts of the early twentieth-century theatre, *The American Stage of Today* (New York, 1908) and *At the New Theatre and Others* (Boston, Mass., 1910). Philip C. Lewis, *Trouping, or How the Show Came to Town* (New York, 1973), provides useful information on the peripatetic American theatre and its problems.

(c) *From 1915 to the present*

There has been such a profusion of books on theatre in recent years that the following should be regarded only as a beginning reading list. Arthur Hopkins, *Reference Point* (New York, 1948), provides a charming insight into the work of one of the most creative producers in the early twentieth century. Jerry Stagg, *The Brothers Shubert* (New York, 1968), not only reports the astute, and sometimes shady, business practices of this amazing trio, but also provides a rich picture of the commercial Broadway theatre.

(Even more details about the Shubert empire will now become known; all of their papers have been given to the Theatre Collection of the New York Public Library.) The extraordinary career of a leading playwright-director is well told in Howard Teichman, *George S. Kaufman* (New York, 1972), and Scott Meredith, *George S. Kaufman and His Friends* (New York, 1974). The Katharine Cornell–Guthrie McClintic management, together with Cornell's substantial career as an actress, is sketched in her autobiography, *I Wanted to be an Actress* (New York, 1939). The life of Eva Le Gallienne and her Civic Repertory Theatre is well told in her *At 33* (New York, 1934) and *With a Quiet Heart* (New York, 1953). The best record of the Group Theatre, sometimes called 'The Odets Theatre', is found in Harold Clurman's *The Fervent Years* (New York, 1945). There are two excellent accounts of the Federal Theatre: Hallie Flanagan, *Arena* (New York, 1940, 1965), and Jane de Hart Mathews, *The Federal Theatre, 1935–1939* (New York, 1967). John Houseman's *Run-Through* (New York, 1972) relates the story of the Negro unit of the Federal Theatre and tells of the author's association with Orson Welles at the Mercury Theatre. Other recent analyses of the American political theatre are Malcolm Goldstein, *The Political Stage: American Drama and the Theatre of the Great Depression* (New York, 1974), Jay Williams, *Stage Left* (New York, 1974), and Sam Smiley, *The Drama of Attack* (Columbia, Mo., 1972).

Three accounts will provide an introduction to the academic theatre and the theatre outside New York City: Kenneth Macgowan's *Footlights Across America: Towards a National Theatre* (New York, 1929) chronicles the explosion of activity in little theatres in the 1920s. Wisner Payne Kinne, *George Pierce Baker and the American Theatre* (Cambridge, Mass., 1954), and Norris Houghton, *Advance from Broadway* (New York, 1941), provide useful perspectives, as do two books on the Off-Broadway theatre, Stuart W. Little, *Off-Broadway, the Prophetic Theatre* (New York, 1972), and Howard Greenberger, *The Off-Broadway Experience* (Englewood Cliffs, NJ, 1971).

(iv) THE ART THEATRE

The so-called 'art theatre' movement has been the subject of a number of studies, beginning with Sheldon Cheney, *The New Movement in Theatre* (New York, 1914) and *The Art Theatre* (New York, 1916). The work of Samuel J. Hume has formed the study of a doctoral dissertation by John Seely Bolin, *Samuel Hume, Artist and Exponent of the American Art Theatre* (Ann Arbor, Mich., 1970). Maurice Browne's account of the pioneering

Chicago Little Theatre is to be found in his autobiography, *Too Late to Lament* (Bloomington, Ind., 1956). Browne's work has also been made the subject of a study by Bernard F. Dukore, *Maurice Browne and the Chicago Little Theatre* (Ann Arbor, Mich., 1974). The Provincetown Theatre is discussed by Susan Glaspell in *The Road to the Temple* (New York, 1927) and by Helene Deutsch and Stella Hannau, *The Provincetown* (New York, 1931). *The Theatre of Tomorrow* (New York, 1921) by Kenneth Macgowan and *Continental Stagecraft* (New York, 1922) by Kenneth Macgowan and Robert Edmond Jones are seminal works. The rise of the Theatre Guild has been chronicled by Lawrence Langner, *The Magic Curtain* (New York, 1951); Walter Prichard Eaton, *The Theatre Guild, The First Ten Years* (New York, 1929); Roy S. Walden, *Vintage Years of the Theatre Guild, 1928–1939* (Cleveland, Ohio, 1972); and Theresa Helburn, *A Wayward Quest* (Boston, Mass., and Toronto, 1960). *Don't Put Your Daughter on the Stage* (New York, 1972), the second volume of Margaret Webster's autobiography, details the author's long and valuable service to the American theatre. *If You Don't Dance, They Beat You* (Boston, Mass., and Toronto, 1974) is José Quintero's autobiographical account of the development of the Circle-in-the-Square Theatre and the Eugene O'Neill revival. For intelligent commentary on the theatre of the 1920s and 1930s, the reader is directed to a variety of essays in collections by the critics George Jean Nathan, Stark Young and Alexander Woollcott.

(v) THE MUSICAL THEATRE

For a detailed survey of the major works of the popular American musical theatre, see David Ewen, *The Complete Book of the American Musical Theatre* (New York, 1958). Alec Wilder's analysis, *The American Popular Song* (New York, 1972), provides many helpful musical insights. The fullest account of the collaboration of Richard Rodgers with Lorenz Hart and with Oscar Hammerstein II is in Rodgers's *Musical Stages* (New York, 1975).

III The dramatists and their plays

(i) GENERAL CRITICAL STUDIES

Hudson Long's bibliography, *American Drama from its Beginning to the Present* (New York, 1970), provides a good starting point. Contemporary periodical reviews and commentary on nineteenth-century American drama are reproduced in the American Periodical Series by University Microfilms at Ann Arbor, Michigan (in progress). Carl J. Stratman lists all *American Theatrical Periodicals, 1799–1967* (Durham, NC, 1970) according to title, editor, dates of issues and present location of the periodical. Clarence Gohdes, *Literature and Theater of the States and Regions of the U.S.A.* (Durham, NC, 1967), provides a checklist of monographs, pamphlets and anthologies from 1900 to 1964. James Salem's *A Guide to Critical Reviews*, I: *American Drama*, 2nd ed. (Metuchen, NJ, 1973) lists reviews from American and Canadian periodicals plus the *New York Times* from 1900 to the present. *American Dramatic Criticism, 1890–1965* (Hamden, Conn., 1967), with Supplement I (Hamden, Conn., 1970), compiled by Helen Palmer and Jane Dyson, fills in some gaps. Another area is covered by Fred M. Litto, *American Dissertations on the Drama and Theatre, A Bibliography* (Kent, Ohio, 1969). Continuing bibliographies appear in the *MLA International Bibliography*, *American Literature, Educational Theatre Journal*, select years of *Modern Drama* and the essay on 'Drama' in the *American Literary Scholarship Annual*.

There are five histories which consider the entire scope of American drama. The standard history is still Arthur Hobson Quinn's *A History of the American Drama from the Beginning to the Civil War*, rev. ed. (New York, 1943) and its continuation, *A History of the American Drama from the Civil War to the Present Day*, rev. ed. (New York, 1936). Montrose J. Moses's *The American Dramatist* (Boston, Mass., 1925) was the first important study of American drama and still has value. Margaret G. Mayorga's *A Short History of the American Drama* (New York, 1932) adds little that is original. Walter J. Meserve's *An Outline History of American Drama* (Totowa, NJ, 1965) provides some new material and a useful organization in terms of a developing drama. *Three Hundred Years of American Drama and Theatre* (Englewood Cliffs, NJ, 1973) by Garff B. Wilson is an attempt to synthesize the development of American drama and theatre, but insufficient account is taken of recent research.

Most scholars and critics have felt that American drama became truly interesting only after Eugene O'Neill started writing, and for this modern period there are a number of valuable general sources. An early book, Thomas H. Dickinson's *Playwrights of the New American Theatre* (New York, 1925), considers O'Neill's early contemporaries. Alan S. Downer, *Fifty Years of American Drama 1900–1950* (Chicago, Ill., 1951), provides a quick review of the first half of the century, while Brooks Atkinson's *Broadway* (New York, 1970) gives anecdotal commentary and some knowledgeable observations on the same period. A more substantial survey, although of a shorter period, is Joseph Wood Krutch's *The American Drama Since 1918*, rev. ed. (New York, 1957), the history being continued very effectively by Gerald Weales's *American Drama Since World War II* (New York, 1962) and by the same author's *The Jumping-Off Place, American Drama in the 1960s* (New York, 1969). In each of these last three volumes the chapters are largely essays on playwrights, or groups of playwrights; some of them have appeared earlier in periodicals. Eleanor Flexnor's *American Playwrights, 1918–1938* (New York, 1938) is written from the point of view of a Marxist critic. Three other books which present particular views of the drama of the 1930s are Morgan Y. Himmelstein's *Drama as a Weapon* (New Brunswick, NJ, 1963), Gerald Rabkin's *Drama and Commitment* (Bloomington, Ind., 1964) and Malcolm Goldstein, *The Political Stage: American Drama and Theatre of the Great Depression* (New York, 1974). Louis Broussard's *American Drama, Contemporary Allegory from Eugene O'Neill to Tennessee Williams* (Norman, Okla., 1962) is an excellent study of selected dramatists during the period between the two World Wars.

(ii) COLLECTIONS OF AMERICAN PLAYS

For American plays of the eighteenth and early nineteenth centuries one must use the Readex Microprint reproductions of plays listed in *Three Centuries of English and American Plays, 1714–1830* (New York, 1963), edited by William G. Bergquist, although one should also check attributions in Jacob Blanch's *Bibliography of American Literature*. Another valuable source of old texts is the series of microprint reproductions, by the American Antiquarian Society, of items from the Evans and Shaw and Shoemaker collections. Many of the older American plays are reprinted in *America's Lost Plays*, edited by Barrett Clark, originally published in 1941 in twenty volumes (Princeton, NJ) and now reissued in ten volumes (Bloomington, Ind., 1965), plus one additional volume entitled *Satiric Comedies* (Bloomington, Ind., 1969). *Trumpets Sounding* (New York, 1972), edited by Norman Philbrick, collects seven plays of the American Revolution. There are three collections which attempt to span the history of American drama. Arthur H. Quinn's *Representative American Plays*, 7th ed. (New York, 1953), is the most representative, while Richard Moody's *Dramas from the American Theatre 1762–1909* (Cleveland, Ohio, 1966) has the most complete introductions. Montrose J. Moses's *Representative Plays by American Dramatists*, 3 vols (Boston, Mass., 1918), includes plays from 1765 to 1819, 1815 to 1858 and 1856 to 1917. A fourth volume by Moses, *Representative American Dramas, National and Local* (Boston, Mass., 1925), covers the period from 1894 to 1924. To this list and covering the same period must be added *SRO : The Most Successful Plays in the History of the American Stage* (Garden City, NY, 1944), edited by Bennett Cerf and Van H. Cartmell. For the entire modern and contemporary drama the several anthologies edited by John Gassner, *Best American Plays* (either alone or with collaborators), provide an excellent sampling of the most popular and best plays of the American stage.

(iii) HISTORY AND CRITICISM BY PERIODS

(a) *From the beginnings to 1800*

For seventeenth- and eighteenth-century drama there are two standard essays: F. L. Gay's 'The First American Play', *Nation* (11 February 1909), 88; and Herbert Brown's 'Sensibility in Eighteenth Century American Drama', *American Literature* (March 1932), 4. Dramatists of this period are few in number. *Robert Munford, America's First Comic Dramatist* (Athens, Ga., 1967) by Rodney M. Baine provides a thorough study of this dramatist's plays which appear in *A Collection of Plays and Poems, by the late Colonel Robert Munford, of Mecklenberg, in the State of Virginia* (Petersburg, Va., 1798). The major playwright of the Revolution, Mercy Warren, is the subject of two biographies: Alice Brown, *Mercy Warren* (New York, 1896), and Katherine Anthony, *First Lady of the Revolution: The Life of Mercy Otis Warren* (Port Washington, NY, 1958). The best biography of Royall Tyler is G. Thomas Tanselle's *Royall Tyler* (Cambridge, Mass., 1967). A standard source for the study of William Dunlap is Oral Sumner Coad's *William Dunlap* (New York, 1917). Robert H. Canary's *William Dunlap* (New York, 1970) is a brief study but contains a good bibliography. None of these dramatists has a collected edition; all are considered in the standard histories of American literature.

(b) *From 1800 to the Civil War*

General studies of the drama particularly relevant to this period are Richard Moody's *America Takes the Stage* (Bloomington, Ind., 1955); Francis Hodge's study of the Yankee in drama and on the stage, *Yankee Theatre: The Image of America on the Stage, 1825–1850* (Austin, Texas, 1964); the standard work on American minstrelsy, Carl Wittke's *Tambo and Bones* (Durham, NC, 1930), and a recent study, Robert C. Toll's *Blacking Up* (New York, 1971); Harry Birdoff's *The World's Greatest Hit – Uncle Tom's Cabin* (New York, 1947); and David Grimstead's *Melodrama Unveiled: American Theatre and Culture, 1800–1850* (Chicago, Ill., 1968). All these books are more concerned with theatrical tradition than with dramatic literature, but the authors frequently provide plots and some discussion of the drama.

Among the major dramatists of this period only George Henry Boker's *Poems and Plays* have been collected (New York, 1883). The authoritative critical study of Boker is still E. Scully Bradley's *George Henry Boker: Poet and Patriot* (Philadelphia, Pa., 1927). Paul H. Musser's *James Nelson Barker, 1784–1858* (Philadelphia, Pa., 1929) is the standard critical biography of this dramatist. John Howard Payne is treated sympathetically in Gabriel Harrison's *John Howard Payne* (Philadelphia, Pa., 1885); Grace Overmyer's *America's First Hamlet* (New York, 1957) is a more even biography of the actor-playwright. An authoritative study, Clement Foust's *The Life and Dramatic Works of Robert Montgomery Bird* (New York, 1919) is well supplemented by Curtis Dahl's *Robert Montgomery Bird* (New York, 1963), which provides a comprehensive analysis of his plays. David F. Haven's *The Columbian Muse of Comedy* (Carbondale, Ill., 1973) examines selected plays by Tyler, Dunlap, Barker, Bird, Ritchie and others. Eric Barnes's biography of A. C. M. Ritchie, *The Lady of Fashion: Anna Cora Mowatt* (New York, 1954), should be read in conjunction with Anna Cora Mowatt's (Mrs Ritchie's) *The Autobiography of an Actress* (Boston, Mass., 1854). Townsend Walsh's *The Career of Dion Boucicault* (New York, 1915) remains a standard work, while Robert Hogan provides a good bibliography in *Dion Boucicault* (New York, 1969). This latter volume is one of Twayne's United States Authors Series (as are Dahl's on Bird and Canary's on Dunlap) which are usually slight studies of a summary rather than provocative nature.

(c) *From the Civil War to 1915*

Of particular interest for this period is an essay entitled 'American Playwrights on the American Drama', published in *Harper's Weekly* (2 February 1889), 33. Belasco's work is adequately treated in *The Bishop of Broadway: The Life and Work of David Belasco* (New York, 1954) by Craig Timberlake. The best study of Daly is *The Theatre of Augustin Daly: An Account of the Late Nineteenth Century Stage* (Cambridge, Mass., 1956) by Marvin Felheim, although the *Life of Augustin Daly* (New York, 1917) by Daly's brother, Joseph F. Daly, is still a standard account. *The Complete Plays of W. D. Howells* (New York, 1960) has a critical introduction by Walter J. Meserve, the editor. The work of Edward Harrigan and Tony Hart is assessed in E. J. Kahn's *The Merry Partners: The Age and Stage of Harrigan and Hart* (New York, 1955). Percy MacKaye's *Epoch: The Life of Steele MacKaye* (New

York, 1927) tells a great deal about the drama of the period as well as being an authoritative biography. *James A. Herne: The Rise of Realism in American Drama* (Orono, Me., 1964) by Herbert J. Edwards and Julia A. Herne is slight but interesting with notes from Herne's daughter. The major study of Sheldon is *The Man Who Lived Twice: The Biography of Edward Sheldon* (New York, 1956) by Eric Barnes. Montrose Moses edited a four-volume collection of *The Plays of Clyde Fitch* (Boston, Mass., 1915); Archie Bell's *The Clyde Fitch I Knew* (New York, 1909) is a personal and revealing view of the playwright. In *Estranging Dawn, The Life and Works of William Vaughn Moody* (Carbondale, Ill., 1973) Maurice F. Brown provides a thorough analysis of the dramatist's work.

(d) *From 1915 to 1945*

During this period the most significant playwright is Eugene O'Neill. The definitive biography is Louis Sheaffer's, in two volumes, entitled *O'Neill, Son and Playwright* and *O'Neill, Son and Artist* (New York, 1968 and 1973). Other valuable biographical studies are *O'Neill* by Arthur and Barbara Gelb (New York, 1960) and Agnes Boulton, *Part of a Long Story* (Garden City, NY, 1958). Oscar Cargill, N. Bryllion Fagin and William J. Fisher have edited a useful anthology of critical work by and about O'Neill, *O'Neill and his Plays* (New York, 1961). Among critical studies, readers may wish to consult the following: John Henry Raleigh's analysis of O'Neill's place in the mainstream of the classic American literary tradition, *The Plays of Eugene O'Neill* (Carbondale, Ill., 1965); two psychologically oriented inquiries by Doris Falk, *Eugene O'Neill and the Tragic Tension* (New Brunswick, NJ, 1958), and Egil Törnquist, *A Drama of Souls* (Uppsala, Sweden, 1968); and two works which concern themselves specifically with O'Neill as a writer for the theatre, Travis Bogard, *Contour in Time, the Plays of Eugene O'Neill* (New York, 1975), and Timo Tiusanen, *O'Neill's Scenic Images* (Princeton, NJ, 1968). See also Clifford Leech, *Eugene O'Neill* (New York, 1963), Frederick Ives Carpenter, *Eugene O'Neill* (New York, 1964), and Edwin Engel, *The Haunted Heroes of Eugene O'Neill* (Cambridge, Mass., 1953). A valuable checklist has been provided by Jordan Y. Miller, *Eugene O'Neill and the American Critic: A Summary and Bibliographical Checklist* (Hamden, Conn., 1962).

Of the other playwrights, Maxwell Anderson is the subject of Mabel D. Bailey's *Maxwell Anderson: The Playwright as Prophet* (New York, 1957) and Barrett H. Clark's early, brief study, *Maxwell Anderson: The Man and His Plays* (New York, 1933). Philip Barry receives somewhat limited critical and biographical treatment in Joseph Rappolo's *Philip Barry* (New York, 1965); see also Walter J. Meserve's 'Philip Barry: A Dramatist's Search', *Modern Drama* (May 1970), 13. Marc Connelly comments on his own career in *Voices Off Stage* (New York, 1968). Agatha Boyd Adams's *Paul Green of Chapel Hill* (Chapel Hill, NC, 1951) is a standard biography; Vincent S. Kenny's *Paul Green* (New York, 1971) is most effective in the analysis of the folk plays. Richard Moody presents a play-by-play analysis of the work of *Lillian Hellman, Playwright* (New York, 1972). Sidney Howard's brief career is surveyed in Joseph Wood Krutch's 'The Dramatic Variety of Sidney Howard', *Nation* (1933), 137, and Walter J. Meserve's 'Sidney Howard and the Social Drama of the Twenties', *Modern Drama* (September 1963), 6. The best study of George S. Kaufman is Howard Teichmann's somewhat popular *George S. Kaufman: An Intimate Portrait* (New York, 1972). There are several book-length studies of Clifford Odets. The best analysis is provided by Gerald Weales in *Clifford Odets, Playwright* (New York, 1971) and Edward Murray in *Clifford Odets: The Thirties and After* (New York, 1968). Frank Durham evaluates Elmer Rice's contribution to American drama in *Elmer Rice* (New York, 1970), but Rice's own *Minority Report* (New York, 1963) also provides an interesting view. Two volumes by John Mason Brown assess the life and career of Robert Sherwood: *The Worlds of Robert E. Sherwood: Mirror to His Times, 1896–1939* (New York, 1965) and *The Ordeal of a Playwright* (New York, 1970). For another view read *Robert E. Sherwood, Reluctant Moralist* (New York, 1970) by Walter J. Meserve. Howard R. Floan's *William Saroyan* (New York, 1966) gives mainly play plots and reviews. Both Malcolm Goldstein in *The Art of Thornton Wilder* (Lincoln, Neb., 1965) and Donald Haberman, *The Plays of Thornton Wilder* (Middletown, Conn., 1967), provide sound, perceptive assessments.

(e) *From 1945 to the present*

There are already several book-length studies of Edward Albee. Anne Paolucci's *From Tension to Tonic: The Plays of Edward Albee* (Carbondale, Ill., 1972) is sensible and thorough. Gilbert Debusscher's *Edward Albee, Tradition and Renewal* (Brussels, 1967) provisionally assesses Albee's place in the development of American drama. Ruby Cohn's pamphlet appraisal, *Edward Albee* (Minneapolis, Minn., 1969) is brief but excellent. Jordan Y. Miller gives a good overall assessment of Inge's career in 'William Inge: Last of the Realists?', *Kansas Quarterly* (1970), 2 (2). Signi Falk considers the drama of *Archibald MacLeish* (New York, 1965); *Archibald MacLeish, A*

Checklist (Kent, Ohio, 1973) by Edward J. Mullaly gives a fair selection of criticism. Arthur Miller published his *Collected Plays* (New York, 1957). Dennis Welland's *Arthur Miller* (New York, 1961), the first full-length appraisal, is still a standard work, supplemented by Benjamin Nelson's *Arthur Miller, Portrait of a Playwright* (New York, 1970), a well-documented analysis of the plays. Benjamin Nelson's study of *Tennessee Williams: The Man and His Work* (New York, 1961) dwells upon Williams's particular kind of genius; *The Broken World of Tennessee Williams* (Madison, Wisc., 1965) by Esther Jackson provides a general appraisal of his works; and Gerald Weales's brief analysis in *Tennessee Williams* (Minneapolis, Minn., 1965) is the most penetrating. One of the best general approaches to black drama is *The Black American Writer*, Volume II: *Poetry and Drama* (Deland, Fla., 1969), edited by C. W. E. Bigsby; this provides a good evaluation of the foremost black dramatists. Theodore R. Hudson's *From LeRoi Jones to Amiri Baraka: The Literary Works* (Durham, NC, 1973) traces the development of the major spokesman for black drama. A number of contemporary dramatists are discussed in *Plays, Politics, and Polemics* (New York, 1973) by Catherine Hughes, who surveys their contribution to the developing drama.

Index